They Are Dead and Yet They Live

Studies in War, Society, and the Military

GENERAL EDITORS

Kate Lemay
Smithsonian Institution

Richard S. Fogarty
University at Albany, State University of New York

EDITORIAL BOARD

Peter Maslowski
University of Nebraska–Lincoln

David Graff
Kansas State University

Reina Pennington
Norwich University

THEY ARE DEAD AND YET THEY LIVE

Civil War Memories in a Polarized America

EDITED BY **JOHN M. KINDER** AND **JENNIFER M. MURRAY**

University of Nebraska Press   Lincoln

© 2026 by the Board of Regents of the University of Nebraska

All rights reserved

The University of Nebraska Press is part of a land-grant institution with campuses and programs on the past, present, and future homelands of the Pawnee, Ponca, Otoe-Missouria, Omaha, Dakota, Lakota, Kaw, Cheyenne, and Arapaho Peoples, as well as those of the relocated Ho-Chunk, Sac and Fox, and Iowa Peoples.

For customers in the EU with safety/GPSR concerns, contact:
gpsr@mare-nostrum.co.uk
Mare Nostrum Group BV
Mauritskade 21D
1091 GC Amsterdam
The Netherlands

Library of Congress Cataloging-in-Publication Data
Names: Kinder, John M. (John Matthew), 1975– editor. | Murray, Jennifer M., editor.
Title: They are dead and yet they live: Civil War memories in a polarized America / edited by John M. Kinder and Jennifer M. Murray.
Other titles: Studies in war, society, and the military.
Description: Lincoln: University of Nebraska Press, [2026] | Series: Studies in war, society, and the military | Includes bibliographical references and index.
Identifiers: LCCN 2025016639
ISBN 9781496235824 (hardback)
ISBN 9781496245649 (paperback)
ISBN 9781496245656 (epub)
ISBN 9781496245663 (pdf)
Subjects: LCSH: Collective memory—United States. | United States—History—Civil War, 1861-1865—Influence. | BISAC: HISTORY / United States / Civil War Period (1850-1877) | SOCIAL SCIENCE / Popular Culture
Classification: LCC E468.9 .T448 2026
LC record available at https://lccn.loc.gov/2025016639

Designed and set in Minion Pro by L. Welch.

FOR PETER S. CARMICHAEL
Passionate educator, dedicated mentor, supportive colleague,
and incomparable friend

Contents

List of Illustrations ix
Acknowledgments xi

Introduction: The Governor and the Palmetto Patriots 1
JOHN M. KINDER AND JENNIFER M. MURRAY

PART 1. LOST CAUSES

1. To Understand Where You Are Going, Remember Where You Have Been: Reconstruction's Reverberations in Twenty-First-Century America 19
BROOKS D. SIMPSON

2. The Republican Party, the Lost Cause, and the Transformation of American Politics 44
TIM GALSWORTHY

PART 2. RECLAMATION PROJECTS

3. The Politics of Civil War Memory in America's Military: The Battles to Rename Nine U.S. Army Bases 65
JENNIFER M. MURRAY

4. Freedom on the Fringes: Interpreting the Civil War and Relevancy at Camp Nelson 93
STEVE T. PHAN

5. Ghosts of Atchison: The Lynching of George Johnson 111
JOSHUA WOLF

PART 3. CONSUMING MEMORY

6. Confederates in the Record Cabinet: Civil War Memory and the Historical Turns in Modern Country Music......131
   JOSEPH M. THOMPSON

7. Love Is a Battlefield: Civil War Memory in Modern Romance Novels......152
   SARAH HANDLEY-COUSINS

8. Dixie Chic: Hoodies and Embodying Confederate Exceptionalism......170
   NICOLE MAURANTONIO

PART 4. CIVIL WAR MEMORY IN THE AGE OF BLACK LIVES MATTER

9. "This Battle Was Fought Because Black Lives Matter": How Black Lives Are (or Aren't) Remembered at Gettysburg......189
   SCOTT HANCOCK

10. The Black Confederate Myth and Civil War Memory in the Trump Era......217
    KEVIN M. LEVIN

PART 5. THE NEXT CIVIL WAR

11. The Confederate Battle Flag's Symbolic Shorthand: Appropriation, Dissemination, and Proliferation by U.S.-Based White Supremacists in Post–Civil War America......235
    BRETT A. BARNETT

12. Dylann Roof's Civil Wars......254
    JOHN M. KINDER

    Epilogue: "Wow, That Was a Big Mistake"......275
    JENNIFER M. MURRAY AND JOHN M. KINDER

    Timeline of Key Events from the Civil War Centennial to 2025......283
    Contributors......285
    Index......287

Illustrations

Intro.1. Barack Obama in front of portrait of
Abraham Lincoln ... 5

1.1. Storming of the U.S. Capitol ... 31

4.1. Memorial obelisk at Graveyard No. 1 at
Camp Nelson ... 104

4.2. Luminaria at Camp Nelson ... 106

8.1. Unite the Right Rally, Charlottesville, Virginia ... 173

9.1. Gettysburg, June 2022 ... 190

9.2 & 9.3. Black Lives Matter flags at Virginia
State Memorial ... 193

9.4. Stephen Lang at Virginia State Memorial ... 196

9.5. African American teamsters, Bermuda
Hundred, Virginia ... 202

9.6. Civil War dead at Fort Mahone ... 203

9.7. *Supply Train* by Edwin Forbes ... 204

9.8. Seventy-fifth anniversary, Battle of
Gettysburg ... 210

9.9. Marker at North Carolina Memorial ... 211

12.1. Museum and Library of Confederate History,
Greenville, South Carolina ... 258

12.2. Elmwood Cemetery, Columbia,
South Carolina ... 261

12.3. Slave quarters at McLeod Plantation,
Charleston, South Carolina ... 268

Epi.1. Counterprotesters at KKK rally, Columbia,
South Carolina ... 278

Acknowledgments

For starters, I want to thank my collaborator Jen Murray, who has forgotten more about the Civil War than I'll ever know; the individual chapter contributors, from whom I've learned so much; and Bridget Barry and the other hardworking people at the University of Nebraska Press, without whom this project might never have come to fruition. Next, I want to acknowledge my colleagues in the History Department and American Studies Program at Oklahoma State University, especially Brian Hosmer and Rebecca Sheehan, both of whom contributed to the lecture event at which this project took root. Finally, I want to recognize the people who, knowingly or not, sacrificed their lives to rid chattel slavery from the American landscape. We owe them our undying gratitude. —JOHN K.

This project originated from a public lecture at Oklahoma State University in November 2021 that explored the various threads of Civil War memory and its manifestations in modern America. I could not have imagined that the afternoon program would lead to this distinguished collection of essays.

My deepest thanks to my colleague John Kinder for conceptualizing this idea and suggesting we work on a volume about Civil War memory together. It has been an intellectually rewarding journey to collaborate with John, and I have learned much along the way. Additional notes of gratitude to the contributors who shared their time and expertise in this volume and to Bridget Barry at the University of Nebraska Press for supporting our project. A special thanks to Ken Noe for reading my chapter, as he has many of my other scholarly endeavors. I am profoundly honored to teach and write about our nation's most transformative event, the American Civil War, and share the stories of countless men and women who fought for democracy.

—JENNIFER M.

They Are Dead and Yet They Live

Introduction

The Governor and the Palmetto Patriots

JOHN M. KINDER AND JENNIFER M. MURRAY

In February 2023, shortly after former South Carolina Governor Nikki Haley announced her run for president, CNN uncovered an interview she had granted over a decade earlier to the Palmetto Patriots, a neo-Confederate group with ties to avowed white supremacists. The video clip, viewed hundreds of thousands of times on YouTube, prominently showcases Haley defending the Confederate battle flag as part of the state's heritage. The then-rising politician described the controversial Confederate History Month as "part of tradition," likening it to Black History Month, a nationally recognized initiative with roots dating back to the 1920s. Most notable was Haley's take on the Civil War itself. "I think you have one side of the Civil War that was fighting for tradition, and I think you have another side of the Civil War that was fighting for change," she told the gathering. In Haley's retelling of the deadliest epoch in our nation's history, the Civil War was not about slavery—it was a conflict rooted in debates about "individual rights and liberty," with good people on both sides.[1]

In retrospect, Haley might seem an unusual choice to invite to a meeting of aging Southern apologists. Born Nimarata Nikki Randhawa to immigrant Sikh parents in 1972, Haley rose quickly through the ranks of establishment Republican politics in South Carolina. In 2004 she was elected to the first of three terms in the South Carolina House of Representatives. Perhaps her most high-profile act as governor came in 2015, when she called for the removal of the Confederate flag from the state capitol after wannabe Nazi Dylann Roof massacred nine people at Charleston's Emanuel African Methodist Episcopal Church. Four years later, however, she continued to equivocate about the flag's meaning and, by extension, the legitimacy of the Confederate rebellion. Writing in an op-ed in the *Wash-*

ington Post, she claimed, "Everyone knows the flag has always been a symbol of slavery, discrimination and hate for many people. But not everyone sees the flag that way. That's hard for non-Southerners to understand, but it's a fact."[2]

To the cynic, Haley's desire to have it both ways is evidence of the politician's willingness to say anything to anybody to win votes. But the South Carolina governor's 2010 flirtation with the Lost Cause—and the 2023 media frenzy it engendered—also speak to a larger set of questions about the use and abuse of the Civil War today. What accounts for the lingering power of the Civil War in American political life? Why does the conflict's meaning continue to spark public outrage and fierce debate? And why do so many Americans view the Civil War of 1861–65 as a template of the United States' current political polarization?

They Are Dead and Yet They Live: Civil War Memories in a Polarized America locates the answers to such questions in the realm of contemporary battles over memory, the production of a usable past through public rituals, mass media representations, and civic engagement.[3] According to scholar Michael Kammen, "Societies . . . reconstruct their pasts rather than faithfully record them, and . . . they do so with the needs of contemporary culture clearly in mind—manipulating the past in order to mold the present." Even as, in historian David Blight's words, President Donald Trump gave birth to a "new 'Lost Cause' myth," plenty of observers have looked back at the old one, repurposing Confederate mantras about "liberty" and "honor" in anticipation of future violence.[4] At a time of heightened political polarization, the Civil War has taken on new significance, from the ongoing and vitriolic disputes over the removal of Confederate monuments, to the sight of an election-denier carrying a Confederate battle flag into the halls of Congress on January 6, 2021, to the scores of armed militiamen draped in Trump attire and Confederate flags menacing the battlefield at Gettysburg. Indeed, more than 160 years after General Robert E. Lee's surrender at Appomattox Court House, battles over Civil War memory continue to play out across the political and cultural landscape—in establishment politics, at former battlefields and U.S. Army bases, in popular music and literature, and in the murderous actions of white supremacists.

Ultimately, this collected volume argues that Civil War memory plays a vital role in twenty-first-century America, framing the past in ways that both exacerbate and undercut the divisions of our hyperpolarized present.

Civil Wars Past and Present

Battles over the Civil War's memory are not new. The guns were barely cool before groups were actively trying to shape the war's memory to suit their personal and ideological purposes. Consider Nikki Haley's home state of South Carolina. Explaining their decision to leave the Union in December 1860, Palmetto State secessionists made preserving slavery central to their argument. In a "Declaration of Immediate Causes," they cited an "increasing hostility on the part of the non-slaveholding States to the Institution of Slavery."[5] Their fellow enslavers and secessionists agreed, crafting a constitution that protected the "right of property in negro slaves."[6] According to newly installed Confederate Vice President Alexander Stephens, the "cornerstone" of the Southern Confederacy was built "upon the great truth that the negro is not equal to the white man; that slavery, subordination to the superior race, is his natural and moral condition."[7] After the war, however, the fight to preserve slavery was quickly and deliberately erased in the memory of defeated Southerners. Now they insisted the war had been fought for other principles: constitutional liberty, self-government, and, above all, states' rights. Over time, through a mix of power politics, willful forgetting, and concerted mythmaking, Southern apologists sought to transform the Civil War from a war to protect slavery to a tragic "Lost Cause."

Subsequent generations of Americans followed suit, cultivating memories of the war to suit their interests, at times with complete disregard to historical accuracy. In his groundbreaking *Race and Reunion: The Civil War in American Memory* (2001), David Blight identified three dominant strands of memory at play in the decades following the surrender at Appomattox: reconciliationist, white supremacist, and emancipationist. Reconciliation was achieved through sectional harmony—the reuniting of white Northerners and white Southerners around shared ideas of race and nation—at the deliberate exclusion of the millions of newly emancipated African Americans. This reconciliationist tradition reached an apogee in veterans' reunions in the late nineteenth and early twentieth century. At the fiftieth anniversary of the Battle of Gettysburg on July 4, 1913, President Woodrow Wilson declared, "We have found one another again as brothers and comrades, in arms, enemies no longer, generous friends rather, our battles long past, the quarrel forgotten." Although several historians have since taken issue with some of Blight's interpretations, most recognize the role of whiteness in cementing the postwar reunion of North and South.[8]

Few African Americans shared Wilson's optimism. On July 4, 1875, Frederick Douglass commented on the prevailing racial tensions when he questioned, "If war among the whites brought peace and liberty to the blacks, what will peace among the whites bring?"[9] The answer, generations of African Americans discovered, was decades of Jim Crow exploitation, terror, and abuse. While white Americans reconciled their brotherhood, millions of African Americans struggled to situate their complex memories of slavery, war, and emancipation within the national narrative of fracture and healing. In time, Black scholar-activists such as W. E. B. Du Bois sought to resurrect a memory of the war that not only recognized the experiences of African Americans but also highlighted the war's failure to end systemic racial oppression in American society.[10]

Historically, battles over the war's memory are especially tense in periods of social turmoil, when memory of the past conflict often serves as a stand-in for the divisions of the present. The 1960s, for instance, witnessed the simultaneous collision of the civil rights movement and the commemorations (or often celebrations) of the Civil War Centennial. Even as both white and Black citizens renewed efforts to dismantle the architecture of racial discrimination, a Civil War subculture flourished, much of it tinged with an air of nostalgia and romance. Throughout the decade, Americans found myriad avenues to consume the Civil War, from Civil War round tables and reenactments to the popular histories of Bruce Catton, whose colorful storytelling and penchant for human drama captivated millions of readers.[11] On August 28, 1963, Martin Luther King Jr. stood in the shadows of the Lincoln Memorial to deliver an impassioned plea for racial harmony, an oration that reminded listeners of the Civil War's "unfinished business." Overall, however, the pageantry of the conflict's centennial further solidified the Lost Cause narrative in nation's collective consciousness, the legacies of which continue to resonate into the present.

In the twenty-first century, Americans continue to call on competing visions of the Civil War to frame the politics of the present. On February 10, 2007, Barack Obama, then a junior U.S. senator from Illinois, announced his bid for the presidency on the steps of the Old State House in Springfield. This was a deliberate choice. In 1858 Abraham Lincoln had begun his quest for the U.S. Senate at the same spot. Invoking the rhetoric of Lincoln's Gettysburg Address, Senator Obama addressed the Civil War's legacies and its promises of a more just and equitable future when he declared, "Together, starting today, let us finish the work that needs to be done, and usher in a

Fig. Intro.1. Barack Obama speaking in front of a portrait of Abraham Lincoln at a dinner celebrating the Lincoln bicentennial in Springfield, Illinois, on February 12, 2009. Obama's supporters attempted to link the two presidents in the public imagination, culminating in the visual trope of "Abraham Obama." Courtesy of the Executive Office of the President of the United States. Photographer Pete Souza.

new birth of freedom on this Earth." That campaign season, connections between Obama and Lincoln proliferated on social media, while urban artist and Illinois native Ron English melded the two men's faces in his iconic series of *Abraham Obama* paintings and busts. Some two years later, on January 20, 2009, Obama was sworn in as the forty-fourth president of the United States, with his hand on the same Bible that Lincoln had used during his inauguration ceremony. The moment was historic: Obama's election as our nation's first African American president held the promise of Lincoln's vision of a "new birth of freedom."[12]

We attribute the recent interest in and heated rhetoric about Civil War memory to several factors. The first is the nearly unprecedented levels of polarization in contemporary American politics.[13] "Americans are angrier, more fearful, less trusting of one another and more polarized than at any time in generations and perhaps since the 1850s," writer Peter Wehner observed in 2021. "Families, friendships, churches and communities are being ripped apart by the savagery of our politics." Although this process began decades ago, it has recently gained traction with the rise of social media and explicitly ideological news outlets, which stoke partisan anger to garner ratings.[14] The election of Donald Trump in 2016 and again in 2024 on campaigns of racial grievance and sectional resentment further exacerbated these tendencies.

Second, memories of the American Civil War have inspired predictions of new battles—some metaphorical, others literal—among contemporary Americans, highlighting a heightened threat of widespread political violence in modern America. Forecasts of the "next Civil War" date back to the end of the first one, but recent decades have inspired new waves of violence—with predictions of even more on the horizon.[15] "In the United States in 2019," notes writer Steven Marche in *The Next Civil War: Dispatches from the American Future* (2022), "domestic anti-government extremists killed forty-two people; in 2018 they killed fifty-three people; in 2017, thirty-seven; in 2016, seventy-two; and in 2015, seventy." By this count, he reckoned, "America is already in a state of civil strife, on the threshold of a civil war."[16] From mainstream news outlets to the fever dreams of the right-wing blogosphere, Americans of all political stripes gaze into the near future and see a nation on the verge of violent collapse.[17] An article in *Time* in October 2022 was boldly headlined "The U.S. Is Heading Toward a Second Civil War. Here Is How We Avoid It."[18]

For many observers, the first battle of this latest conflict took place on January 6, 2021, when thousands of supporters of President Donald

Trump stormed the Capitol in Washington DC to prevent the lawful election of Joe Biden. As hundreds of millions of viewers looked on, crowds of insurrectionists—some waiving Confederate battle flags, some wielding firearms and cloaked in protective armor, nearly all white—attacked Capitol police, broke windows, looted offices, and chased lawmakers into hiding, all with the tacit permission of the sitting president. Maryland's Democratic Representative Jamie Raskin defined the events of January 6 as "extraordinary and unprecedented," adding, "You really have to go back to the Civil War to understand anything like [it]." It was a fitting analogy. In the weeks after the November 1860 election, impassioned bellows of voting fraud spread like a tumor across the Deep South, centering on the belief that Abraham Lincoln won the presidency because of "illegal" Black votes in Northern states.[19] Some 160 years later, similar beliefs in election conspiracy and voting fraud propelled scores of misguided and angry Americans—with untold others cheering them on from afar—to wanton destruction.

Third, we view the reignited urgency of Civil War memory as a product of the nation's forced reckoning with racial injustice. Outraged by state-sanctioned violence against Black bodies—including the police killings of Michael Brown (2014), Eric Garner (2014), Tanisha Anderson (2014), Ezell Ford (2014), Freddie Gray (2015), Sandra Bland (2015), Deborah Danner (2016), Keith Lamont Scott (2016), Breonna Taylor (2020), and George Floyd (2020), among many others—and enraged by continued efforts to deny the effects of systemic racism, Black activists and allies have demanded transformative change in all walks of life, from policing and housing to education and health. Among members of the Black Lives Matter movement, the Civil War and Reconstruction are both sources of inspiration and reminders of promises unkept. Not all Americans are willing to make such connections, particularly when discussions of the nation's racist past (and present) are often dismissed as "wokeness" run amok. Nevertheless, growing numbers of antiracist activists, scholars, and public figures draw a direct line between the Civil War-era and the present.[20] As historian Michael Landis recently observed, "Black lives were the cause, conduct, and consequence of the Civil War. The Civil War was fundamentally a Black Lives Matter event."[21]

Beyond the Monument Debate

No doubt the most visible manifestation of our current memory battles involves the fate of Confederate monuments, many of which were erected in the early twentieth century to shore up the forces of Jim Crow. "The heyday of monument building, between 1890 and 1920, was also a time of extreme racial violence, as Southern whites pushed back against what progress had been made by African Americans in the decades after the Civil War," writes historian Karen L. Cox. "As monuments went up, so did the bodies of black men, women and children during a long rash of lynching." Violence stalks contemporary monument debates as well. A plan to remove a statue of Robert E. Lee in Charlottesville, Virginia, in 2017 inspired a deadly white nationalist rally in which Heather Heyer was fatally struck by a car driven by James Alex Fields Jr., who intentionally drove into the group of antiracist protesters. Following the murder of George Floyd, demonstrators across the nation unleashed decades of pent-up fury on Confederate statues and monuments, reigniting sentiments that had flared up five years earlier after the massacre in Charleston.[22] By one counting, 168 Confederate symbols were removed in 2020, the majority after Floyd's murder in late May. While an important step forward, some seven hundred monuments to traitors and enslavers continue to mar our national landscape, not to mention the hundreds of other memorial tributes—named schools and roads, for instance—to the Confederate past.[23]

Yet the debate over Confederate monuments is but one manifestation of a larger reckoning with the Civil War. Thus, we've chosen to highlight some of the other places—several expected, others not—where public battles over Civil War memory continue to be waged. In the recent decades, Civil War memory has played an important role in realm of *politics*, particularly within the Republican Party and the conservative movement at large. As Tim Galsworthy notes, beginning in the 1960s, Republicans have made a concerted effort to distance themselves from Unionist ancestors, embracing Lost Cause ideals of "states' rights" to realign their party ideology. Memories of Reconstruction politics, as Brooks D. Simpson shows, have been mobilized to sanction contemporary antidemocratic actions and further widen the ideological gulf between Democrats and Republicans.

Battles over the Civil War are simultaneously taking place at what historians often call *memory spaces*, sites where people individually or collectively engage in the active work of narrating the past.[24] Apart from Confederate monuments, the naming of U.S. military bases for Confederate officers remained the most visible tribute to enslavers and traitors. Jennifer M. Murray explores the controversy surrounding the renaming of nine army bases in 2023 and the Department of Defense's efforts to rid itself of this tangible manifestation of white supremacy. Steve T. Phan examines the establishment of Camp Nelson National Monument and the National Park Service's commitment to interpret the story of the recruitment and training of United States Colored Troops and the challenges of doing so in Kentucky, a loyal slave state and a state with tangled strands of Civil War memory. Joshua Wolf tracks similar dynamics in rural Kansas, where community activists tried to uncover the history of an 1870 lynching after a century of deliberate forgetting.

Of course, the production of Civil War memory is not limited to political parties or stone memorials. It also takes place in the realm of *consumption*. Even as the war was being fought, savvy merchants sought to sell the conflict to anyone willing to plunk down a few pennies for a photograph, flyer, or kitschy souvenir. Today, the mass marketing of Civil War memory is big business, especially if one is willing to fudge the facts. Country music, as Joseph M. Thompson shows us, continues to trade in Confederate mythmaking and apologies to the Lost Cause. Sarah Handley-Cousins reveals the on-again off-again relationship between romance novels and Civil War plots. Meanwhile, Nicole Maurantonio's textured analysis of North Carolina-based brand Simply Dixie reminds us that the memory of the Civil War is stitched into the most ordinary products.

Unsurprisingly, the intersection of Civil War memory and political polarization is especially visible around issues of *race*. In the era of Black Lives Matter, more Americans are connecting Civil War–era questions over racial equality and citizenship to contemporary issues of racial injustice. Scott Hancock demonstrates how both white supremacists and Black Lives Matter activists have sought to lay claim to the Gettysburg battlefield as symbolic home turf. Likewise, Kevin M. Levin shows how Confederate apologists conjure myths of "Black Confederates" to downplay the horrors of the slave system and, in the process, claims of systemic racism in the present.

Hanging over all of this is the threat of *violence*. In recent years, battles over the Civil War's memory and meaning have inspired hate crimes, murder, and terrorism. The Confederate battle flag, Brett A. Barnett shows, has become a kind of symbolic shorthand, taken up by white nationalists, neo-Nazis, and others to signal their commitment to using violent means to carry out their agendas. Indeed, it's wrong to dismiss talk of future "civil wars" as keyboard fearmongering. John M. Kinder uses the story of mass murderer Dylann Roof to show how the toxic combination of conspiracy, bad history, and cheap weapons can turn online fantasies into real-life bloodshed.

Writing in 1961, Robert Penn Warren, a Kentucky-born poet and novelist, proclaimed, "The Civil War is our only 'felt' history—history lived in the national imagination." More than any other event in the nation's history, the Civil War—its gestation, its violence, its horrors, its perceived pageantry, its promises and failures—continues to touch people's lives. "This is not to say that the War is always, and by all men, felt in the same way," Warren added. "Quite the contrary." Today, Civil War memory remains as powerful and fractured as ever. Collectively and individually, these twelve essays show the eclectic and multifaceted ways that the Civil War permeants our national culture and fabric, far beyond the tributes in granite and stone, and distinctly remains our nation's "felt history."[25]

The Stakes of Memory

This book is driven by several distinct goals, some scholarly and others motivated by contemporary concerns.

For starters, it aims to explore the "mystic chords of memory" of the Civil War in the contemporary era, focusing on the Civil War Centennial through the present day. In the 1990s, historians began to shift their attention from the events of 1861–65 to questions of how the participants remembered the conflict. Consequently, memory studies began to grow and then ultimately flourish as a subfield of Civil War scholarship. Much of the work on Civil War memory examines the process of remembering (and forgetting) immediately following the conflict's end. Few scholars have considered the strands of memory beyond the early twentieth century, when the war's veterans and participants began to die out.[26] This book addresses this shortcoming in the vast sea of Civil War historiography by exploring how the Civil War continues to manifest itself in modern society, culture, and political discourse. Indeed, as the past few years have demonstrated, the war's memory is unquestionably relevant in twenty-first-century American culture.

Similarly, this collection of essays offers a counterweight to the notion that discussions of Civil War memory should be consigned to the built environment. Of the relatively few works published on Civil War memory in contemporary America, most focus on the construction and removal of Confederate monuments. Others consider the establishment and preservation of Civil War battlefields. Scholars writing on the war's battlefields remind us that while these once bloody grounds were used as sites of reconciliation for the veterans of the Blue and the Gray, Civil War battlefields have been—and remain—platforms to debate the war's meaning, interpretation, and consequences.²⁷ *They Are Dead and Yet They Live* moves the conversation beyond the "monument debates" to examine other manifestations of Civil War memory witnessed in the last fifty to sixty years. In doing so, our collective chapters consider new battles in Civil War memory taking place in contemporary politics, popular culture, and public history, while simultaneously underscoring the enduring relevance of America's most defining epoch.

Finally, we hope to use this volume to reiterate the stakes of Civil War memory in the present—why memory matters not despite America's fracture but because of it. As this book goes to print, conservatives across the nation are working to delegitimize African American studies in public schools and higher education and ban all mention of the nation's ugly history of white supremacy. Early into his second term, President Donald Trump signed an executive order, "Restoring Truth and Sanity to American History," which aims to provide what the administration considers an important corrective to the "widespread effort to rewrite our Nation's history, replacing objective facts with a distorted narrative driven by ideology rather than truth." Efforts to eliminate what Trump considers "corrosive ideology" are widespread and have ushered in considerable instability on the interpretation of American history in public and digital spaces managed by the federal government. This directive requires the National Park Service, for example, to evaluate and report all "inappropriate content" and to remove information that "inappropriately disparages Americans past or living (including persons living in colonial times)" by mid-September 2025. The installation of QR codes in each of the 433 national parks allows visitors to report offensive content. At present, the National Park Service oversees some ninety sites associated with the Civil War, not to mention other sites with complex and painful history, like Manzanar National Historic Site, which tells the story of Japanese American internment during World War II. Put simply, Trump's policies do more than threaten our ability to freely and honestly interpret the complexity of the Civil War—they encourage the kind of political fracture and historical amnesia that fueled the first civil war. Sanitizing "inappropriate content" at our historical sites allows citizens to reject any recognition of the nation's complicated past.²⁸

Americans of all political stripes continue to debate the Civil War's meaning and legacies, drawing upon the Civil War era as a touchstone for understanding the divisions of contemporary American life. These debates are neither abstract nor divorced from everyday life but resonate in our politics, on our nation's military bases, in the lyrics of our songs, and in our public spaces. Indeed, as we show throughout this book, twenty-first-century Americans' conflicts over the memory of the Civil War are fraught with high-stakes implications about our nation's past and our collective identity.

On September 11, 1889, Chaplain J. C. Truesdale provided a lengthy oration at the dedication of the 105th Pennsylvania Infantry Monument at Gettysburg. Imploring listeners to remember the heroic deeds and sacrifices of his comrades who sacrificed their life for the preservation of the Union, Truesdale extolled, "They are dead, and yet they live. In the homes and communities from which they went out to die, and in all our land today they live." Aging veterans gathered around the newly erected monument along Emmitsburg Road some twenty-six years after the Federal victory at Gettysburg and pondered the legacy of their service to the Union, their suffering, and their sacrifice. Chaplain Truesdale's words resonate as deeply in modern America as they did in 1889. Those soldiers who wore Blue and those who donned the Gray have long since passed, but their legacy and memory live among us.[29]

NOTES

1. Andrew Kaczynski, "Nikki Haley Defended Right to Secession, Confederate History Month and the Confederate Flag in 2010 Talk," CNN, February 21, 2023, https://www.cnn.com/2023/02/21/politics/nikki-haley-secession-confederate-history-month-flag-kfile/index.html.
2. Nikki Haley, "My Position on the Flag Has Been Constant. Our Country's Culture Has Changed," *Washington Post*, December 11, 2019, https://www.washingtonpost.com/opinions/nikki-haley-todays-climate-wouldnt-allow-us-to-remove-the-confederate-flag-in-south-carolina/2019/12/11/67373682-1c3c-11ea-8d58-5ac3600967a1_story.html. For a powerful response to Haley, see Adam H. Domby's "Nikki Haley Gets the History of the Confederate Flag Very Wrong," *Washington Post*, December 8, 2019, https://www.washingtonpost.com/opinions/2019/12/08/nikki-haley-gets-history-confederate-flag-very-wrong/.
3. Contributors to this volume employ an expansive understanding of the concept of memory, one that encompasses both formal and informal practices of memorialization, commemoration, and remembrance. For more on the topic of "memory," particularly as it pertains to war, see Piehler, *Remembering War the American Way*; Sturken, *Tangled Memories*; Winter, *Remembering War*.
4. David Blight, "Trump Has Birthed a Dangerous New 'Lost Cause' Myth. We Must Fight It," *The Guardian*, January 8, 2022, https://www.theguardian.com/commentisfree/2022/jan/08/trump-has-birthed-a-dangerous-new-lost-cause-myth-we-must-fight-it.
5. "Confederate States of America—Declaration of the Immediate Causes Which Induce and Justify the Secession of South Carolina from the Federal Union" (December 24, 1860), Lillian Goldman Law Library, *Avalon Project—Documents in Law, History and Diplomacy*, 2008, https://avalon.law.yale.edu/19th_century/csa_scarsec.asp.

6. "Constitution of the Confederate States; March 11, 1861," Lillian Goldman Law Library, *Avalon Project—Documents in Law, History and Diplomacy*, 2008, https://avalon.law.yale.edu/19th_century/csa_csa.asp.
7. Quoted in Kytle and Roberts, *Denmark Vesey's Garden*, 31.
8. See Janney, *Remembering the Civil War*; and Harris, *Across the Bloody Chasm*.
9. Frederick Douglass, "What to the Slave is the Fourth of July?" (1875 edition), quoted in Blight, "What Will Peace Among the Whites Bring?"
10. Du Bois, *Black Reconstruction in America*.
11. Blight, "Bruce Catton." Edward Tabor Linenthal coined the term "Civil War subculture"; see Linenthal, *Sacred Ground*, 97–98.
12. On the connection between Obama and Lincoln, see Deysine, "Obama, homme providentiel?"; and Evans, "Lincoln-Obama Moment." On Abraham Obama, see Goede, *Abraham Obama*; Cook, *Civil War Memories*, 197–200; and Matthew Dalleck, "The Comparisons Between Barack Obama and Abraham Lincoln," *US News*, November 20, 2008, https://www.usnews.com/opinion/articles/2008/11/20/the-comparisons-between-barack-obama-and-abraham-lincoln.
13. See Mason, *Uncivil Agreement*; Klein, *Why We're Polarized*; Michael Dimock, "America Is Exceptional in Its Political Divide," *Pew Trust Magazine*, March 29, 2021, https://www.pewtrusts.org/en/trust/archive/winter-2021/america-is-exceptional-in-its-political-divide; and Robinson, *Dangerous Instrument*.
14. Quoted in Russomanno, *"Stench" of Politics*, 17. See also Persily and Tucker, *Social Media and Democracy*; Kubin and von Sikorski, "Role of (Social) Media."
15. See Kinder, "Dylann Roof's Civil Wars," in this volume.
16. Marche, *Next Civil War*, 3.
17. See, for example, Carlos Lozada, "Is America Headed to a New Civil War?" *Washington Post*, January 6, 2022, https://www.washingtonpost.com/outlook/2022/01/06/civil-war-books/; "Is America Headed for Another Civil War?" *New York Times*, October 12, 2022, https://www.nytimes.com/2022/10/12/opinion/the-argument-america-civil-war.html; Tim Dickinson, "Is America Already in a Civil War?" *Rolling Stone*, June 15, 2023, https://www.rollingstone.com/politics/politics-features/donald-trump-far-right-brad-onishi-america-civil-war-interview-1234772017/.
18. Peter T. Coleman, "The U.S. Is Heading Toward a Second Civil War. Here Is How We Avoid It," *Time*, October 20, 2022, https://time.com/6222633/second-civil-war-us-how-to-avoid/.
19. Elizabeth R. Varon, "The Secessionist Roots of the Jan. 6 Insurrection," *Washington Post*, June 15, 2022, https://www.washingtonpost.com/outlook/2022/06/15/secessionist-roots-jan-6-insurrection/. These claims were, of course, inaccurate; voting rights of Black men in Northern states were severely limited, and their paltry votes in November 1860 did not swing the election in favor of Lincoln.
20. See Liz Vinson, "'A New Dawn': How Four Young Black Activists Powered Movement to Remove Confederate Emblem from Mississippi Flag," Southern Poverty Law Center, November 13, 2020, https://www.splcenter.org/news/2020/11/13/new-dawn-how-four-young-black-activists-powered-movement-remove-confederate-emblem; Joseph, *Third Reconstruction*; Lebron, *Making of Black Lives Matter*.

21. Michael Landis, "The US Civil War as the Ultimate BLM Protest," *Dr. Michael Landis* (blog), September 11, 2020, https://drmichaellandis.com/2020/11/09/the-us-civil-war-as-the-ultimate-blm-protest/.
22. Karen L. Cox, "Why Confederate Monuments Must Fall," *New York Times*, August 15, 2017, https://www.nytimes.com/2017/08/15/opinion/confederate-monuments-white-supremacy-charlottesville.html; Aimee Ortiz and Johnny Diaz, "George Floyd Protests Reignite Debate over Confederate Statues," *New York Times*, June 3, 2020, https://www.nytimes.com/2020/06/03/us/confederate-statues-george-floyd.html. Such actions are not new, as historian Karen Cox notes in her discussion of student activism against Confederate monuments following the murder of Tuskegee student Sammy Younge Jr. in 1966; see "Black Protesters Have Been Rallying Against Confederate Statues for Generations," *Smithsonian Magazine*, April 12, 2021, https://www.smithsonianmag.com/history/black-protestors-have-been-rallying-against-confederate-statues-generations-180977484/.
23. Rachel Treisman, "Nearly 100 Confederate Monuments Removed in 2020, Report Says; More Than 700 Remain," NPR, February 23, 2021, https://www.npr.org/2021/02/23/970610428/nearly-100-confederate-monuments-removed-in-2020-report-says-more-than-700-remain.
24. The concept of the "memory space" or "site of memory" (*lieux de mémoire*) was initially developed by French historian Pierre Nora; see "Between Memory and History."
25. Warren, *Legacy of the Civil War*, 4.
26. Notable exceptions to this trend include Coski, *Confederate Battle Flag*; Cook, *Troubled Commemoration*; and Levin, *Searching for Black Confederates*. Hilary Green and Andrew Slap's edited volume *Civil War and the Summer of 2020* provides a thoughtful collection of essays that explore some of the intersecting trends of Civil War memory and race during the summer of 2020.
27. Recent standouts on the "monument debate" include Brown, *Civil War Monuments and the Militarization of America*; and Cox, *No Common Ground*. Scholarship on the relationship between battlefield and memorialization includes Zenzen, *Battling for Manassas*; Smith, *Golden Age of Battlefield Preservation*; Smith, *Altogether Fitting and Proper*; and Murray, *On a Great Battlefield*.
28. Lisa Friedman, "National Parks Are Told to Delete Content That 'Disparages Americans,'" *New York Times*, June 13, 2025, https://www.nytimes.com/2025/06/13/climate/national-parks-trump-americans-censorship.html.
29. Truesdale, "Dedication Address, 105th Pennsylvania," 537.

BIBLIOGRAPHY

Blight, David. "Bruce Catton." *American Heritage* 62, no. 1 (Spring 2012). https://www.americanheritage.com/bruce-catton.

———. *Race and Reunion: The Civil War in American Memory*. Belknap Press of Harvard University Press, 2001.

———. "'What Will Peace Among the Whites Bring?': Reunion and Race and the Struggle Over the Memory of the Civil War in American Culture." *Massachusetts Review* 34, no. 3 (Autumn 1993): 393–410.

Brown, Thomas J. *Civil War Monuments and the Militarization of America*. University of North Carolina Press, 2020.

Cook, Robert J. *Civil War Memories: Contesting the Past in the United States since 1865*. Johns Hopkins University Press, 2017.

———. *Troubled Commemoration: The American Civil War Centennial, 1961–1965*. Louisiana State University Press, 2007.

Coski, John M. *The Confederate Battle Flag: America's Most Embattled Emblem*. Belknap Press of Harvard University Press, 2005.

Cox, Karen L. *No Common Ground: Confederate Monuments and the Ongoing Fight for Racial Justice*. University of North Carolina Press, 2021.

Deysine, Anne. "Obama, homme providentiel?" *Parlements[s], Revue d'histoire politique* 1, no. 13 (2010): 87–210. https://www.cairn.info/revue-parlements1-2010-1-page-87.htm.

Du Bois, W. E. B. *Black Reconstruction in America, 1860–1880*. 1935. Oxford University Press, 1998.

Evans, C. Wyatt. "The Lincoln-Obama Moment." In *Remixing the Civil War: Meditations on the Sesquicentennial*, edited by Thomas Brown. Johns Hopkins University Press, 2011.

Goede, Don. *Abraham Obama: A Guerilla Tour Through Art and Politics*. Last Gasp, 2009.

Green, Hilary, and Andrew Slap, eds. *The Civil War and the Summer of 2020*. Fordham University Press, 2024.

Harris, M. Keith. *Across the Bloody Chasm: The Culture of Commemoration Among Civil War Veterans*. Louisiana State University Press, 2014.

Janney, Caroline E. *Remembering the Civil War: Reunion and the Limits of Reconciliation*. University of North Carolina Press, 2016.

Joseph, Peniel E. *The Third Reconstruction: America's Struggle for Racial Justice in the Twenty-First Century*. Basic, 2022.

Kammen, Michael. *Mystic Chords of Memory: The Transformation of Tradition in American Culture*. Knopf, 1991.

Klein, Ezra. *Why We're Polarized*. Avid Reader, 2020.

Kubin, Emily, and Christian von Sikorski. "The Role of (Social) Media in Political Polarization: A Systemic Review." *Annals of the International Communication Association* 45, no. 3 (2021): 188–206.

Kytle, Ethan J., and Blain Roberts. *Denmark Vesey's Garden: Slavery and Memory in the Cradle of the Confederacy*. The New Press, 2018.

Lebron, Christopher J. *The Making of Black Lives Matter: A Brief History of an Idea, Updated Edition*. Oxford University Press, 2023.

Levin, Kevin M. *Searching for Black Confederates: The Civil War's Most Persistent Myth*. University of North Carolina Press, 2019.

Linenthal, Edward Tabor. *Sacred Ground: Americans and Their Battlefields*. University of Illinois Press, 1991.

Marche, Stephen. *The Next Civil War: Dispatches from the American Future*. Avid Reader, 2022.

Mason, Lilliana. *Uncivil Agreement: How Politics Became Our Identity*. University of Chicago Press, 2018.

Murray, Jennifer M. *On a Great Battlefield: The Making, Management, and Memory of Gettysburg National Military Park, 1933–2023*. 2nd ed. University of Tennessee Press, 2023.

Nora, Pierre. "Between Memory and History: Les Lieux de Mémoire." *Representations*, no. 26, Special Issue: Memory and Counter-Memory (Spring 1989): 7–24.

Persily, Nathaniel, and Joshua A. Tucker, eds. *Social Media and Democracy: The State of the Field and Prospects for Reform*. Cambridge University Press, 2020.

Piehler, G. Kurt. *Remembering War the American Way*. Smithsonian Institution Press, 1995.

Robinson, Michael A. *Dangerous Instrument: Political Polarization and U.S. Civil-Military Relations*. Oxford University Press, 2023.

Russomanno, Joseph. *The "Stench" of Politics: Polarization and Worldview on the Supreme Court*. Lexington, 2022.

Smith, Timothy B. *Altogether Fitting and Proper: Civil War Battlefield Preservation in History, Memory, and Policy, 1861–2015*. University of Tennessee Press, 2017.

———. *The Golden Age of Battlefield Preservation: The Decade of the 1890s and the Establishment of America's First Five Military Parks*. University of Tennessee Press, 2008.

Sturken, Marita. *Tangled Memories: The Vietnam War, the AIDS Epidemic, and the Politics of Remembering* University of California Press, 1997.

Truesdale, J. C. "Dedication Address, 105th Pennsylvania." September 11, 1889. In *Pennsylvania at Gettysburg: Ceremonies at the Dedication of the Monuments Erected by the Commonwealth of Pennsylvania to Mark the Positions of the Pennsylvania Commands Engaged in Battle*, vol. 2. E. K. Meyers, 1893.

Warren, Robert Penn. *The Legacy of the Civil War*. Random House, 1961.

Winter, Jay. *Remembering War: The Great War between Memory and History in the Twentieth Century*. Yale University Press, 2006.

Zenzen, Joan. *Battling for Manassas: The Fifty-Year Preservation Struggle at Manassas National Battlefield Park*. Penn State University Press, 1997.

PART I
Lost Causes

On April 9, 1865, General Robert E. Lee met Lieutenant General Ulysses S. Grant in the parlor of a home owned by Wilmer McLean to surrender the Army of Northern Virginia, the Confederacy's principal instrument of war. There, as the generals sat at two separate tables in this farmhouse in Appomattox, Virginia, the American Civil War came to an end, at least in the Eastern Theater. The following day, Lee issued General Order No. 9, the general's famous farewell address, which not only spoke to his tattered—and now defeated—soldiers but also laid the foundation for generations of explanations and debates over the nature of the conflict itself. "After four years of arduous service marked by unsurpassed courage and fortitude, the Army of Northern Virginia has been compelled to yield to overwhelming numbers and resources," Lee penned.[1] In this explanation, Lee helped frame the reason for the Confederacy's defeat—the loyal Federal states simply overwhelmed the agrarian South with its abundant resources and plentiful manpower. The following year, Edward Pollard, editor of the *Richmond Examiner*, authored *The Lost Cause: A New Southern History of the War of the Confederates*, which helped perpetuate a version of the Civil War that ignored slavery as its principal cause and championed Confederate soldiers as heroic defenders of the malleable "states' rights."

The myth of the Lost Cause is one of the most powerful currents in American history and still holds considerable sway in some sectors of the country. In the decades that followed Lee's surrender, echoes of the Lost Cause could be seen in the erection of scores of Confederate monuments across the South, read in textbooks approved by the United Daughters of the Confederacy, consumed on-screen in the 1915 silent film *The Birth of a Nation*, or heard in the soaring rhetoric of white Southern politicians of the nineteenth and twentieth centuries. The Lost Cause is more than an artifact of the conquered Confederacy, however: modern Republicans have perpetuated elements of the original Lost Cause, primarily its racial tenets that privileged white Americans. Contemporary Republicans have also fashioned a "new Lost Cause" that promotes the lie that the 2020 election was stolen. Historian Richard Slotkin suggested, "MAGA's use of myth gives its adherents the sense of righteous empowerment that comes from association with a deeply rooted historical tradition. But its embrace of Lost Cause symbolism carries with it a commitment to the myth's political action script of cultural and political authoritarianism."[2] The original Lost Cause polluted an accurate narration of the causes and consequences of the American Civil War, and the "new Lost Cause" has the potential to be just as toxic and corrosive to fundamental ideas of American democracy, liberty, and history.

NOTES

1. "General Orders No. 9," April 10, 1865, available on the National Park Service website at https://www.nps.gov/apco/general-order-9.htm.
2. Richard Slotkin, "Trump's New Lost Cause," Illiberalism, April 3, 2024, https://www.illiberalism.org/trumpisms-new-lost-cause-national-myth-and-the-struggle-for-america/.

1

To Understand Where You Are Going, Remember Where You Have Been

Reconstruction's Reverberations in Twenty-First-Century America

BROOKS D. SIMPSON

Reconstruction does not rouse the same degree of interest in the American popular mind as does the Civil War. It rarely attracts writers who prefer to cater to the Civil War popular history market, and it lacks the compelling visual portrayal offered in Ken Burns's famed 1990 *The Civil War*, with its cursory treatment of Reconstruction. For decades the most vivid views of Reconstruction in the American popular mind came from two films, *The Birth of a Nation* (1915) and *Gone with the Wind* (1939). Although mainstream academic historians undertook a fundamental reassessment of Reconstruction starting in the late 1950s, the fact that even recent scholarly accounts still devote space to undermining the credibility of interpretations a century old suggests the degree to which newer understandings, now in place for more than six decades, have struggled to supplant what came before.

Nor has Reconstruction often served as a reference point in discussions of American politics. For decades the most one could hope for was an observation about election results in the former Confederate states, where pundits would note that one candidate was the first African American elected from somewhere since Reconstruction or that someone else was the first Republican elected to some office since Reconstruction (these were not always the same people). Even at the turn of the last century, when both a presidential impeachment and a disputed election brought Reconstruction parallels to mind, discussions of the Civil War's aftermath rarely informed present-day politics. The same can be said for the prolonged process of regime change and nation-building that characterized the American military presence in Afghanistan and Iraq, which in certain ways reflected the experience of the U.S. government in rebuilding Southern state governments after the Civil War with a prolonged military presence.

The exception to the rule was the public discussion about terrorism in the wake of the events of September 11, 2001. The notion that terrorism was foreign to the American historical experience was quickly dispelled by several scholars, many of whom highlighted what had happened in the American South in the wake of the Civil War. Reconstruction was recast partly as a war against terrorism, with historians offering new accounts of the period that focused on Reconstruction violence (building on some previously underrecognized work). However, such scholarship failed to make much impact on the larger popular mind, which still viewed Reconstruction as some dark, unfathomable part of the American past that one rushed over, often shielding one's eyes, in leaving the Civil War for the Gilded Age and the road to world power.[1]

Likewise, Reconstruction was rarely emphasized in the field of Civil War memory studies, in which historians explored how Americans constructed and reconstructed understandings and interpretations of the Civil War to suit various constituencies and agendas in forming a more serviceable past. Properly understood, such studies were really about the place that slavery, race, secession, and war played in Americans' understanding of the Civil War era, including the coming of the war and Reconstruction. Often the needs of sectional reconciliation required a recasting of the history of the period to sidestep certain divisive issues to promote harmony, at least among most white people. Yet there was very little scholarship that specifically addressed Reconstruction memory, even as scholars recognized that one of the purposes of memory studies was to learn more about how people understood the past than the past they were attempting to understand and explain.[2]

How Americans observed the Civil War Sesquicentennial of 2011–15 led to far more attention being devoted to Reconstruction than had been paid to it during the commemoration of the war's centennial between 1961 and 1965. Over the next fifty years, American historical scholarship firmly set aside an interpretive paradigm that claimed that the war was a clash of economic systems and differences over federalism and states' rights in favor of one that emphasized the role of slavery as a moral, political, and economic institution in dividing the American republic. This revolution in mainstream Reconstruction scholarship emphasized the wartime and postwar effort to define liberty and equality for Black Americans, both free and freed; it also treated sectional reconciliation between whites as coming at the expense of Black Americans. Studies on how Americans remembered the Civil War debated the degree to which tales of Confederate brilliance and bravery and

Union victory through overwhelming resources (managed by inferior and sometimes inept leaders) endeavored to assuage wounded white Southerners' egos and bring white Americans together. Analytical studies of the Lost Cause myth explored how interpretations of the coming, conduct, and consequences of the conflict of 1861–65 had been shaped by political and social agendas of the later nineteenth and early twentieth century that privileged the defeated over the victors, embraced white supremacist perspectives concerning race and slavery, and questioned whether the freedpeople were capable of seizing advantage of the opportunity offered by emancipation.

Although much changed during the half century after the passage of civil rights and voting rights legislation in 1964–65, resistance remained to these new narratives, especially among those whites who still romanticized both the antebellum South and the Confederacy and saw Reconstruction primarily in terms of Northern vengeance against white Southerners. Some self-described heritage groups defiantly waived the Confederate battle flag, claiming that their efforts were expressions of heritage, not hate, despite the willingness of white supremacist groups to appropriate the flag for purposes that contradicted such benign explanations (see Brett A. Barnett's chapter herein). Moreover, scholarly reassessments of Reconstruction and some of its chief figures did not easily infiltrate the historical consciousness of many Americans, especially white Americans. The nation was as divided over historical memory when it came to the Civil War and Reconstruction as it had been over the events that they were remembering and explaining.

The sesquicentennial of the American Civil War navigated these divisions uneasily. Despite the efforts of the National Park Service and various professional historical organizations and scholars to shape commemorations to reflect the changing nature of historians' understandings of the Civil War era, obstinate resistance remained, while many Americans choose not to probe too deeply into why Americans fought and killed each other with such intensity. The fact remained that in the wake of the celebration of the 150th anniversary of the Battle of Gettysburg in 2013, what interest there was in the history of the conflict steadily declined, despite ceremonies and conferences covering the last two years of the war.

The year 2015 proved pivotal, bringing to the fore issues that had been heretofore far less salient during the sesquicentennial itself. On June 17, 2015, in Charleston, South Carolina, the very city that had fired the first shots against U.S. authority some 150 years before, a white North Carolinian, Dylann Roof, murdered nine Black South Carolinians and wounded a tenth inside Emanuel African Methodist Episcopal Church. Roof's embrace of white supremacy and his embrace of the Confederate battle flag ignited a national debate about the meaning of Confederate icons, including monuments and places named to honor former Confederate heroes as well as flags (see John M. Kinder's chapter). What once seemed to be a debate between scholars, extremists, and heritage groups quickly evolved into something quite different. In communities where the display of Confederate icons was already a subject of debate, the events of 2015 accelerated and escalated matters. Within a month South Carolina removed the Confederate flag from the grounds of the state capital; in New Orleans, city officials, led by Mayor Mitch Landrieu, removed three monuments dedicated to Confederate leaders.

New Orleans officials did not stop there. They also decided that it was finally time to remove a monument that specifically honored the triumph of white supremacy during Reconstruction. In September 1874 insurrectionists had tried to overthrow the state's Republican government in what became known as the Battle of Liberty Place; in 1891, as part of local authorities' desire to commemorate the state's takeover by Democrats in 1877, the city erected a monument on Canal Street. In 1932 the city approved a commission's decision to add to the monument descriptive language that explicitly linked the event to the triumph of white supremacy through violence.[3]

The obelisk soon became a point of controversy. Removed from Canal Street in 1989, it was relocated four years later to a back lot near railroad tracks, bearing additional wording designed to suggest that not everyone agreed with the characterization of events framed over six decades earlier. Original inscriptions were augmented by other inscriptions and markers, some of which took issue with the interpretation initially offered by the monument or which sought to distance it from later generations.[4] In the debates that followed, this monument was often grouped with its three Confederate counterparts as a Civil War monument, an implicit admission that not all the issues of the war had been decided in 1865 with the collapse of the Confederacy. It also renewed attention to the role of white supremacist violence in overthrowing Reconstruction. The Battle of Liberty Place monument joined its Confederate brethren in storage in 2017.

By the time New Orleans placed its Confederate monuments in storage, most people were turning their attention to Charlottesville, Virginia, where the city council had decided to authorize the removal of equestrian statues to Robert E. Lee and Thomas J. "Stonewall" Jackson. A lawsuit seeking to keep the monuments in place provided Confederate heritage advocates and other groups with time to act. On August 11, 2017, protesters gathered at the University of Virginia under the rallying cry of "Unite the Right," bringing together white nationalists and white supremacists, many with ties to activist Confederate heritage groups. Many of the same people appeared the next day in downtown Charlottesville around the Lee monument. They were met by counterprotesters. The ensuing clash reached a tragic climax when an avowed white supremacist, James Alex Fields, drove his car into a crowd, killing one of the counterprotesters, Heather Heyer, and injuring dozens more.[5]

Charlottesville completed what Charleston began in earnest. Confederate heritage would never be the same once it was so clearly identified with extremism, racism, and violence. That this was primarily the doing of Confederate heritage advocates was ironic, given their embrace of the slogan "heritage, not hate." There had been protests against the display of Confederate images and celebration of Confederate icons for decades, but the events at Charleston and Charlottesville escalated the struggle and tipped the balance in favor of the critics of Confederate heritage. No longer was there talk of compromises or contextualization: Whatever middle ground had ever existed had given way, largely due to the assertiveness of community leaders. One sign of how emotional and extreme the debate had become was to be seen in the videos shot by the *Washington Post* to accompany its account of the melting of the Lee statue in October 2023.[6]

New understandings of the Civil War, especially concerning race, violence, and white supremacy, had their impact on renderings of Reconstruction, especially when the two were linked in the form of prominent individuals. The fate of a statue in Memphis honoring Nathan Bedford Forrest was a case in point. While Americans associated Lee and Jackson most closely with the American Civil War, Forrest's historical significance included his activities during Reconstruction, especially his association with the Ku Klux Klan. A slave trader before the war, Forrest gained notoriety when his command slaughtered Black Union soldiers attempting to surrender after Forrest's Confederates overran Fort Pillow, Tennessee, just outside Memphis, on April 12, 1864. After the war, Forrest's affiliation with the Klan became the subject of much contention, although one wonders why, if Forrest had nothing to do with the Klan, his defenders assert as a point of pride that he ordered it disbanded. In the eyes of many observers, Forrest linked together the Civil War and Reconstruction, uniting Confederates and Klansmen in a common struggle to preserve white supremacy through violence.

At the beginning of the twentieth century white residents of Memphis, supported by the United Daughters of the Confederacy, decided to commemorate Forrest as a Confederate hero. An equestrian statue had been erected over the gravesite of Forrest and his wife, Mary, in a Memphis public park by 1905. The statue and the site had been a point of open controversy since the 1980s, but an effort in 2015 to secure the monument's removal failed due to a Tennessee law prohibiting the removal of such monuments. That the city renamed the park Health Sciences Park, dropping the name Forrest Park, seemed the best critics could do. In the wake of Charlottesville, Memphis's city council tried again to secure removal. This time they took advantage of a loophole in the law that allowed them to sell public land to a private buyer who would not be subject to the state law barring the removal of monuments. On December 20, 2017, the monument was removed; the Forrests' remains were exhumed in 2021 and eventually reinterred on the grounds of the National Confederate Museum in Columbia, Tennessee, with plans to re-erect the monument atop the gravesite.[7]

Debates over the place of Confederate iconography in twenty-first-century America marked a major shift in how many Americans viewed the Civil War—one that had consequences for how they viewed Reconstruction. Scholars increasingly identified the Confederacy as an insurrection rooted in Southern whites' desire to defend slavery. It thus followed that Americans increasingly viewed Reconstruction through new eyes that reflected the same emphasis on race and violence. By placing race at the center of the narrative, replacing sectional reconciliation, historians presented Reconstruction as part of a continuing conflict over the meaning of emancipation in the wake of the destruction of slavery in a world characterized by voter suppression and terrorist violence carried out in large part by Confederate veterans against African Americans and their white allies (including the occasional Confederate veteran, such as James Longstreet).[8] Having long cast aside the white supremacist assumptions about Black inferiority that characterized the work of the first generation of mainstream Reconstruction scholars (sometimes known as "the Dunning School," after Columbia University Professor William A. Dunning), historians in the twenty-first century shifted their focus from debates over the framing of Reconstruction policy to Reconstruction as a "continuing Civil War," replete with stories of violence and terrorism. They now questioned whether Reconstruction failed or was overthrown.

At the same time, scholarly examination of Civil War memory provided new contexts for understanding Confederate iconography, which can often tell us less about Lost Cause heroes and more about those who celebrate them. The debate over the monument to the Confederate dead at Arlington National Cemetery made this explicit. Defenders of the monument highlighted its Reconstruction and post-Reconstruction origins by claiming that it commemorated national reconciliation, despite the fact that no one had ever referred to it that way before it was suggested that the memorial be moved.[9] In other words, debates about Civil War memory are often at least as much debates about how white Americans during and after Reconstruction chose to remember the Civil War, and how those decisions reflected contemporary concerns, agendas, and preferences that reflected the political situation at the time.

To be sure, it takes time for evolutions in scholarly understandings to make their way into popular understandings of American history. While scholars, through books, presentations, or use of social media, drove home their points with vigor, it was not until Charleston, Charlottesville, and subsequent events that those understandings found expression in the popular consciousness, making them part of a broader discourse about the history of the Civil War and Reconstruction era, which now assumed new relevance for many people.

One example of the pace at which such changes take place was the reassessment of the presidency of Ulysses S. Grant in historical scholarship, especially when it came to Reconstruction. The reputation of Grant's presidency did not benefit from the first wave of reassessments about Reconstruction in the 1960s and 1970s, which did much to revise downward the historical standing of his predecessor, Andrew Johnson. Dissenters such as John A. Carpenter, David H. Donald, William R. Brock, and Richard N. Current failed to gain a foothold in scholarship, while William S. McFeely's harshly critical biography of the eighteenth president won the Pulitzer Prize in 1982.[10] However, starting in 1991, a series of studies sought to revise the mainstream assessment. Over the next twenty-five years Grant's stock began to rise, largely because most of these studies offered new understandings of Grant's efforts to promote racial equality and justice during his presidency. Some of these studies went further than others: scholars ranking Grant's performance as president lifted him from the bottom of the barrel to rest in the middle.[11] By the time of the appearance of Ron Chernow's popular synthesis biography in 2017, Grant's rehabilitation seemed complete, aided in part by Chernow's own popularity in the wake of the phenomenon known as Lin Manuel Miranda's *Hamilton: A*

Musical, based in part on Chernow's 2004 biography of Alexander Hamilton. Much as Chernow and the ensuing musical had made much (perhaps too much) of Hamilton's antislavery feelings, now Chernow advanced Grant's greatness as a civil rights president past earlier assessments, which had balanced shortcomings, failures, and limits against laudatory sentiments and successes. What the public and uninformed reviewers found to be new in Chernow had long been known to many scholars, illustrating the tensions between professional scholarship and popular accounts and biographies (as well as the way in which publishers promote their products).

Playing a notable role in transforming Americans' understandings of the Civil War and Reconstruction, ironically, were the efforts by Confederate heritage groups to contest these emerging narratives as they promoted the preservation and display of Confederate iconography in ways that ultimately proved counterproductive. Their claims that their display of the Confederate flag was historical and neither political nor racial in motivation collapsed when investigation revealed their links between these groups and white supremacists and white nationalists, inquiries often enhanced by the tendency of Confederate heritage groups to use social media to publicize their messages and images, which offered rather easy proof of such associations. For example, one such group, the Virginia Flaggers, celebrated their association with noted white supremacists such as Matthew Heimbach in blogs and photographs. Later efforts to disavow and distance themselves from such people proved futile when they celebrated the comradeship of still other white supremacists and white nationalists, thus providing the best evidence of the people with whom they associated.[12]

The fervent efforts of such self-styled Confederate heritage groups to preserve Confederate iconography proved disastrous to their cause. They resisted efforts to address the presence of such images in the aftermath of Charleston and Charlottesville, refusing to give an inch. They also rejected discussions about contextualizing Confederate icons on public display through signs and displays, which empowered those groups seeking removal by making removal the only alternative to leaving statues, flags, and names untouched—a position that became far more unlikely once blood had been shed.

The confrontation at Charlottesville came during the first year of Donald J. Trump's presidency. The president's comments that "there is blame on both sides" and that there were "very fine people, on both sides" sparked fierce controversy.[13] Over the next four years the actions of the forty-fifth president and his supporters offered many opportunities for people to present historical comparisons grounded in understandings of Reconstruction. People witnessed two impeachments; a disputed election; an abortive insurrection; racial unrest, especially during the summer of 2020; and a president whose extreme language and willingness of engage his opponents through name-calling and denigration brought to mind none other than Andrew Johnson, especially in 1866.

In 2019 Trump was impeached on charges of abuse of power and obstruction of justice concerning his attempt to manipulate foreign aid to secure information about his political rival, Joseph R. Biden Jr., who had already declared his intent to run for president in 2020 (Biden said what had happened in Charlottesville moved him to run). Although some commentators offered parallels with the experiences of Richard Nixon and William Jefferson Clinton, others pointed to the 1868 impeachment of Andrew Johnson as offering much more insight and better historical context.[14] As Tim Murphy suggested, Trump as president resembled Andrew Johnson, especially in his combative behavior. There were other parallels, but Murphy's piece sought to bring readers up to speed on current understandings of Reconstruction during Johnson's presidency.[15] Occasionally there was reference to the Johnson impeachment, notably by Alan Dershowitz, a member of Trump's defense team, who cited the strategy of Johnson's defense team in setting forth his arguments on behalf of his client—namely, that mere abuse of power was insufficient grounds on which to indict a president through the impeachment process without assessing the seriousness of the offense as rising to a "high crime and misdemeanor."[16]

In February 2020 the U.S. Senate acquitted Trump in an impeachment trial whose result was a foregone conclusion. As with other impeachment trials, including Johnson's, partisan politics played a role. Several months later, however, the nation, already battling the impact of a widespread pandemic, reeled in the face of widespread protests sparked by the murder of George Floyd on May 25, 2020, by a policeman in Minneapolis, Minnesota. During the next several months of increasing friction and confrontations, spurred in part by Trump's aggressive response to the protests, debates over Confederate symbols and iconography emerged anew, even as Americans debated over the commemoration by statues of other Americans, including Ulysses S. Grant and Theodore Roosevelt. While some scholars compared 2020 with the 1960s, others reached back once more to Reconstruction, emphasizing issues of structural racism and violence. Some even talked of a new or third Reconstruction that directly addressed these issues.[17]

One outcome of the protests in the summer of 2020 was that state and local governments as well as the federal government again moved to address prominent Confederate symbols. Residents of Richmond, Virginia, had long debated the existence of statuary tributes to Confederate leaders along famed Monument Avenue. The monuments were targeted by protesters, who covered them in graffiti and decorated them to advance their message. In one case, protesters managed to topple the Jefferson Davis statue from its position atop a tall pillar. Within weeks, the process of removing the statues and surrounding monumentation began, with several city-controlled statues being removed in July 2020; the statue of Robert E. Lee, which had assumed symbolic importance as the center of the protests, was removed in September 2021.[18]

The federal government soon followed in undertaking the dismantling of Confederate symbols. In 2020 the House of Representatives voted to remove statues of people who had served in the Confederacy; several states also chose to replace statues of Confederate leaders from their states.[19] The following year Congress provided for the establishment of the Commission on the Naming of Items, commonly known as the Naming Commission. Its charge was to consider renaming federal military installations and the fate of other commemorations of prominent Confederates on properties controlled by the Department of Defense (see Jennifer M. Murray's chapter). In some cases, the removals affected Reconstruction heritage as well, as in the case of renaming a fort that originally honored Confederate general and later Ku Klux Klan leader John B. Gordon as Fort Eisenhower. The commission also called for the removal of the Confederate Memorial at Arlington National Cemetery and the removal or renaming of various places at the United States Military Academy at West Point (often replacing Lee with Grant). As a sign of the times, a new statue of Ulysses S. Grant was commissioned for display on the academy grounds at West Point. During 2023 nine U.S. military bases were renamed, thus losing their association with Confederate leaders; the Confederate Memorial in Arlington was removed at year's end.[20]

Not everyone agreed with the renaming decision. Two candidates for the 2024 Republican presidential nomination, Florida Governor Ron DeSantis and former Vice President Mike Pence, spoke against renaming Fort Bragg (named after Confederate general Braxton Bragg) as Fort Liberty in remarks delivered at North Carolina's 2023 Republican state convention.[21] The following year, Trump, by then the de facto Republican presidential nominee, faced ridicule when he spoke of Robert E. Lee and the Battle of Gettysburg at a rally in Pennsylvania.[22] For Trump, who had previously claimed without any basis in fact that his golf course in northern Virginia was the site of a Civil War battle, who had mangled Ulysses S. Grant's first name in speaking of the Union commander, and who had repeatedly spoken highly of Lee and his fellow Confederates once it seemed such comments would appeal to many of his supporters, the renaming exercise was a deplorable destruction of history.[23]

Many of Trump's comments became fodder for the campaign trail as he commenced his quest for reelection. On Election Day 2020, it remained unclear as to whether Trump or Biden would ultimately prevail. Given the variation in how states counted mail-in votes—which had become a more popular way of voting given the risks associated with the COVID-19 pandemic—full sets of returns would not be available in some cases for days, raising tensions still more given the closely contested nature of the election. Yet it did not take long for Trump to declare that widespread and systematic fraud would deprive him of reelection. Such talk reminded observers of the disputed election of 1876. White supremacist violence worked to suppress the Republican vote in 1876, while Democratic state regimes, in control of the process of counting ballots and protecting citizens, kept those states in the Democratic column. Meanwhile, in those former Confederate states where the Republicans claimed control of the governor's seat and the statehouses, returning boards more than undid evidence of voter suppression and reported Republican majorities that were products of creative counting. Trump and his supporters claimed that voting machines and the actions of state and local officials had stolen the election from him through outright fraud.

Whatever one made of such claims, attention soon focused on how the electoral vote would be counted. Trump supporters in several closely contested states where Biden had been certified the winner decided to authorize the creation of alternative electors pledged to Trump. If such slates of electors were recognized as legitimate by Vice President Mike Pence, Trump's running mate in 2016 and 2020, Trump might still claim victory; Pence might also rule that the disputes in various states should be settled by state legislatures, which in several cases were controlled by Republicans. Other scenarios supposed that congressional Republicans could challenge the counting of the electoral vote in key states, leading to stalemate, chaos, or a Trump triumph.

Here the obvious comparison was to the resolution of the disputed election of 1876 far more than it was to the contest between George W. Bush and

Albert Gore Jr. in 2000. In the former election, the president of the Senate was a Republican, Thomas W. Ferry (Vice President Henry Wilson had died during Grant's second term, and the Twenty-Fifth Amendment was some nine decades away). In 1877 Congress improvised a resolution by establishing the Electoral Commission; a decade later it passed the Electoral Count Act to avoid another crisis in the counting of the electoral vote. Despite a few minor controversies, that act largely served its purpose, even during the 2000 presidential contest. However, in the aftermath of the election of 2020, Trump supporters, including the president's legal advisers, attempted to formulate a theory that would empower Vice President Pence to act unilaterally, either to decide which slate of electors was legitimate or to send back the competing slates for adjudication by Republican-controlled state legislatures. Pence refused to cooperate with such schemes, although multiple accounts suggest that he was not totally unwilling to act had a more persuasive case been made as to the amount of discretion he could exercise. It would be left to a small group of Republicans in each chamber as to whether they could derail the process of counting the electoral vote.

Events overtook this process on January 6, 2021. Right-wing extremist groups, largely supportive of Trump, and other Trump supporters had planned a rally in Washington under the name "Stop the Steal." In the morning Trump, his supporters, and prominent Republicans addressed a crowd of protesters; that afternoon that crowd advanced upon the Capitol, broke into the building, and sought to disrupt the counting of the electoral vote by both houses of Congress. Members of Congress evacuated their chambers and retreated to secure places shortly before protesters entered both chambers. Confrontations with law enforcement authorities escalated and turned violent, with one protester shot and killed.

Once more Civil War symbols were evident as the nation watched on television. In approaching the Capitol, protesters swarmed around the Ulysses S. Grant Memorial, erecting a gallows across the reflecting pool from the recently restored monument. Confederate flags were scattered throughout the mob of protesters, and one memorable photograph captured a protester carrying a Confederate flag into the Capitol itself. For viewers acquainted with Reconstruction, the protest-turned-insurrection recalled events in New Orleans in 1874 and 1875, the Brooks–Baxter War in Little Rock, Arkansas, and the tense confrontation in Columbia, South Carolina, as the Republican regime, lacking sustained federal support, gave way to the Red Shirt Democrats of incoming Governor (and former Confederate General) Wade Hampton.[24]

Fig. 1.1. The storming of the U.S. Capitol by supporters of President Donald Trump on January 6, 2021. Note the Confederate flag on the left side of the image. Tyler Merbler from USA, CC BY 2.0, https://creativecommons.org/licenses/by/2.0, via Wikimedia Commons.

In the immediate aftermath of the January 6 assault on the U.S. Capitol, journalists scurried to find historical context for such an event. They found it in Reconstruction. Several writers advised incoming President Joseph R. Biden Jr. to emulate Ulysses S. Grant and employ a firm hand to punish insurrectionists. Their point of comparison was how Grant went after terrorists and insurrectionists during Reconstruction. Within days, Ryan Cooper of *The Week* highlighted historical parallels between January 6 and Reconstruction, focusing on Grant's use of the Third Enforcement Act, commonly known as the Ku Klux Klan Act, to subdue Klan activity in the South Carolina upcountry. He warned that unless insurrectionary acts were persistently punished, the insurrectionists would eventually prevail as they had during Reconstruction.[25]

At *Politico*, Casey Michel tended to blur the lines between white supremacist violence against Blacks and the white allies with efforts to overthrow Republican regimes. Michel also focused on Grant's intervention in South Carolina in 1871, claiming that the eighteenth president "relied on a combination of brute military force and a drastic curtailment of civil liberties," and that his failure to persist in his efforts helped lead to Reconstruction's undoing. Although Michel cited the efforts of Phil Sheridan to subdue the effort to overthrow Louisiana's Republican-controlled state legislature in January 1875, he did so to suggest that Grant realized that he lacked the public support to continue such enforcement efforts.[26]

Perhaps the loudest of the journalists who invoked Reconstruction parallels to January 6 was Jamelle Bouie, who returned repeatedly to these themes, first on the social media platform Twitter, then in the *New York Times*.[27] Bouie's initial column in the *Times* focused on the September 1874 insurrection in Louisiana, the 1875 "Mississippi Plan," and political violence in South Carolina in 1876, overlooking the January 1875 Louisiana attempted coup d'état that most closely resembled what happened in Washington in 2021.[28]

Cooper based his historical research on a reading of Eric Foner's scholarship; Michel, with more time at his disposal, cast a wider net, contacting several scholars for quotes. Bouie was not always so careful in citing the sources of his historical understanding. Historians also weighed in, even if they did not always agree with journalists' historical comparisons.[29] In a critical assessment of Ron Chernow's Grant biography, Brook Thomas cautioned that Grant's record in punishing white Southern terrorists was not as successful or as persistent as some accounts made it out to be, singling out Chernow for special attention.[30]

What was significant in retrospect is that people who recounted what happened on January 6 commonly referred to it as an insurrection. While not, strictly speaking, a coup d'état, because it did not seek to overthrow a regime, it was widely understood to be an attempt to overturn an election result through violent means as well as disrupting and abusing the political process to the point that, if successful, the American experiment in representative democracy would have been seriously and perhaps irreparably damaged. Reconstruction comparisons thus emphasized the degree to which violence was a political weapon that was used to overthrow state Republican governments and thus secure states' electoral votes for the Democratic Party through voter suppression, intimidation, and murder. Grant received too much credit for supposedly destroying the Ku Klux Klan, given that white supremacist terrorism in the former Confederacy eventually carried the day, but at least commentators were now taking his presidency seriously and reconsidering the challenges of Reconstruction considering the events both in the 1870s and the 2020s. If anything, Grant's later reluctance to battle Southern violence due to multiple factors offered a cautionary tale for anyone advising amnesty and reconciliation. In turn, defenders of the insurrection, like Reconstruction Democrats and many early scholars of the Reconstruction period, sought either to minimize the violence or justify it. For members of the party of Lincoln and Grant to discount what had happened was remarkable indeed.

In the wake of the events of January 6, 2021, the House of Representatives once more impeached Trump, this time on January 13, 2021, for inciting an insurrection. Although a few House Republicans supported impeachment, fewer Senate Republicans voted for conviction in a proceeding that took place after Trump had left office. There was even debate on whether Trump as a former president had to face impeachment. Scholars of impeachment, the Grant presidency, and Reconstruction recalled that in 1876 Grant's secretary of war, William W. Belknap, had been impeached by the House and tried by the Senate even after he had resigned his cabinet post (Grant later regretted accepting the resignation, having not yet been alerted to the serious nature of the charges against Belknap). In Belknap's case, he was acquitted by the Senate, but a majority of those who voted for acquittal claimed that they did so because they questioned jurisdiction even though they believed that Belknap was guilty of an impeachable offense.[31] In 2021 most Senate Republicans would not go that far, in part because political considerations caused them to temper their criticism of Trump even when they chose not to defend him.[32]

Two years later, the former president faced a wave of indictments for his actions while president concerning the election of 2020 (as well as for private acts and business transactions). Commentators immediate brought out Ulysses S. Grant as a point of comparison, reminding readers that Grant was once arrested for speeding in Washington (a tale some scholars began to question upon closer examination) and that the basis for indicting Trump reached as far back as the Enforcement Act of 1870, passed during the Grant administration.[33] Grant was also cited in relation to Trump's legal problems concerning his business transactions, reviving stories of the failure of Grant and Ward in 1884.[34] Given the resurgence in Grant's reputation during the twenty-first century, especially concerning his performance as president, perhaps such references were to be expected. Commentary usually offered a far more sympathetic, even positive view of the eighteenth president in comparing him to his successor.

Just when it seemed that references to Reconstruction in American politics showed signs of dying down, along came another argument that refocused attention on the Fourteenth Amendment. This time it concerned section 3, which disqualified from holding state or federal office people who had served or supported the Confederacy after having taken an oath to "support" the Constitution of the United States. Congress could remove this disability by a two-thirds vote in each house. The purpose of that clause was to prevent the return of many leading former Confederates to political office; it prevented them from holding offices (members of Congress, members of the Electoral College, or "any office, civil or military under the United States, or under any State," wording which seemed specific enough for most people). Left undefined was who would judge whether someone had indeed violated any oath they took and whether they, in fact, had "engaged in insurrection or rebellion."

The clause received new attention in the aftermath of the events of January 6, 2021. In 2022 a federal district judge ruled that an effort to disqualify a North Carolina Republican congressman, Madison Cawthorn, from eligibility for reelection due to his support of the insurrection of January 6 was in error, using the curious reasoning that the Amnesty Act of 1872 removed Cawthorn's disqualification.[35] That logic, such as it was, did not remain unchallenged for long: Less than three months later, an appeals court overturned the ruling. By that time Cawthorn had been defeated in the Republican primary; efforts to take the same action against several other Republican members of the House of Representatives, including Marjorie Taylor Greene (Georgia), Andy Biggs (Arizona), and Paul Gosar (Arizona), failed, as well as Arizona state legislator Mark Finchem.[36] Whether state courts could invoke section 3 to disqualify candidates for state office was another matter entirely. In September 2022 New Mexico district court Judge Francis Mathew ruled that Otero County Commissioner Couy Griffin's actions on January 6 constituted an act of insurrection and barred him from ever serving in public office again.[37]

In August 2023 two legal scholars, William Baude and Michael Stokes Paulsen, each identified as politically conservative, argued that section 3 disqualified Donald J. Trump Jr. from again becoming president because of his actions in contesting the result of the 2020 presidential election, specifically those involving the insurrection of January 6, 2021.[38] They asserted that the clause was "self-executing" and should be enforced. They were not the first to do so: less than two weeks after January 6, Daniel J. Hemel raised the issue in *Lawfare*, an online legal commentary and analysis publication associated with the Brookings Institution, citing several commentaries that had already appeared by then.[39] But Baude and Paulsen renewed the case for application: "Taking Section Three seriously means excluding from present or future office those who sought to subvert lawful government authority under the Constitution in the aftermath of the 2020 election by engaging in insurrection or rebellion or giving aid or comfort to enemies of the lawful constitutional order."[40]

Not everyone agreed with Baude and Paulsen. Within days of the appearance of their article, David E. Weisberg challenged the notion that section 3 applied to presidents or vice presidents.[41] Other critics claimed that the presidential oath of office called upon the president to "preserve, protect, and defend" the Constitution but not to "support" it, as section 3 would have it.[42] There were arguments that Congress's later amnesty legislation, although it specifically applied to former Confederates, might also apply to the January 6 insurrections, an argument that seemed on its face flawed, even desperate, as the Cawthorn example suggested. Inevitably the debate became entangled with Trump's ambition to be reelected, a desire that became more difficult to realize as he faced multiple indictments in multiple jurisdictions for various offenses, including his efforts to overturn the 2020 election result in Georgia and his role in inciting the insurrection on January 6 as part of a larger plot to steal the very election he claimed was stolen from him.

The legal arguments pro and con seemed endless.[43] Before long, however, several lawsuits filed in various states sought to test the proposition that Trump could be disqualified from running for president through a vigorous application of section 3.[44] Attention soon centered on Colorado, where the state supreme court ruled in favor of a petition offered by several registered Republicans and independents seeking to remove Trump's name from the 2024 Colorado Republican primary ballot due to his supposed disqualification. Trump appealed the decision to the Supreme Court of the United States, which decided to hear the case.

Groups of historians and legal scholars, as well as other parties, rushed to submit amicus briefs to support various arguments, with the majority of scholarly briefs taking the position that section 3 did in fact apply to Trump because he had inspired and encouraged (and may have helped plan) the events of January 6, 2021, which amounted to committing an insurrectionary act.[45] The briefs also offered a number of opinions as to whether section 3 was self-executing, or whether implementing it required additional congressional action. The Supreme Court heard arguments on February 8, 2024. It soon became clear over the course of questioning that the entire court agreed that whatever the merits of the section 3 argument, it should not be left to a state to interpret its applicability to a national election, lest that give rise to a "patchwork" diversity of outcomes and confusion. However, the court did not restrict itself to considering that question, choosing also to explore whether the clause was self-executing, or whether, following a decision issued in federal circuit court in 1869 by Chief Justice Salmon P. Chase, *Ex parte Caesar Griffin*, Congress had to legislate to apply the clause to specific cases. While several of the briefs had touched on that decision, it assumed an importance few had anticipated.[46]

On March 4, 2024, the Supreme Court issued its ruling. As expected, it was unanimous in deciding that state courts could not use section 3 to disqualify presidential candidates or other candidates for federal office from appearing on a state's ballot (although state courts could invoke the clause to disqualify candidates for state office). Nor could a state act against a federal officeholder. It was Congress's responsibility to apply section 3 to specific cases as provided by section 5. That in practice section 3 was self-executing (as were several other pieces of Civil War legislation concerning the actions of individuals who participated in insurrection against the United States) did not move the court. However, the ruling did not exclude the president of the United States from the provisions of section 3; moreover, it also held that the clause of the Second Confiscation Act of 1862 that engaging in insurrection or rebellion, which was a crime punishable by disqualification from holding federal office, also remained in force.[47]

Not every justice agreed with every aspect of the majority's opinion. Associate Justice Amy Coney Barrett argued that the court's opinion need not have gone beyond the immediate issue before it, which was whether a state could enforce section 3 when it came for candidates for federal office. Three other justices (Sonia Sotomayor, Elena Kagan, and Ketanji Brown Jackson) went further in using Chief Justice Roberts's endorsement of judicial restraint in a case involving reproductive rights (*Dobbs v. Jackson Women's Health Organization*, 597 U.S. 215, [2022]) to argue that their five male colleagues, all nominated by Republican presidents, went beyond the matter before them to specify how Congress (and only Congress) could enforce section 3. The trio specifically cast aside Griffin's Case (as *Ex parte Caesar Griffin* came to be known) in asserting that the section was, in fact, self-executing. Judicial overreach by the majority, they concluded, "attempts to insulate all alleged insurrectionists from future challenges to their holding federal office."[48]

A careful reading of the decision reveals that the court did not rule on whether then-President Trump engaged in insurrection as a finding of fact;

the majority left that to Congress to so decide. Nevertheless, it accepted that someone occupying the office of the president of the United States fell under the provisions of the clause in question, meaning that Congress could act to disqualify Trump from holding office again. A second Supreme Court decision, *Trump v. United States*, decided July 1, 2024, may further complicate matters in its efforts to define qualified presidential immunity from prosecution, although the opinions made no reference to its previous ruling on section 3. Still, questions remain. Was Trump operating in his official capacity on January 6, 2021, in all of his actions, or simply some of them? Would the immunity granted in this decision also immunize him from actions taken by Congress under section 3 of the Fourteenth Amendment given the court's previous ruling in *Trump v. Anderson*? One would think not, given that these are qualitatively different categories of behavior. Such speculations were rendered moot when Trump secured a second term as president in the 2024 election: That Republicans won majorities, however slim, in both houses of Congress effectively ended whatever chance there was of exploring the possibilities of section 3. Still, one wonders whether understandings of congressional intent during the Civil War and Reconstruction will resurface in future cases concerning the actions of federal officials.

That Reconstruction, understood and misunderstood, has enjoyed renewed interest is suggested in how it has been invoked in several recent accounts, including those composed by scholars not known for possessing any special expertise in Reconstruction, who have sought to render accounts of Reconstruction in light of contemporary events. These studies included Jeremi Suri's *Civil War by Other Means: America's Long and Unfinished Fight for Democracy* (2022); Kermit Roosevelt III's *The Nation That Never Was: Reconstructing America's Story* (2022); and Heather Cox Richardson's *How the South Won the Civil War* (2020).[49] Of these three writers, only Richardson possesses a track record of previous publication in the field as the author of several critically acclaimed books on the politics of the Civil War and Reconstruction. Each book offered an understanding of Reconstruction that focused on the ways in which white Americans battled against Blacks' struggle for equality and opportunity during Reconstruction, sometimes as part of larger themes. Reviewers familiar with the history of Reconstruction have not always been kind in their assessments of these books, and it remains to be seen how much they are more products of the time in which they were written than studies of the time they purport to describe and interpret.[50]

A more recent study of Grant's actions against the Ku Klux Klan, published in 2023, suggested that just as observers had been citing Reconstruction contexts for present-day events, other scholars saw the past from the perspective of the present in terms of the issues explored and the questions raised. Fergus M. Bordewich moved carefully between past and present in his narrative. "The urgency of containing domestic terrorism and racial zealotry have not gone away," he observed. "Nor has the need to protect basic civil rights, including the right to vote." To be sure, Bordewich observed, he was writing about the past, but his account "shows that forceful political action can prevail over violent extremism," but "when political courage succumbs to partisan self-interest the darker impulses that are always present in America inherit a fertile ground on which to thrive."[51] In *The Rise and Fall of the Second American Republic: Reconstruction, 1860–1920* (2024), Manisha Sinha reminded readers that many of the issues of Reconstruction were still present in the twenty-first century, balancing hope for the future against concern that reactionary forces might well carry the day in an era of "renewed challenges to American democracy."[52]

The story of Reconstruction once stood in the shadow of the history of the Civil War proper. In recent years, however, scholars and commentators have decided the period has much to contribute to helping us grasp what is happening in twenty-first-century America. This is attributable in part to the nature of recent events, which echo, even if sometimes in distorted fashion, key moments in Reconstruction history; it is also because our changing understanding of the meaning of the Civil War era and the fundamental ways in which the themes of slavery and coercion, race and political violence, resistance and insurrection, as well as the tendency of popular historical memory to reshape understandings of the past to fit present agendas, bring the Civil War and Reconstruction together as part of a larger struggle over the fundamentals of the American experiment that remain relevant.

NOTES

1. See, for example, Keith, *Colfax Massacre*; Emberton, *Beyond Redemption*; Hogue, *Uncivil War*; Egerton, *Wars of Reconstruction*. Nor was this shift limited to academic historians: see Lemann, *Redemption*; Lane, *Day Freedom Died*; Budiansky, *Bloody Shirt*.
2. Blight's *Race and Reunion* offered an approach that incorporated Reconstruction, but the emphasis on military events in some studies overshadowed how memories about the Civil War were just as much about Reconstruction. Domby's *False Cause* is one study of memory that addresses Reconstruction.

3. Gordon Chadwick, "The Creation of the Battle of Liberty Place Monument," New Orleans Historical, accessed June 10, 2024, https://neworleanshistorical.org/items/show/150.
4. Adolph Reed Jr., "The Battle of Liberty Monument," The Free Library, accessed June 10, 2024, https://www.thefreelibrary.com/The+battle+of+Liberty+Monument.-a013773324.
5. See Nelson and Harold, *Charlottesville 2017*.
6. "Charlottesville's Lee Statue Meets Its End, in a 2,250-Degree Furnace," *Washington Post*, October 26, 2023, https://www.washingtonpost.com/dc-md-va/interactive/2023/civil-war-monument-melting-robert-e-lee-confederate/.
7. See "A Confederate General's Remains Are Being Moved Out of Memphis," Associated Press, June 19, 2021, https://www.npr.org/2021/06/19/1008371491/confederate-general-remains-memphis-moved; Clint Confehr, "Nathan Bedford Forrest Statue, Graves, and Memorial to Be Reconstructed," *Tennessee Tribune*, September 7, 2023, https://tntribune.com/nathan-bedford-forrest-statue-graves-and-memorial-to-be-reconstructed/.
8. For example, Varon's *Longstreet* emphasized Longstreet's views on race before, during, and after the Civil War and emphasized Longstreet's career during Reconstruction.
9. Erin L. Thompson, "The Arlington National Cemetery Will Finally Remove Its Racist Monument," *The Nation*, May 9, 2023, https://www.thenation.com/article/society/arlington-national-cemetery-racist-monument/. For the "reconciliation" website, see OneClickPolitics, accessed October 28, 2023, https://oneclickpolitics.global.ssl.fastly.net/messages/edit?promo_id=18074.
10. See Carpenter, *Ulysses S. Grant*; Brock, *Conflict and Transformation*; Donald, *Liberty and Union*; Current, *Arguing with Historians*; McFeely, *Grant*.
11. See Simpson, *Let Us Have Peace*; Scaturro, *President Grant Reconsidered*; Smith, *Grant*; Bunting, *Ulysses S. Grant*; White, *American Ulysses*.
12. "Matthew Heimbach," Southern Poverty Law Center, accessed July 1, 2024, https://www.splcenter.org/fighting-hate/extremist-files/individual/matthew-heimbach.
13. See "Trump Said 'Blame on Both Sides' in Charlottesville, Now the Anniversary Puts Him on the Spot," ABC News, August 12, 2018, https://abcnews.go.com/Politics/trump-blame-sides-charlottesville-now-anniversary-puts-spot/story?id=57141612.
14. See, for example, Patrick Rael, "By the Standard of Andrew Johnson's Impeachment, Trump's Would Be a No-Brainer," *Muster*, September 1, 2017, https://www.journalofthecivilwarera.org/2017/09/by-standard-of-johnsons-impeachment-trumps-no-brainer/; Aaron Astor, "'Disgrace, Ridicule, Hatred, Contempt and Reproach': The Impeachments of Andrew Johnson and Donald Trump," *Muster*, November 26, 2019, https://www.journalofthecivilwarera.org/2019/11/disgrace-ridicule-hatred-contempt-and-reproach-the-impeachments-of-andrew-johnson-and-donald-trump/.
15. Tim Murphy, "Trump's Not Richard Nixon. He's Andrew Johnson," *Mother Jones*, January/February 2020, https://www.motherjones.com/politics/2019/12/trumps-not-richard-nixon-hes-andrew-johnson/.
16. Bruce Ackerman, "Trump's Lawyers Are Getting Andrew Johnson's Impeachment All Wrong," *Politico*, January 25, 2020, https://www.politico.com/news/magazine/2020/01/25/trump-impeachment-andrew-johnson-104066.
17. Adam Serwer, "The New Reconstruction," *The Atlantic*, September 2020, https://www.theatlantic.com/magazine/archive/2020/10/the-next-reconstruction/615475/.

18. Sarah Rankin and Denise Lavoie, "Gen. Lee Statue Comes Down in Former Confederate Capital," Associated Press, September 8, 2021, https://apnews.com/article/robert-e-lee-statue-virginia-removed-92955a351d9fda6319f379ddc28df8a0.
19. Catie Edmondson, "House Votes to Remove Confederate Statues from U.S. Capitol," *New York Times*, July 22, 2020, https://www.nytimes.com/2020/07/22/us/politics/confederate-statues-us-capitol.html; Matthew Daly, "Pelosi Orders Removal of Confederate Portraits from Capitol," PBS News, June 18, 2020, https://www.nytimes.com/2020/07/22/us/politics/confederate-statues-us-capitol.html.
20. "Congressional Naming Commission Report"; "Confederate Memorial," Arlington National Cemetery, accessed July 1, 2024, https://www.arlingtoncemetery.mil/Explore/Monuments-and-Memorials/Confederate-Memorial.
21. Jay Price, "Presidential Campaign Talking Point: Fort Bragg's Name Change," *Morning Edition*, NPR, June 26, 2023, https://www.npr.org/2023/06/26/1184268004/presidential-campaign-talking-point-fort-braggs-name-change.
22. Margaret Hartman, "Trump's Gettysburg Address Featured a Pirate Impression," *Intelligencer*, April 15, 2024, https://nymag.com/intelligencer/article/trumps-gettysburg-address-uphill-lee.html.
23. Nicholas Fandos, "In Renovation of Golf Club, Donald Trump Also Dressed Up History," *New York Times*, November 24, 2015, https://www.nytimes.com/2015/11/25/us/politics/in-renovation-of-golf-club-donald-trump-also-dressed-up-history.html; Libby Cathey, "Trump's History of Defending Confederate 'Heritage' Despite Political Risk," ABC News, June 11, 2020, https://abcnews.go.com/Politics/trumps-history-defending-confederate-heritage-political-risk-analysis/story?id=71199968; Trump, Remarks, CBS News, October 13, 2018, https://youtu.be/z0ERwowRYZk; Sushma Karra, "Trump Mispronounces Ulysses Grant as 'Ulysseus' Twice in Speech at Mount Rushmore, Internet Says He's a 'Moron,'" *Meaww*, July 4, 2020, https://meaww.com/donald-trump-mt-rushmore-rally-specch-ulysses-ulyssius-mispronounce-mocked-twitter-fans-react.
24. Two television hosts turned their hand to writing about the events of Ulysses S. Grant's second administration concerning violence and the overturning of elections: Baier, *To Rescue the Republic*; Bash, *America's Deadliest Election*. Each author also had a coauthor who was not always recognized in publicity; while Baier's book received laudatory comments from blurbers and Amazon reviewers, it was riddled with mistakes and took much of his story from existing scholarship.
25. Ryan Cooper, "What Joe Biden Can Learn from Ulysses S. Grant," *The Week*, January 8, 2021, https://theweek.com/articles/959430/what-joe-biden-learn-from-ulysses-s-grant.
26. Casey Michel, "What Ulysses Grant Can Teach Joe Biden About Putting Down Violent Insurrections," *Politico*, January 31, 2021, https://www.politico.com/news/magazine/2021/01/30/what-ulysses-grant-can-teach-joe-biden-about-putting-down-violent-insurrections-463976.
27. Jamelle Bouie (@jbouie), "I'll keep saying this but for example look no further than the ku klux klan, theatrical and silly and also deadly serious," Twitter (now X), January 7, 2021, https://twitter.com/jbouie/status/1347177083177496576.
28. Jamelle Bouie, "Running Out the Clock on Trump Is Cowardly and Dangerous," *New York Times*, January 8, 2021, https://www.nytimes.com/2021/01/08/opinion/trump-capitol-riot-impeachment.html.

29. Hilary N. Green, "Civil War Eera Scholars Respond to January 6, 2021 Events and Aftermath," *Muster*, January 12, 2021, https://www.journalofthecivilwarera.org/2021/01/civil-war-era-scholars-respond-to-january-6-2021-events-and-aftermath/.
30. Brook Thomas, "Grant's Mixed Legacy," *Muster*, February 11, 2021, https://www.journalofthecivilwarera.org/2021/02/grants-mixed-legacy/. More recently, Cwiklik emphasized the failure to stop such violence in *Sheridan's Secret Mission*.
31. See Calhoun, *Presidency of Ulysses S. Grant*, 532.
32. Belknap's impeachment received new attention in 2024, when House Republicans impeached Homeland Security Secretary Alejandro Mayorkas, although Mayorkas did not face trial in the Senate—the indictment was dismissed. See Zachary B. Wolf, "Mayorkas Impeachment Effort Is Nothing Like the Only Other Cabinet Impeachment for 1876," CNN Politics, February 6, 2024, https://www.cnn.com/2024/02/06/politics/mayorkas-impeachment-cabinet-what-matters/index.html.
33. "Ulysses S. Grant Was the First President to Be Arrested," *Morning Edition*, NPR, April 3, 2023, https://www.npr.org/2023/04/03/1167683136/ulysses-s-grant-was-the-first-president-to-be-arrested; Meilan Solly, "When President Ulysses S. Grant Was Arrested for Speeding in a Horse-Drawn Carriage," *Smithsonian Magazine*, March 31, 2023, https://www.smithsonianmag.com/smart-news/when-president-ulysses-s-grant-was-arrested-for-speeding-in-a-horse-drawn-carriage-180981916/; "Was General Grant Arrested for Speeding in Washington, DC?" Ulysses S. Grant National Historical Site, National Park Service, April 26, 2023, https://www.nps.gov/articles/000/was-general-grant-arrested-for-speeding-in-washington-d-c.htm; Joshua Zeitz, "If Trump Gets Convicted, Blame Ulysses S. Grant," *Politico*, August 3, 2023, https://www.politico.com/news/magazine/2023/08/03/enforcement-acts-trump-00109622.
34. James Barron, "Once Before, an Ex-President Was in Jeopardy in New York," *New York Times*, March 23, 2023, https://www.nytimes.com/2023/03/31/nyregion/ulysses-grant-trump.html.
35. "Judge Blocks Effort to Disqualify Cawthorn from Ballot as 'Insurrectionist,'" *New York Times*, March 4, 2022, https://www.nytimes.com/2022/03/04/us/politics/madison-cawthorn-north-carolina-insurrectionist.html.
36. Martin Pengelly, "Blow to Madison Cawthorn as Appeals Court Reverses 'Insurrectionist' Ruling," *The Guardian*, May 25, 2022, https://www.theguardian.com/us-news/2022/may/25/madison-cawthorn-appeals-court-insurrection-ruling.
37. Ashley Lopez, "A New Mexico Judge Cites Insurrection in Barring a County Commissioner from Office," NPR, September 6, 2022, https://www.npr.org/2022/09/06/1121307430/couy-griffin-otero-county-insurrection-fourteenth-amendment.
38. Baude and Paulsen, "Sweep and Force of Section Three."
39. Daniel J. Hemel, "Disqualifying Insurrectionists and Rebels: A How-to Guide," *Lawfare*, January 19, 2021, https://www.lawfaremedia.org/article/disqualifying-insurrectionists-and-rebels-how-guide. Among the commentaries cited by Hemel were Eric Foner, "Impeachment May Not Work. Here's the Next Best Way to Dump Trump," *Washington Post*, January 12, 2021, https://www.washingtonpost.com/outlook/2021/01/12/14th-amendment-impeachment-alternative/; Michael Macagnone, "Excluding Lawmakers Under 14th Amendment No Easy Task," *Roll Call*, January 12, 2021, https://rollcall.com/2021/01/12/14th-amendment-section-3-capitol-riot/; and Michael S. Rosenwald, "There's an Alternative to Impeachment or 25th Amendment for Trump, Historians Say," *Washington Post*, January 12, 2021,

https://www.washingtonpost.com/history/2021/01/11/14th-amendment-trump-insurrection-impeachment/.
40. Baude and Paulsen, "Sweep and Force of Section Three," 7.
41. David E. Weisberg, "Baude and Paulsen Are Mistaken: Section 3 Has Never Barred Anyone from Serving as President," SSRN, September 12, 2023, https://papers.ssrn.com/sol3/papers.cfm?abstract_id=4549928.
42. Mead Gruver and Nicholas Riccardi, "Colorado Judge Strikes down Trump's Attempt to Toss a Lawsuit Seeking to Bar Him from the Ballot," Associated Press, October 12, 2023, https://apnews.com/article/trump-insurrection-14th-amendment-ballot-colorado-c699e7c00687be6bc4bedbaf4182e451.
43. Mark Brown, "Trump and Section 3 of the Fourteenth Amendment: An Exploration of Constitutional Eligibility," *Jurist*, October 12, 2023, https://www.jurist.org/features/2023/10/12/trump-and-section-3-of-the-fourteenth-amendment-an-exploration-of-constitutional-eligibility/.
44. Marshall Cohen and Devan Cole, "Takeaways from Day 1 of the Trump Disqualification Trial in Colorado," CNN, October 31, 2023, https://www.cnn.com/2023/10/30/politics/takeaways-trump-14th-amendment-trial-colorado/index.html.
45. The collection of briefs may be found on the Supreme Court webpage for case no. 23-719 at https://www.supremecourt.gov/docket/docketfiles/html/public/23-719.html. For a summary of the positions taken by the various briefs, see Hyemin Han et al., "Breaking Down the Amicus Briefs in Trump v. Anderson," *Lawfare*, February 7, 2024, https://www.lawfaremedia.org/article/breaking-down-the-amicus-briefs-in-trump-v.-anderson. The author was one of twenty-five historians who signed the brief titled "Brief for Professors Orville Vernon Burton, Allan J. Lichtman, et al." concerning whether section 3 included the president of the United States and was self-executing.
46. For the case in question, see the *American Law Register* 17, no. 6, new series volume 8 (June 1869): 358–67, via the Internet Archive, accessed July 1, 2024, https://archive.org/search?query=external-identifier%3A%22urn%3Ajstor-articleid%3A10.2307%2F3303523%22. See also William Hogeland, "'Griffin's Case' and Trump," *Hogeland's Bad History*, February 7, 2024, https://williamhogeland.substack.com/p/griffins-case-and-trump.
47. Trump v. Anderson, 601 U.S. 100 (2024).
48. Trump v. Anderson, 601 U.S. 100 (2024).
49. Suri, *Civil War by Other Means*; Roosevelt, *Nation That Never Was*; Richardson, *How the South Won the Civil War*.
50. See, for example, Mark W. Summers's critical review of Richardson (*H-Net Reviews*, February 2021, https://www.h-net.org/reviews/showpdf.php?id=55850) and of Suri (*H-Net Reviews*, October 2023, https://www.h-net.org/reviews/showrev.php?id=58746).
51. Bordewich, *Klan War*.
52. Sinha, *Rise and Fall of the Second American Republic*.

BIBLIOGRAPHY

Baier, Bret, with Catherine Whitney. *To Rescue the Republic: Ulysses S. Grant, the Fragile Union, and the Crisis of 1876*. Mariner, 2021.

Bash, Dana, with David Fisher. *America's Deadliest Election: The Cautionary Tale of the Most Violent Election in American History*. HarperCollins, 2024.

Baude, William, and Michael Stokes Paulsen. "The Sweep and Force of Section Three." *University of Pennsylvania Law Review* 172, no. 3 (2024). https://scholarship.law.upenn.edu/penn_law_review/vol172/iss3/1/.

Blight, David W. *Race and Reunion: The Civil War in American Memory*. Belknap, 2001.

Bordewich, Fergus M. *Klan War: Ulysses S. Grant and the Battle to Save Reconstruction*. Knopf, 2023.

Brock, William R. *Conflict and Transformation: The United Sates, 1844–1877*. Penguin, 1973.

Budiansky, Stephen. *The Bloody Shirt: Terror After Appomattox*. Viking, 2008.

Calhoun, Charles W. *The Presidency of Ulysses S. Grant*. University Press of Kansas, 2017.

Carpenter, John A. *Ulysses S. Grant*. Twayne, 1970.

"Congressional Naming Commission Report." United States Military Academy at West Point. https://www.westpoint.edu/naming-commission-report.

Current, Richard. *Arguing with Historians*. Wesleyan University Press, 1987.

Cwiklik, Robert. *Sheridan's Secret Mission: How the South Won the War*. Harper, 2024.

Donald, David Herbert. *Liberty and Union: The Crisis of Popular Government, 1830–1890*. Little, Brown, 1978.

Domby, Adam H. *The False Cause: Fraud, Fabrication, and White Supremacy in Confederate Memory*. University of Virginia Press, 2020.

Egerton, Douglas R. *The Wars of Reconstruction: The Brief, Violent History of America's Most Progressive Era*. Bloomsbury, 2014.

Emberton, Carole. *Beyond Redemption: Race, Violence, and the American South after the Civil War*. University of Chicago Press, 2013.

Hogue, James K. *Uncivil War: Five New Orleans Street Battles and the Rise and Fall of Radical Reconstruction*. Louisiana State University Press, 2006.

Keith, LeeAnna. *The Colfax Massacre*. Oxford University Press, 2008.

Lane, Charles. *The Day Freedom Died: The Colfax Massacre, the Supreme Court, and the Betrayal of Reconstruction*. Henry Holt, 2008.

Lemann, Nicholas. *Redemption: The Last Battle of the Civil War*. Farrar, Straus, and Giroux, 2006.

McFeely, William S. *Grant: A Biography*. W. W. Norton, 1981.

Nelson, Louis P., and Claudrena N. Harold, eds. *Charlottesville 2017: The Legacy of Race and Inequity*. University of Virginia Press, 2018.

Richardson, Heather Cox. *How the South Won the Civil War*. Oxford University Press, 2020.

Roosevelt, Kermit, III. *The Nation That Never Was: Reconstructing America's Story*. University of Chicago Press, 2022.

Scaturro, Frank J. *President Grant Reconsidered*. University Press of America, 1998.

Simpson, Brooks D. *Let Us Have Peace: Ulysses S. Grant and the Politics of War and Reconstruction, 1861–1868*. University of North Carolina Press, 1991.

Sinha, Manisha. *The Rise and Fall of the Second American Republic: Reconstruction, 1860–1920*. Liveright, 2024.

Smith, Jean Edward. *Grant*. Simon and Schuster, 2001.

Suri, Jeremi. *Civil War by Other Means: America's Long and Unfinished Fight for Democracy*. Public Affairs, 2022.

Varon, Elizabeth R. *Longstreet: The Confederate General Who Defied the South*. Simon and Schuster, 2023.

White, Ronald C. *American Ulysses: A Life of Ulysses S. Grant*. Random House, 2016.

2

The Republican Party, the Lost Cause, and the Transformation of American Politics

TIM GALSWORTHY

On January 6, 2021, as the world watched in horror at the attempted overthrow of American democracy, many commentators drew attention to an insurrectionist carrying a Confederate battle flag into the U.S. Capitol.[1] Historians opined that this flag-wielding insurgent—alongside the cadre of rioters accompanying him—were adherents to a "new Lost Cause," believing (wrongly) that the 2020 election was stolen and Donald Trump remained the rightful president.[2] According to journalist Mary C. Curtis, devotees of this new Lost Cause make up "a substantial minority" that "doubts duly elected leaders as legitimate and blames Black and brown voters for the imaginary injustice."[3] While the case for the new Lost Cause is compelling, the relationship between the Republican Party and Lost Cause–style sentiments is not reserved to Trumpites and their denial of democratic norms. Throughout the twentieth century, and up until the present day, Republicans have engaged extensively with the *original* Lost Cause—the white Southern–friendly, pro-Confederate memory narrative of the Civil War era that deliberately avoids genuine assessments of slavery and secession.

This chapter reveals how Southern Grand Old Party (GOP) candidates and activists, and subsequently national Republican leaders, used Lost Cause memories instrumentally to promote Republicanism below the Mason–Dixon line and mobilize the party's white, racially conservative base. It first considers how, during the civil rights revolutions of the 1960s, Southern Republicans relied on pro-Confederate memories in their strategies to foster two-party competition in a region long hostile to the GOP. From there, this chapter underscores how during Richard Nixon's presidency the Lost Cause was transformed from the preserve of incipient Southern partisans to become part of national Republican efforts to realign the former Confederacy. Finally, it analyzes contemporary Republicans' engagement with Lost

Cause allusions, showing how pro-Confederate sentiments now underpin the GOP's racialized appeals nationwide. Focusing on the Lost Cause allows us to consider the transformations wrought within the GOP in the last sixty years, as the so-called Party of Lincoln became increasingly white, Southern, and (racially) conservative. As the Republican Party has conducted a steady, tactical retreat from its Lincolnian, emancipationist roots, the Lost Cause has been—and continues to be—part and parcel of its positioning on the right of U.S. politics.

The Lost Cause and Southern Republicanism

In the early 1960s, Black activists succeeded in making the cause of racial equality a central animating factor in American politics. As the national Democratic Party—under the leadership of John F. Kennedy and subsequently Lyndon B. Johnson—associated itself increasingly with civil rights, Southern Republicans spied an opportunity to realign their region. Since the overthrow of Reconstruction, the former Confederacy had been overwhelmingly Democratic, constituting the so-called Solid South. In the Deep South especially, Republicans were few and far between. During the 1960s, the South "changed from the nation's most reliable Democratic area to the bedrock of conservative Republicanism," in what some historians style "The Great White Switch."[4]

Southern Republicans engaged recurrently with Lost Cause sentiments as they distanced themselves from the Civil War–era GOP and portrayed themselves to the region's voters as steadfast segregationists. They employed Civil War memories to tackle the GOP's negative image in the South and advance their racially conservative vision of Republicanism. Dixie partisans viewed the Lost Cause as a politically useful instrument to enhance their electoral campaigns, realign Southern politics, and remake the national GOP into a party that appealed to white Southerners.

Southern Republicans' appeals in this period were rooted firmly in racial resentment, hoping to profit from dissatisfaction with the Kennedy administration. Like Southern Democrats, they condemned the president's actions—particularly his deployment of federal troops to integrate Southern universities, and eventually his decision to send a comprehensive civil rights bill to Congress—as a radical challenge to segregation. Southern Republicans hoped Kennedy's moves in support of civil rights would lead white voters to look again at the GOP.[5]

If Republicans hoped to attract white Southerners away from their traditional partisan home, addressing the GOP's poor standing among white Southerners would be a key task. Their party's role in prosecuting the Civil War and Reconstruction engendered transgenerational disdain for Republicanism and ingrained Democratic loyalty. Many white Southerners understood Reconstruction as a "Tragic Era" in which newly enfranchised Blacks, their white Republican allies, and the GOP-dominated federal government subjected white Southerners to corruption and oppression. The terms "carpetbagger" and "scalawag" remained evocative insults.[6] Southern Republicans had no choice but to engage with Lost Cause memories to unshackle their party from its historical burden. The growing impetus behind the civil rights movement, especially the bitter opposition which Black activism provoked among white Southerners, afforded Southern Republicans an opportunity. The concurrent context of the Civil War Centennial, which led many Americans—both politicians and ordinary citizens, both North and South—to compare contemporary clashes over civil rights and states' rights to the battles of the 1860s, furthered increased the functionality of historical references.[7]

Two significant Southern Republicans who sought to upend their region's political identity were William Workman, the South Carolina GOP's 1962 candidate for the U.S. Senate, and Rubel Phillips, who ran for Mississippi governor in 1963. In unequivocally segregationist campaigns, they channeled white Southern ire about the Kennedy administration and its growing association with Black civil rights.[8] Workman encouraged white South Carolinians to "forget old stands" and "old labels" and recognize that Republicans now best represented the values of states' rights and segregation.[9] Launching his campaign in December 1961, Workman declared that although his "Grandpappy" might be "turning over in [his] grave" because of his party switch, his ancestor would understand because he too "fought for what he believed in." Workman cited a December 1860 address from South Carolina's secessionist convention, including sections bemoaning the "the gradual and steady encroachment on the part of the people of the North," to describe his grandpappy's beliefs. In line with mainstream Lost Cause narratives, he elided sections of the original text referencing slavery.[10] Workman understood that many Southern whites worried voting Republican would besmirch their Confederate forebears. Supporters warned of the "stigma" and "prejudice" felt deeply toward Republicans.[11] Therefore, Workman presented desertions to the GOP as compatible with white voters' traditional views—implying that a new secession, a partisan secession, was necessary.

Phillips also urged Mississippians to focus on present-day problems rather than dwell in the past. At one boisterous rally in Jackson, Phillips accepted a Lost Cause caricature of the GOP, asserting that "[a] hundred years ago, the Republican Party came down to this state and put its feet on the necks of Mississippians." Offering "no apology" for his Republican "label," he launched a defense of the two-party system because the supposed horrors of Reconstruction were "done under a one-party system."[12] Phillips also compared Radical Republicans with contemporary Northern Democrats. "Today the shoe is on the other foot," he argued; "the Democrats in Mississippi are doing exactly what the Republicans did 100 years ago."[13] Southern Republicans had no interest in challenging Tragic Era or Lost Cause narratives. Rather, their intentions were to transfer white Southern animosity from the GOP of the 1860s to the Democrats of the 1960s.

Both candidates adopted common Southern political trappings. Workman spoke in front of Confederate battle flags, which supporters waved at his rallies. Strains of "Dixie" were common, with Workman leading crowds in renditions of the Confederate anthem.[14] The Confederate flag also served as a backdrop during Phillips's appearances, and he made at least one speech "in the shadow of a Confederate monument."[15] Through these actions, alongside their use of Lost Cause and Tragic Era narratives, Workman and Phillips hoped to associate the GOP firmly with the South's segregationist political norms. These Southern Republicans, just like GOP partisans since, were not necessarily strict adherents to all of the Lost Cause's tenets. Instead, they perceived the political utility of pro-Confederate sentiments.

Although both candidates were unsuccessful in their campaigns—Phillips received 38 percent of the vote and Workman 43 percent, impressive showings in such firmly Democratic states—these results fostered growing enthusiasm about Southern Republicanism's potential.[16] Workman and Phillips were representative of Deep South Republicans in the early 1960s. Their willingness to associate themselves with Lost Cause memories was part of a strategy that acknowledged the continuing relevance of the past in Southern politics but hoped to place Democrats on the back foot by presenting contemporary civil rights concerns as more significant than transgenerational partisan hatred.

Yet some Southern Republicans went even further in their use of Lost Cause references. In 1962 James Martin challenged veteran Alabama Democrat Lister Hill for his Senate seat. He made white anger at the president's civil rights liberalism the centerpiece of his appeals, berating Hill as a Kennedy lackey.[17] Martin explicitly compared his Senate bid to Confederate secession and wartime exertions. He told voters to "go to the polls with a Rebel yell," announcing that the South would "rise again" if he was triumphant.[18] Accepting the party's nomination in June 1962, Martin called for a "return to the spirit of '61—1861, when our fathers formed a new nation." He continued, "God willing, we will not again be forced to take up rifle and bayonet to preserve these principles."[19] Later in the campaign, during a jubilant rally at Montgomery's state capitol, a spotlight flashed to Martin standing on the star that marked where the Confederacy's president had been inaugurated. Bounding down the steps to address supporters waving Confederate battle flags, he noted the spectacle of a Republican standing "where Jefferson Davis stood on that historic moment" and declared his victory would be "a drastic change" and "new page in Alabama history," comparable to "the inauguration of Davis."[20] Martin used Lost Cause emotions to associate historical Confederate veneration with contemporary Republican support, positioning himself firmly as a Confederate legatee.

Although Workman and Phillips had not been tentative in embracing Rebel symbols, they focused chiefly on the millstone of Reconstruction. Martin adopted Lost Cause, pro-Confederate sentiments more forthrightly and aggressively. While Workman and Phillips sought to look beyond the past, Martin was more comfortable looking backward to stir white voters' emotions. Like Workman and Phillips, Martin went down to eventual electoral defeat. Yet, by capturing 49 percent of the vote—losing by fewer than seven thousand votes—his campaign was a highlight for early 1960s Southern Republicanism.[21] Martin's bid reveals the extent to which Republican candidates could make the Lost Cause a valuable element of their campaigns.

These segregationist Republicans challenged the GOP's negative image in the South and, to varying degrees, connected their party with the Lost Cause. Civil War memories offered Southern candidates an important lexicon to demonstrate to voters their shared racial values, serving as a key prong in their efforts to overcome long-engrained contempt for Republicanism. Aiming to address the Republican elephant in the room, Dixie Republicans made common cause with the Lost Cause to realign Southern politics and attract white voters.

In the wake of these earlier campaigns, Barry Goldwater's 1964 presidential campaign cemented the importance of Lost Cause memories in Southern GOP designs. The Arizona senator was a staunch conservative and the Republican Right's figurehead. His nomination represented the culmination of grassroots conservative activists' efforts to capture the GOP and reorient it in a determinedly rightward direction. Appeals to white Southerners antagonistic to civil rights, and the belief that a Goldwater-led GOP could carry the former Confederacy, was at the core of Goldwaterism—as typified by the senator's vote against the landmark 1964 Civil Rights Act, calculated to assure support below the Mason-Dixon line.[22]

Goldwater's ardent Southern supporters deployed Lost Cause, pro-Confederate memories to justify their shifting allegiances, both to themselves and fellow Southerners, associating the Republican nominee with their Civil War–era ancestors. Dick McCool, an elderly GOP convert in Canton, Mississippi, informed Goldwater's running mate that his "maternal and paternal grandfathers and my Uncles were all proud Confederate soldiers . . . with Lee and with Forrest." He claimed that "they would pat me on the back if they were here for voting for you; and better than that, they would also cast their's for you, too."[23] Mississippian Florence Sillers Ogden, a prominent commentator on Southern affairs, likewise instructed her readers: "If our fathers should rise up out of their graves and take a look around, they wouldn't recognize the party of their fathers. . . . I know what my father would do. He would vote for Goldwater. So would my two Confederate grandfathers."[24] When South Carolina's Democratic senator—and 1948 "Dixiecrat" presidential candidate—Strom Thurmond announced he was switching parties and backing Goldwater, he expressed similar sentiments. "The Party of our fathers is dead. Those who took its name are engaged in another Reconstruction, this time not only of the South but of the entire nation," the segregationist figurehead declared in a mid-September 1964 televised address.[25]

In his Southern campaign appearances, while avoiding explicitly Lost Cause references, Goldwater acclaimed the same white supremacist Democrats as his supporters. "There is nothing left . . . of the principles that your fathers, grandfathers and great-grandfathers stood for in the Democratic Party," he told one raucous crowd in Greenville, South Carolina. "I wonder how many votes Hubert Horatio Humphrey would have gotten in the Deep South of your fathers and grandfathers?" the senator asked, chastising Lyndon Johnson's liberal running mate.[26] Although Goldwater was not as openly segregationist as his allies, he was willing to invoke the white supremacist history of Southern Democratic politics—(dog-)whistling "Dixie"—in the pursuit of votes.

Despite a crushing defeat, Goldwater did succeed in the Deep South. He carried Alabama, Georgia, Louisiana, Mississippi, and South Carolina. He won comfortably in these states, capturing 59 percent of the vote in South Carolina, 69 percent in Alabama, and 87 percent in Mississippi.[27] The 1964 election was one of realignment, as many white Southerners, motivated by the two parties' changing positions on civil rights, switched to the GOP. By rupturing the Democratic Solid South, Goldwater reoriented the GOP toward racial conservatism and white Southerners.[28] Republican politicians and ordinary white Southerners used historical memories, particularly the Lost Cause, as they shaped the region's changing identity. References to the Confederacy, Reconstruction, and the South's Democratic traditions allowed politicians and voters to depict the GOP as the region's legitimate home.

Although the passage of the 1965 Voting Rights Act caused some Southern Republicans to temper their rhetoric in the face of an integrated electorate, many GOP politicians and activists continued employing Lost Cause narratives to soothe lingering white hostility toward their party. Building on Goldwater's beachhead, they positioned Civil War memories at the heart of their efforts to foster an enduring two-party South. During a March 1965 event, Strom Thurmond acknowledged that Albert Watson—a Goldwater-supporting Democratic congressman who had recently switched to the Republican Party, prompting a special election—would be "the first Republican to be elected to Congress from South Carolina . . . since Reconstruction days." "Only today the tables are turned," he continued; "now the Reconstruction Party is the Democratic Party. Scalawags are back on the scene today, as are carpetbaggers." Thurmond labeled Robert Kennedy a carpetbagger, which thrilled the crowd, given his role in desegregating Southern institutions.[29]

By the mid- to late 1960s, pro-Confederate memories and iconography had become ubiquitous in Southern Republicanism. Confederate flags, Rebel yells, "Dixie," and salutes to Confederate heroism were common.[30] One 1966 television advertisement placed Thurmond squarely in the footsteps of South Carolina's secessionists, Confederate soldiers, and Wade Hampton, a prominent Redeemer politician and Confederate soldier.[31] As Republicans became more prominent in the region's political milieu, often seeking to outflank Democrats on race, they adopted customary symbolic elements of Lost Cause Southern campaigning.

The instrumental deployment of Lost Cause memories significantly aided the thawing of relations between white Southerners and the GOP. While the region was not realigned overnight, and Southern Democrats persisted as an effective electoral force into the first decade of the 2000s, outright hostility toward Republicans began dissipating in the 1960s. In the 1968 presidential election, despite facing the third-party challenge of Alabamian George Wallace, Richard Nixon carried the states of Florida, North Carolina, South Carolina, Tennessee, and Virginia.[32] Four years later, he was reelected with the support of every former Confederate state.[33] Although his win was not solely the result of Republicans' Lost Cause rhetoric, the party's willingness to tackle the GOP's negative historical perceptions head-on contributed markedly to its improving fortunes below the Mason–Dixon line.

It would be wrong to conclude that the GOP was uniformly conservative, or that the Lost Cause was the only memory narrative circulating in the party, during the 1960s and 1970s. Indeed, ideological and historical plurality persisted. Throughout this period, the GOP was a broad, perhaps unsustainable, coalition that encompassed both Southern ex-segregationists like Thurmond and racially liberal Republicans, sometimes dubbed "Rockefeller Republicans" after New York governor Nelson Rockefeller. For progressives, notably Black Republicans like Massachusetts Senator Edward Brooke, the GOP's status as the Party of Lincoln and emancipation informed their pro–civil rights philosophy and partisan identity deeply.[34] Full ideological polarization between a conservative Republican Party and moderate-to-liberal Democratic Party was not immediate. Yet Southern Republicans' employment of Lost Cause memories helped create favorable conditions for a two-party South—a realignment fundamental to the (racially) conservative transformation of Republicanism specifically, and U.S. politics more broadly.

Southern Republicans maintained their use of pro-Confederate memories in the late twentieth and early twenty-first centuries, furthering the GOP's rightward trend. They aimed to demonstrate unmistakably to white voters that the GOP best represented their interests and beliefs, still perceiving Lost Cause references as a useful vehicle to boost Southern Republicanism and secure the region's partisan shift. Speaking before the Sons of Confederate Veterans in 1984, Mississippi congressman Trent Lott declared proudly that "the spirit of Jefferson Davis lives in the 1984 Republican Platform." Lott, the Senate majority leader between 1996 and 2001, also moved Davis's former desk into his congressional office. The Mississippian understood these tributes as a vehicle to cement white Southern support for the GOP and overcome any remaining resentments toward his party.[35]

As divisive "culture wars"—conflicts between social and political groups related to different value systems—came to the fore in the 1990s, many Republicans made Civil War memory part of their polarizing appeals.[36] In South Carolina, Republicans led the fight to keep the Confederate battle flag flying above the state capitol. State Senators Glenn F. McConnell, John E. Courson, and Arthur Ravenel Jr. resisted pressure from civil rights groups to move the emblem, which had been raised in 1962 in resistance to the civil rights movement. Palmetto State Republicans, who still faced a Democratic-controlled state senate, saw the Confederate flag as a provocative issue to rally white voters.[37] Ravenel was so associated with Lost Cause sentiments that his unapologetic defense of the Confederate battle flag was emphasized in his January 2023 funeral eulogy, given by McConnell. His recessional song was "Dixie."[38]

Twenty-first-century GOP politicians still perceive overt pro-Confederate stances as an effective means to mobilize Southern white conservatives. For example, Corey Stewart, an avidly pro-Trump Republican in Virginia, based his 2017 gubernatorial bid and his 2018 Senate campaign almost entirely on defending Confederate monuments and the Confederate flag from their detractors.[39] Appearing at the 2017 Old South Ball in Danville, just a few months before the infamous Unite the Right Rally in Charlottesville, Stewart told supporters: "I'm proud to be next to the Confederate flag. That flag is not about racism. . . . It's not about hatred. It's not about slavery. It's about our heritage. . . . Over my dead body . . . are we ever going to take down the statues of Robert E. Lee and Stonewall Jackson."[40] Facing calls to alter the region's memorial landscape, Southern Republicans have passed a slew of heritage protection laws restricting the removal of Confederate monuments.[41] In June 2021, 120 House Republicans also voted against removing Confederate statues from Congress.[42]

It has become common in contemporary campaigns for Southern GOP candidates to have high-profile controversies related to Civil War memory—specifically, Republicans associating themselves positively with the Confederacy and attracting widespread media attention and condemnation. During her 2018 reelection bid, Mississippi Senator Cindy Hyde-Smith was criticized by her opponents when a photo surfaced of her posing gleefully with artifacts at former Confederate President Jefferson Davis's home.[43] The same year, South Carolina Republican Catherine Templeton—who unsuccessfully sought her party's nomination for governor—continued to express pride in the Confederacy and her family's Confederate service even after learning that one of her ancestors was a prominent slaveholder.[44] In October 2022 Georgia congresswoman and staunch Confederate monuments defender Marjorie Taylor Greene was roundly mocked after she tweeted photographs of herself at the Chickamauga battlefield. "Tonight, I stopped at the Wilder Monument in Chickamauga, GA, which honors the Confederate soldiers of the Wilder Brigade. I will always defend our nation's history!" she wrote—ignoring, perhaps deliberately, that the marker commemorated a brigade in the Union's Army of the Cumberland from the September 1863 battle.[45] More than simply being faux pas offering ammunition to their liberal detractors, such examples betray the established relationship between present-day Republicans and the Lost Cause, alongside the prominence of Civil War allusions in the GOP's white identity politics. The Lost Cause is certainly not gone with the wind for Southern Republicans seeking to motivate their party's white conservative base. They still rely on pro-Confederate expressions as a political strategy in a racially polarized region.

Civil War memory serves a particular purpose for Southern Republicans with national ambitions, as the 2024 election cycle made abundantly clear. Former South Carolina Governor Nikki Haley attracted widespread attention and derision when, during a December 2023 campaign stop in New Hampshire, she (once again) failed to describe slavery as the cause of the Civil War.[46] Similarly, when Tim Scott launched his exploratory presidential committee in April 2023, his glossy video managed to avoid using the words "slavery" or "Confederacy"—despite being filmed at Fort Sumter.[47] The South Carolina senator reflects the staunchly conservative nature of modern Black Republicans. After the civil rights era, the small remaining band of African American partisans overwhelming adjusted to their party's conservatism—especially on issues of race and affirmative action—rather than continuing as the progressive, racially liberal intraparty force Edward Brooke and his colleagues had been in the 1960s and 1970s.[48] Given that disassociating slavery from the Civil War is central to Lost Cause mythology, Haley and Scott's silences are as telling about the status of Civil War memory in the modern GOP as Republicans' shouting loudly about Confederate monuments or flags. Celebrating the role Republicans played in ending slavery or advancing Radical Reconstruction does not easily complement the racially conservative ideology, and racialized campaign appeals, of the modern-day GOP.

Making the Lost Cause National

Perhaps the most significant element of the GOP's relationship with the Lost Cause is that it is no longer reserved for Republican operatives in the former Confederacy. Lost Cause invocations have come to offer rhetorical value to non-Southern Republicans and national GOP leaders. This is principally the result of Nixon's presidency. Pursuing a "Southern Strategy," which sought to secure the white South's enduring realignment, Nixon selected Southerners for important administration positions, attempted unsuccessfully to appoint two conservative Southern justices to the Supreme Court, and denounced the use of "forced busing" to achieve racial balance in schools.[49]

The Lost Cause was a valuable touchstone for the Nixon administration's Southern Strategy, primarily in the speechmaking of Vice President Spiro Agnew. Nixon had chosen the combative Maryland governor as his running mate in 1968 to further inspire support for his "law-and-order" platform.[50] As Agnew wooed white Southerners, he embraced the Lost Cause in his rhetoric. This is best exemplified in his May 1970 appearance at Stone Mountain, Georgia. Speaking at the dedication of massive stone reliefs of Robert E. Lee, Thomas "Stonewall" Jackson, and Jefferson Davis, Agnew celebrated the Confederate luminaries' "loyalty, dignity and honor." Repeating common Lost Cause myths, including the claim that Lee "opposed slavery," the vice president depicted the secessionist triumvirate as model Americans. The reliefs had long been an aspiration of Confederate heritage groups and were highly controversial, especially given the second Klan's founding at Stone Mountain in 1915.[51]

Nixon also engaged with the Lost Cause himself. During a May 1971 visit to West Point, he stated that the U.S. Army's service academy should have a statue honoring Confederates. The president's suggestion, which was resisted successfully by West Point's Black cadets, was part of his designs to further improve the GOP's standing with white Southerners.[52] During the 1960s, pro-Confederate memories had primarily been the preserve of Southern Republicans promoting the GOP from the bottom up. Agnew and Nixon helped make the Lost Cause a top-down Republican political weapon. They instigated the use of Lost Cause memories by national Republican leaders in appeals to white voters—a mobilization technique that remains common in the twenty-first century, particularly by Donald Trump.

Across his turbulent first presidency, Trump frequently embraced Lost Cause sentiments. He extolled Robert E. Lee at his rallies, at which Confederate flags were common.[53] Moreover, Trump steadfastly opposed the removal of Confederate monuments. In his infamous August 15, 2017, press conference, Trump labeled the far-right protesters gathered in Charlottesville to defend a statue of Lee as "very fine people." The chaos and violence of that summer afternoon resulted in dozens of people being injured and the death of one counterprotester, Heather Heyer. Trump also used this erratic speech to oppose the removal of statues of Lee, Jackson, George Washington, and Thomas Jefferson.[54] A week later, at a rally in Arizona, he continued in a similar vein, warning that "they are trying to take away our culture. They are trying to take away our history."[55]

Trump relied on pro-Confederate memory to enliven his base during critical moments of his White House tenure, underscoring the Lost Cause's prominence at the very top of the modern GOP. He fervently resisted moves, begun subsequently by President Joe Biden, to rename ten U.S. Army bases named after Confederate generals—a wedge issue Trump resurrected during his 2024 presidential bid (see Jennifer M. Murray's chapter in this volume). When Biden launched his presidential campaign in April 2019 with a clip from Trump's notorious post-Charlottesville press conference, the president doubled down on his defense of Robert E. Lee, labeling him "one of the great generals."[56] Facing reelection in 2020, Trump responded to reinvigorated Black Lives Matter protests, which had increasingly targeted Confederate monuments and statues of other controversial figures in the wake of George Floyd's murder, by defending the United States' memorial landscape unequivocally. "We must build upon our heritage, not tear it down," he told one June 2020 audience.[57] Later that month, Trump signed an executive order reinforcing state laws which protected statues—especially Confederate monuments—from removal. He even called on the Park Service to re-erect a monument of Confederate Albert Pike that protesters had forcibly toppled in Washington DC.[58] Trump cast himself and his supporters as the patriotic defenders of national heritage, resisting an allegedly un-American opposition. This intransigence on Confederate monuments helped him foment the cultural, racial, and political divisions that underpinned his electoral strategies. During the 2024 presidential election, Trump's enduring comfort with Lost Cause sentiments was again demonstrated by the playing of "Dixie" at a Madison Square Garden rally and his praise of Robert E. Lee during a speech in Pennsylvania (see epilogue).

But Trump is not the only contemporary non-Southern Republican who has demonstrated an affinity for the Confederacy. In November 2021 Arizona State Senator Wendy Rogers, a staunch Trumpite conservative, tweeted her support for Virginia gubernatorial candidate Glenn Youngkin. She encouraged Virginians to vote Republican and "Make General Lee proud."[59] Mike Pence, Trump's Hoosier vice president, echoed his boss's defense of Confederate memorials, calling for "more monuments, not less."[60] Of the 120 House Republicans who opposed removing Congress's Confederate statues in 2021, more than half were from states outside the former Confederacy.[61] While the Lost Cause is far from the only memory narrative in GOP circles today—indeed, Trump has often been at pains to stress communality between Abraham Lincoln and himself—the embrace of pro-Confederate sentiments by non-Southern Republicans, especially national leaders, is crucial for explaining its prominence in the modern Party of Lincoln.[62]

For Trump and many other contemporary Republicans, Lost Cause references are not primarily about securing white Southern support. Today, the former Confederacy resembles a key bastion of Republicanism.[63] It is not necessary, as it was for earlier GOP candidates, to address lingering hostilities toward the party of Reconstruction—although pro-Confederate allusions do no harm in solidifying Republican votes in the South. The Lost Cause is now useful as part of Republican appeals nationwide. Pro-Confederate sentiments, along with defenses of Confederate statues and symbols, have become a useful wedge issue. Southern and non-Southern GOP politicians alike view Confederate totems as expedient culture war stimuli that will rally white conservatives against their "woke" liberal opponents, who supposedly want to erase America's history. During the 1950s and 1960s, segregationist politicians and ordinary Americans deployed Confederate battle flags and other Lost Cause memories to resist the transformations which the Black freedom struggle portended for the South.[64] Today, die-hard defenses of Confederate monuments, flags, and symbols perform a similar role on a national scale. They provide, especially to Republican politicians, a shared language and set of cultural references points for Americans antagonistic to the United States' diverse, multiracial democracy.

During the civil rights era, Southern Republicans introduced Confederate memories to the GOP to a significant degree. When national politicians like Goldwater and Nixon played on the white backlash and appealed for Southern support, they capitalized on established memories in the region's politics. During the Nixon administration, especially through Agnew's Southern speechmaking, GOP leaders normalized the presence of Lost Cause sentiments in Republican appeals on a national level. Throughout the second half of the last century, building on foundations laid in the 1960s, many white politicians and voters, especially in the South, switched to the GOP. Southern converts brought their Lost Cause sentiments with them; the Republican Party became a safe space and breeding ground for the Lost Cause. The pro-Confederate memories deployed by Trump and his supporters, therefore, are the end result of the GOP's evolving relationship with

Civil War memory—especially Southern Republicans' use of Lost Cause invocations—since the 1960s. Trump and most Trumpites have no deep ideological connection with the Lost Cause. Instead, they perceive the political utility of pro-Confederate sentiments to energize white conservatives as part of their emotional grievance politics.

Republicans' historical and contemporary relationships with the Lost Cause reveal much about modern Republicanism. During the 1960s, reacting to the civil rights movement and the Democratic Party's increased support for Black equality, pro-Confederate invocations were essential to Republican efforts to realign the South. To win white Southern support, GOP candidates below the Mason–Dixon line embraced the Lost Cause and denounced their party's Civil War and Reconstruction heritage. As national Republican leaders pursued regional realignment, the Lost Cause transitioned from the domain of Dixie Republicans to being an important rhetorical prong in top-down Southern Strategies. The Lost Cause maintains its currency for Southern and non-Southern Republicans today. Donald Trump and like-minded contemporary Republicans often invoke Lost Cause sentiments—particularly celebrations of Confederate heroism or defenses of Confederate memorialization—to mobilize white conservatives in all corners of the country, believing, quite justifiably, that pro-Confederate references motivate much of their base. The GOP, the political institution that led the fight against Confederate secession, now comfortably hosts those who wave Rebel flags, defend Confederate statues, and speak of "heritage, not hate." The insurrectionist who carried the Confederate battle flag into the U.S. Capitol on January 6, 2021, was undoubtedly a disciple of the *new* Lost Cause of Trump's stolen victory in 2020. Nevertheless, his willingness to embrace Confederate iconography, without any hint that it was out of place in the Party of Lincoln, demonstrates just how far elements of the *original* Lost Cause have become common in the modern Republican Party.

NOTES

1. Kevin Seefried was ultimately found guilty of felony and misdemeanor offenses. "Man Who Carried Confederate Flag in US Capitol and Son Found Guilty of Felonies," CNN, June 15, 2022, https://edition.cnn.com/2022/06/15/politics/kevin-hunter-seefried-confederate-flag-capitol-riot/index.html.
2. Karen Cox, "What Trump Shares with the 'Lost Cause' of the Confederacy," *New York Times*, January 8, 2021, https://www.nytimes.com/2021/01/08/opinion/trump-confederacy-lost-cause.html. David Blight, "Trump Has Birthed a Dangerous New 'Lost Cause' Myth. We

Must Fight It," *Gilder Lehrman Center*, January 13, 2022, https://glc.yale.edu/news/trump-has-birthed-dangerous-new-lost-cause-myth-we-must-fight-it.

3. Mary C. Curtis, "Donald Trump, Confederates and the GOP—Brethren in the New Lost Cause," *Roll Call*, December 3, 2020, https://rollcall.com/2020/12/03/donald-trump-confederates-and-the-gop-brethren-in-the-new-lost-cause/.
4. Bullock et al., *South and the Transformation*, vi–vii, 14–18, 50–55, 68–70, quote 1 on p. 50; Black and Black, *Rise of Southern Republicans*, 24–29, 138–52, 171–73, 205–22, quote 2 on p. 205.
5. Thurber, *Republicans and Race*, 173–84.
6. Baker, *What Reconstruction Meant*, 1–12, 21–43, 69–90.
7. Cook, *Troubled Commemoration*.
8. Merritt, "Senatorial Election of 1962," 284–94; Hathorn, "Challenging the Status Quo," 240, 245–46.
9. "Text of Speech by W.D. Workman, Jr. Statewide Television Network," September 11, 1962, Speeches, Television, Elections, U.S. Senate, Johnston vs. Workman, Box 5, Campaign Files, William D. Workman Jr. Papers (hereafter WDW).
10. "Lexington—9 Dec 61," Republican Party, Box 26, Speeches, WDW; "Address of the People of South Carolina, Assembled in Convention, to the People of the Slaveholding States of the United States" (December 25, 1860), Teaching American History, https://teachingamericanhistory.org/library/document/address-of-south-carolina-to-slaveholding-states/.
11. C. B. Pegram to William Workman, July 21, 1962, Box 2, General Papers, WDW; M. B. Swayze to William Workman, April 14, 1962, General, Elections, U.S. Senate, Johnston vs. Workman, Box 4, Campaign Files, WDW.
12. "Address of Rubel Phillips—K.O. Kennedy Dinner—Mississippi State Coliseum," October 17, 1963, Speeches—1967, b. Rubel Phillips, 1967, Box D-6, Individual Candidates/Campaigns, Series D: Mississippi Elections, Mississippi Republican Party Records.
13. "Rubel Wants Two Parties," *Clarion-Ledger* (Jackson MS), October 16, 1963, 16.
14. Merritt, "Senatorial Election of 1962," 291–94; "Senate Race Is On in South Carolina," *New York Times*, March 18, 1962, 53; "State GOP Brings Its Drive to Tumultuous Finish Here," *Greenville News*, November 6, 1962, 1–2.
15. "Phillips Campaigns Throughout Mississippi," *Mississippi Conservative Challenge*, July 1967, 2A, Box Y-1, Series Y: Publications, Mississippi Republican Party Records; "Routine for Red-Necks," *Newsweek*, October 14, 1963, 35–36 (quote); for more on the Rebel flag, see Coski, *Confederate Battle Flag*.
16. "Political Profiles of the States: Revised," September 1965, Frames 230–81, Reel 4, Kesaris, *Papers of the Republican Party*.
17. Hathorn, "James Douglas Martin," 53–56; "Martin Stresses Anti-Kennedyism," *Birmingham Post-Herald*, October 24, 1962, 24; "Martin Is the Man We Need in the U.S. Senate," *Brewton Standard*, November 1, 1962, 14.
18. "Cheering Crowd Hears Martin Predict Victory," *Montgomery Advertiser*, November 2, 1962, 1–2A; "Need for Strong 2-Party System," *Montgomery Advertiser*, September 29, 1962, 12; "Hill, Martin Begin Final Stumping Tours," *Alabama Journal*, November 3, 1962, 9.
19. "Alabama Republicans," *Congressional Quarterly Weekly Report*, June 22, 1962, 1072.
20. "Martin Says Victory 'Near,'" *Birmingham News*, November 2, 1962, 29.

21. "Hill Winner by 6,845," *Decatur Daily*, November 15, 1962, 1.
22. Perlstein, *Before the Storm*, 190–94, 203–29, 333–402, 418–70, 508–15; Mason, *Republican Party and American Politics*, 182–201.
23. Dick McCool to William Miller, September 10, 1964, Mississippi, State Correspondence, Box 60, William Edward Miller Papers.
24. "Go with Goldwater Is Cry of Democrat Without Party," *Clarion-Ledger*, August 9, 1964, F3–4.
25. "Television Address of Senator Strom Thurmond to the People of South Carolina on the 1964 Presidential Race," September 16, 1964, South Carolina, Campaign Material, Box 4, F. Clifton White Papers.
26. "'Whitewash' Charged by Goldwater," *Los Angeles Times*, September 18, 1964, 1–2.
27. "The 1964 Elections: A Summary Report with Supporting Tables," October 1965, Frames 379–443, Reel 4, Kesaris, *Papers of the Republican Party*; "1964 Presidential General Election Results," Atlas of U.S. Presidential Elections, accessed August 8, 2024, https://uselectionatlas.org/RESULTS/national.php?year=1964.
28. Lamis, *Two-Party South*, 18–28.
29. "Address by Senator Strom Thurmond (R-SC) Before the South Carolina Republican Convention in Columbia, S.C.," March 6, 1965, Folder 64, Box 30, Series 11: Speeches, Strom Thurmond Collection.
30. "S.C. Demos Can't Stomach State GOP," *The State* (Columbia SC), April 21, 1966, 17; "Hopes Dim for Alabama G.O.P. as Party Opens Its Convention," *New York Times*, July 30, 1966, 10; "GOP Poised for Capitol Battle," *Anniston Star*, July 30, 1966, 1.
31. "Products of Freedom," [November 7,] 1966, Publicity—Campaign Material, Box 16, 1966 Campaign, Series 9: Campaigns, Strom Thurmond Collection.
32. "The 1968 Elections: A Summary Report with Supporting Tables," April 1969, Frames 1–214, Reel 8, Kesaris, *Papers of the Republican Party*.
33. Mason, *Republican Party*, 236–39.
34. Brooke, *Challenge of Change*. On the GOP's internal groupings, see Reichley, *Conservatives in an Age of Change*, 22–36.
35. Maxwell and Shields, *Long Southern Strategy*, 15; Cook, *Civil War Memories*, 196.
36. On U.S. culture wars, see Hartman, *War for the Soul of America*.
37. Prince, *Rally 'Round the Flag Boys!*, 31–49, 138–94.
38. "'He Was Born to Serve': Former SC Congressman Arthur Ravenel Jr. Is Laid to Rest," *Post and Courier* (Charleston SC), January 20, 2023, https://www.postandcourier.com/politics/he-was-born-to-serve-former-sc-congressman-arthur-ravenel-jr-is-laid-to-rest/article_7c204f20-983a-11ed-afcc-87d0201d66e6.html.
39. "Did a Republican Running for Va. Governor Really Dress Up Like a Confederate Gent?" *Washington Post*, April 11, 2017, https://www.washingtonpost.com/local/virginia-politics/did-a-republican-running-for-va-governor-really-dress-up-like-a-confederate-gent/2017/04/11/bbffcaca-1eca-11e7-ad74-3a742a6e93a7_story.html; "Virginia Republicans Just Nominated an Alt-Right Hero to Run for Senate," *Vox*, August 8, 2018, https://www.vox.com/2018/6/13/17458452/alt-right-corey-stewart-virginia-gop.
40. "Corey Stewart Proud of Confederate Flag, Claims It Isn't Racist (4/8/17)," lowkell, YouTube, April 9, 2017, https://www.youtube.com/watch?v=t4rk6a1za4Y.

41. "Republican Legislators Want You to Think Confederate Monuments Aren't Political," *The Nation*, June 15, 2017, https://www.thenation.com/article/archive/republican-legislators-want-you-to-think-confederate-monuments-arent-political/.
42. "Full List of 120 House Republicans Who Voted Against Removing Confederate Statues," *Newsweek*, June 30, 2021, https://www.newsweek.com/confederate-statues-full-list-house-republicans-voted-against-removing-1605439.
43. "Photo Surfaces of Cindy Hyde-Smith Posing with Confederate Artifacts," CNN, November 20, 2018, https://edition.cnn.com/2018/11/20/politics/hyde-smith-confederate-artifacts-facebook-post.
44. "South Carolina Candidate 'Proud' of Confederacy and Slave-holding Ancestor," *Daily Beast*, March 12, 2018, https://www.thedailybeast.com/south-carolina-candidate-proud-of-confederacy-and-slave-owning-ancestor.
45. Greene's tweet was widely condemned by historians. Gregory Downs accused the congresswoman of dishonoring American veterans and treating the Civil War dead as political "props." "Marjorie Taylor Greene's Confederacy Remark Trashed by Civil War Historians," *Newsweek*, October 21, 2022, https://www.newsweek.com/marjorie-taylor-greenes-confederacy-remark-trashed-civil-war-historians-1754011.
46. "Nikki Haley Doesn't Cite Slavery as Cause of the Civil War After Question at Campaign Stop," ABC News, December 28, 2023, https://abcnews.go.com/amp/Politics/nikki-haley-doesnt-cite-slavery-cause-civil-war/story?id=105956626.
47. "Tim Scott | Faith in America," Tim Scott, YouTube, April 12, 2023, https://www.youtube.com/watch?v=pqu52y1B6qc&t=5s.
48. Farrington, *Black Republicans and the Transformation of the GOP*, 223–31.
49. Lowndes, *From the New Deal*, 116–39.
50. Carter, *Politics of Rage*, 330–31.
51. "Address by the Vice President Dedication of Confederate Monument Stonemountain, Georgia," May 9, 1970, Folder 32, Box 3, Sub-Series 3.7: Public Statements, Series 3: Vice President of the United States, Spiro T. Agnew Papers; "Agnew Mellow in Talk Hailing Confederate Heroes," *New York Times*, May 10, 1970, 69.
52. Seidule, *Robert E. Lee and Me*, 205–7.
53. "Trump Calls on Blacks to 'Honor' Republicans with Votes, Then Praises Confederate General Robert E. Lee," *Washington Post*, October 12, 2018, https://www.washingtonpost.com/politics/trump-calls-on-blacks-to-honor-him-with-votes-then-praises-confederate-general-robert-e-lee/2018/10/12/ab819a9c-ce33-11e8-a360-85875bac0b1f_story.html; "As Trump Rises, So Do Some Hands Waving Confederate Battle Flags," *New York Times*, November 18, 2016, https://www.nytimes.com/2016/11/19/us/confederate-flag-trump.html.
54. "Full Text: Trump's Comments on White Supremacists, 'Alt-Left' in Charlottesville," *Politico*, August 15, 2017, https://www.politico.com/story/2017/08/15/full-text-trump-comments-white-supremacists-alt-left-transcript-241662; "Charlottesville: White Supremacist Gets Life Sentence for Fatal Car Attack," *The Guardian*, June 28, 2019, https://www.theguardian.com/us-news/2019/jun/28/charlottesville-james-fields-life-sentence-heather-heyer-car-attack.
55. "President Trump Ranted for 77 Minutes in Phoenix. Here's What He Said," *Time*, August 23, 2017, https://time.com/4912055/donald-trump-phoenix-arizona-transcript/.
56. "Trump's History of Defending Confederate 'Heritage' Despite Political Risk," ABC News, June 11, 2020, https://abcnews.go.com/amp/Politics/trumps-history-defending-confederate

-heritage-political-risk-analysis/story?id=71199968; "Trump Pledges to Rename Army Base After Confederate General," *Politico*, October 4, 2024, https://www.politico.com/news/2024/10/04/trump-rename-army-confederate-general-00182606.

57. "Trump Says 'We Must Build upon Our Heritage, Not Tear It Down' amid Confederate State Removals," Fox News, June 16, 2020, https://www.foxnews.com/politics/trump-build-upon-our-heritage-not-tear-it-down.amp.

58. "Donald Trump Signs an Executive Order Calling to Prosecute anyone who Damages Federal Monuments 'to the Fullest Extent Possible,'" *Artnet News*, June 29, 2020, https://news.artnet.com/art-world/trumps-latest-executive-order-protects-monuments-1890691/amp-page; "Trump Requests Toppled Confederate Statue in DC to be Restored," *The Guardian*, June 25, 2020, https://www.theguardian.com/world/2020/jun/25/trump-requests-toppled-confederate-statue-albert-pike-restored.

59. Tim Galsworthy, "How the Party of Lincoln Became the Party of Lee," *Muster*, November 23, 2021, https://www.journalofthecivilwarera.org/2021/11/3880/.

60. "Pence: Confederate Monuments Help US 'Remember Our History,'" CNN, August 22, 2017, https://edition.cnn.com/2017/08/22/politics/mike-pence-confederate-monuments/index.html.

61. "Full List of 120 House Republicans."

62. "Presidential Candidate Donald Trump Remarks in Gettysburg, Pennsylvania," C-SPAN, October 22, 2016, https://www.c-span.org/video/?417328-1/donald-trump-unveils-100day-action-plan-gettysburg-address; "Trump Says '100 Percent of the Black People Should Vote for Trump,'" *Rolling Stone*, March 9, 2024, https://www.rollingstone.com/politics/politics-news/donald-trump-claims-black-people-should-vote-for-him-1234984486/.

63. In 2016 and 2024 Trump won every ex-Confederate state except Virginia. Georgia joined the Democratic column in 2020.

64. Cook, *Troubled Commemoration*, 51–87, 193–200.

BIBLIOGRAPHY

Archives and Manuscript Materials

F. Clifton White Papers. Cornell University Library, Division of Rare and Manuscript Collections, Ithaca, New York.

Mississippi Republican Party Records. Mississippi State University Libraries, Congressional and Political Research Center, Starkville.

Spiro T. Agnew Papers. University of Maryland Libraries Archival Collections, College Park.

Strom Thurmond Collection. Clemson University Libraries Special Collections and Archives, Clemson, South Carolina.

William D. Workman Jr. Papers. South Carolina Political Collections, University of South Carolina, Columbia.

William Edward Miller Papers. Cornell University Library, Division of Rare and Manuscript Collections, Ithaca, New York.

Published Works

Baker, Bruce E. *What Reconstruction Meant: Historical Memory in the American South*. University of Virginia Press, 2007.

Black, Earl, and Merle Black. *The Rise of Southern Republicans*. Harvard University Press, 2002.

Black Demographics. "Black Party Affiliation." Accessed August 8, 2024. https://blackdemographics.com/culture/black-politics/.

Brooke, Edward. *The Challenge of Change: Crisis in Our Two-Party System*. Little, Brown, 1966.

Bullock, Charles S., Susan A. MacManus, Jeremy D. Mayer, and Mark J. Rozell. *The South and the Transformation of U.S. Politics*. Oxford University Press, 2019.

Carter, Dan T. *The Politics of Rage: George Wallace, the Origins of New Conservatism, and the Transformation of American Politics*. Louisiana State University Press, 2000.

Cook, Robert J. *Civil War Memories: Contesting the Past in the United States since 1865*. Johns Hopkins University Press, 2017.

———. *Troubled Commemoration: The American Civil War Centennial, 1961–1965*. Louisiana State University Press, 2007.

Coski, John M. *The Confederate Battle Flag: America's Most Embattled Emblem*. Harvard University Press, 2005.

Farrington, Joshua D. *Black Republicans and the Transformation of the GOP*. University of Pennsylvania Press, 2016.

Hartman, Andrew. *A War for the Soul of America: A History of the Culture Wars*. University of Chicago Press, 2015.

Hathorn, Billy B. "Challenging the Status Quo: Rubel Lex Phillips and the Mississippi Republican Party (1963–1967)." *Journal of Mississippi History* 47, no. 4 (November 1985): 240–64.

———. "James Douglas Martin and the Alabama Republican Resurgence, 1962–1965." *Gulf Coast Historical Review* 8, no. 2 (Spring 1993): 52–73.

Kesaris, Paul, ed. *Papers of the Republican Party, Part II: Reports and Memoranda of the Research Division of the Headquarters of the Republican National Committee, 1938–1980*. University Publications of America, 1986. Microfilm.

Lamis, Alexander P. *The Two-Party South*. Oxford University Press, 1990.

Lowndes, Joseph E. *From the New Deal to the New Right: Race and the Southern Origins of Modern Conservatism*. Yale University Press, 2008.

Mason, Robert. *The Republican Party and American Politics from Hoover to Reagan*. Cambridge University Press, 2012.

Maxwell, Angie, and Todd Shields. *The Long Southern Strategy: How Chasing White Voters in the South Changed American Politics*. Oxford University Press, 2019.

Merritt, Russell. "The Senatorial Election of 1962 and the Rise of Two-Party Politics in South Carolina." *South Carolina Historical Magazine* 98, no. 3 (July 1997): 281–301.

Perlstein, Rick. *Before the Storm: Barry Goldwater and the Unmaking of the American Consensus*. Hill and Wang, 2001.

Prince, K. Michael. *Rally 'Round the Flag Boys! South Carolina and the Confederate Flag*. University of South Carolina Press, 2004.

Reichley, A. James. *Conservatives in an Age of Change: The Nixon and Ford Administrations*. Brookings Institution, 1981.

Seidule, Ty. *Robert E. Lee and Me: A Southerner's Reckoning with the Myth of the Lost Cause*. St. Martin's, 2020.

Thurber, Timothy N. *Republicans and Race: The GOP's Frayed Relationship with African Americans, 1945–1974*. University Press of Kansas, 2013.

PART 2
Reclamation Projects

On a sunny afternoon in early August 2024, Justin Vernon, lead guitarist of the indie folk band Bon Iver, walked onto a small makeshift stage in Eau Claire, Wisconsin, and began a stirring acoustic rendition of "Battle Cry of Freedom." It was an appropriate choice for the occasion. Some twelve thousand people had gathered that day for a rally of Kamala Harris and Tim Walz, the Democratic ticket for the 2024 presidential election. As scores of American flags billowed against the breeze, Vernon began, "While we rally round the flag, boys, we rally once again, shouting the battle cry of freedom!" The song was written in July 1862 by composer George Frederick Root as a response to President Abraham Lincoln's call for three hundred thousand volunteers. No tune is more emblematic of the American Civil War, the Union cause, and of course, freedom. Justin Vernon, himself a native of Eau Claire, tapped into the region's strong Union tradition. Between 1861 and 1865, some ninety-one thousand Wisconsin men rallied around the flag; three of the state's regiments (the Second, Sixth, and Seventh Wisconsin) formed part of the Army of the Potomac's famous Iron Brigade, one of most fierce, battle-hardened units to serve during the war.[1]

In the wake of the January 6 insurrection, the line "Down with the traitors, up with the stars" resonates in ways not seen in the country since the secession winter of 1860–61. "We're here for the right reasons," Vernon told listeners eager to reclaim freedoms lost in previous years or to rally once again for the Union and democracy. Reclamation of Civil War memory occurs in a variety of ways. It's heard in the soulful lyrics of a pro-Union tune at a political rally for the first woman president in the country's history. Reclamation occurs in the establishment of a national park site to tell the story of the United States Colored Troops during the Civil War. Reclamation happens when the Department of Defense removes the names of Confederates from U.S. Army bases, bringing "down with the traitors, up with the stars" into a literal reality in the twenty-first century.[2]

NOTES

1. David Browne, "Bon Iver's Justin Vernon Endorses Harris-Walz: 'I've Been Feeling Patriotic,'" *Rolling Stone*, October 9, 2024, https://www.rollingstone.com/music/music-features/bon-iver-justin-vernon-kamala-harris-tim-walz-1235120521/; Brett D. Griffiths, "Bon Iver's Lead Man Sings Civil War-Era Anthem at a Harris Rally," *Business Insider*, August 7, 2024, https://www.businessinsider.com/bon-iver-justin-vernon-battle-cry-of-freedom-harris-rally-2024-8; "Wisconsin's Involvement in the Civil War," Wisconsin Historical Society, https://www.wisconsinhistory.org/Records/Article/CS3355.
2. Browne, "Bon Iver's Justin Vernon Endorses Harris-Walz"; Griffiths, "Bon Iver's Lead Man."

3

The Politics of Civil War Memory in America's Military

The Battles to Rename Nine U.S. Army Bases

JENNIFER M. MURRAY

On April 27, 2023, officials gathered in Virginia for a ceremony that renamed the U.S. Army base Fort Lee to honor Lieutenant General Arthur Gregg and Lieutenant Colonel Charity Adams, two African American veterans with distinguished careers in uniform. For over one hundred years, this installation had borne tribute to Confederate General Robert E. Lee, a man who resigned his commission in the U.S. Army, served a government committed to sustaining slavery and dissolving the Union, and between June 1862 and April 1865 led an army that killed or wounded hundreds of thousands of American soldiers. The event at what was once Fort Lee marked part of the Department of Defense's efforts to undo its practice of celebrating and honoring the Confederacy. Six months later, the renaming of the nine U.S. Army bases that once honored traitors and enslavers was complete.[1]

This change had been a long time coming. In the fall of 2022, Secretary of Defense Lloyd Austin, the first African American to hold the position, approved the renaming of nine U.S. Army bases bearing the names of Confederate officers. All nine were located in states of the former Confederacy. Six of the nine installations honored men who had graduated from West Point, served in the antebellum army, and subsequently fought for the Confederacy. No longer would our nation's soldiers, individuals who took the solemn oath to "support and defend the Constitution of the United States against all enemies, foreign and domestic," walk through the grounds of army installations bearing names of men who broke their own loyalty oath and participated in a four-year-long civil war. Nor could it be overlooked that these bases long paid tribute to enslavers, and by retaining the names of people who owned, bought, and sold human beings, the U.S. Army and Department of Defense further perpetuated the toxic—and now firmly rejected—notion of the Lost Cause that for generations perverted the cause of our nation's bloodiest war.[2]

Stripping the names of former Confederates, men who took up arms against the United States of America, from U.S. Army bases underscores the complex ways in which the contested memory of the Civil War, and its legacy of racism, permeate American society and politics. And even though President Donald Trump announced in June 2025, just months into his second term, that he would undo this historic renaming achievement, the stakes of Civil War memory remain no less significant. Indeed, while the nine army bases will again receive new names, they will not pay tribute to Confederate officers. Years of the debates concerning naming tributes of military installations parallel contemporary discussions over the Civil War's enduring legacy and the eclectic ways that these "mystic chords of memory" continue to resonate in modern America.[3]

The precedent and historical origins of naming U.S. Army installations in honor of individuals began during the American Revolution with the establishment of Forts Washington and Lee in 1776. Strategically positioned on the Hudson River, these two forts paid tribute to the top generals in the Continental Army, George Washington and Charles Lee. For the next one hundred years or so, the designation of a fort's name was left to the local commander. Then, in 1878, the War Department revamped its policies on base naming, stating that division commanders were "authorized at their discretion, to name and style all posts permanently occupied by troops."[4]

The United States' entrance into World War I and the rapid mobilization of the army necessitated the establishment of scores of training camps. On July 16, 1917, Brigadier General Joseph E. Kuhn, assistant to the army's chief of staff and chief of the War College Division of the Army staff, crafted a memo that further institutionalized the process of base naming. One criterion stated that efforts would be "made to select names of Federal commanders for camps of divisions from northern states and of Confederate commanders for camps of divisions from southern states." This led, for instance, to the creation of Camp Sheridan in Anniston, Alabama, which became the home of the Thirty-Seventh Division, whose soldiers came from Ohio and West Virginia. Should a Civil War name be "impracticable," names of officers from other wars would be adopted.[5]

This naming impulse was squarely rooted in the trends of reconciliation, a phenomenon best articulated by historian David Blight in his classic *Race and Reunion*. Indeed, World War I provided white Southerners with an opportunity to revitalize the Lost Cause trope of Confederate soldiers as loyal and patriotic Americans. Consequently, World War I "restored" the reputation of Confederate soldiers. Actions of Southern white men on the battlefields of Western Europe, combined with the efforts of Southern white women on the home front, "served primarily as a vindication of southern patriotism." Of the nineteen camps initially established in the Southern states, four were named after Confederate officers—Lee (Virginia), Beauregard (Louisiana), Gordon (Georgia), and Wheeler (Georgia). In reporting on the naming of these newly established camps, the *Richmond Times-Dispatch* boasted that the U.S. War Department, "for the first time since the War Between the States, officially paid a tribute to the military genius of noted Confederate war chieftains."[6]

The United States Military Academy in New York soon became the scene of similar naming policies. Criticized by Radical Republicans during the Civil War as being a bastion of secession, in the postwar years West Point students and faculty held profoundly anti-Confederate beliefs. Then, starting in the 1930s, West Point's leadership allowed organizations like the United Daughters of the Confederacy to memorialize men who fought against the United States, namely Robert E. Lee. Soon tributes to Lee came in the form of Lee Barracks, Lee Housing Area, Lee Road, Lee Gate, and Lee Area Child Development Center.[7]

On the eve of World War II, the War Department again reevaluated its policy on the naming of bases and on July 1, 1939, stipulated that "all military posts will be named by the Secretary of War." Then, in December 1942, one year after the bombing of Pearl Harbor, the War Department clarified that the name of the base should be "identified with the locality of the post by birth or distinguished service." A plethora of army installations were established during World War II to meet the mobilization of some twelve million American soldiers. The U.S. Army elected to name bases in the South to honor Confederate generals—Camp Polk, Camp Hill, Camp Gordon, Camp Pickett, Camp Rucker, Camp Hood, Camp Forrest, and Camp Van Dorn.[8]

Those bases, with naming traditions that lay in World War I and World War II, remained untouched for decades, like many Confederate tributes on our national landscape. The fatal shooting of nine Black worshippers in Charleston, South Carolina, in the summer of 2015, sparked passionate debates about the appropriate place of commemorations to the Confederacy. Yet the U.S. Army initially stood firm on the tributes to former Confederate officers. In an official statement, Brigadier General Malcolm Frost, then the army's chief of public affairs, proclaimed that "every Army installation is named for a soldier who holds a place in our military history." Frost added, "Accordingly, these historic names represent individuals, not causes or ideologies." And while Frost was correct to observe that the "naming occurred in the spirit of reconciliation, not division," such a statement conveniently obscures the persuasion of the Lost Cause. It is intellectually dishonest to separate the individual—Robert E. Lee, George Pickett, Leonidas Polk, Henry Benning—from the cause for which they fought: slavery. In selecting names of enslavers and traitors, the federal government and War Department bolstered white supremacist ideologies and the perversion of Civil War history. Frost's statement signaled the army's unwillingness to divorce itself from commemorating the Confederacy even in the wake of a racially charged mass murder.[9]

In mid-August 2017 two Democratic New York lawmakers, Senator Kirsten Gillibrand and Representative Sean Patrick Maloney, reopened the issue by publicly voicing their support for the renaming of Lee Barracks at West Point.[10] This announcement came just days after the Unite the Right Rally in Charlottesville, Virginia, a gathering of white supremacists from across the nation ostensibly to defend the removal of the Lee monument in the city's Lee Park. That incident resulted in the death of one counterprotester and the wounding of more than thirty others. In the summer of 2020, the murder of George Floyd further reinvigorated conversations in cities and communities to remove Confederate tributes. One survey reported that ninety-four Confederate statues came down in 2020. Historian Karen Cox explained the connection between what happened in Minneapolis and Confederate monuments: "What protestors saw in George Floyd's death was what they saw symbolized by Confederate monuments—white supremacy and systemic racism."[11]

The same can be said of these nine army bases. One month after the murder of Floyd, Democratic Senator Elizabeth Warren introduced a bill to remove all Confederate names, displays, and symbols from Department of Defense assets. Thirty-five Senate Democrats co-sponsored the Removing Confederate Names and Symbols from Our Military Act of 2020. Senator Gillibrand supported the initiative, declaring, "We know that removing these names and symbols won't erase the ugly stain of slavery from our nation's history, but it will help us build a future where members of the military—no matter their skin color—can proudly serve our country without the glorification of the legacy of white supremacy."[12]

Then, on December 20, 2019, Congress passed the National Defense Authorization Act (NDAA) for Fiscal Year 2020, setting the budget and policies for the Department of Defense for the upcoming fiscal year. One short sentence, section 1749, plainly addressed Civil War naming traditions and reads, "Prohibition on names related to the Confederacy." This language became critically important, as will be discussed, in another round of renaming initiatives.[13] The second step in the path toward addressing the bases named for Confederate officers came in the following year's National Defense Authorization Act. Section 370 of the 2021 NDAA established the Commission on the Naming of Items of the Department of Defense that Commemorate the Confederate States of America or Any Person Who Served Voluntarily with the Confederate States of America—more commonly referred to as the Naming Commission. The committee consisted of eight members, four of whom were appointed by the secretary of defense and four chosen by the chair and ranking members of the Committee on Armed Services of the Senate and Committee on Armed Services of the House. The legislation charged the commission to review "assets" within the Department of Defense bearing names of individuals who served in the Confederacy or the name of Confederate battlefield victories. Assets for review included all military bases, installations, aircraft, ships, streets, buildings, or "any other property owned or controlled by the Department of Defense." The act also charged the commission with five specific duties. Foremost among them was to establish a plan for the removal of "names, symbols, displays, monuments, or paraphernalia that commemorates the Confederate States of America or any person who served voluntarily with the Confederate States of America from assets of the Department of Defense." The act required the secretary of defense to implement the recommendations from the Naming Commission within three years—no later than January 1, 2024.[14]

Predictably, this amendment in the defense policy bills amplified political discord that had already defined the current political landscape. Much of the opposition, unsurprisingly, came from the ultra-right wing of Republican politics. For example, Missouri Senator Josh Hawley, a Republican later linked to the January 6, 2021, insurrection, voted against Warren's amendment to the bill, asserting, "Congress should not be mandating renaming of our bases and military installations." In a nine-minute speech on the Senate floor, Hawley claimed that removing the names of Confederate generals would not unite the country but rather intensify division. Oklahoma Senator James Inhofe, then armed services chair, also resisted the proposal. Not all Republicans opposed the initiative, however. Indeed, Missouri's other Republican senator, Roy Blunt, lent his support for the base renaming, adding, "If you want to name them after soldiers, there's been lots of great soldiers since the Civil War." In the final tally, the opposition failed to mount the necessary sixty votes to remove the renaming amendment from the defense bill.[15]

President Donald Trump had repeatedly commented that he opposed the renaming of installations affiliated with the Confederacy. Such a stance was not surprising. In the wake of the rally in Charlottesville, Trump defended the white nationalists, declaring them "very fine people." Now he pledged to retain the base names honoring Confederate officers, proclaiming, "These monumental and very powerful bases have become part of a great American heritage, and a history of winning, victory, and freedom." In a Twitter post, Trump promised that he would "not even consider the renaming of these Magnificent and Fabled Military Installations."[16] Trump lashed out against Senator Warren in another tweet: "Seriously failed presidential candidate, Senator Elizabeth 'Pocahontas' Warren, just introduced an Amendment on the renaming of many of our legendary Military Bases from which we trained to WIN two World Wars." How the naming of military bases after soldiers who committed treason contributed to victory in World War I and World War II remained unclear. Asserting that the establishment of the Naming Commission was a politically motivated attempt to "wash away history," Trump vetoed the act. With considerable bipartisan support, the House overrode the president's veto on December 28, 2020, as did the Senate on January 1, 2021. This was not insignificant and represented, at least for the time being, a political setback for the president.[17]

On March 2, 2021, the eight members of the Naming Commission were sworn in and held their first commission meeting. Retired Admiral Michelle Howard, U.S. Navy, chaired the committee, and retired Brigadier General Ty Seidule, U.S. Army, served as the commission's vice chair. Members quickly established guidelines for the renaming process. It soon became apparent that because of the sheer quantity of Confederate-affiliated assets within the Department of Defense, especially within the army, the commission would focus its efforts on the renaming of nine army bases bearing names of Confederate officers. Additionally, the commission would provide recommendations to the military services for the disposition of thousands of other assets bearing Confederate tributes. To critics who charged that renaming the nine bases equated to the erasing of history, the committee correctly asserted that "although Americans owe much of their modern identity to the Civil War, they do not owe equal commemoration to both sides." The army retained a heritage deeply intertwined with the Confederacy and the renaming of these bases represented a significant step in cleansing the army's institutions and traditions of honoring men who were traitors to their country.[18]

The Naming Commission adopted a methodology that was fully transparent and engaged the public throughout the process. First, the commission established a public website to solicit naming recommendations for the nine bases. When the nomination period closed on December 1, 2021, more than 34,000 potential names were recorded, representing 3,663 unique options. The sheer volume of submissions underscored one clear fact: The U.S. Army had no shortage of people who had served their country bravely and honorably and were worthy of commemoration. Submissions ranged the gamut from distinguished and well-known officers, such as Dwight D. Eisenhower and Ulysses S. Grant, to a myriad of common soldiers, to the farcical suggestions of actor Tom Cruise, rapper Eminem, the fictional Vietnam veteran John Rambo, and singer Britney Spears. Terms associated with values were also accepted, including words such as "allegiance," "brotherhood," and "resilience." Location or military operation recommendations included names such as Gettysburg, Wounded Knee, and Yorktown. Ultimately, the Naming Commission trimmed the initial list to 461 candidates and then to a list of 87 names, with 10 names and 2 values identified for each of the 9 bases.[19]

Public buy-in was imperative for the process to gain credibility. Commission members visited each base and participated in frank discussions with senior leaders, military personnel, and community stakeholders. With the initial site visits complete, the commission held a second round of "virtual listening sessions" in March and April 2022 to gain feedback on the list of proposed names provided to each site. Input from the local stakeholders "featured prominently" in the discussions of the commission members, who held the final decision for the chosen name.[20]

The Naming Commission submitted its final report to Congress in three parts and, with its congressional duties fulfilled, disbanded on October 1, 2022. After an extensive review of these reports, Secretary Austin announced his intention to proceed with the renaming agenda. Then, on January 5, 2023, William A. LaPlante, under secretary of defense for acquisition and sustainment, announced that the Department of Defense would begin implementing the recommendations; the renaming would be complete by the January 1, 2024, deadline.[21]

When considering potential names, the Naming Commission identified seven criteria. Individuals had to be deceased and had to have "distinguished themselves through courageous and valorous acts." Because today's army is a racially diverse institution, another criterion required the "aggregated list of candidates reflects the Armed Forces population." A 2021 report indicated that 32 percent of active-duty army members identified with a racial minority group and an additional 17 percent identified as Hispanic or Latino. In sum, half of the U.S. Army active-duty officers and enlisted are non-white.[22] While the commission members stated that they did not select names of minority soldiers just for the sake of diversity, their final choices suggest an attempt to redress some historical inequities and an effort to reflect the composition of today's military. Before the renaming efforts, for instance, not a single base in the nation honored a woman, an African American, or a Latino.[23] Of the nine bases, three would bear the names of women, two of African Americans, one of a Native American, and one of a Latino American. As it turns out, the nine bases only held their new names for a short time—until, early in his second term, Trump decided they needed to be renamed once again. Consistent with the president's elimination of diversity and inclusion initiatives early in his second term, none of the bases renamed in the Trump administration will honor a woman.

The 2023 renaming process first played out in Virginia. Perhaps this was appropriate; no state's history is as deeply intertwined with the Civil War as Virginia's. From the war's first battle, Bull Run, to Lee's surrender at Appomattox, the farm fields and communities of Virginia played host to the ravages of war for four long, deadly years. No state recorded more battles and skirmishes than Virginia, and no state produced generals—Robert E. Lee, Thomas "Stonewall" Jackson, J. E. B. Stuart—who were as honored and glorified. Three of the nine bases that were eventually renamed were in the Commonwealth. Mark Warner, Virginia's Democratic senator, enthusiastically supported the renaming of installations in his state, asserting, "It really doesn't make sense to name our military bases after soldiers who fought against America."[24]

On March 24, 2023, Fort Pickett became the first base to receive a new name. When Camp Pickett, near Blackstone, Virginia, opened in 1941, the U.S. Army bypassed an opportunity to name the installation in honor of American Revolutionary hero Daniel Morgan in favor of Major General George E. Pickett. Graduating last in his West Point class of 1846, Pickett's service in the Army of Northern Virginia was, in many ways, ignoble. Pickett's name is forever associated with the failed Confederate charge at Gettysburg on July 3, 1863, which cost Pickett half of his division. In February 1864 Pickett's decision to execute twenty-two Union soldiers at Kinston, North Carolina, further mired his reputation, and finally, after negligible behavior at the Battle of Five Forks, April 1, 1865, Pickett's military career came to an end when he was relieved of command.[25]

Now named Fort Barfoot, this installation was the first army base in the continental United States named after a Native American soldier. While serving with the Forty-Fifth Infantry Division at the Battle of Anzio, on May 23, 1944, Technical Sergeant Van T. Barfoot, who was of Choctaw descent, single-handedly overpowered and silenced three German machine gun nests. During a German counterattack later that day, Barfoot disabled an enemy tank and then destroyed an abandoned German artillery gun. Barfoot also escorted two seriously wounded American soldiers to the rear. For these meritorious efforts, Barfoot received the Medal of Honor. In a postwar interview, Barfoot reflected on his actions that day, stating, "I never lost my head." When the war ended, Barfoot remained in the army and served tours of duty in Korea and Vietnam. He retired after thirty-four years of service and died in 2012.[26]

The second Virginia base to receive a new name was Camp Lee. Located in Virginia's Prince George's County, Camp Lee opened in 1917. No Confederate general holds a more prominent place in Southern (or perhaps American) consciousness than Robert E. Lee. After thirty-six years of service as either a cadet or regular army officer, Lee resigned his commission on April 20, 1861. A popular Lost Cause trope emphasizes this decision as a simple matter of Lee's allegiance to his state, but Lee was the only one of the eight army colonels from Virginia to abrogate his oath to the U.S. Constitution and cast his allegiance with the Confederacy. On June 1, 1862, Lee assumed command of the Army of Northern Virginia, the Confederacy's most powerful instrument of war, which he led until its surrender at Appomattox on April 9, 1865. During these three years, Lee's army fought against Federal soldiers at places like Antietam, Fredericksburg, Gettysburg, Spotsylvania, and Petersburg. Lee's tenure in command meant "no other enemy officer in American history was responsible for the deaths of more U.S. Army soldiers than Robert E. Lee."[27]

On April 27, 2023, Fort Lee became Fort Gregg–Adams, the first U.S. Army fort named to honor an African American. Arthur Gregg enlisted in the army in 1945 at the age of seventeen. After serving thirty-five years, including a stint at Fort Lee, Gregg retired at the rank of lieutenant general, the first African American to achieve the rank. In 1942, meanwhile, Charity Adams suspended her career as a teacher and graduate student earning a master's degree in psychology to volunteer for service in the Women's Army Auxiliary Corps. Upon completing Officer Candidate School, Major Adams assumed command of the inaugural unit of all African American women serving overseas, the 6888th Central Postal Directory in England. She persevered through gender and racial discrimination before leaving the army in 1946.[28] As the base is home to the army's Quartermaster, Ordnance, and Transportation Corps and the army's Sustainment Center of Excellence, Gregg and Adams were fitting selections.

The third base located in Virginia that honored a Confederate general was Fort A. P. Hill. A graduate of the West Point class of 1847, Ambrose Powell Hill resigned his commission in the U.S. Army on March 1, 1861. Rising to command one of the corps in Lee's army, Hill was mortally wounded during the Petersburg Campaign on April 2, 1865. Located just southeast of the 1862 battlefields of Fredericksburg, this installation opened in April 1941, when the War Department earmarked seventy thousand acres for the establishment of a military base.[29]

In late August 2023 this site was renamed to honor Dr. Mary Edwards Walker, a New Yorker who served as a U.S. Army surgeon during the Civil War. Fort Walker became the only base renamed to honor an individual from the Civil War, a reflection of a desire to select more contemporary soldiers to inspire today's military personnel. When the Civil War began, Walker offered her medical services but was denied because of the strict regulations that allowed women only to serve as nurses. Undeterred, Walker volunteered at the U.S. Patent Office Hospital in Washington, and in December 1862 she volunteered to treat Federal soldiers wounded in the Battle of Fredericksburg. In September 1863 Walker's expertise was finally accepted, and she headed to Tennessee to work in the Army of the Cumberland, becoming the first woman surgeon in the history of the U.S. Army.[30]

In recognition for her services to the Union war effort, President Andrew Johnson signed a bill to award Walker the Medal of Honor. The federal government rescinded this distinction, however, in 1917. Walker died two years later—the medal still in her possession. In 1977, through the urging of her descendants, President Jimmy Carter reinstated Walker's Medal of Honor. To this date, Walker is the only woman in history to receive our nation's highest military honor.[31]

Other bases to be renamed were scattered throughout the South. Fort Benning, located in Columbus, Georgia, is home to the U.S. Army Infantry. For over one hundred years, this installation honored Henry Benning, an antebellum politician and secession commissioner, who fervently spread the message of disunion and unequivocally advocated for secession as the only means to prevent the abolition of slavery. At one point during the war, Benning owned eighty-nine enslaved people. Unlike other Confederates with bases named in their honor, Benning never served in the U.S. Army. Rather, Benning's military career began in the summer of 1861 when he received an appointment as the colonel of the Seventeenth Georgia Infantry.[32] In 1918, when Secretary of War Newton Baker selected Benning as the installation's namesake, he acquiesced to the naming preference of local interest groups, including Confederate veterans and the Lizzie Rutherford Chapter of the United Daughters of the Confederacy.[33]

On May 11, 2023, Fort Benning was officially named Fort Hal and Julia Moore. It was a particularly fitting choice. Moore spent thirty-two years in the army, from 1945 until 1977. In November 1965 then–Lieutenant Colonel Moore led the Seventh Cavalry Regiment at the Battle of Ia Drang, dramatically captured in the 2002 movie *We Were Soldiers*. For his leadership during that battle, Moore received the Distinguished Service Cross. Meanwhile, back at Fort Benning, with her husband in Southeast Asia, Julia devoted her energies to supporting army families. Frustrated with the impersonal system of casualty notifications that used taxi drivers to inform family members of the loss of a loved one, Julia accompanied drivers to deliver casualty notices. She also urged the Pentagon to improve this process. Her dedication paid off; the army changed its procedure and delegated uniformed personnel to deliver the notice, a practice that continues today. Dave Moore, the general's youngest child and himself an army veteran, proclaimed that "it had to be Mom and Dad together."[34]

In addition to Fort Benning, another army installation created during World War I and named for a Confederate was North Carolina's Fort Bragg. Developed as a site for field artillery training, Major General William J. Snow, the army's chief-of-artillery, chose Braxton Bragg's name because of Bragg's distinguished services as an artillery officer during the Mexican American War. Bragg's Civil War career, however, was considerably less illustrious. He served in several capacities during the war, but his most notable position was at the head of the Army of Tennessee between June 1862 and December 1863. The Confederacy's main army in the western theater, the Army of the

Tennessee, lost more battles than it won. On top of contemporary debates about the appropriate place of Confederate tributes on our national landscape, the irony of naming bases after commanders who generally *lost* in battle seemed increasingly absurd. David Petraeus, retired U.S. Army general, emphasized this point by observing, "Most of the Confederate generals for whom our bases are named were undistinguished, if not incompetent, battlefield commanders."[35]

On June 2, 2023, Fort Bragg, the nation's largest military base became Fort Liberty, the only base to be renamed for value not an individual. While several distinguished names were on the short list, including Colin Powell and Matthew Ridgway, Bragg's personnel insisted on the naming of the base for a value. "Fort Liberty symbolizes the U.S. Army's defense of liberty for almost 250 years within our nation and throughout the world," the Naming Commission declared.[36] The naming of this installation became a hot topic during the 2024 presidential election, and as will be discussed, it was renamed once again in early 2025.

In one case, the Naming Commission decided to replace one local military figure with another. Located in central Texas, Fort Hood, named for John Bell Hood, opened in 1942 and became the home of the army's Third Armored Corps. Unlike other Confederate generals, Hood was rarely commemorated in the postwar years, and perhaps with good reason. A native of Kentucky and graduate of West Point's class of 1853, Hood resigned his commission in the wake of the firing on Fort Sumter. As the commander of the famed Texas Brigade, Hood developed a reputation as an aggressive fighter. Wounded at Gettysburg, Hood lost the use of his left arm and was wounded again at the Battle of Chickamauga, which resulted in the amputation of his right leg. Appointed to command the Army of Tennessee in July 1864, Hood ultimately evacuated Atlanta and then suffered a stunning defeat at the Battle of Nashville and near-annihilation of his army two weeks later at the Battle of Franklin.[37]

On May 9, 2023, this installation received a new name—Fort Cavazos. Born in Kingsville, Texas, First Lieutenant Richard E. Cavazos, deployed to Korea commanding E Company, Second Battalion, Sixty-Fifth Infantry Regiment, a unit composed primarily of Puerto Rican soldiers. In one of the war's final campaigns, Cavazos led his men in a frontal assault against an entrenched enemy position on Hill 412. As enemy artillery poured devastating fire into his ranks, Cavazos returned to the front five times to escort wounded soldiers to the rear, despite being wounded himself. For these selfless actions, he received the Distinguished Service Cross.[38]

Sent to Vietnam in 1967, then–Lieutenant Colonel Cavazos commanded the 1st Battalion, Eighteenth Infantry Regiment. Cavazos continued to exhibit an active style of leadership. When his unit was ambushed near Lộc Ninh, Cavazos rallied his men into a successful counterattack. For this action, Cavazos again received the Distinguished Service Cross. In the years following the Vietnam War, Cavazos's career witnessed historic achievements when, in 1982, he became the first Hispanic American to achieve the rank of four-star general.[39]

The decision to rename Fort Hood to Fort Cavazos offered a fitting opportunity to honor an individual who paved the way for ethnic diversity in the U.S. military. Major General Alfred Valenzuela reflected on Cavazos's impact, remarking, "We all looked up to him as an American soldier, a Hispanic soldier. He was the guy we wanted to be." That Cavazos was a proud Texan and former commander of the Third Corps at Fort Hood made the choice all the more appropriate.[40]

Other renamed army bases once honored two of the lesser-known Confederate officers. In 1941 the U.S. Army established Fort Polk, named after Leonidas Polk, "the Fighting Bishop." After graduating from West Point in 1827, Polk pursued a career as an Episcopal minster. At one time Polk owned, by a conservative estimate, approximately 215 enslaved people. In June 1861 Polk accepted an appointment as a major general in the Confederate military; he fell mortally wounded on June 14, 1864, during the Atlanta Campaign.[41]

Located in western Louisiana, Fort Polk was renamed on June 13, 2023, to honor Sergeant William Henry Johnson. Born in Winston-Salem, North Carolina, Johnson, an African American, moved to Albany, New York, sometime in his early teens. In early June 1917, at the age of twenty-six, he enlisted in the Fifteenth New York Infantry Regiment, an all–African American National Guard unit, which then mobilized into Federal service and was redesignated the 369th Infantry Regiment. The 369th was attached to the Ninety-Third Infantry Division, one of two divisions made up of African American soldiers. Societal segregation and prevailing racial philosophies, including a widespread belief that African Americans were not capable soldiers, led General John J. Pershing to create an expeditionary force of only white soldiers. African Americans would be relegated to supporting roles. When Johnson and the 369th Infantry Regiment arrived in Europe in March 1918, however, they were sent to augment a disseminated French colonial unit then positioned in the Champagne region.⁴²

On the night of May 14–15, 1918, Johnson and Private Needham Roberts were standing sentry at a forward redoubt in the Argonne Forest when they were ambushed by a German raiding party. Although he was dangerously outnumbered, Johnson defended his position until he ran out of ammunition. Johnson then used his rifle as a club and fended off two enemy soldiers with his bolo knife as they tried to capture Roberts, who had been wounded in the melee. Johnson single-handedly fought some twenty-four enemy soldiers, killing at least four. Although these men called themselves Harlem's Rattlers, Germans later described the soldiers in the 369th Infantry as Hollenkampfer—the German word for "hellfighter."⁴³

For these gallant efforts, Johnson received the French Croix de Guerre, that nation's highest military honor, and became the first American to receive such an award. His comrades took to calling him "Black Death." If Johnson's efforts inspired African Americans on the battlefront or the home front, his heroism did not translate to racial justice and equity at home. When he returned to the United States, he faced prevalent discrimination that underscored the hypocrisy of a nation that pledged to fight a war to make the world "safe for democracy." During his fight in the Argonne, Johnson sustained twenty-one separate wounds, which severely limited his ability to work. In July 1929, at the age of thirty-seven, Sergeant Johnson died.⁴⁴

Of the nine bases honoring Confederate officers, none was as obscure to Civil War history as Colonel Edmund Rucker, the namesake of Fort Rucker in Dale County, Alabama. Amassing a rather indistinctive military career, Rucker spent the final year of the war serving in Nathan Bedford Forrest's cavalry unit. The installation opened on May 1, 1942, and eventually became home to army aviation. Renamed on April 10, 2023, Fort Novosel briefly honored army aviator Michael J. Novosel Sr., a fitting tribute to the base's aviation heritage.⁴⁵

Born in western Pennsylvania to Croatian immigrants, Novosel enlisted in the U.S. Army Air Corps at the age of nineteen and flew B-29 Superfortresses during World War II, rising to the rank of captain. He left active duty in the postwar period and fought in the Korean War with the U.S. Air Force Reserves. Then, as the nation's commitment in Southeast Asia deepened, Novosel returned to the army as a Dustoff pilot, responsible for evacuating wounded soldiers from combat zones. During his two tours in Vietnam, Novosel recorded 2,543 extraction missions that rescued more than 5,500 wounded soldiers. The most daunting moment of Novosel's tour in Vietnam occurred on October 2, 1969, when Novosel flew his helicopter into an active combat zone, sustaining severe ground fire that damaged his aircraft. His operations that day lasted eighteen hours, and Novosel rescued twenty-nine soldiers. For these heroic actions, Novosel received the Medal of Honor.[46]

The last U.S. Army base renamed as part of this effort was Fort Gordon, which became Fort Eisenhower on October 27, 2023. Established in 1941, Fort Gordon, located southwest of Augusta, Georgia, honored the state's native son John B. Gordon. Born into a prominent slaveholding family, Gordon studied law, and although he had no formal military training, he rose to the rank of major general in the Army of Northern Virginia. In the postwar years, Gordon ardently resisted Reconstruction policies, opposed measures of social and political equality for freedpeople, and is acknowledged as the state's leader of the Ku Klux Klan.[47] Home to the U.S. Army Signal Corps, Cyber Command, and Cyber Center of Excellence, the installation now honors one of the nation's most illustrious generals, Dwight D. Eisenhower. Guests gathered for the ceremony at Fort Eisenhower on October 27, 2023, marking the last of the army's nine bases slated for renaming. Among those present included Army Secretary Christine Wormuth, who rightfully observed that continuing to honor Confederate generals through these naming practices was "only deepening our social and political divides."[48]

This renaming was not without controversy. While few could dispute Eisenhower's exceptional military record, at least one writer believed that the commission missed an opportunity to select a person of color. Alex Horton, columnist for the *Washington Post*, surmised, "The selection of a prestigious White man is at best a missed opportunity, and at worst a failure of the renaming commission's goal to not merely kill off the military's racist relics but also elevate minorities in the process." Proposed names were indeed diverse and included five African Americans, other meritorious people of color, and two women. Selecting the name of a minority would have been particularly fitting—Augusta-Richmond County is over 55 percent African American.[49] While the selection of a meritorious African American soldier to rename Fort Gordon would in no way minimize the systemic racism, it would offer an important corrective and a rebuke of the racist ideologies that John Gordon stood for.

The *Washington Post* columnist raised a valid point. Historically, bases in the South, like Fort Gordon, were scenes of racial violence. When the Department of Defense selected the names of traitors—some of whom were also enslavers—for these bases, they embraced not only the Lost Cause but also white supremacy. Locating army bases in the Jim Crow South, where the climate would be conducive to year-round training, virtually ensured that Black soldiers would be subjected to racial violence. Racial discrimination and violence toward African American soldiers are an inescapable part of the history of America's military and have been well documented by historians. For instance, in November 1946, after being honorably discharged at Fort Gordon, Sergeant Isaac Woodard was brutally beaten by a local police chief. Woodard was left permanently blinded, but after a fifteen-minute deliberation by an all-white jury, the police officer was acquitted.[50] Lieutenant Jackie Robinson's incident with a bus driver en route to Camp Hood represented another example of the racial discrimination of Black servicemen stationed at bases in the former Confederacy.[51]

While the desegregation of the military in 1948 by President Harry Truman's executive order was an imperative for a democratic nation to live up to its ideals of justice and equality, integration of the armed services did not erase racism within the ranks.[52] Such sentiments continue in the modern day. A poll conducted in the fall of 2019 by the *Military Times*, reported that active-duty personnel believed that white-supremacy and racism were on the rise. This poll revealed that over half of service members of color reported personally experiencing or witnessing incidents of racism. On February 11, 2020, Lecia Brooks, a senior member of the Southern Poverty Law Center, testified before Congress about the increase of white supremacy in the nation, and specifically in the U.S. military. An editorial in the *New York Times* forcefully observed, "Bases named for men who sought to destroy the Union in the name of racial injustice are an insult to the ideals servicemen and women are sworn to uphold—and an embarrassing artifact of the time when the military itself embraced anti-American values."[53]

Stripping the names of traitors and enslavers from installations where today's military men and women train, live, and work was controversial. Perhaps this is not surprising considering the heightened polarization of contemporary American politics and the continual debates over Civil War memory in modern America. One poll conducted by *Military Times* recorded that 49 percent of respondents believed the renaming necessary, while 37 percent opposed the renaming. On the other hand, one witness to the 2023 renaming ceremonies at two bases believed the change was enthusiastically welcomed. While some veterans and soldiers insisted on clinging to the original naming as a token of nostalgia and their "glory days," optimistic forecasting suggested that the renaming would become less controversial. After all, some ten thousand new recruits enter the army each month, and new generations of soldiers begin to train and work at these installations. "We do not live in a country," Petraeus asserted, "to which Braxton Bragg, Henry L. Benning, or Robert E. Lee can serve as an inspiration."[54]

Although these nine bases were perhaps the most visible commemorative tribute to the Confederacy within today's military, hundreds of other vestiges remain woven into the tapestry of the U.S. military. Tangible objects like signs, gates, paintings, roadways, and buildings, for instance, were also to be renamed. In the fall of 2023, for instance, workers removed the street sign for Lee Road at West Point, replacing it, appropriately, with one that read "Grant Road." Additionally, scores of heraldry items (uniform insignia, a unit's coat of arms, mottos, or crests) include aspects that represent or honor the Confederacy. Approximately two hundred army heraldic items contain saltires, a diagonal cross, that resemble the Confederate battle flag.[55]

The army's heritage is more deeply woven to the Civil War than any other branch of the military, but the other services are not immune.[56] At the Naval Academy in Annapolis, Maryland, the superintendent's house, once named after Confederate Commander Franklin Buchanan, became the Farragut House, to honor Admiral David Farragut, a native Tennessean who remained loyal to the Union during the Civil War and became the hero of the Battle of Mobile Bay. The most significant changes in the navy came through the renaming of two ships. The USS *Chancellorsville*, named after Lee's victory in May 1863 on that battlefield, was renamed the USS *Robert Smalls*, honoring an enslaved man who commandeered a Confederate ship in 1862 and sailed himself and sixteen others to the Union line. Additionally, the USNS *Maury* has been renamed USNS *Marie Tharp*, in honor of the ocean cartographer who helped map the Atlantic Ocean floor and document the continental drift.[57]

While relatively few high-ranking elected officials have publicly decried the renaming, some MAGA Republicans have used these nine army bases as talking points in their rallies, rhetoric that escalated in the months leading up to the 2024 presidential election. In early October 2024, while speaking at a town hall meeting in Fayetteville, North Carolina, presidential candidate Donald Trump pledged that, if reelected, he would return Fort Liberty's name to Fort Bragg. Many gathered that day no doubt had ties to Fort Liberty, inspiring Trump to add, "We have a great military, and we have a military that's not woke."[58] Such rhetoric (cleverly labeled as "base pander" by one columnist) appealed to the conservative base; on November 5, 2024, some 77.3 million people cast their ballot for the Republican ticket, ushering Trump into the White House for the second time.[59]

Less than one month following Trump's inauguration, the new president made good on his campaign pledge to restore the name of Fort Bragg... well, sort of. On February 10, 2025, Secretary of Defense Pete Hegseth, an army veteran, issued an order that would rename Fort Liberty to Fort Bragg. This North Carolina base will now honor not the blundering Confederate general but Private First Class Roland L. Bragg, a World War II paratrooper who earned the Silver Star for his actions at the Battle of the Bulge.[60] While the decision came as a surprise to Bragg's descendants, including his daughter, a Trump supporter, it was welcome news. Yet there can be no denying that Roland Bragg too is a victim in the current political circus and the battle for Civil War memory.[61]

The Trump Republicans had found a clever loophole in the law. As noted, section 1749 of the 2020 NDAA clearly prohibited "names related to the Confederacy," and while the re-renaming violated the "spirit of the law," it was not illegal.[62] Hegseth's team did not have to search too far, however, to find a worthy serviceman with the surname Bragg. Roland L. Bragg was one of the original thirty-four thousand individual names submitted to the Naming Commission.[63]

Undoubtedly, Hegseth and other Republicans saw this as a victory in their perpetual quest to "own the libs" and end "wokeness." Even before his confirmation to the cabinet post, Hegseth had made clear his opposition to the renaming, calling these initiatives "garbage" and expressing concern that the name changes broke a "generational link." Yet in honoring Roland Bragg, as Ty Seidule observed, "Hegseth upheld the most important decision from Congress and the Naming Commission. Confederates like the old namesake, Braxton Bragg, do not deserve commemoration in the Defense Department."[64] This is true. Hegseth's proclamation came under fire from some sectors of the far right. Several Confederate heritage groups loudly denounced the name change calling it an act of "cowardice" and "another political bait and switch." One Sons of Confederate Veterans camp in Texas opined in a social media post, "Hegseth is a joke."[65]

Arguably, renaming Fort Liberty was the easiest of the new names to change because it honored not an individual but a value. But MAGA Republicans would not stop with Fort Liberty. Their next target was Fort Hal and

Julia Moore. On March 3, 2025, Hegseth signed an order restoring the name of Fort Benning to the Georgia base. Rather than honoring the Southern enslaver, however, the installation will now pay tribute to Corporal Fred G. Benning, a World War I soldier.[66]

Trump's next declaration came three months later, June 10, 2025, during his visit to Fort Bragg. The event, ostensibly a celebration of the U.S. Army's 250th anniversary, mirrored a Trump rally. Vendors set up booths selling all varieties of Trump and MAGA merchandise. As the president ranted about the 2020 "stolen" election and the perceived fallacies of Democratic politicians and their policies, uniformed men and women eagerly clapped and cheered him on. Without question, this spectacle marked an uncomfortable exhibition of partisanism in the armed forces, violating long-standing tendencies for uniformed personnel to remain nonpartisan.[67] Then, standing before his followers, Trump announced that he would rename all of the bases that had been stripped of their Confederate tributes. "We won a lot of battles out of those forts. It's no time to change," Trump proclaimed.[68]

Thus, as this book goes to print, this latest renaming effort is under way. The seven remaining bases not yet renamed under the Trump administration will receive new names. While the bases will return to their original designations—Fort Benning, Fort Hill, Fort Pickett—they will not honor enslavers or Confederates, thereby abiding by the letter of the law as defined by the NDAA, if boldly defying the spirit. Rather, this latest renaming effort will honor other servicemen with the (conveniently) same surnames. Fort Gregg–Adams, for instance, will once again be Fort Lee. This time, however, the base will be named in honor of Private Fitz Lee, an African American soldier who received the Medal of Honor for his service in Cuba during the Spanish American War.[69]

The 2025 renaming initiative falls within Trump's larger agenda of "Restoring Names That Honor American Greatness." This includes, for instance, the restoration of the name Mount McKinley from Denali and changing the name of the Gulf of Mexico to the Gulf of America.[70] But this is a matter of graver import than substituting one name for another, or rolling back achievements from the Biden administration.[71] There are real Civil War memory issues at stake here. The decision to name nine military bases after traitors and enslavers sent a specific message about the racial hierarchy in the post–Civil War South, one that implied that using the names of Confederate officers was, for its time, "politically correct." A century later, the decision to rename these bases after ten meritorious American service members signaled a different set of values made through the service and sacrifice of generations of American soldiers—individuals like Mary Edwards Walker, William Henry Johnson, Hal and Julia Moore, and Charity Adams. And even though the Trump administration deemed these servicemen and women unworthy of naming tributes in a vindictive effort to terminate "woke garbage" and "political correctness," even the 2025 names recognize that Confederate officers have no place of honor in today's military.[72]

In the aftermath of the Civil War, Union veterans spoke openly about the causes of the war—slavery and treason. At a dedication speech for the First Michigan Infantry Monument at Gettysburg on June 12, 1889, Captain Clinton Spencer proclaimed, "Disloyalty to the old flag was, is, and shall always be TREASON, deep, dark, and damnable."[73] The power of the Lost Cause too often subserviated the voices of Federal soldiers to sweepingly heroic—but inaccurate—versions of Confederate soldiers. And for generations the U.S. Army willingly entangled itself in the memory of the soldiers and officers of the Confederacy. The renaming of these nine army bases, including the 2025 renaming of Fort Liberty, and other Department of Defense assets rightfully divorces the army's tendency to honor officers who owned, bought, and sold peoples and finally removes the stain of treason from the American military.

NOTES

1. Antonio Olivo, "U.S. Army Renames Fort Lee in Virginia After Two Black Former Officers," *Washington Post*, April 27, 2023, https://www.washingtonpost.com/dc-md-va/2023/04/27/fort-lee-rename-gregg-adams/.
2. "Oaths of Enlistment and Oaths of Office," U.S. Army, https://history.army.mil/faq/oaths.html; "Why Does the U.S. Military Celebrate White Supremacy?" *New York Times*, May 23, 2020, https://www.nytimes.com/2020/05/23/opinion/sunday/army-base-names-confederacy-racism.html. Benning, Rucker, and Gordon did not attend West Point and were not in the antebellum U.S. military.
3. Cox, *No Common Ground*, 6.
4. "Naming of U.S. Army Posts," U.S. Army Center of Military History, 2017, https://history.army.mil/faq/naming-of-us-army-posts.htm; "Naming Army Installations," U.S. Army Center of Military History, 2006, https://history.army.mil/faq/army-posts-documents/Naming_Army_Installations.pdf.
5. Joseph E. Kuhn, "Memorandum for the Chief-of-Staff, July 16, 1917," U.S. Army, https://history.army.mil/faq/army-posts-documents/005a-Names_for_cantonments_and_posts_with-policy_statement_1917_orig_scan.pdf; "Naming of U.S. Army Posts."
6. Cox, *No Common Ground*, 54; Janney, *Remembering the Civil War*, 281. For a groundbreaking discussion of postwar memory, see Blight, *Race and Reunion*. "Southern Military Heroes

Are Honored by War Department," *Richmond Times-Dispatch*, July 16, 1917; "Naming of U.S. Army Posts."
7. Seidule, "'Treason Is Treason'"; Naming Commission, Final Report to Congress, Part II, 10–11. The Naming Commission determined that tributes to Lee in Federal uniform, which would reflect his service there as a major while superintendent of the academy, are "historical artifacts" and can remain.
8. "Naming of U.S. Army Posts." In October 1945 the U.S. Army closed Camp Van Dorn and the following year closed Camp Forrest.
9. Mark Thompson, "U.S. Flag Waves Over Ten Army Bases Proudly Named for Confederate Officers," *Time*, June 23, 2015, https://time.com/3932914/army-bases-confederate/.
10. Mike Randall, "West Point's Lee Barracks Under Scrutiny," *Times Herald-Record* (Middletown NY), August 16, 2017, https://www.recordonline.com/story/news/2017/08/16/west-point-s-lee-barracks/18963116007/. Both Gillibrand and Maloney were then serving as members of West Point's advisory board.
11. Rachel Treisman, "Nearly 100 Confederate Monuments Removed in 2020, A Survey Says," NPR, February 23, 2021, https://www.npr.org/2021/02/23/970610428/nearly-100-confederate-monuments-removed-in-2020-report-says-more-than-700-remai; Cox, *No Common Ground*, 6.
12. "Gillibrand, Colleagues Introduce Legislation to Rename All Bases and Other Military Assets for Confederacy Within One Year," June 24, 2020, https://www.gillibrand.senate.gov/news/press/release/gillibrand-colleagues-introduce-legislation-to-rename-all-bases-and-other-military-assets-for-confederacy-within-one-year/; s.4076, Removing Confederate Names and Symbols from Our Military Act of 2020, 116th Congress, https://www.congress.gov/bill/116th-congress/senate-bill/4076/text?r=43&s=1.
13. National Defense Authorization Act for Fiscal Year 2020, December 20, 2019, 116th Congress, https://www.congress.gov/116/plaws/publ92/PLAW-116publ92.pdf.
14. Naming Commission, Final Report to Congress, Part I, 74; s.4076, Removing Confederate Names and Symbols from Our Military Act of 2020; William (Mac) Thornberry National Defense Authorization Act for Fiscal Year 2021, 116th Congress, https://www.congress.gov/bill/116th-congress/house-bill/6395/text.
15. Austin Huguelet, "Hawley Opposes Renaming Army Bases Honoring Confederate Generals," *Springfield News Leader*, June 11, 2020, https://www.news-leader.com/story/news/2020/06/11/missouri-senator-hawley-opposes-renaming-confederate-named-military-bases/5346912002/; Bryan Lowry, "Hawley Quotes Lincoln to Defend Confederate Named Military Bases," *Kansas City Star*, June 13, 2020; Timothy Bella, "Trump Vows to Veto Defense Bill," *Boston Globe*, July 2, 2020.
16. Rosie Gray, "Trump Defends White Nationalist Protesters: 'Some Very Fine People on Both Sides,'" *The Atlantic*, August 15, 2017, https://www.theatlantic.com/politics/archive/2017/08/trump-defends-white-nationalist-protesters-some-very-fine-people-on-both-sides/537012/; Alex Horton, "Trump Won't Rename Army Posts That Honor Confederates," *Washington Post*, June 11, 2020, https://www.washingtonpost.com/national-security/2020/06/10/trump-confederate-bases/; Bella, "Trump Vows to Veto Defense Bill"; "Milley Calls for 'Hard Look' at Renaming Bases Honoring Confederates," *New York Times*, July 9, 2020, https://www.nytimes.com/2020/07/09/us/politics/milley-trump-confederate-base-names.html.

During the 2024 presidential election, some debate emerged as to whether Trump actually said "very fine people," or what he meant by that term if he did. For a discussion of this, see Philip Bump, "What Trump Said with His 'Very Fine People' Comments vs. What He Meant," *Washington Post*, June 28, 2024.

17. Allison Pecorin, "Senators Move to Change Names of Military Bases, Set Stage for a Showdown with Trump," ABC News, June 11, 2020, https://abcnews.go.com/Politics/senators-move-change-names-military-bases-set-stage/story?id=71201478; Rebecca Kheel, "Pentagon Appoints Commissioners to Scrub Confederate Base Name," *The Hill*, January 8, 2021, https://thehill.com/policy/defense/533443-pentagon-appoints-commissioners-to-scrub-confederate-base-names/; Connor O'Brien, "House Democrats Consider Slower Timeline for Renaming Bases That Honor Confederates," *Politico*, November 20, 2020, https://www.politico.com/news/2020/11/20/house-democrats-confederate-bases-renaming-438784; Heather Caygle, "Dem Divide Over Confederate Bases Threatens Massive Defense Bill," *Politico*, November 23, 2020, https://www.politico.com/news/2020/11/23/confederate-bases-democrats-defense-bill-439818; "Vetoes by President Donald J. Trump," U.S. Senate, https://www.senate.gov/legislative/vetoes/Trumpdj.htm; "Roll Call Vote," U.S. Senate, 116th Congress, 2nd Session, https://www.senate.gov/legislative/LIS/roll_call_votes/vote1162/vote_116_2_00264.htm. The House voted 322–87, and the Senate voted 81–13. Among those who supported Trump's veto included the predictable likes of John Kennedy (LA), Tom Cotton (AR), Josh Hawley (MO), and Rand Paul (KY).

18. Naming Commission, "Media Roundtable Transcript," May 21, 2021, author's collection, formerly available at www.thenamingcommission.gov; Naming Commission, Final Report to Congress, Part I, 4–5.

19. Naming Commission, "Recommend a Name," available via the WayBack Machine, https://web.archive.org/web/20211128084623/https://www.thenamingcommission.gov/recommend-a-name; Naming Commission, Final Report to Congress, Part I, 6, 10–11, 78–85.

20. Naming Commission, Final Report to Congress, Part I, 5–6, 10, 14; Ty Seidule, interview, May 25, 2023.

21. "Secretary of Defense Lloyd J. Austin III Directs Implementation of the Naming Commission's Recommendation," U.S. Department of Defense, October 6, 2022, https://www.defense.gov/News/Releases/Release/Article/3182169/secretary-of-defense-lloyd-j-austin-iii-directs-implementation-of-the-naming-co/; "DoD Begins Implementation of Naming Commission Recommendations," U.S. Department of Defense, January 3, 2023, https://www.defense.gov/News/Releases/Release/Article/3259966/dod-begins-implementation-of-naming-commission-recommendations/.

22. Naming Commission, Final Report to Congress, Part I, 8, 11, 14; "2021 Demographics Profile: Army Active Duty Members," Demographics Profile of the Military Community (Department of Defense), https://download.militaryonesource.mil/12038/MOS/Infographic/2021-demographics-active-duty-army-members.pdf; Naming Commission, "Media Roundtable Transcript," May 24, 2022, author's collection, formerly available at www.thenamingcommission.gov. The gender diversity, however, is not as pronounced. Eighty-five percent of active-duty U.S. Army personnel are men, and 15 percent are women.

23. Fred Kaplan, "Good News About Those Military Bases Named After Confederate Officers," *Slate*, July 9, 2023, https://slate.com/news-and-politics/2023/07/military-bases-confederate-officers-renamed.html.

24. "Search for Battles," National Park Service, https://www.nps.gov/civilwar/search-battles.htm. The NPS tallied 124 battles in Virginia. The state with the second most, Tennessee, counts 38. Olivo, "U.S. Army Renames Fort Lee."
25. Memorandum for Brigadier General Harry L. Twaddle, June 12, 1941, U.S. Army Center of Military History, https://history.army.mil/faq/army-posts-documents/270-Camp_Picket_1941.pdf; Gordon, *Pickett*, 129–33, 160–61; Naming Commission, Final Report to Congress, Part I, 8. These men once served in North Carolina's home guard but had switched to the Union side to avoid conscription. In the postwar years, the federal government sought to charge him accordingly, but because of the intervention of Grant, Pickett's old West Point buddy, Pickett was spared from being held accountable for war crimes. Pickett wrote to Grant asking him to intervene on his behalf. Grant wrote President Andrew Johnson explaining that while Pickett had acted poorly, he requested the president overlook such transgressions. The Naming Commission assert that Pickett committed war crimes in his decision to execute the North Carolina soldiers.
26. Chris Cameron, "Army Base Renamed for Native American War Hero," *New York Times*, March 24, 2023, https://www.nytimes.com/2023/03/24/us/politics/army-base-pickett-barfoot.html; Naming Commission, Final Report to Congress, Part I, 53–59; Tre'Vaughn Howard, "Virginia Army Base Named in Honor of Native American War Hero," CBS News, March 24, 2023, https://www.cbsnews.com/news/virginia-army-base-renamed-fort-barfoot-native-american-war-hero-first-of-9-to-drop-confederate-name/.
27. Seidule, *Robert E. Lee and Me*, 216–19.
28. Olivo, "U.S. Army Renames Fort Lee"; Scott Neuman, "An Army Fort Named After Robert E. Lee Now Honors 2 Pioneering Black Officers," NPR, April 27, 2023, https://www.npr.org/2023/04/27/1172126808/fort-gregg-adams-army-fort-lee; Naming Commission, Final Report to Congress, Part I, 47–52.
29. Warner, *Generals in Gray*, 134–35; "History of Fort A.P. Hill," U.S. Army, https://home.army.mil/aphill/application/files/6215/3374/1729/CreationOfFortAPHillBrochure.pdf.
30. Naming Commission, Final Report to Congress, Part I, 35–40; "Dr. Mary Edwards Walker," National Park Service, https://www.nps.gov/people/mary-walker.html. Walker earned a medical degree from Syracuse University in 1855. After being captured and arrested for being a spy, Walker spent four months in Castle Thunder, a prisoner of war camp near Richmond, Virginia, before she was released in a prisoner exchange.
31. Katie Lange, "Meet Dr. Mary Walker," U.S. Army, March 7, 2017, https://www.army.mil/article/183800/meet_dr_mary_walker_the_only_female_medal_of_honor_recipient. In 1917, however, the federal government reviewed its process of awarding the Medal of Honor to civilians and rescinded the medals of 911 recipients, including Walker.
32. Henry Benning, November 19, 1860, in Freehling, *Secession Debated*, 143. In 1922 this site became Fort Benning. Tim Chitwood, "Fort Benning Is Named for a Slave Owning Secessionist. That Could Soon Change," *Ledger-Enquirer*, December 23, 2020, https://www.ledger-enquirer.com/news/local/military/article247853965.html; "Naming of U.S. Army Posts"; Warner, *Generals in Gray*, 26.
33. "Name It Benning," *Columbus Ledger*, September 30, 1918; "Ladies Endorse Camp Benning," *Columbus Ledger*, August 19, 1918; "Confederate Veterans Adopt Resolution," *Columbus Ledger*, August 15, 1918; Memorandum for the Chief of Staff, August 26, 1918, and October 5, 1918, U.S. Army Center of Military History, https://history.army.mil/faq/army-posts

-documents/035-Camp_Benning_1918.pdf; Henry Benning, November 19, 1860, in Freehling, *Secession Debated*, 143. The local Rotary Club and local Confederate veterans also endorsed this selection. In 1922 this site became Fort Benning. A resident of Columbus, Georgia, Elizabeth Rutherford is often credited as the originator of Confederate Memorial Day and was active in postwar Ladies Memorial Associations.

34. Naming Commission, Final Report to Congress, Part I, 15–21; Corey Dickstein, "When Fort Benning Becomes Fort Moore, It Will 'Honor the Army Family,'" *Stars and Stripes*, February 22, 2023, https://www.stripes.com/branches/army/2023-02-22/fort-benning-confederates-fort-moore-9219684.html.

35. "Naming of U.S. Army Posts"; Hess, *Braxton Bragg*, 4, 266, 276. Camp Bragg became Fort Bragg in 1922. David Petraeus, "Take the Confederate Names Off Our Army Bases," *The Atlantic*, June 9, 2020, https://www.theatlantic.com/ideas/archive/2020/06/take-confederate-names-off-our-army-bases/612832/.

36. Naming Commission, Final Report to Congress, Part I, 22–26.

37. Miller, *John Bell Hood*, xvi–xvii, 40–41.

38. Suzanne Gamboa, "Fort Hood to Officially Drop Its Confederate Name and Become Fort Cavazos," NBC News, March 24, 2023, https://www.nbcnews.com/news/latino/fort-hood-drops-confederate-name-fort-cavazos-may-9-rcna76561; "Fort Hood Redesignates Fort Cavazos," U.S. Army, https://home.army.mil/hood/index.php/about/fort-cavazos-redesignation; "Richard E. Cavazos," National Museum of the United States Army, https://www.thenmusa.org/biographies/richard-e-cavazos/.

39. Naming Commission, Final Report to Congress, Part I, 42–46; "Fort Hood Redesignates Fort Cavazos"; "Richard E. Cavazos."

40. "Richard E. Cavazos"; Gamboa, "Fort Hood to Officially Drop Its Confederate Name."

41. "Cities for Soldiers," *Shreveport Times*, May 4, 1941; "Louisiana Camps Named for Famous Men," *Shreveport Times*, April 6, 1941; Warner, *Generals in Gray*, 242–43; Robins, *Bishop of the Old South*, 96.

42. Kim Bellware and Brittany Shammas, "Army Base in Louisiana Sheds Confederate Name for Black War Hero," *Washington Post*, June 14, 2023, https://www.washingtonpost.com/national-security/2023/06/14/army-fort-johnson-polk-renamed/; Sergeant Henry Johnson, Medal of Honor, U.S. Army, https://www.army.mil/medalofhonor/johnson/; Naming Commission, Final Report to Congress, Part I, 60–61; "Who Are They? Men in the 369th Infantry Iconic Photo," National Park Service, https://www.nps.gov/articles/000/iconic369thphoto.htm.

43. Sergeant Henry Johnson, Medal of Honor; Naming Commission, Final Report to Congress, Part I, 60–61; Richard Goldenberg, "Medal of Honor Monday: Army Sgt. Henry Johnson," U.S. Department of Defense, https://www.defense.gov/News/Feature-Stories/story/Article/2201270/medal-of-honor-monday-army-sgt-henry-johnson/.

44. Naming Commission, Final Report to Congress, Part I, 61; Goldenberg, "Medal of Honor Monday"; Naming Commission, Final Report to Congress, Part I, 60–65; "Ceremony Set for Fort Polk Name Change," KALB, March 30, 2023, https://www.kalb.com/2023/03/30/ceremony-set-fort-polk-name-change/. In 1996 Johnson was posthumously awarded the Purple Heart.

45. Phil Gast, "Fort Rucker Was Named for a Confederate," CNN, April 11, 2023, https://www.cnn.com/2023/04/10/us/fort-rucker-name-change-novosel/index.html.

46. Naming Commission, Final Report to Congress, Part I, 66–71; Gast, "Fort Rucker Was Named."
47. W. Todd Groce, "John B. Gordon," New Georgia Encyclopedia, https://www.georgia encyclopedia.org/articles/government-politics/john-b-gordon-1832-1904/.
48. Aisha Frazier, "Georgia's Fort Gordon Becomes Last of 9 US Army Posts to be Renamed," ABC News, October 27, 2023, https://abcnews.go.com/US/georgias-fort-gordon-9-us-army-posts-renamed/story?id=104371264.
49. Alex Horton, "How Black Troops Lost Out in Bid to Sever Army Post's Confederate Ties," Washington Post, October 7, 2022, https://www.washingtonpost.com/national-security/2022/10/07/fort-gordon-confederate-eisenhower-augusta-national/.
50. "South Carolina Sheriff Acquitted in Blinding of Isaac Woodard," St. Paul Recorder, November 15, 1946; "South Carolina Police Chief Acquitted in Blinding Case," The Tennessean, November 6, 1946; Audra D. S. Burch, "Why a Town Is Finally Honoring a Black Veteran Attacks by Its White Police Chief," New York Times, February 8, 2019, https://www.nytimes.com/2019/02/08/us/sergeant-woodard-batesburg-south-carolina.html. Shull was the chief of police of Batesburg, South Carolina.
51. Bristol, "Terror, Anger, and Patriotism," 22–23.
52. America's military is an institution that changes at a glacial pace, and significant change is not often generated from within the military itself but mandated by the federal government. For instance, racial integration occurred when President Harry Truman signed Executive Order 9981 on July 26, 1948. On September 20, 2011, President Barack Obama repealed the Don't Ask, Don't Tell policy, which had for seventeen years prohibited openly gay people from serving in the military.
53. Leo Shane, "Signs of White Supremacy, Extremism Up Again in Poll of Active Duty Troops," Military Times, February 6, 2020, https://www.militarytimes.com/news/pentagon-congress/2020/02/06/signs-of-white-supremacy-extremism-up-again-in-poll-of-active-duty-troops/. The poll found that 36 percent responded that they have witnessed signs of white supremacy compared to 22 percent the previous year, 2018. "SPLC Testifies Before Congress on Alarming Incidents of White Supremacy in the Military," Southern Poverty Law Center, February 11, 2020, https://www.splcenter.org/news/2020/02/11/splc-testifies-congress-alarming-incidents-white-supremacy-military; "Why Does the U.S. Military Celebrate White Supremacy?"
54. Leo Shane, "Nearly Half of Troops Polled Support Changing Names of Bases Honoring Confederate Leaders," Military Times, September 3, 2020, https://www.militarytimes.com/news/pentagon-congress/2020/09/03/nearly-half-of-troops-polled-support-changing-names-of-bases-honoring-confederate-leaders/; Ty Seidule, interview, May 25, 2023; Petraeus, "Take the Confederate Names."
55. Ty Seidule, interview, May 25, 2023; "West Point Residents Receive New Street Signs, Addresses," West Point, October 31, 2023, https://www.westpoint.edu/news/community-news/west-point-residents-receive-new-street-signs-addresses; Naming Commission, Final Report to Congress, Part I, 12–13; Naming Commission, Final Report to Congress, Part III, 7–11. This report includes the listing of all assets.
56. "SECNAV Renames United States Naval Academy Campus Building After Former President Carter," U.S. Navy, February 17, 2023, https://www.navy.mil/Press-Office/Press-Releases/display-pressreleases/Article/3301924/secnav-renames-united-states-naval-academy-campus-building-after-former-preside/.

57. Geoff Ziezulewicz, "Navy Drops Confederate Namesake from Naval Academy Residence," *Navy Times*, May 2, 2023; Sam LaGrone, "USS *Chancellorsville* to Be Renamed After Former Slave Who Captured Confederate Ship," *USNI News*, February 27, 2023, https://news.usni.org/2023/02/27/uss-chancellorsville-to-be-renamed-after-former-slave-who-stole-confederate-ship; Emily Schmall, "Stripping Confederate Ties, the U.S. Navy Renames Two Vessels," *New York Times*, March 11, 2023, https://www.nytimes.com/2023/03/11/us/navy-ship-confederate-robert-smalls.html.

58. Irie Sentner, "Trump Pledges to Rename Army Base After Confederate General," *Politico*, October 4, 2024, https://www.politico.com/news/2024/10/04/trump-rename-army-confederate-general-00182606; Ronald G. Shafer, "Who Was Fort Bragg Named After? The South's Worst, Most Hated General," *Washington Post*, June 16, 2023, https://www.washingtonpost.com/history/2023/06/16/fort-bragg-renamed-fort-liberty-braxton-bragg/; Kaplan, "Good News About Those Military Bases"; Steve Beynon, "DeSantis, Pence Campaign on Reversing Fort Liberty Designation," *Military Times*, June 12, 2023, https://www.military.com/daily-news/2023/06/12/gop-hopefuls-vow-scrap-fort-liberty-return-confederate-namesake-fort-bragg.html. Republican presidential candidates Mike Pence and Ron DeSantis both pledged, if elected, to reinstate the name Fort Bragg.

59. Charles Lane, "Even by Trump-Era GOP Standards, This Is Base Pander," *Washington Post*, June 14, 2023, https://www.washingtonpost.com/opinions/2023/06/14/pence-desantis-pander-fort-bragg/; "Election 2024 Presidential Results," CNN, https://www.cnn.com/election/2024/results/president.

60. "Secretary of Defense Pete Hegseth Renames Fort Liberty to Fort Bragg," U.S. Department of Defense, February 10, 2025, https://www.defense.gov/News/Releases/Release/Article/4062245/secretary-of-defense-pete-hegseth-renames-fort-liberty-to-fort-bragg/.

61. Akilah Davis, "Daughter of World War II Veteran Roland Bragg Reacts to Fort Liberty Name Change: 'Very Proud of My Father,'" ABCNews11, February 12, 2025, https://abc11.com/post/fort-bragg-daughter-wwii-veteran-pfc-roland-reacts-liberty-name-change-proud-father/15894581/.

62. National Defense Authorization Act for Fiscal Year 2020, 116th Congress, https://www.congress.gov/116/plaws/publ92/PLAW-116publ92.pdf; Tom Vanden Brooke and Cybele Mayes Osterman, "Fort Liberty Now Fort Bragg," *USA Today*, February 11, 2025, https://www.usatoday.com/story/news/politics/2025/02/11/hegseth-fort-liberty-bragg-name-change/78408328007.

63. Naming Commission, Final Report to Congress, Part I, 76, 78.

64. Brooke and Osterman, "Fort Liberty Now Fort Bragg"; Ty Seidule and Connor Williams, "Fort Bragg Is Back. Stop the Re-Naming of Army Bases There," *Washington Post*, February 11, 2025, https://www.washingtonpost.com/opinions/2025/02/11/hegseth-fort-bragg-commission-confederate/.

65. Kevin Levin, "Thank You, Pfc. Roland L. Bragg, for Your Service," *Slate*, February 12, 2025, https://slate.com/news-and-politics/2025/02/fort-bragg-name-alvin-trump-pete-hegseth-liberty.html.

66. Matthew Olay, "Hegseth Restores Fort Moore to Fort Benning in Honor of World War I Soldier," U.S. Army, March 5, 2025, https://www.army.mil/article/283521/hegseth_restores_fort_moore_to_fort_benning_in_honor_of_wwi_soldier.

67. Stephen Saideman, "Trump's Fort Bragg Speech Was a Serious Step Toward Ending Democracy," MSNBC, June 11, 2025, https://www.msnbc.com/opinion/msnbc-opinion/trump-fort-bragg-military-republican-civil-war-rcna212215; Anne Flaherty, "Trump Merchandise Sold at Fort Bragg for President's Speech Now Under Review," ABC News, June 12, 2025, https://abcnews.go.com/US/trump-merchandise-sold-army-base-presidents-speech-now/story?id=122764288.
68. Joe Walsh and Eleanor Watson, "Trumps Says He's Restoring the Original Confederate Names of These Army Bases—but with New Namesakes," CBS News, June 10, 2025, https://www.cbsnews.com/news/trump-restoring-confederate-names-army-bases/.
69. Carol Rosenberg, "No, Not That Lee. Pentagon Finds Black Hero to Rechristen Base Long Named for Robert E.," *New York Times*, June 11, 2025; Walsh and Watson, "Trump Says He's Restoring the Original Confederate Names." Fort Gordon will now honor Master Sergeant Gary I. Gordon, a Medal of Honor recipient killed in Mogadishu, Somalia. To recapture the tribute to A. P. Hill, that Virginia installation will now honor three Civil War Medal of Honor recipients (Lieutenant Colonel Edward Hill, Sergeant Robert A. Pinn, and Private Bruce Anderson). Fort Hood will now be named for Colonel Robert B. Hood, a World War I soldier, and Fort Pickett will honor World War II soldier Vernon W. Pickett. Louisiana's Fort Polk will be named for World War II General James H. Polk, and Alabama's Fort Rucker will pay tribute to World War I aviator Captain Edward W. Rucker.
70. Donald J. Trump, "Restoring Names That Honor American Greatness," White House, January 20, 2025, https://www.whitehouse.gov/presidential-actions/2025/01/restoring-names-that-honor-american-greatness/; Tara Copp and Lolita C. Baldor, "Hegseth Renames North Carolina Military Base Fort Roland L. Bragg and Signals More Change Coming," Associated Press, February 11, 2025, https://apnews.com/article/bragg-base-confederate-rename-a73e96565617830cf3b22c33fc845ab4.
71. Naming Commission, Final Report to Congress, Part I, 76–77; Levin, "Thank You, Pfc. Roland L. Bragg"; Seidule and Williams, "Fort Bragg Is Back."
72. Seidule and Williams, "Fort Bragg Is Back"; Carol Rosenberg, "No, Not That Lee. Pentagon Finds Black Hero to Rechristen Base Long Named for Robert E.," *New York Times*, June 11, 2025, https://www.nytimes.com/2025/06/11/us/politics/army-bases-trump-confederate.html?unlocked_article_code=1.OE8.ZkJ1.H2Yy8jmu5ncb.
73. Spencer, "Address of Captain Clinton Spencer," 72–73.

BIBLIOGRAPHY

Blight, David. *Race and Reunion: The Civil War in American Memory*. Harvard University Press, 2001.

Bristol, Douglas Walter, Jr. "Terror, Anger, and Patriotism: Understanding the Resistance of Black Soldiers during World War II." In *Integrating the US Military: Race, Gender, and Sexual Orientation since World War II*, edited by Douglas Walter Bristol Jr. and Heather Marie Stur. Johns Hopkins University Press, 2017.

Cox, Karen. *No Common Ground: Confederate Monuments and the Ongoing Fight for Racial Justice*. University of North Carolina Press, 2021.

Freehling, William, ed. *Secession Debated: Georgia's Showdown in 1860*. Oxford University Press, 1992.

Gordon, Lesley J. *Pickett: General George E. Pickett in Life and Legend*. University of North Carolina Press, 1998.

Hess, Earl J. *Braxton Bragg: The Most Hated Man in the Confederacy*. University of North Carolina Press, 2016.

Janney, Caroline E. *Remembering the Civil War: Reunion and the Limits of Reconciliation*. University of North Carolina Press, 2013.

Miller, Brian Craig. *John Bell Hood and the Fight for Civil War Memory*. University of Tennessee Press, 2010.

Naming Commission. Final Report to Congress, Part I, United States Army Bases. August 2022.

———. Final Report to Congress, Part II, U.S. Military Academy and U.S. Naval Academy. August 2022.

———. Final Report to Congress, Part III, Renaming Department of Defense Assets. September 2022.

Robins, Glenn. *The Bishop of the Old South: The Ministry and Civil War Legacy of Leonidas Polk*. Mercer University Press, 2006.

Seidule, James Tyrus. "'Treason Is Treason': Civil War Memory at West Point, 1861–1902." *Journal of Military History* 76, no. 2 (April 2012): 427–52.

Seidule, Ty. *Robert E. Lee and Me: A Southerner's Reckoning with the Myth of the Lost Cause* St. Martin's, 2020.

Seidule, Ty, and Connor Williams. *A Promise Delivered: Ten American Heroes and the Battle to Rename Our Nation's Military Bases*. St. Martin's, 2025.

Spencer, Clinton. "Address of Captain Clinton Spencer." In *Michigan at Gettysburg, July 1st, 2nd, 3rd, 1863. June 12, 1889. Proceedings Incident to the Dedication of the Michigan Monuments upon the Battlefield of Gettysburg, June 12th, 1889*. Winn & Hammond, Printers and Binders, 1889.

Warner, Ezra. *Generals in Gray: Lives of the Confederate Commanders*. Louisiana State University Press, 1959.

4

Freedom on the Fringes

Interpreting the Civil War and Relevancy at Camp Nelson

STEVE T. PHAN

The Southern terminal of the Kentucky Central Railroad ended at Nicholasville—a small community just seventeen miles south of Lexington. Another half dozen miles south, travelers came to Camp Nelson, a burgeoning U.S. Army supply depot straddling the Lexington-Danville Turnpike at the confluence of the Kentucky River and Hickman Creek. The base, established in April 1863, served as a staging area for the Army of the Ohio's long-anticipated East Tennessee Campaign, which aimed to liberate civilian Unionists suffering under Confederate occupation in the region. Camp Nelson was a temporary stop for U.S. Army soldiers, civilian employees, and refugees escaping war-ravaged areas and enslavement. It was a dramatic and tragic space that was developed, expanded, and dismantled in a span of three years. During its short existence, Camp Nelson was a crossroads that witnessed the intersection of military necessity, conditional Unionism, and emancipation that directly impacted national policies and the collective memory of the Bluegrass State. The martial infrastructure that spanned four thousand acres and featured more than three hundred wooden buildings is gone, long replaced by grazing animals and the plowshare. But beneath the native grasses and karst geology are the stories of people—free and enslaved, civilian and soldier—who were determined to find their place in a country torn asunder. Their experiences are integral to our understanding of the complexities of emancipation, the postwar struggle for civil rights, and the contested legacy of the Civil War in a border state.

Camp Nelson speaks to the "mystic chords of memory" in modern America. It's a place that is difficult to label and categorize, existing outside the boundary of traditional military scholarship and preservation in a state brimming with Confederate iconography and monuments. Few Civil War enthusiasts have visited or even heard of the site, but there's something unique here; it serves as an intermediary between the war's complex legacies and the nation's paradoxes regarding race and equality. At Camp Nelson, civilians and enslaved African American families navigated the dangers of Unionism and emancipation in a region raided by Confederate military forces and marauded by guerrillas. Their stories are an important and overlooked facet of Civil War history that speaks to the root cause of America's most divisive conflict.

This chapter tells the story of efforts to preserve and protect Camp Nelson as a site of Civil War history and memory. Camp Nelson is a site filled with hope, self-determination, broken promises, and an unfiltered glimpse of our imperfect union. It serves on the front line of interpreting the conflict by bringing the stories of marginalized people into our Civil War narrative and modern memories. The accounts of white civilian refugees and enslaved African Americans who poured by the thousands into the army base exist on the fringes of public discourse and the interpretation at Civil War sites, especially in Kentucky—a pro-Union and pro-slavery border state during the war that adopted a Lost Cause ideology in the years after Appomattox. Today, Camp Nelson Monument not only memorializes the Bluegrass State's complex past but also provides "opportunities for research and scholarship related to military history, race, identity, and gender during the Civil War."[1] Above all else, Camp Nelson reflects recent interpretive efforts to understand the Civil War as not just a conflict of "brother against brother" but as a battle over civil rights.

The Making of Camp Nelson in Civil War Kentucky

Kentucky is positioned on the periphery of Civil War memory and commemoration despite the state's strategic and political significance during the conflict. It's the birthplace of the war's chief executives: Abraham Lincoln, born in Hodgenville, and Jefferson Davis, born in Fairview. First Lady Mary Todd Lincoln was born to a prominent family in Lexington. The state's contested landscape witnessed the Confederate army's capture of Frankfort—the only U.S. state capital to fall—and the inauguration of a pro-Confederate governor. Confederate cavalry raids, meanwhile, penetrated deep into the country's interior, stirring fear and chaos in Ohio and Indiana.

The war's legacy can perhaps be articulated by two often-quoted remarks spoken six decades apart. The first was reportedly uttered by President Abraham Lincoln in 1861: "I hope to have God on my side, but I must have Kentucky."[2] The statement has become a source a pride for Kentuckians, and adorns an assortment of memorabilia, kitschy home decor, T-shirts, and street art in the Bluegrass State. The second was penned in *The Civil War and Readjustment in Kentucky* (1926) by historian E. Merton Coulter, who contended that the state "waited until after the war was over to secede from the Union." According to Coulter, the post-Appomattox shift was rooted in Federal authorities' perversion of "the purposes and promises of the war."[3] Historians have repeatedly referenced Coulter's thesis to explain Kentucky's dramatic adoption of a pro-Confederate identity. The arguments range from "antifederal sentiments" to the "the supposed distinctiveness of its citizens," explained Anne E. Marshall.[4] In both reality and practice, Kentucky's turn hinged on the emancipation of the 225,490 enslaved African Americans who resided in the state and the tidal wave of consequences it generated. The ripple effect shaped political power and the war's memorialization for a century and a half. The legacy endures to this day. Camp Nelson exists in this complicated and conflicted setting, where perception and truth were separated at birth but also where they may be reunited and find relevance, an idealistic goal in a polarized America.

To some degree, the roots of Camp Nelson's intentional exclusion from Kentucky's Civil War legacy can be traced to the state's noted ambivalence about joining the conflict. At the war's outbreak in April 1861, Kentucky Governor Beriah Magoffin, a Confederate sympathizer, firmly rejected the War Department's call for state volunteers to suppress the rebellion, which he described as "the wicked purpose of subduing [Kentucky's] sister Southern States."[5] Despite Magoffin's obstinance, many white Kentuckians desired a cautious and practical approach to the war. Others openly supported the Confederacy and secession. As a result, the Commonwealth of Kentucky adopted a policy of neutrality a month after Fort Sumter, "pledging to remain independent of both sides" and prohibiting the entrance of blue- or gray-clad troops into the state.[6] The state's neutrality was short-lived, as military operations along the Kentucky-Tennessee border resulted in a Confederate invasion on September 2, 1861.[7] The state legislature passed several resolutions, including expelling Confederate soldiers from Kentucky and seeking military assistance from the Federal government. Magoffin vetoed all measures and advocated neutrality and the removal of all non-Commonwealth soldiers from the state, but his actions were overridden by the General Assembly. Kentucky affirmed its allegiance to the United States on September 18.[8]

However, Kentucky's loyalty was tenuous and conditionally tied to the Federal government's continued protection of their state's rights regarding slavery, especially the Fugitive Slave Act and other legislation.⁹ Patrick Lewis described this malleable commitment to the defense of the Union and the Constitution as "loyalty *because of* and *for the benefit of slavery*."¹⁰ The institution underpinned Kentucky's economy and racial and social order. The loss of the latter, explained James W. Finck, was what white Kentuckians feared most, and drove tens of thousands of them into the ranks of the Union.¹¹

Kentucky's fragile and contested alliance with the United States was reflected in the military enlistment. In her study of Civil War Kentucky, Anne Marshall found that "between 66,000 and 76,000 white Kentuckians fought for the Union, and an estimated 25,000 to 40,000 enlisted in the Confederate ranks."¹² The addition of nearly 24,000 African American men who enlisted in the United States Colored Troops (USCT) beginning in 1864 increases the number of Kentuckians who served in the Union to over 90,000 men. The number does not include Black men who enlisted in neighboring states in 1863, especially Indiana and Ohio, where more than 6,600 joined the ranks.¹³ However, the numbers are misleading, especially when examining the percentage of white Kentuckians who didn't serve. "Of Kentucky's eligible white males," explained Marshall, "71 percent chose not to fight at all."¹⁴ The Federal government's attempt to draft white men also proved unsuccessful, with fewer than 25 percent of eligibles responding to the calls.¹⁵ In contrast, according to one estimate, 57 percent of able-bodied Black Kentuckians joined the U.S. Army, an astonishing percentage despite the resistance from state officials, enslavers, guerrillas, and the delay in recruitment.¹⁶

The enlistment numbers reveal the evolution of the Civil War in Kentucky, especially Federal policy affecting slavery that sparked a dramatic turn of white citizens against the Lincoln administration. Those who flocked to Union camps and carried the Stars and Stripes into battle in 1861 and 1862 served "not only for the interests of the Union," wrote Patrick Lewis, "but for the interests of the state itself."¹⁷ Kentucky's Unionists volunteers rallied on the battle cry, the Union as it was, the Constitution as it is.¹⁸ But internal and external forces threatened and eventually destroyed the institution of slavery, severing Kentucky's precarious ties to the Union.

Camp Nelson was founded as a result of the commingling of the Lincoln administration's political and military objectives. The base, officially established on April 29, 1863, laboriously supplied Major General Ambrose E. Burnside's East Tennessee Campaign. The offensive, launched from Camp Nelson on August 16, 1863, achieved both strategic and political goals long desired by Lincoln, Andrew Johnson, and the War Department. It fulfilled three major objectives: liberating loyal civilian Unionists; establishing a U.S. stronghold in the region; and threatening the East Tennessee and Virginia Railroad that "link[ed] Virginia with the western part of the Confederacy."[19] The army organized seven white Kentucky and East Tennessee regiments at Camp Nelson in 1863; the latter was largely composed of refugees fleeing areas controlled by the Confederate army. The Federal government embarked on a radical course the following year: Black enlistment. It set the uneven course to emancipation and "stirred up a hornet's nest" in the Bluegrass State, the ramifications of which persist to this day.[20]

The U.S. Army's development of Camp Nelson, one of the largest supply depots constructed during the Civil War, involved enslaved African Americans at the onset. Upon selecting the site for the supply depot, Major James H. Simpson, chief engineer for the Department of the Ohio, was instructed by Major General Ambrose E. Burnside "to fortify the area."[21] Army engineers designed an elaborate system of fully connected earthworks that spanned one and a half miles from the Kentucky River east to Hickman Creek, guarding every approach to the base from the north. Secondary fortifications defended Hickman Valley and the Kentucky River (Hickman Bridge). Burnside's army, consisting of Ninth Corps and Twenty-Third Corps, were scattered to occupy and secure strategic areas across Kentucky. Consequently, to fill the labor void, the War Department enforced military necessity to authorize the impressment of enslaved African Americans.

Black men began to be impressed in June 1863, but Brigadier General Jeremiah T. Boyle, commander of the District of Kentucky, expanded the practice when he issued General Orders No. 41 on August 10, impressing six thousand enslaved people from fourteen counties. The order targeted Black males ages sixteen to forty-five to construct fortifications and roads at Camp Nelson and roads through Central Kentucky to support military operations for an unspecified period. Enslavers were "paid for the services of the laborers" at the end of each month by voucher, averaging fifteen dollars per month.[22] White Kentuckians' attempt to resist "the military use of slave labor" proved futile, as more than 1,900 enslaved Blacks were impressed at Camp Nelson and the surrounding area.[23] Lasting from mid-1863 to March 1864, impressed labor laid the foundation for U.S. military operations in the region for the remainder of the war. It also set the course for slavery's destruction.

Enslaved African Americans' self-determination to escape bondage combined with Kentucky's inability to fill draft quotas with white men began the process of slavery's demise in the Bluegrass State. In the late spring and early summer of 1864, the evolution of Federal military policies provided an opportunity for Black men to self-emancipate by enlisting in the U.S. Army. The birth of the USCT in Kentucky sparked a powder keg. State officials, supported by loyal civilians and soldiers, had long opposed any form of African American military service in the Commonwealth, including the enlistment of free Blacks. They keenly understood that it portended government-sanctioned emancipation across the state. The War Department initially set limits on Black recruitment in 1864, but the restrictions were ultimately lifted, allowing any enslaved man to enlist, and authorizing the organization of USCT regiments at eight recruiting centers in Kentucky. Camp Nelson, the largest station, experienced a flood of enslaved African Americans into army lines. Men physically fit for military service were enlisted and assigned to one of eight USCT regiments. The men were not alone; thousands of women, children, and men unfit for military service also arrived at the base. However, unlike their husbands, sons, and brothers who were mustered into Federal service, they were branded as refugees.

The prospect of emancipation induced thousands of enslaved people to make the hazardous journey to Camp Nelson. White Kentuckians directly targeted the family members of USCT soldiers, especially wives and children, who were physically punished as retribution for their husbands' enlisting. Freedom seekers were subject to exposure, illness, and violence. "They stopped at nothing: torturing, maiming, and even murdering their victims," wrote Richard D. Sears.[24] After arriving at Camp Nelson, Black refugees were not afforded protection or allocated the supplies provided to East Tennessee refugees, especially medical care, food, and shelter. Their status was precarious, and they were subject to forced removal, known as expulsions, from the base. On at a least eight separate occasions in 1864, the U.S. Army issued orders "that all negro women and children, old and inform, negro men unfit for any military duty who have voluntarily come into Camp, be at once sent beyond the lines with instructions not to return."[25] The November 1864 expulsion of four hundred Black refugees included the wives and children of USCT soldiers. The expulsion sparked outrage from several army officers, notably Captain Theron S. Hall, chief quartermaster, who disclosed the incident to the War Department and eastern newspapers. The order was quickly rescinded, but not before the deaths of at least 102 refugees. It proved to be the last forced removal of Black refugees, revealing the tragic paradox of Camp Nelson as a bastion of freedom for men of military age and fitness and a perilous, ambiguous space for their families. However, the expulsion inspired the establishment of the Home for Colored Refugees at Camp Nelson in 1865. The home, a government-sanctioned and government-funded site, featured a school, hospital, offices, and cottages for all Black refugees who made it to Union lines, and it remained active until 1866. According to Captain Hall, "Good resulted from the evil."[26]

Joseph Simpson, a native of Manchester and a member of the Friends' Central Committee for the Relief of the Emancipated Negroes based in London, England, toured several American cities to inspect and document the condition of formerly enslaved people in the spring and summer of 1865. After crossing the Atlantic, Simpson arrived at New York City on April 19, ten days after the Confederate Army of Northern Virginia's capitulation to the Armies of the United States at Appomattox, Virginia. In the coming weeks, Simpson's whirlwind tour took him to Philadelphia, Baltimore, Richmond, Cincinnati, and the Mississippi Delta. After visiting the Queen City, Simpson's journey took him to an institution "in the very heart of Kentucky," Camp Nelson.[27] His itinerary included meeting the camp's commandant, inspecting the facilities and cottages, and interviewing refugee women on why they had made the decision to escape enslavement. The visit was highlighted by a meeting organized by Reverend John G. Fee, abolitionist minister and founder of Berea College, at a mess hall in the Home for Colored Refugees that was attended by an estimated six hundred freedmen, including USCT soldiers. The meeting featured statements from the Black soldiers, who spoke in an earnestness and ease about their experiences from slavery to freedom, especially their "much prize[d] liberty," reported Simpson.[28]

It was at this meeting where Simpson recorded a remark from an unknown USCT sergeant major about Camp Nelson's position as Kentucky's bastion of freedom. "It used to be five hundred miles to git to Canada from Lexington, but now it's only eighteen miles! *Camp Nelson* is now *our* Canada."[29] The quote has been widely circulated by local historians in recent decades and is featured prominently in the park's interpretive publications and exhibits. The meeting also featured a few appropriate remarks from Theron Hall, the former chief quartermaster who served as the first superintendent at the Home of Colored Refugees. Victory without emancipation was not possible, proclaimed Hall, whose personal experience as a soldier and impassioned advocacy for African Americans was manifested at Camp Nelson. For Hall, Fee, and enslaved people, the war to for the Union was a consecrated struggle to destroy slavery. "Look at Bull's [R]un! Had we succeeded there, slavery would still have been rampant. Look at our other battles! We were never victorious till we were earnest in this sacred cause. I know myself that I speak the truth about these battles; for I was there, and saw myself."[30]

From Civil War to Civil Rights

Nationally, the camp's revival coincided with a period of renewed interest in the Civil War and its legacies on American life.[31] Beginning in the 1970s, this heightened attention—spurred by documentaries, feature films, and other media—fueled land preservation and visitor services development at several Civil War sites in Kentucky, including Mill Springs Battlefield, Fort Duffield, Richmond Battlefield, and Camp Nelson. The preservation of Camp Nelson was also tied to local and regional factors, including the planned realignment of U.S. Route 27 and the installation of a new fiber optic line near Camp Nelson's former location. Over the final three decades of the twentieth century, the highway's expansion spurred a series of cultural resource investigations, especially archaeological surveys and excavations.

Camp Nelson was not the only Civil War site in the Bluegrass State to draw the interest of preservationists. "Since 1991, the landscape of Kentucky has changed, nearly 3,000 acres of land that contains portions of numerous Civil War battlefields or sites have been preserved," writes Joseph Brent, former historian at the Kentucky Heritage Council.[32] Federal initiatives, notably the Civil War Sites Advisory Commission and the American Battlefield Protection Program, "change[d] the face of Civil War sites preservation in Kentucky," explains Brent.[33] In 1991 the Kentucky Heritage Council formed the Kentucky Civil War Sites Preservation "to develop partnerships between state and local governments entities that [worked] closely with area residents and national Civil War preservation organizations to preserve, protect, and interpret Kentucky's other Civil War sites."[34] The same year, the congressionally mandated Civil War Sites Advisory Commission Survey began, "designed to examine 384 principle battlefields in 26 states," including eleven sites in Kentucky.[35] Camp Nelson was not featured, as the base did not witness a military engagement during the war; rather, its preservation was a testament to "public-private partnership" that proved remarkably successful in the setting defined by battlefield protection.[36]

The earliest steps to preserve Camp Nelson, then under private ownership, occurred in 1994, when the Kentucky Heritage Council, in partnership with the county and the newly formed Camp Nelson Preservation and Restoration Foundation, completed a preservation plan and developed a driving tour and interpretive waysides. In total, Camp Nelson received "nearly $1 million in transportation enhancing funding" that was used to purchase more than four hundred acres of the original four-thousand-acre site, culminating in the establishment of Camp Nelson Heritage Park by Jessamine County in 1998.[37] In the ensuing years, county staff and the Camp Nelson Foundation constructed a visitor center, museum, and walking trails. Camp Nelson's national significance was further cemented when it was listed on the National Register of Historic Places (1998) and National Underground Railroad Network to Freedom (2007) and declared a National Historic Landmark District (2013).

In 1998 National Park Service (NPS) Civil War site managers met in Nashville to discuss, in large part, "the need to more fully interpret the causes and consequences of the war, as well as the experiences of African Americans, women, and civilians, and others, in order to help the public better understand the relevance of the Civil War today."[38] The meeting spurred a fundamental shift in how the NPS interpreted slavery as the central cause of the war, especially at venerated battlefields, and produced the publication, *Holding the High Ground: A National Park Service Plan for the Sesquicentennial of the American Civil War* (2008). Report author Robert K. Sutton stated that the agency had made substantial strides "by interpreting not only the issue of slavery, but other causational themes as well."[39] Sutton admitted that NPS "interpreters and managers have deftly skirted such issues as why the North won the Civil War."[40] As a result, the iconic battlefield sites commemorate engagements and the deeds of courageous soldiers and became "laboratories to study the military actions that took place there."[41] This narrative remains deeply entrenched at NPS Civil War sites.

However, incremental progress has been made, and the Civil War 150th (2011–15) commemorations at NPS units served as a testing ground for this interpretive shift. *Holding the High Ground* served as "the foundational document for envisioning and planning the agency's approach to the [sesquicentennial] commemoration."[42] The NPS's framework evolved from the "Civil War 150" to feature the fiftieth anniversary of the civil rights movement and was retitled Civil War to Civil Rights.[43] The agency's commemoration desired to fulfill six major goals: "move beyond the battlefield; move beyond the facts; expand outreach; offer unmatched visitor experiences; create a lasting legacy; and leverage partnerships."[44] The process to achieve the aims included the design and installation of new interpretive exhibits, waysides, and digital and visual media products; the publication of handbooks, including *Hispanics and the Civil War*, *American Indians and the Civil War*, and

Asians and Pacific Islanders and the Civil War; and special event programming, especially sixteen signature events. According to the NPS Civil War to Civil Rights Report, the commemorations generated momentum "to expand the Service's understanding and interpretation of the Reconstruction/Jim Crow Eras and to preserve more of the sites that tell these stories." Civil War to Civil Rights inspired the next service-wide effort—Arc to Equality—an ongoing effort by the NPS to "be an agent of understanding, healing, and change in the world today."[45]

Camp Nelson's national significance and relevance is found beyond the battlefield. "African American people, particularly soldiers and those women and children who entered the camp, are a critical part of the story," wrote W. Stephen McBride in 2013—just five years before Camp Nelson's establishment as a national monument.[46] County staff, archaeologists, and historians, supported by a cadre of stakeholders, supporters, and descendants, attempted to "change Kentucky and the nation's Civil War narrative and public memory from one created in support of sectional (white) reconciliation and racism, to one of Union victory and emancipation."[47] Their efforts proved fruitful and set the foundation for the established of Camp Nelson National Monument. The site was listed on the National Underground Railroad Network to Freedom (2008) and the Reconstruction Era National Historic Network (2020), both administered by the NPS. Camp Nelson's elevation from a county park to a unit of the NPS in 2018 "provide[s] a national platform for preserving this history."[48]

The park's path to federal status involved stakeholders at the local, state, and national level, and was codified during a firestorm of political exigencies. "National monuments help preserve and tell our nation's history, and Camp Nelson is one of the places where our nation was made stronger and history was made," wrote Secretary of the Interior Ryan Zinke, recommending Camp Nelson's designation as a national monument on December 5, 2017.[49] The Department of the Interior's recommendation was in response to the Camp Nelson Heritage Park Study Act introduced by U.S. Representative Andy Barr of Kentucky's Sixth Congressional District and co-sponsored by Congresswoman Marica L. Fudge (D-OH) on August 18, 2016. The act, and subsequent legislation, initiated a two-year process that transformed Camp Nelson from a county to a national park. The Camp Nelson Heritage National Monument Act was passed by House of Representatives on June 5, 2018, and it was approved by a vote of 376–4. HR 5655 gained the support of U.S. Senator Mitch McConnell, who introduced companion legislation to the Committee on Energy and Natural Resources on July 26, 2018. The committee met on October 2 and recommended passage upon the adoption of three major amendments—boundary, name, and definitions. Before the Senate could take up the debate, the executive branch intervened. On October 26, 2018, President Donald Trump issued Proclamation 9811, declaring Camp Nelson National Monument as the 418th unit of the NPS.

The action was not without its detractors, who criticized Trump for employing the Antiquities Act to create the national monument after shrinking Bears Ears and Grand Staircase–Escalante National Monuments in Utah in 2017.[50] "We wholeheartedly support designating national monuments that honor the fight for equality and justice such as Camp Nelson," writes Dan Hartinger, national monuments campaign director for the Wilderness Society, echoing the sentiment of several conservation organization's endorsement of Camp Nelson's addition to the national park system.[51] However, continues Hartinger, "all national monuments that recognize our diverse history must be protected and honored—including Bears Ears National Monument in Utah, where a coalition of sovereign tribal nations proposed and advocated for the monument."[52] Critics charged that it made little sense to honor Camp Nelson's role in advancing equality while simultaneously working to strip protections from sites like Bears Ears.[53] Even so, Camp Nelson's addition to the NPS reflected the proliferation of recognition for African American historical sites beginning in the 1990s and continued under the Barack Obama administration, especially units affiliated with the Civil War and Reconstruction, including Fort Monroe National Monument (2011), Charles Young Buffalo Soldiers National Monument (2013), and Reconstruction Era National Historical Park (2017).[54] Camp Nelson National Monument's realization was attained through grassroots efforts and bipartisanship at the congressional level, the endorsement of Senate Republicans, and the enactment of the Antiquities Act by President Trump that stirred universal approval and charges of mendacity. Camp Nelson's history, both historical and modern, remains contradictory and mysterious.

The Monument That Never Materialized

Today, Camp Nelson National Monument is a civil rights park. According to the foundation document, the site's purpose is to "preserve[] and interpret[] the historic and archeological resources of a Union Army supply depot that became one of the largest Civil War-era recruitment and training centers for USCTs and an African American refugee camp."[55] NPS staff are in the

Fig. 4.1. Memorial obelisk at Graveyard No. 1, burial ground for African American and white refugees who died at Camp Nelson in Kentucky. Courtesy of National Park Service.

process of reframing the park's purpose and interpretive themes from Civil War to Civil Rights to Civil War *for* Civil Rights, and a site that witnessed nontraditional battles—a struggle for freedom, emancipation, and the rights of citizenship, and the contested memory of the war's legacies.

This dramatic recalibration is reflected in the park's Long Range Interpretive Plan, public programs, digital and visual media, and cultural landscape projects. The Long Range Interpretive Plan, finalized in 2023–24, serves as the guideline for interpretive and education programs, exhibits, and projects. It modified the park's purpose and significance statements, and features new interpretive themes, especially the impact of Lost Cause ideology on the distortion of historical memory; the power of self-determination and community in postwar Black settlements; the civilian and refugee experience, including white Unionists and the U.S. Army's role as liberator; the impact of military service on Black families; and the park's elevation as the USCT center for NPS. These themes amplify the voices and narratives of underserved and marginalized communities and provide nuance and relevance to understudied historical scholarship. Beginning in 2021 NPS staff organized thematic and appropriate public programs, notably the annual Luminaria and Memorial Walk, which pays tribute to the enslaved African Americans expelled from Camp Nelson, and the 160th Anniversary of Camp Nelson commemorations. New interpretive exhibits emphasize the individual and collective experience of soldiers, civilians, refugees, and enslaved people. NPS staff collaborate diligently with descendants, local and national organizations, educational institutions, and a philanthropic partner to uncover and tell new stories about the people—men and women, combatant and noncombatant, Black and white—whose lives intersected with Camp Nelson.

The story of one proposed monument offers a useful coda for understanding changing sentiments around Camp Nelson. It was meant to honor the life and service of Frank Wolford, a native Kentuckian and battle-scarred Union veteran who earned notoriety for publicly opposing emancipation and Black enlistment. Wolford's insubordination resulted in an unceremonious dismissal from the U.S. Army in June 1864, but it also elevated him as a heroic martyr in the estimation of many white Kentuckians who felt betrayed by President Abraham Lincoln and the War Department for undermining the institution of slavery by enlisting African American soldiers. "We lost our bravest and most generous foe in war, our best friend in peace," wrote J. H. Miller, a Confederate veteran who served in the 6th Kentucky Cavalry, eulogizing Wolford in the *Semi-weekly Journal* (Stanford KY) on March 13, 1896.[56] Miller's remarks were part of a short biography of Wolford's controversial Civil War military service titled "To Every Kentucky Survivor of 'The Lost Cause.'" It concluded with a proposal "that the Confederates erect a monument to his memory." The inscription featured the text, "Our Closest Enemy in War. Our Closet Friend in Peace. Kentucky moved the hand that restored the South and Wolford moved Kentucky."[57]

Fig. 4.2. The U.S. Army expelled more than 400 African American refugees from Camp Nelson on November 23, 1864. At least 102 people, including the wives and children of United States Colored Troops, died as a direct result of the largest and final expulsion of Black freedom seekers. The 102 flags represent the named and unknown people who died and are surrounded by 400 luminaria. Courtesy of National Park Service.

The monument never materialized. On May 7, 1896, two months after J. H. Miller's tribute to Wolford, the *Daily Public Ledger* in Maysville—General William "Bull" Nelson's hometown—reported that eighty miles to the southwest the "ground for the erection of a monument in memory of the Confederate dead was broken in the courthouse."[58] The monument, originally designed to honor a U.S. soldier, was refurbished to resemble a Confederate and sold at discount to the Jessamine Confederate Memorial Association. It was dedicated with great enthusiasm and fanfare in front of the courthouse in Nicholasville on June 15, 1896. Colonel Bennett H. Young served as the keynote speaker, and he paid homage to the sacrifice and privations bore by Southern women during the war. The monument, "which we trust will remain forever," remarked Young, honored the illustrious deeds of the Confederate soldier.[59]

LEX18, an NBC affiliate, reported on June 9, 2023, that a group of Jessamine County pastors are "coming together, under Christian principles, to heal the community's racial divides" by removing the Confederate monument from the courthouse and relocating it to Maple Grove Cemetery, the interment site of the county's Southern soldiers.[60] Pastor Moses Radford, First Baptist Church (African American), is leading the coalition. For many in the community, "passing by here every day is a hurtful reminder that they're not being heard."[61] Radford's church is located two blocks from the courthouse. Six miles down the road from the courthouse is a new monument—Camp Nelson. It exists on a conflicted landscape, both historical and present. It's a place where visitors can grapple with the contradictions of our imperfect union, a rumination particularly timely in a day of such heightened polarization of American society and find relevance in the triumphs and tragedies of the human condition.

NOTES

1. Proclamation 9811.
2. Harrison, *Lincoln of Kentucky*, 134–35.
3. Coulter, *Civil War and Readjustment in Kentucky*, 439.
4. Marshall, *Creating a Confederate Kentucky*, 4–5.
5. *War of the Rebellion*, Serial 122, Correspondence, 70.
6. Marshall, *Creating a Confederate Kentucky*, 16–17.
7. Finck, *Divided Loyalties*, 169–70.
8. Finck, *Divided Loyalties*, 171–72.
9. Finck, *Divided Loyalties*, 50–51.
10. Lewis, *For Slavery and Union*, 2–3.
11. Finck, *Divided Loyalties*, 50.
12. Marshall, *Creating a Confederate Kentucky*, 20.
13. Astor, *Rebels on the Border*, 126.
14. Marshall, *Creating a Confederate Kentucky*, 20.
15. Marshall, *Creating a Confederate Kentucky*, 20.
16. Astor, *Rebels on the Border*, 126.
17. Lewis, *For Slavery and Union*, 74.
18. Lewis, *For Slavery and Union*, 74.
19. Hess, *Knoxville Campaign*, 1–2.
20. "Arrested for Treason," *Columbia Democrat and Bloomsburg General Advertiser* (Bloomsburg PA), April 30, 1864, https://chroniclingamerica.loc.gov/lccn/sn85025181/1864-04-30/ed-1/seq-1.
21. *War of the Rebellion*, Serial 035, Chapter 35, 349.
22. "Orders by Gen. J. T. Boyle," *Dollar Weekly Bulletin* (Maysville KY), August 20, 1863, https://chroniclingamerica.loc.gov/lccn/sn86069123/1863-08-20/ed-1/seq-2.
23. Lee, *Wolford's Cavalry*, 219.
24. Sears, *Camp Nelson, Kentucky*, 1.
25. Sears, *Camp Nelson, Kentucky*, 111.

26. Sears, *Camp Nelson, Kentucky*, 148.
27. Simpson, *Letters on the State of Slaves*, 24.
28. Simpson, *Letters on the State of Slaves*, 21.
29. Simpson, *Letters on the State of Slaves*, 23.
30. Simpson, *Letters on the State of Slaves*, 2.
31. Noe, *Perryville*, 365–66.
32. Brent, "Power to the People," 1.
33. Brent, "Power to the People," 1.
34. Camp Nelson National Monument Cultural Landscape Report, 163–64.
35. Brent, "Power to the People," 1.
36. Brent, "Power to the People," 7–8.
37. Brent, "Power to the People," 8.
38. Civil War to Civil Rights, 5.
39. Sutton, "Holding the High Ground," 47.
40. Sutton, "Holding the High Ground," 49.
41. Sutton, "Holding the High Ground," 49.
42. Civil War to Civil Rights, 6.
43. Civil War to Civil Rights, 6–7.
44. Civil War to Civil Rights, 8.
45. Civil War to Civil Rights, 8–13, 19.
46. McBride, "Camp Nelson," 78.
47. McBride, "Camp Nelson," 78.
48. Proclamation 9811.
49. Andy Barr, "Interior Department Recommends Designating Camp Nelson as a National Monument," December 5, 2017, https://barr.house.gov/2017/12/interior-department-recommends-designating-camp-nelson-as-a-national.
50. Thomas Burr, "Remember the Antiquities Act Trump Despised When He Shrank Utah's Grand Staircase and Bears Ears? Well, He Just Used That Law to Create a Monument," *Salt Lake Tribune*, October 27, 2018, https://www.sltrib.com/news/politics/2018/10/27/remember-antiquities-act/.
51. Dan Hartinger, "Response to Camp Nelson Designation: All Monuments Must Be Protected," Wilderness Society, October 27, 2018, https://www.wilderness.org/articles/press-release/response-camp-nelson-designation-all-monuments-must-be-protected.
52. Hartinger, "Response to Camp Nelson Designation."
53. Hartinger, "Response to Camp Nelson Designation."
54. Weber and Sultana, "Civil Rights Movement," 6–8.
55. Camp Nelson National Monument Foundation Document, 6.
56. J. H. Miller, "Gen Wolford. To Every Kentucky Survivor of 'The Lost Cause,'" *Semi-weekly Interior Journal* (Stanford KY), March 13, 1896, https://chroniclingamerica.loc.gov/lccn/sn85052020/1896-03-13/ed-1/seq-2.
57. Miller, "Gen Wolford. To Every Kentucky Survivor."
58. "Will Honor Dead Heroes," *Daily Public Ledger* (Maysville KY), May 7, 1896, https://chroniclingamerica.loc.gov/lccn/sn86069117/1896-05-07/ed-1/seq-2.
59. Young, *A History of Jessamine County*, 137.

60. Rachel Richardson, "Jessamine County Clergy Work Together to Remove Confederate Stature from Courthouse," LEX18, June 9, 2023, https://www.lex18.com/news/jessamine-county-clergy-work-together-to-remove-confederate-statue-from-courthouse.
61. Richardson, "Jessamine County Clergy Work Together."

BIBLIOGRAPHY

Astor, Aaron. *Rebels on the Border: Civil War, Emancipation, and the Reconstruction of Kentucky and Missouri*. Louisiana State University Press, 2012.

Brent, Joseph E. "Power to the People: The Modern Era of Civil War Sites Preservation in Kentucky, 1991–2003." Unpublished article. Versailles KY, March 2024.

Camp Nelson National Monument Cultural Landscape Report. National Park Service, Interior Region 2: South Atlantic–Gulf, September 2022.

Camp Nelson National Monument Foundation Document. National Park Service, Interior Region 2: South Atlantic–Gulf, 2020. https://npshistory.com/publications/foundation-documents/cane-fd-2020.pdf.

Civil War to Civil Rights Commemoration Summary Report. National Park Service, Washington Support Office, Cultural Resources, Partnerships and Science, Interpretation, Education and Volunteers, May 2020.

Coulter, Ellis Merton. *The Civil War and Readjustment in Kentucky*. University of North Carolina Press, 1926.

Finck, James W. *Divided Loyalties: Kentucky's Struggle for Armed Neutrality in the Civil War*. Savas Beatie, 2012.

Harrison, Lowell H. *Lincoln of Kentucky*. University Press of Kentucky, 2000.

Hess, Earl J. *The Knoxville Campaign: Burnside and Longstreet in East Tennessee*. University of Tennessee Press, 2012.

Lee, Dan. *Wolford's Cavalry: The Colonel, the War in the West, and the Emancipation Question in Kentucky*. University of Nebraska Press, 2016.

Lewis, Patrick A. *For Slavery and Union: Benjamin Buckner and Kentucky Loyalties during the Civil War*. University Press of Kentucky, 2015.

Marshall, Anne E. *Creating a Confederate Kentucky*. University of North Carolina Press, 2010.

McBride, W. Stephen. "Camp Nelson and Kentucky's Civil War Memory." *Historical Archaeology* 47, no. 3 (2013): 69–80. https://link.springer.com/article/10.1007/BF03376909.

Noe, Kenneth W. *Perryville: This Grand Havoc of Battle*. University Press of Kentucky, 2001.

Proclamation 9811: Establishment of Camp Nelson National Monument. October 26, 2018. American Presidency Project. https://www.presidency.ucsb.edu/documents/proclamation-9811-establishment-the-camp-nelson-national-monument.

Sears, Richard D. *Camp Nelson, Kentucky: A Civil War History*. University of Kentucky Press, 2003.

Simpson, Joseph. *Letters on the State of Slaves in the United States*. Friends' Central Committee for the Relief of the Emancipated Negroes, 1865. https://play.google.com/store/books/details/Joseph_SIMPSON_of_Manchester_Letters_on_the_state?id=WUW9YrvvgFQC.

Sutton, Robert K. "Holding the High Ground: Interpreting the Civil War in National Parks." *George Wright Forum* 25, no. 3 (2008): 47–57. http://www.npshistory.com/publications/battlefield/253sutton.pdf.

The War of the Rebellion: Original Records of the Civil War. Ohio State University. Digitized from *The War of the Rebellion: A Compilation of the Official Records of the Union and Confederate*

  Armies. 70 vols. in 128 parts. Washington DC, 1880–1901. https://ehistory.osu.edu/books/war-rebellion-official-records-civil-war.

Weber, Joe, and Selima Sultana. "The Civil Rights Movement and the National Park System." *Tourism Geographies* 15, no. 3 (2013): 444–69. https://libres.uncg.edu/ir/uncg/f/S_Sultana_Civil_2013.pdf.

Young, Bennett H. *A History of Jessamine County, Kentucky: From Its Earliest Settlement to 1898*. Courier-Journal, 1898.

5

Ghosts of Atchison

The Lynching of George Johnson

JOSHUA WOLF

Atchison, Kansas, is a small Midwestern city that sits on western bank of the Missouri River. Once the town was a burgeoning railroad hub, but today Atchison is best known as "the most haunted city in Kansas."[1] There are ghost stories and haunted houses all about town. Every autumn, the historical society sponsors a haunted trolley ride, taking visitors to the spookiest sites the city has to offer. The most infamous haunt is the Sallie House. This quaint residence on Second Street was once the home and office of a town physician. Years ago, a child died by the doctor's negligence, and her malignant spirit still plagues the home.

The haunting of Molly's Hollow in Jackson Park is a particularly memorable ghost story. The hollow is an isolated ravine in the heavily wooded municipal park. Legend holds a young woman named Molly died there in the early 1900s. Generations of Jackson Park patrons claim to have seen the young woman's apparition, though the more common experience is to hear Molly's nocturnal, ear-splitting death wail. There are numerous versions of the Molly legend. One depicts her death as an accident, another as suicide. Most commonly, Molly is portrayed as the victim of mob violence. In this version of the ghost story, Molly was an African American woman lynched by the people of Atchison for engaging in an interracial relationship.[2]

Researching Atchison's past, however, complicates Molly's ghost story. There was never any woman named Molly; that name evolved from the 1850s original—Milo's Hollow. Until a shooting in 1979, nobody had ever died in Jackson Park by accident, by suicide, or by violence.[3] There was a brutal lynching in Atchison, but not in a secluded, wooded ravine. On the night of January 4, 1870, a man named George Johnson was murdered by a mob of at least fifty men on the busiest street in town. Atchisonians proved not only less inclined to remember Johnson's haunting tale but went a step further and distorted, diminished, and ultimately deleted the event from town history.

This chapter will trace Johnson's fate and the lynching's erasure from Atchison's collective memory, offering just one example of the malleable nature of Civil War memory, both in the past and the present. What unfolded in the eastern Kansas railroad town was reflective of larger national trends and statewide priorities that required the chaotic violence unleashed on the freedpeople to be reduced or omitted from the historical narrative. As a result, the carnage of Reconstruction continues to be an area of national ignorance. There are methods of asserting a more accurate narrative, though, some of which are rooted in local history.

Around dusk on Friday, December 31, 1869, Patrick Cox was making his way from Atchison to Walnut Township, just a few miles south of town. Cox, a former Atchison resident, had moved to Walnut several years earlier, but local commerce, politics, and sociability caused him to visit town often. That evening, as Cox rode his horse southward, a gunshot rang out from the underbrush, hitting Cox in the back and knocking him off his horse. The New Year's Day edition of the *Atchison Daily Champion* reported, "Cox . . . reached a point just south of city limits . . . when a negro, armed with a rifle, stepped out of the brush, and fired at him. . . . The assassin then approached him, took a look at him as he lay on the ground, then moved into the brush and disappeared."[4] Cox was seriously wounded and expected to die as a result of his wounds. Marshal Jesse Crall was in pursuit of the gunman. The next day, January 2, local African American George Johnson surrendered at home to Crall and Constable Philip Weber.[5]

Johnson was a young man, only twenty-three years old, and rather poor. A former-Missouri-slave-turned-Atchison-day-laborer, Johnson lived in a rented house with his wife Eliza Ann and their extended family. In all there were ten people living in the house, eight of them employed in some kind of unskilled, manual labor. An assessment of all property owned by the adults in the house had a total value of just three hundred dollars.[6] Johnson vacillated when first confronted by Marshal Crall about the shooting, but he soon admitted to wounding Cox. He insisted, however, that the shooting had been an accident. According to Johnson's version of events, he was hunting for small game in the brush, shot at a pheasant, but accidentally hit Cox. Johnson panicked once he realized what he had done and fled the scene.[7]

On evaluation, Johnson's version of events was more logical than an attempted robbery or deliberate act of violence, as initially reported by the *Daily Champion*. There were immediate inconsistencies with the highwayman explanation. Cox was by himself, and there were no eyewitnesses to the shooting. The only people there were Cox and Johnson, so the first description of the shooting as a deliberate act of banditry had to be pure speculation. By January 3 John Martin, *Daily Champion* editor, was willing to concede that a hunting accident was a reasonable story. The evidence aimed strongly in that direction. Patrick Cox had been hit by buckshot from a single-barrel shotgun and not gunned down with a rifle, as initially reported. Johnson had his hunting dog with him—a fact confirmed by Cox. If Johnson was planning on murder and robbery, bringing his canine companion along was an odd choice. The poverty of Johnson's household certainly supports the claim he was hunting to feed his family. The time of day—early evening—coincides with one of the best times for hunting pheasant. Had Johnson intended to kill Cox, why did he not wait until it was full dark, thereby reducing the odds of being seen? Finally, Johnson took nothing from Cox, a strange choice if his intention had been robbery. And if Johnson's motive wasn't robbery, why shoot Cox at all? By all accounts George Johnson and Patrick Cox were strangers, so there was no explanation for a deliberate act of violence.[8]

Atchison County Attorney Colonel P. L. Hubbard recommended a ten-day continuance before any criminal charges be filed against Johnson. One problem was what charges to file. Despite reports indicating Patrick Cox was at death's door, he was alive, recovering from his injuries, and well enough to cooperate in the investigation. A continuance was granted, but a $15,000 bail was also set. Johnson, unable to pay his bail, was ordered held in the Atchison jail house until January 12. The jail was located at the intersection of Sixth and Santa Fe streets.[9]

Atchison was a relatively new community in 1870 but had experienced a decade of tremendous growth due to its increasing importance as a Missouri River railroad town. Each year there was more work and more opportunity, for the intelligent and the ignorant, skilled and unskilled laborers, Irish immigrants and freedmen. In 1860 there were 2,616 people residing in the town. By 1870 that number had more than doubled, to 7,054. The growth of the Black community had been even more dramatic. In 1860 there were only 29 free Blacks in Atchison, and a decade later that number had risen to 840. In wider Atchison County, the population expansion was comparable;

from a populace of 5,113 in the year of Lincoln's election to 8,453 ten years on. Likewise, the Black inhabitants grew from only 7 Blacks residing outside the county seat to a total rural population of 296.[10]

The tensions caused by a rapidly expanding African American population could be gleaned by reading the local papers, especially the *Daily Patriot*, Atchison's Democratic organ. In the months before Johnson's lynching, the *Patriot* ran stories with the central purpose, seemingly, of dehumanizing African Americans. One story, reprinted from the *New York World*, claimed that more than two hundred white men had been robbed and murdered by freedmen in Washington since 1865. "As a whole, these negroes are a mass of thieves, murderers, and bawds, the lowest of the low and the vilest of the vile." The piece bluntly stated, "Negros . . . have no regard for human life."[11] At other times, the *Patriot* emphasized the seemingly endless benefits and perquisites visited upon the undeserving freedmen, while earnest white people suffered. A typically grim tale told of the treatment doled out to Robert Anderson, the hero of Fort Sumter, whom the *Patriot* described as disease riddled, penniless, and homeless. Meanwhile, "Able bodied, ignorant n——s are appointed foreign consulates and ministries—salaries payable in gold! Such is Radical love for the soldiers of whom they made n——r-freeing, white-man-enslaving cats paws."[12] The most consistent grievance pressed by the *Daily Patriot* was impending ratification of the Fifteenth Amendment and Black men's suffrage. The paper alternately warned that Radical Republicans were attempting to create an autocracy maintained by negro votes, or that the United States was headed toward Black rule—"negro-ocracy."[13]

Atchisonians who read the *Daily Patriot* and moved in Democratic circles must have had a gloomy outlook of national affairs by the end of 1869. Freedmen were depicted as a plague of locusts that invaded cities and drained resources; they were violent, inhumane, indolent, a persistent threat to white job security and white womanhood. When George Johnson shot Patrick Cox on New Year's Eve, it must have seemed to some in town the inevitable result of local shifting demographics. The swelling Black population had to be kept in line. An example had to be made. The impulse to vigilantism must have grown in urgency when it was reported that the shooting might be determined an accident and Johnson had not been charged with any crime.

The rumor mill churned in Atchison. Throughout town, word spread that Johnson might not have meant to shoot Cox, but he surely meant to shoot somebody. Gossip claimed Johnson was trying to rob a man of three hundred dollars and had accosted the wrong person, but what man? What three hundred dollars? The Republican paper in town was the *Daily Champion*, and an editorial pointed out that there had been a number of false rumors surrounding the entire event. "This shooting is a singular one. We give all stories respecting it that seem to have any foundation in fact or reason. We hope that a full investigation will clear away the mystery connected with it."[14] At the same time, the *Champion*, though never calling for violence against Johnson, fed the gossip-mongering. On New Year's Day, it was the *Daily Champion* that spread the rumor Johnson was trying to rob a different man. Three days later, editor John Martin stoked the flames again by writing, "The negro did not intend to shoot Mr. Cox, but the question is, did he intend to shoot some one else? And this is not so clear."[15] Intimations and speculation kept up the pretense that George Johnson was a violent menace.

Another rumor began to circulate in Atchison on Tuesday, January 4. A lynch mob was being organized, and it was coming for Johnson that night. The newest bit of gossip proved all too true.[16]

George Johnson had been in the county jail for just over forty-eight hours on the night of January 4. At 11:30 p.m. a group of approximately fifty men stormed the Atchison jail. Despite whispers of a lynch mob throughout the day, there was only one deputy sheriff guarding the jailhouse. He offered little resistance to the mob, but he rang the fire bell as he fled. The ringing bell drew a crowd as "dozens of people rushed to the firehouse." The crowd assembled, "unarmed and unorganized," just in time to witness the lynching commence. Inside the jail, the mob shot at Johnson three times before pulling him out of the building by a rope tied around his neck. The vicious horde dragged Johnson from the intersection of Sixth and Santa Fe to Fourth and Commercial, approximately five hundred yards.[17] Johnson was beaten as he was hauled through town, his body further torn as he was dragged over the rocky ground.[18] Upon reaching Fourth and Commercial, the mob halted and fired twelve more shots. The lynching reached a crescendo: "The mob . . . rushed on to the Fifth Street Bridge, where they hanged the helpless, wounded, bruised, and mangled victim of their brutal fury over the railing, and then left as suddenly as they came."[19] The entire affair concluded in less than thirty minutes.

Many in Atchison were quick to condemn the violence. W. J. Scott raged that "the barbarous treatment that was dealt upon that man [Johnson] by that clan of inhuman wretches is almost dark enough to bedim the brightest rays of the noonday sun."[20] John Bakewell, minister of Trinity Episcopal Church, felt compelled to issue a statement on the lynching since his house of worship sat at the south end of the Fifth Street Bridge: "As one of the ministers of this town, who knows at all events how the Bible regards the unlawful shedding of a man's blood, I hope that the officials will prosecute the matter with such vigor as the awfully heinous nature of the crime deserves."[21] The city council and Mayor John Price issued a joint statement decrying mob rule and stating that "such conduct evinces a degree of moral turpitude and a reckless disregard for the law of the land and well-being of society."[22] The paper also reported that clergymen in town used their Sunday sermon to preach against the violence.

Undoubtedly, these strong objections to the violence of January 4 were sincere, but just as quickly the people of Atchison tried to distance themselves, and their town, from the lynching. From the first report in the *Daily Champion*, it was asserted that the "mob of people . . . came into the city from Walnut and Mt. Pleasant townships." The city council took up the argument and stated in their condemnation of the event that the mob was composed of "largely non-residents of the city of Atchison." The composition of the mob meant the city bore no culpability. "We condemn in the most solemn manner such an outrageous and unlawful proceeding and . . . we deny on the part of the city of Atchison any responsibility therewith."

For two years, town leaders continued to assert that the violence of January 4, 1870, was the work of outsiders. Future U.S. Senator John J. Ingalls insisted, "The crimes were committed by persons who are well known and pecuniarily responsible, not the citizens of the city. Our citizens unanimously condemned the transaction and would have prevented its consummation had they been aware of the intention of its perpetration."[23] Ingalls's assertion that Atchison citizens would have stopped the lynching had they known defies all evidence. The *Daily Champion* reported the rumor of a lynch mob had been circulating throughout town all day on January 4. Johnson's death was foretold, but no measures were taken by any civic leaders in Atchison to protect him; no extra deputies were placed on duty, nor was Johnson removed to a secret location. Instead, George Johnson was left "poor and friendless. There was no effort made to clear, or save him."[24]

Civic leaders and citizens, by denying any culpability and instead foisting blame onto a vaguely identified mob of outsiders, set the immediate tone for remembrance. This was the first step of erasure. It was a nonevent: tragic certainly, but an outburst of vigilantism by a group of outsiders perpetrated against an outsider, so nothing Atchisonians need concern themselves over. In case there was lingering doubt or guilt, esteemed lawyer John Ingalls assured his neighbors that not only was there no collective responsibility, but they were all latent heroes simply denied opportunity.

The next step of narrative control was the failure of the Atchison justice system to ever hold anyone accountable for the events of January 4. George Johnson's lynching was a well-witnessed event. The fire bell brought dozens of townsfolk to the jail. The mob moved down a Commercial Street in 1870 lined with boardinghouses, hotels, saloons, and parlors. The tumult caused by the lynch mob must have drawn the patrons of those businesses to the windows and into the street. When the mob halted and fired off a dozen shots at Fourth and Commercial, curious but late-arriving residents had a chance to reach the source of discord. As much as a quarter of the town saw some part of the lynching. Witnesses from the night of January 4 stepped forward. Members of the lynch mob were identified. Multiple arrest warrants were issued. One of the leaders was identified as city resident Matthew Collins. He absconded. So did many other participants, according to the *Daily Champion*: "Several of those concerned in the late brutal mob, have fled the county. The Sheriff has been after them, but they could not be found."[25] In fact, only one man was ever brought into custody for Johnson's murder. Mount Pleasant Township resident Martin Donnelly was arrested a week after the lynching, but the charges against him were dismissed when Donnelly was able to produce an alibi. Lynch mob members were always capable of finding an alibi—usually another member of the lynch mob.[26] It was rare for a lynch mob member to be prosecuted anywhere in America. Nothing unique about Atchison in that regard, but the lack of any criminal prosecutions also ensured that the details of January 4 never had to be revisited. There was no court record. There were no newspaper stories from the trial offering readers accounts of lurid eye-witness testimony.

Besides the lack of criminal accountability, the city of Atchison tried to wiggle out of any fiscal responsibility. An 1868 Kansas law stated, "Cities and towns shall be liable for all damages that may occur in consequence of the action of mobs within their incorporated limits."[27] The Atchison lynching was the first time the law was exercised. Eliza Ann Johnson, widowed by the mob, secured legal representation after her husband's death and sued the city for $10,000. The trial was held at the district court in Doniphan, Kansas, and took place over five days, from September 21 to 26, 1870. The jury deliberated for two days before deciding in Eliza Ann Johnson's favor and awarded her $450 for the wrongful death of her husband. It was a small settlement, but nonetheless, the city appealed. The appeal was denied, however, and the amount in damages owed was increased in January 1872 to $726.05.[28]

The financial settlement concluded the George Johnson affair. After January 1872, Johnson's name was forgotten in Atchison, and the events surrounding his death faded from popular memory until all local knowledge disappeared. There was an occasional shadow of George Johnson in the pages of the local newspaper, but even these faint references were further obfuscations of the truth.

To celebrate the fortieth anniversary of Atchison's founding, in 1894 the *Atchison Daily Globe* (the paper that succeeded the *Patriot*) ran a special edition that focused on Atchison history. The anniversary paper featured a column about incidents of mob violence in the city's history. The article focused on the 1863 hanging of four violent thieves, who were given a drumhead trial, defended by prominent lawyer John J. Ingalls, and found guilty before their execution at the hands of the citizenry. Tacked on to the very end of feature was a three-sentence acknowledgment of the lynching of George Johnson: "Several years later a negro was taken from jail by a mob . . . and hanged on the Fifth Street bridge. His offense was shooting a man named Cox . . . and it was believed by many that the shooting was accidental."[29] The *Globe* mention may be brief, but it was nonetheless important because it was a rare acknowledgment of the event by a local authority or institution. The *Globe* article also entertained the idea that the lynching proceeded despite the absence of a crime. There was a stark difference between the two incidents of communal violence covered in the article, however. The hanging of the four white thieves was covered in detail—their names, crimes, neighborhood of residence, even specifics on the trial and hanging. Conversely, Johnson was not identified by name (though Patrick Cox was), no date was provided, and the torment that preceded the hanging was omitted. Johnson's life and his death were no more than an aside. Thirty-five years later the *Daily Globe* reprinted the exact same column under a new headline in the special city of Atchison seventy-fifth-anniversary edition.[30]

A more intimate and direct connection to Johnson's lynching was Patrick Cox, who lived a long life after the events of January 1870. In fact, he lived so long that twenty-eight years after George Johnson's death, the *Atchison Daily Champion* ran a story about the longevity of Cox's life and marriage. The column featured the tale of Cox's 1869 wounding. Nearly three decades later, though, the circumstances surrounding the shooting were presented as the deliberate actions of an assassin. "He [Cox] met a colored man carrying a Winchester rifle and accompanied by two dogs. . . . After he had passed, THE FATAL SHOT was fired. . . . As he looked back the smoking rifle still lay in the fork of the tree from which the deadly aim was sighted." In this updated, dramatic retelling of the New Year's Eve incident, there was not even a suggestion that what happened was an accident. Additionally, the shot was neither fatal nor deadly as the newspaper described in 1898—otherwise there would have been no article. Johnson was presented to have been carrying a Winchester rifle instead of a single-barrel shotgun. Perhaps most shocking about the retrospective was Johnson (who the article referred to once, by last name only) was made out to have successfully fled town. "Jesse Crall was at that time city marshal, but all efforts to discover the whereabouts of Johnson, the colored man, proved futile." Patrick Cox knew the truth of the shooting, and he knew the truth of George Johnson's fate. There must have been hundreds of people around town who remembered January 4, 1870. Yet the *Daily Champion* deliberately presented a falsified account of the events and wrote the lynching out of the story.[31]

The participation of print media is one of the key developments in the distortion and deletion of Reconstruction-era violence. Although there were national publications and powerful urban newspapers in the 1870s, the dissemination of news remained highly localized and cooperative. Most of the nation's newspapers were local, the editor was usually the owner and often the only writer. There was generally a column or two on local matters (in a town as large as Atchison local affairs could receive an entire page), and the rest of the paper consisted of stories reprinted from other newspapers across the country. If events were never initially reported in any paper, other editors could not pick up the story. For example, the *Patriot* produced no issues in January 1870 while events played out in town. As a result, no Democratic newspapers in Missouri or Kansas ever ran a story about what happened with Patrick Cox or George Johnson. Editors could also choose not to reprint a news item, stifling dissemination, and keeping knowledge of affairs hyperlocal.[32]

The process extended beyond the press. Local historians play their part in suppressing unsavory knowledge. In Atchison the writings of prominent locals produced no account of George Johnson. Sheffield Ingalls penned a massive, thousand-page tome, *The History of Atchison County*, when the county was only fifty years old. Ingalls had a chapter on the "Afro-American Race in Atchison" but not a word on George Johnson. Stan Alexander's work "Atchison, an Early History" and all of historian George Anderson's writings that focused on Atchison failed to include the lynching of George Johnson, despite both historians covering the exact time period during which the event occurred.[33] The brief, three-sentence summation of Johnson's death in the 1894 *Daily Globe* article, reprinted in 1929, was the only local recognition the lynching received after the conclusion of Eliza Johnson's lawsuit in 1872.[34]

Atchison could not escape the specter of George Johnson entirely and his final whisper in local memory may well be the Molly's Hollow ghost story itself. Local myths, often called urban legends, can serve various purposes to the communities that produced them. Legends, among other roles, can serve as an expression of alienation between past and present, confirmation of self-identity, and as "a mechanism for concealing reality in the historical memory" of the local population.[35] Does the Molly's Hollow ghost fulfill any of these purposes for Atchison?

The story of a murdered girl haunting Jackson Park was not mentioned in print until 1947. Her name was Molly, "and the echo of her ghostly screams could be heard in the hollow." How, when, and why Molly was murdered were not mentioned, but in the same story it was related that a man once hanged himself in Molly's Hollow. Although his body was taken down, the hanging strap remained tied around the tree limb for years. Interestingly, the author stated that these two local legends would best be remembered by "old timers," likely referencing individuals in their sixties, dating the legends to the turn of the century.[36]

The roots of the Molly's Hollow haunting can be found in the combination of half-truths about Johnson's lynching and established local legends. Sometime between the 1920s and 1950s, the murdered Molly, the suicidal hanged man, and the lynched George Johnson morphed into one mythical figure. This process must have been greatly aided by George Johnson's being stripped of any personal identity. After 1872, in those rare instances when the lynching was mentioned, Johnson was only referred to as "a negro." He was a blank canvas, unnamed and ungendered. A lynched negro could become anyone. The hollow itself adds an important component. The ravine was long regarded as spooky and mysterious and was home to several earlier legends among the youth of Atchison. So, while nobody had ever violently perished in the hollow, it was easy for townsfolk to imagine differently. The mythical Molly added a feminine touch, and the tragic romance angle fits well into the tale's creation. As the Molly legend absorbed George Johnson's race and manner of death, there could only be a handful of motives for lynching a woman. A secret, interracial relationship certainly would have fit justifications of the time.[37] Feminizing Atchison's lynching and making it a tale of star-crossed lovers romanticized the killing, softening the reality of a terribly violent event for public consumption. The avenue of evolution was the mile of road between the Fifth Street Bridge, where Johnson was hanged, and Molly's Hollow. If one purpose of myth is to obfuscate historical truths from collective memory, the legend of Molly's Hollow accomplished that objective. The only kernel of truth in the entire tale was that there was a race-based lynching in Atchison. That was an important concession to the historical record. If a person pursued that part of the legend thoroughly enough, it could have led them to George Johnson. Everything else about the legend was false. Molly the lynch victim became an accepted part of local legend, while simultaneously being dismissed as just another ghost story. There was no truth in the tale worth chasing.

Perhaps, though, the purpose of the ghost story was originally darker.

Lynching was a deadly tool used to maintain white supremacy. The public spectacle. The torture that often preceded the final death stroke. The prominent display of the body. It was a message to all local African Americans, not just one. George Johnson's murder was no different.[38]

If lynchings were a mechanism to uphold white social and political control, then ghost stories built around such incidents of race-based violence were surely rooted in the same purpose. Tall tales and local legends serve various causes, and one of those can be to act as a warning, or veiled threat.[39] The oral tradition of a lynched specter in Molly's Hollow was built on the premise that she was killed because of an interracial relationship, a social taboo. The story could easily be interpreted as a cautionary tale that the African American population of Atchison should closely adhere to social expectations or risk severe consequences. Making the lynch victim a woman, instead of the man George Johnson, implied the warning was meant for everyone—no exceptions for the gentler sex. Events in Atchison during the 1920s suggest that could be the decade the Molly's Hollow lynched spirit first materialized.

The 1920s were notable for national race tensions, and Atchison was no exception. The city was a battleground in the war over the Ku Klux Klan's future in the state of Kansas. The Klan targeted Atchison for recruitment, it seems, because it was home to a chapter of the National Association for the Advancement of Colored People. By 1922 there were hundreds of dues-paying Klan members in Atchison, and the group held a mass rally at Atchison's Memorial Hall attended by more than a thousand locals.[40] Meanwhile,

Governor Henry Allen vowed to drive the Klan out of the state of Kansas. Less than four weeks later, Allen visited Atchison as part of his anti-Klan campaign. His rally, held in the same Memorial Hall, was attended by more than two thousand people. He used his platform to belittle and ridicule the KKK, much to the enjoyment of his audience.[41] Despite Allen's best efforts, the Klan was never entirely rooted out of the state. The hate group's presence continued throughout the decade in Atchison as well.

The elements necessary to create a local lynching legend as a means to help enforce social hierarchy seemed to be present during the twenties. This timeline, in turn, allowed the story to grow and develop as part of Atchison's oral tradition until it became so deeply ensconced the ghost of Molly's Hollow was generational. A 1920s creation also meshes well with the final removal of George Johnson from local knowledge. By the end of the decade, people old enough to remember Johnson's lynching were at least sixty-eight years old, with most being in their seventies. The last generation with actual knowledge of the lynching was dying off as the legend of Molly's Hollow was taking root. Hence the last mention of any kind from a local source regarding the events of January 4, 1870, come from the 1929 *Daily Globe* city anniversary reprint: "A negro was taken from jail by a mob . . . and hanged from the Fifth Street bridge."

The Community Remembrance Project is a collaborative effort between the Equal Justice Initiative (EJI) and local communities to "memorialize documented victims of racial violence and foster meaningful dialogue about race and justice." Communities around the United States participate in the project by recognizing and researching a local race-based lynching. The Community Soil Collection Project and the Historical Marker Project are the two halves of the Remembrance Project. In the Community Soil Collection, earth is taken from lynching sites and placed in glass jars—one for the community to keep and the other for the Legacy Museum in Montgomery, Alabama. The Legacy Museum was founded by the EJI and is dedicated to the history of slavery and racism in America.[42] The collected soil from community projects comprises one of the most sobering exhibits in the museum, with hundreds of jars from across country on display. The Historical Marker Project includes the instillation of a narrative historical marker in the partnering city or township and a smaller, corresponding marker at the Legacy.

On June 11, 2021, the city of Atchison began its annual Juneteenth celebration with a soil collection for the George Johnson Community Remembrance Project. Important city, community, and faith leaders participated in the program, while an audience of more than a hundred watched. Soil was gathered from the three main locations of violence against Johnson: the intersection of Sixth and Santa Fe, the intersection of Fourth and Commercial, and underneath the Fifth Street viaduct. At each stop, part of George Johnson's story was told, a prayer was offered, and soil was collected and placed into two large jars.[43] A week later, on June 19, 2021, in front of a crowd of hundreds, a national historical marker memorializing George Johnson was unveiled on Commercial Street.

Before the George Johnson Remembrance Project, the Legacy Museum had no record of Johnson's lynching. He was nowhere among the incidents incorporated into their database. This is not uncommon for lynch victims of the Reconstruction era. To date, the Legacy Museum has confirmed the identity of more than two thousand African Americans killed by mob violence between 1865 and 1876. Every year more names are incorporated into their database, but there will likely never be a full accounting of all Reconstruction casualties. Many freedmen disappeared in the Reconstruction South. Southern newspapers often refused to report on lynchings, and African American witnesses were intimidated and traumatized into silence. In Atchison there was a record that could be recovered, and George Johnson was incorporated into the museum's archive. A partnership with EJI was mutually beneficial; it provided all the resources Atchison needed to make the memorial a reality, while contributing to the Equal Justice Initiative's mission of community education.[44]

The George Johnson Remembrance Project was the first such project in the state of Kansas. Both Leavenworth and Salina have since completed their own community remembrance projects, with Lawrence engaged in the process as well. It is important and necessary to create these public memorials and historical markers in order to combat the still overwhelming power of Reconstruction erasure. In 2022 the Zinn Education Project released a report on the state of Reconstruction education in American schools, which indicated a profound ignorance on the subject. Among their findings, the authors reported that curriculum standards regarding the teaching of Reconstruction were inadequate in all fifty states. The Reconstruction era was the most frequently compressed or skipped over subject in history classrooms. There is little mention of white-on-Black violence, and a majority of school districts still teach some version of the factually incorrect, racist Dunning School. Many teachers themselves do not understand Reconstruction.[45]

The difficulties of effectively educating Americans about Reconstruction through the primary or secondary education system are likely to continue given the increased scrutiny of "controversial" classroom content in many parts of the United States.

If there is going to be a shift in the American public's understanding of Reconstruction, and the unceasing white-on-Black violence that defined the era, it may be most successfully pursued as a local endeavor. Community efforts to forget or obfuscate past events of white-supremacist terrorism, such as in Atchison, helped lead the nation to its present state of ignorance. A grassroots movement like the Community Remembrance Project that strives to correct the local chronicle of race-based violence during the Reconstruction era and beyond can work to ensure community knowledge perseveres, regardless of wider trends. Adding markers like the one that commemorates the lynching of George Johnson is an important corrective in Civil War commemoration and will help ensure a fuller, more accurate narrative of the Civil War and Reconstruction eras are told in communities across the nation.

NOTES

1. Heitz, *Haunted Kansas*, 157–76. Heitz named Atchison the most haunted city in the state. The Atchison Chamber of Commerce has capitalized on the title, as evidenced by the chamber's tourism website, www.visitatchison.com, which strongly emphasizes the city's paranormal reputation.
2. Heitz, *Haunted Kansas*, 173–76; Pregont, *Haunted Atchison*, 37; Kathy Weiser, "Haunted Atchison—Most Ghostly Town in Kansas," Legends of America, www.legendsofamerica.com/ks-hauntedatchison/.
3. "Gathered on Commercial," *Atchison Daily Globe*, February 7, 1974, https://www.newspapers.com/image/4587055; "One Killed and 6 Hurt in Shooting After Dispute at Kansas Park," *New York Times*, May 6, 1979, https://www.nytimes.com/1979/05/06/archives/one-killed-and-6-hurt-in-shooting-after-a-dispute-at-a-kansas-park.html.
4. "The Shooting of Patrick Cox," *Atchison Daily Champion*, January 1, 1870, microfilm, Kansas History Room, Atchison Public Library, Atchison, Kansas (hereafter KHR).
5. "On Saturday Morning," *Atchison Daily Champion*, January 3, 1870, KHR.
6. Microfilm AR 6756, vols. 3 and 4, 1863–1872, District Court Journals, Doniphan County District/Probate Court, Kansas State Archives, Topeka; Webb, *Reports of Cases Argued and Determined*, 350–58; U.S. Census Bureau, Schedule 1.
7. "On Saturday Morning."
8. "On Saturday Morning."
9. "On Saturday Morning."
10. U.S. Census Bureau, Table I; U.S. Census Bureau, Table III.
11. "Cuffee in Clover: The Africanization of the National Capital," *Atchison Daily Patriot*, July 1, 1869, https://www.newspapers.com/image.

12. "Brig. General Robert Anderson," *Atchison Daily Patriot*, May 26, 1869, https://www.newspapers.com/image/80352417.
13. "Died That We May Live," *Atchison Daily Patriot*, May 8, 1869, https://www.newspapers.com/image/80352241.
14. "Shooting of Patrick Cox."
15. "On Saturday Morning."
16. "Last Night," *Atchison Daily Champion*, January 5, 1870, KHR.
17. "Last Night"; "The Mob of Tuesday," *Atchison Weekly Champion*, January 8, 1870, https://www.newspapers.com/image/95928161.
18. "Events of Tuesday Night," *Atchison Daily Champion*, January 6, 1870, KHR.
19. "Last Night."
20. W. J. Scott, "Mobs and Their Work," letter to the editor, *Atchison Daily Champion*, January 6, 1870, KHR.
21. Rev. John Bakewell, letter to the editor, *Atchison Daily Champion*, January 6, 1870, KHR.
22. "Yesterday's Proceedings," *Atchison Daily Champion*, January 6, 1870, KHR.
23. "The Hanging of Johnson," *Atchison Weekly Champion*, January 18, 1872, https://www.newspapers.com/image/80359377.
24. "Mob of Tuesday."
25. "Local Matters," *Atchison Daily Champion*, January 9, 1870, KHR.
26. Martin Donnelly's name was alternately spelled Donnalay. "Local Matters," *Atchison Daily Champion*, January 8, 1870, KHR; "Local Matters," *Atchison Daily Champion*, January 12, 1870, KHR.
27. Dassler, *General Statutes of Kansas*, 341.
28. "Suit Decided," *Atchison Daily Champion*, September 27, 1870, KHR. There were several issues related to the city's appeal to the highest state court. These included another woman falsely claiming to be Johnson's widow, as well as the city attorney's argument that Rev. William Twine, an African American community leader, had improperly acted as substitute plaintiff for Eliza Ann Johnson and that the court had improperly interpreted the 1868 state law on mob violence. Kansas Chief Justice Samuel A. Kingman largely rejected the city attorney's arguments. Webb, "Atchison v Twine," 350–58. Legal scholar James H. Chadbourn demonstrated the Johnson case was the first exercise of the 1868 law. Chadbourn, *Lynching and the Law*, 39.
29. "Historical Paragraphs," *Atchison Daily Globe*, July 16, 1894, KHR.
30. "'Lynch Law' in Early Atchison," *Atchison Daily Globe*, July 11, 1929, https://www.newspapers.com/image/33879562.
31. "Patrick Cox and Wife," *Atchison Daily Champion*, June 15, 1898, KHR.
32. Litwack, *Been in the Storm*, 274–82. Parsons, "Klan Skepticism and Denial," 53–90, demonstrated how this process worked during the Reconstruction era in creating competing views on the nature of the Ku Klux Klan, and her arguments can be applied to all racial violence of the period. Perloff, "Press and Lynchings," 315–30.
33. Ingalls, *History of Atchison*; Alexander, "Atchison, an Early History"; Anderson, "Atchison, 1865–1886," 30–45. Another example of an article on Atchison history covering the 1870s with no mention of Johnson is Wyman, "Atchison," 297–308. Roe, *Atchison Centennial*, the centennial history released by the city in 1954, is another.

34. The dearth of local information or knowledge of Johnson's lynching is even stranger considering his death attracted the attention of national scholars on three separate occasions. Yost, "History of Lynching in Kansas," 182–219, was the first scholarly mention of Johnson. Chadbourn published certain details of the Johnson lynching in his book in 1933. The most recent was Campney, *This Is Not Dixie*, 27. None of these works focused on Atchison or George Johnson. All three historians were operating on a broader scale, and Johnson was used as an illustrative example for these historians. However, these three references make clear that scholarship of Johnson's killing existed.
35. Bomat, "Myth and Oral History," 12–18, quote 13.
36. "How Many Old Timers Remember," *Atchison Daily Globe*, February 8, 1947, https://www.newspapers.com/image/30497318.
37. Wells, *Light of Truth*, 57–82, 218–312. Raper, *Tragedy of Lynching*, details different lynchings of the early 1930s. For more information on women lynching victims, see Bailey and Tolnay, *Lynched*, 32–60, 178–218; Baker and Garcia, "Black Female Lynchings."
38. Wood, *Lynching and Spectacle*.
39. Frank, *Letting Stories Breathe*, argues for the various purposes stories of all kinds play in our lives, how stories help form us, and how they evolve in relation to time and need. Another interesting work on the importance of story and its generational adaptability is Zipes, *Irresistible Fairy Tale*, 1–40; although Zipes is focused on fairy tales, his arguments about the evolutionary nature of a fairy tales is just as applicable to ghost stories.
40. In June the paper advertised for the weekly meeting of the NAACP at the Zion Baptist Church. Weeks later the paper advertised a recruiting drive by the Klan. "Important: Mass Meeting," *Atchison Daily Globe*, June 5, 1921, https://www.newspapers.com/image/480013374/; "Organizer for Ku Klux Klan," *Atchison Daily Globe*, July 27, 1921, https://www.newspapers.com/image/480018253/.
41. "Allen Pokes Fun at Klan," *Atchison Daily Globe*, October 27, 1922, https://www.newspapers.com/image/480204675. For more on Allen's efforts to bar the Ku Klux Klan from the state of Kansas, see Sloan, "Kansas Battles," 393–409.
42. The Equal Justice Initiative was founded in 1989 by Bryan Stevenson as a nonprofit organization with the aim to end mass incarceration. The group provides legal representation to the wrongfully convicted and challenges excessive sentences, including the death penalty. EJI expanded its mission to include education about the lasting impact of chattel slavery and white supremacy on the African American community. "Community Remembrance Project," Equal Justice Initiative, accessed September 19, 2021, https://eji.org/projects/community-remembrance-project/.
43. James Howey, "Atchison Remembers the Tragedy of George Johnson," *Atchison Globe*, June 13, 2021. The George Johnson Community Remembrance Project would not have been possible without the support of several local organizations, including first and foremost Atchison United, as well as the Atchison Art Association, City Council, Historical Association, Juneteenth Committee, and Public Library.
44. "Legacy Museum: From Enslavement to Mass Incarceration," Equal Justice Initiative, accessed September 19, 2021, https://museumandmemorial.eji.org/museum.
45. Ana Rosado, Gideon Cohn-Postar, and Mimi Eisen, with the Zinn Education Project Team, "Erasing the Black Freedom Struggle: How State Standards Fail to the Teach the Truth About Reconstruction," Zinn Education Project, https://www.teachreconstructionreport.org/.

BIBLIOGRAPHY

Alexander, Stan. "Atchison, an Early History." MS thesis, Emporia State University, 1978.

Anderson, George. "Atchison, 1865–1886, Divided and Uncertain." *Kansas Historical Quarterly* 35 (Spring 1969): 30–45.

Bailey, Amy Kate, and Stewart E. Tolnay. *Lynched: The Victims of Southern Mob Violence.* University of North Carolina Press, 2015.

Baker, David V., and Gilbert Garcia. "An Analytical History of Black Female Lynchings in the United States, 1838–1969." *Journal of Qualitative Criminal Justice & Criminology* 8, no. 1 (October 2019). https://doi.org/10.21428/88de04a1.105517eb.

Blight, David. *Race and Reunion: The Civil War in American Memory.* Belknap Press, 2001.

Bomat, Joanna, ed. "Myth and Oral History: Sixth International Oral History Conference." *Oral History* 16, no. 1 (Spring 1988): 12–18.

Campney, Brent. "'Light Is Bursting upon the World!': White Supremacy and Racist Violence Against Blacks in Reconstruction Kansas." *Western Historical Quarterly* 41, no. 2 (Summer 2010): 81–109.

———. *This Is Not Dixie: Racist Violence in Kansas, 1861–1927.* University of Illinois Press, 2015.

Chadbourn, James H. *Lynching and the Law.* University of North Carolina Press, 1933.

Cutler, William, ed. *History of the State of Kansas.* A. T. Andreas, 1883.

Dassler, C. F. W., ed. *The General Statutes of Kansas: Being a Compilation of All the Laws of a General Nature, Based Upon the General Statutes of 1868.* Vol. 1. W. J. Gilbert, 1876.

Egerton, Douglas. *The Wars of Reconstruction: The Brief, Violent History of America's Most Progressive Era.* Bloomsbury, 2014.

Foner, Eric. *Reconstruction: America's Unfinished Revolution, 1863–1877.* Harper and Row, 1988.

Frank, Arthur. *Letting Stories Breathe: A Socio-Narratology.* University of Chicago Press, 2012.

Heitz, Lisa Hefner. *Haunted Kansas: Ghost Stories and Other Eerie Tales.* University Press of Kansas, 1997.

Ingalls, Sheffield. *The History of Atchison County Kansas.* Standard Publishing, 1916.

Litwack, Leon F. *Been in the Storm for So Long: The Aftermath of Slavery.* Vintage, 1980.

McConnell, Stuart Charles. *Glorious Contentment: The Grand Army of the Republic, 1865–1900.* University of North Carolina Press, 1992.

Parsons, Elaine. "Klan Skepticism and Denial in Reconstruction-Era Public Discourse." *Journal of Southern History* 77, no. 1 (February 2011): 53–90.

Perloff, Richard. "The Press and Lynchings of African Americans." *Journal of Black Studies* 30, no. 3 (January 2000): 315–30.

Pregont, Justin, ed. *Haunted Atchison: The Collected Stories.* Mennonite Press, printed for Atchison Area Chamber of Commerce, 2011.

Raper, Arthur F. *The Tragedy of Lynching.* University of North Carolina Press, 1933.

Roe, Catherine, and Bill Roe, eds. *Atchison Centennial, 1854–1954: A Historic Album of Atchison, Kansas.* Centennial Association, 1954.

Sloan, Charles William, Jr. "Kansas Battles the Invisible Empire: The Legal Ouster of the KKK from Kansas, 1922–27." *Kansas History* 40, no. 3 (Autumn 1974): 393–409.

U.S. Census Bureau. Schedule 1: Persons Who during the Year Ending 1st June 1870 in 4th Ward, Atchison City, in the County of Atchison, State of Kansas, enumerated by me, J. L. Fox, Ass't Marshal. 1870 Census. Microfilm, Kansas State Archives.

———. Table I: State of Kansas Population by Age and Sex. Statistics of the Population of the United States. 1860 Census. https://www.census.gov/library/publications/1864/dec/1860a.html.

———. Table III: Population, 1870–1850, in Each State and Territory, by Civil Divisions Less Than Counties, as White and Colored, and Native and Foreign. Statistics of the Populations of the United States. 1870 Census. https://www.census.gov/library/publications/1872/dec/1870a.html.

Webb, W. C. *Reports of Cases Argued and Determined in the Supreme Court of the State of Kansas*. Vol. 9. State Printing Works, 1873.

Wells, Ida B. *A Red Record*. In *The Light of Truth: Writings of an Anti-Lynching Crusader*, edited by Mia Bay. Penguin, 2014.

———. *Southern Horrors: Lynch Law in All Its Phases*. In *The Light of Truth: Writings of an Anti-Lynching Crusader*, edited by Mia Bay. Penguin, 2014.

Wood, Amy Louise. *Lynching and Spectacle: Witnessing Racial Violence in America, 1890–1940*. University of North Carolina Press, 2009.

Wyman, Walker. "Atchison: A Great Frontier Depot." *Kansas Historical Quarterly* 11 (August 1942): 297–308.

Yost, Genevieve. "History of Lynching in Kansas." *Kansas Historical Quarterly* 11 (May 1933): 182–219.

Zipes, Jack. *The Irresistible Fairy Tale: The Cultural and Social History of a Genre*. Princeton University Press, 2013.

PART 3
Consuming Memory

Few cartoon characters love Confederate iconography more than Early Cuyler, the liquor-swigging, truck-boat-truck-driving, foul-mouthed hillbilly anthropomorphic mud squid in Adult Swim's *Squidbillies*. Living in the mountains of north Georgia, Early and his clan—sister Lil, son Rusty, and Granny, a one-time lover of General Robert E. Lee—revel in their violently backward brand of Southern identity.

Hence their surprise and outrage when, in season 10, episode 2 ("Southern Pride and Prejudice"), local business owner and all-around villain Dan Halen decides to ban the sale of all "Confederate mercantile" to drum up much-needed visitors. Arriving at the nearby Ballmart discount store, Early is shocked to see employees emptying the shelves: no more Confederate flag boogie boards, no more Confederate welcome mats—they can't even buy a "Johnnie Reb whites-only hot-rocking Santa in a bubble globe!" After managing to purchase several Confederate-themed items on the sly (a rape whistle and baby's onesie among them), Early joins the EBISSE, the Esteemed Brotherhood of the Institute of Southern South Self Esteem, a makeshift band of modern-day rebels, and eventually gets a Confederate battle flag tattooed across his face. Only at the episode's end does he learn the truth: that his Confederate heroes kept cephalopods as slaves—and that his new "brothers" were conflicted about letting a "lazy welfare-sponging eightlegger" into their ranks.

Removed from both Adult Swim and HBO Max in the aftermath of the Black Lives Matter protests of 2020, "Southern Pride and Prejudice" is as much a celebration of anti-PC humor as it is a pointed critique of Early's self-righteous ignorance. For all that, the episode serves as a telling reminder to those who take pleasure in consuming Civil War memory, whether in the form of music, stories, clothing, or—in Early's case—"imitation crab meat dyed in the colors of the Confederacy." You get what you pay for—and it's far cheaper to sell Lost Cause nostalgia than just about anything else.[1]

NOTES

1. "Southern Pride and Prejudice," *Squidbillies*, season 10, episode 2, Adult Swim, 2016.

6

Confederates in the Record Cabinet

Civil War Memory and the Historical Turns
in Modern Country Music

JOSEPH M. THOMPSON

In 2013 the white country music singer Brad Paisley and the Black hip-hop artist LL Cool J released the duet "Accidental Racist" as a country radio single. The lyrics take the form of a conversation, casting the vocalists as embodiments of race, region, and Civil War memory. Paisley's white Southern character begins with an apology if the Confederate flag on his Lynyrd Skynyrd T-shirt has offended the Black barista at Starbucks. He pleads fandom, not fanaticism, and claims to feel the heavy burden of history in which he is "caught between Southern pride and Southern blame." LL Cool J picks up the next verse, asking the white man to judge him not by his sagging pants but by the content of his character. In his own plea for understanding, the rapper claims pride in wearing gold chain necklaces instead of the iron chains of enslavement. By the song's end, the characters reach an agreement to "Let bygones be bygones." Paisley declares himself reborn as a "son of the new South," and LL Cool J delivers a benediction over the memories of Confederate and Union leaders, intoning, "RIP Robert E. Lee / But I've gotta thank Abraham Lincoln for freeing me."[1] Everyone receives a pardon, regardless of their sins.

Written by the two vocalists and Lee Thomas Miller, "Accidental Racist" looks at history to mend the social and political polarizations that still marked life in the United States at the dawn of the second Obama administration. The lyrics rightly diagnose the conjoined legacies of slavery and the Confederacy as the root malignancies that have threatened to destroy the union. Yet the songwriters' prescription—that everyone should forgive and forget—offers an impotent remedy. Platitudes mask the symptoms. No one has really healed.

Critics panned the song.² While the country-rap collaboration may have aimed for a progressive message, its narrative of letting "bygones be bygones" reflects country music's longstanding connection to the Lost Cause. That version of Civil War memory has celebrated the Confederate military, minimized the horrors of slavery, and prized white reconciliation over racial justice. In fact, for all of country music's odes to honesty, authenticity, and tradition, the genre's industry, artists, and fans have a hard time reckoning with the white supremacy and false historical narratives embedded within the music.³ Paisley felt comfortable releasing this song and believed in its message. After all, the Lost Cause enjoyed such wide acceptance among white Americans as a unifying theme of sectional reconciliation for so long that it infected the nation's politics and pop culture. And although civil rights activists threatened those feel-good narratives by revealing the unfulfilled promise of U.S. democracy, pop culture's blinkered fascination with the war never wavered. Musicians, writers, painters, and filmmakers continually mined the 1860s for inspiration with varying degrees of historical accuracy across the late twentieth century.⁴

Country music was not immune to that influence, and its songs and pervading themes of nostalgia have often echoed positive spins on the Confederacy. Mention this combination of music and memory to any longtime fans, and they will likely recall main offenders from the 1970s and 1980s like Hank Williams Jr., Alabama, or Charlie Daniels. Those artists emblazoned album covers with Confederate battle flags and sang eulogies to Dixie with impunity.⁵ In the political climate of the early twenty-first century, any connections with the Confederate past stir controversy and spur confessions. Country superstar Luke Combs apologized for his past use of a Confederate flag in 2021.⁶ The next year, the Country Music Association banned any reference to the Confederacy at its CMA Fest, the biggest annual country festival in the nation.⁷

No one should mistake musicians waving Rebel flags for deep historical analysis (see Brett A. Barnett's chapter in this volume), but music can function as a primary place where people attain a sense of history. Songs tell listeners about their place in the world, or at least the world of an artist's imagination. This becomes a thornier issue whenever country artists have moved beyond Confederate chauvinism to make seemingly earnest inquiries about the Civil War and have used music to convey their interpretations of historical events to their audiences. This essay identifies two such "historical turns" in country music that can help explain how this genre influenced and was influenced by Civil War memory. The first turn was ushered in by Jimmy Driftwood, a schoolteacher, folklorist, and songwriter who landed in Nashville in the late 1950s, just in time to benefit from the folk revival boom and the centennial anniversary of the Civil War. Country musicians and fans embraced another historical turn in the 1970s, when a generation raised on midcentury Civil War memory once again used the genre to define their cultural and racial politics through the sound of country-rock. British songwriter Paul Kennerley composed two country-rock concept albums titled *White Mansions* (1978) and *The Legend of Jesse James* (1980), which assembled all-star lineups of musicians who grappled with the experiences of everyday Southerners during the Civil War and Reconstruction.

The music industry marketed these historical albums as reverent, near-scholarly studies of the war. While none of this work can be characterized as outright celebrations of the Confederacy, neither Driftwood nor Kennerley could completely dodge the Lost Cause. When these songwriters reached back to the Southern past, they sank their hands into the fertile but blood-stained soil that grew the politics of white supremacy alongside the rich musical cultures that gave birth to country music. Understanding these tangled roots of genre, history, and memory reveals just how much the Lost Cause has shaped the sound, style, and substance of modern country music well into the twenty-first century.

Cold War, Civil War

Country music's connection to the Lost Cause dates to its birth as a commercial genre when record labels called it "hillbilly" or "old-time" music. In 1922 Eck Robertson and Henry Gilliland left a Confederate veterans' reunion at Richmond, Virginia, and traveled to New York City, with Gilliland wearing a Confederate uniform, to make the first recording of Southern fiddle playing ever committed to shellac.[8] Fiddlin' John Carson, an entertainment staple at Confederate reunions around Atlanta and a member of the Ku Klux Klan, launched the hillbilly record genre in 1923 with his recording of the minstrel song "Little Old Log Cabin in the Lane," in which a formerly enslaved man longs for his home on the plantation.[9] The Ryman Auditorium, known as the "Mother Church of Country Music" and home to the Grand Ole Opry from 1943 to 1974, featured a balcony called the Confederate Gallery, originally built to accommodate a United Confederate Veterans reunion in 1897. The seating section retained that name, announced in gold lettering visible from the stage, until 2017.[10] So, even as country musicians on the Grand Ole

Opry infused the genre with electrified sounds and turned Southern folk music into big business, they did so under the sonic and spatial legacies of the Lost Cause.

The specter of the Civil War emerged in force again during the late 1950s, when some country artists embraced elements of the folk revival. That included a return to older instrumental sounds and the reincorporation of narrative songwriting about past events called saga songs. This trend opened the door for historical storylines, including tales of the Civil War, to creep back to the forefront of the genre.[11] A singer-songwriter named Jimmy (or Jimmie) Driftwood inked a recording contract with RCA Victor in 1957 on the strength of his historical saga songs, and the industry pitched him as a "contemporary ancestor," a modern link to some supposedly untouched culture of the Southern hills. A promotional blurb in *The Tennessean* announced this "unique" signing and described Driftwood in a way meant to appeal to fans of folk music. The paper claimed that the singer was "born near the old Kickapoo trail and now living in Snowball, Ark., a valley with high hills and bluffs," insinuating that he belonged to a world that existed beyond the reaches of modernity and market forces. To prove this further, the paper relayed that Driftwood played "the longbow [a large homemade mouth harp], almost a lost art, and sings folk songs of true Shakespearean English."[12]

Driftwood was no missing cultural link, but the press's construction of his persona did reflect his lifelong devotion to folk music. In fact, Driftwood (born James Corbitt Morris) held a college degree and worked as a teacher in the Ozark Mountains of Arkansas. He found his first commercial break with "The Battle of New Orleans," his song about Andrew Jackson's victory over the British troops at New Orleans on January 8, 1815. Driftwood had written the lyrics to teach his students about the conclusion of the War of 1812. He matched his original lyrics with the folk fiddle tune "The Eighth of January," melding tradition and originality. In 1958 he included the song on his debut album, *Jimmie Driftwood Sings Newly Discovered Early American Folk Songs*, where it sat alongside other originals and traditional tunes like "Old Joe Clark."[13] This collapsing of old and new transformed Driftwood from a local schoolteacher into the nation's history teacher, all backed by Nashville's growing influence as the center of the country music industry.

Although Driftwood's first album failed to make a commercial impact, his general approach to songwriting positioned him to take advantage of three overlapping trends in the late 1950s: the consolidation of the country industry in Nashville, the portrayal of country music as evidence of American exceptionalism, and the rising popularity of the folk revival. In 1958 a powerful trade organization called the Country Music Association (CMA) formed in Nashville, Tennessee, with the express purpose of promoting and policing the image of the genre. The CMA's combination of advertising strategies, artistic gatekeeping, and boosterism helped to chart the commercial growth of country music over the coming decades, sealing the promotional side of the music business with the actual production of the records happening along Nashville's famed Music Row.[14]

While the CMA stimulated the genre's commercial growth, Tennessee Governor Frank G. Clement raised the genre's political reputation as a musical style of atavistic Americanism that complemented Cold War politics and the renewed interest in folk music. First elected in 1953, Clement delivered several speeches during his years in office boosting the genre's industry. He usually boasted of the music's pioneer stock, as if country music's origins were synonymous with the nation's founding. Clement's approach made country music seem respectable rather than the music of unlearned hillbillies and, in the process, helped to wed the genre to the creed of American exceptionalism.[15] Driftwood's music meshed well with Clement's selling strategy, as the Arkansas songwriter's work seemed to offer proof of country music's historical bona fides. Similarly, the folk revival, spurred by the release of the *Anthology of American Folk Music* and the Kingston Trio's hit "Tom Dooley," saw U.S. youth embrace the sounds of string bands, country blues, and mountain ballads. This trend primed audiences to hear Driftwood's history lessons as part of the topical song tradition that runs throughout much of American roots music.[16]

Nothing about Driftwood's initial recordings suggested that the artist or country music carried overt connections to the Lost Cause or even the Civil War, but that trajectory changed when Johnny Horton released his single of "The Battle of New Orleans" and placed it on his album *The Spectacular Johnny Horton*. Horton's version bears the ahistorical distinction of beginning with a melodic line from "Dixie" played on a banjo before the rest of the band jumps in over a military-style drumbeat. "The Battle of New Orleans" rocketed to number one on the country and pop charts in 1959, delivering the biggest financial success of Driftwood's long career. His song meant for schoolchildren had found mainstream success. In 1960 Horton included the track again on the album *Johnny Horton Makes History*, where it sat beside Merle Kilgore's "Johnny Reb," a song logging the bravery of common Confederate soldiers, and other historically themed songs about the Comanche, the Chicago Fire, Thomas "Stonewall" Jackson, the sinking of the *Bismarck*, and a flattering account of Abraham Lincoln.[17] With Driftwood's folk-centric country and Horton's mainstreaming of historical songs, the country music industry staked out the common ground shared by Music Row, Cold War patriotism, and midcentury folk revival.

The country music industry has rarely missed an opportunity to profit from copying a hit formula. Horton's popular album landed on the eve of the centennial anniversary of the Civil War, and other country artists dropped a slew of Civil War–themed songs and albums. Country singer Stonewall Jackson released a version of "Mary, Don't You Weep" in 1960 that turned the Black spiritual into a story about a Confederate soldier's last letter to his wife, Mary. Claude King, best known for his version of Merle Kilgore's "Wolverton Mountain," entered the fight with "The Burning of Atlanta" in 1962.[18] Tennessee Ernie Ford, a radio-television personality and purveyor of pop country, released two full albums of Civil War songs in 1961, *Tennessee Ernie Ford Sings Civil War Songs of the South* and *Tennessee Ernie Ford Sings Civil War Songs of the North*.[19]

Bluegrass proved to be an especially verdant corner of the country music field for Civil War memory. In 1960 three friends, Charles R. "Dick" Freeland, Bill Carroll, and Sonny "Zap" Compton, founded a bluegrass label called Rebel Records to promote the subgenre's thriving scene in Washington DC, Virginia, and Maryland. Rebel Records used Confederate flags and Confederate soldiers in its promotions, although Freeland claimed that they chose the name because of the film *Rebel Without a Cause* rather than an expression of neo-Confederate or segregationist sentiment.[20] The bluegrass duo Reno and Smiley released an album on King Records in 1961 with the cumbersome title *New and Original Folk Songs Written in Commemoration of the Centennial of the American Civil War, the War Between the States*. The two men posed as soldiers on the cover, one U.S. and the other Confederate. This album featured lyrics that aimed for historical accuracy written by Dr. Albert J. Russo, a physician and writer from Virginia who held an interest in folklore and Southern history. Despite a stated attempt to present an objective view of the war, Russo's Confederate leanings emerge in lyrics that celebrate Robert E. Lee, mourn the death of Albert Sidney Johnston, and lament the surrender at Appomattox.[21]

Jimmy Driftwood made history once again during the centennial. In 1961 he released *Songs of Billy Yank and Johnny Reb*, a collection of twelve original songs documenting the trials of the war from the perspective of

Confederates, U.S. soldiers, and enslaved Black Southerners. Produced by Chet Atkins, one of the architects of the "Nashville Sound," and recorded with a band of professional studio musicians, Driftwood's album revealed how much Music Row had embraced his brand of country. In keeping with the populist appeal of folk music, Driftwood's songs focus on the shared hardships of soldiering on both sides of the war while landing critiques against the inequalities of military life. His song "Billy Yank and Johnny Reb" works as a series of questions like "Who's that with the blisters / On their feet and mouth? / Not the politicians / In the north and in the south." The correct answer, of course, was "Billy Yank and Johnny Reb," the generic names for the low-ranking soldiers to whom most of the war's labor and fighting fell.[22]

Driftwood showed his interest in the common soldier's experience throughout the album, often routing his commentary through the personal level of an individual's story. His lyrics to "Poor Rebel Soldier" told the tale of a lovesick Confederate in need of affection who plans on abandoning his post to reunite with his woman. By the end of the song, we learn that he has deserted. His fellow soldiers may search, he says, "but me they won't find / I'm going to be south of that old Dixie line." In this candid portrait of a love-deprived Rebel, devotion to making love trumped his devotion to making war.[23]

The album even included Driftwood's commentary on the fate of Black Southerners, heard in the song "My Black Bird Has Gone." The narrator, presumably a man, describes a woman of great tenderness who taught him how to be humble and pray while also possessing sweet lips like "a hummingbird's mouth." The narrator then cries in the chorus, "They came with a chain . . . they carried my blackbird away."[24] Listeners may have assumed they were hearing an enslaved man lamenting the loss of his beloved, but Driftwood refused to confirm such an interpretation. In a demo recording, he introduces the song with the claim, "It might be a white boy or a white girl singing about a black mammy that he might have had. It could be a black boy singing about his sweetheart that's gone. Well, as [folklorist] Alan Lomax says, you have to interpret this song for yourself."[25]

Driftwood's songs may have represented honest efforts to inject discussions of class and race into the Civil War Centennial, but no country artist dared to critique the Confederacy for attempting to destroy the national experiment. Nor did any artist reckon with the true horrors of slavery or its centrality to the cause of the war. With civil rights activists staging protests and organizing across the South, sometimes literally down the street from Music Row in the case of James Lawson and the Nashville Movement, commentary on the state of race relations in the 1860s would have felt too much like commentary on the 1960s.[26] Better then, at least in Driftwood's mind, to let the listeners decipher country music's politics for themselves.

The country music press left little doubt about how listeners should interpret the memory of the Confederacy. In 1964 *Music City News*, a trade paper published in Nashville, contained an admiring write-up about the reenactments of the Battles of Nashville and Franklin. These events enjoyed support by the Civil War Centennial Commission, the Confederate High Command, and the local camps of the United Daughters of the Confederacy and the Sons of Confederate Veterans. Another article detailed the martial and sentimental songs enjoyed by the North and the South during the war.[27] The January 1965 edition of the paper featured a picture of Hank Williams Jr., then a fifteen-year-old musician toiling in his dead father's legacy, while serving as a captain in the Confederate High Command. He participated in the closing events of the reenactments by dressing in a Confederate officer's uniform and placing a wreath on a Confederate monument at Mount Olivet Cemetery in Nashville.[28]

The country music industry had turned to the Southern past during the centennial anniversary and found an opportunity to connect with audiences through the music of and about the Civil War. Tapping into the music's folk roots and telling stories about common foot soldiers played to country audiences well enough to deliver several hits. However, because those centennial observances overlapped with some of the most intense years of the civil rights movement, country artists' willingness to sing songs commemorating the Confederacy, dressing as Confederate soldiers, and placing Confederate flags on their album covers could look like an endorsement of the same states' rights rhetoric used by white supremacists. No one could fault a casual observer for thinking that way when artists like Minnie Pearl, George Morgan, and Hank Thompson campaigned for George Wallace in the 1950s and 1960s.[29] Regardless of the intent of the artists who engaged with Civil War memory, they could not divorce the genre from the racial and political histories of the South.

Civil War, Culture War

As Americans navigated the social and political fractures of the Vietnam era, some musical artists from the genres of rock and folk, including the Byrds, the Sir Douglas Quintet, the Rolling Stones, and the Grateful Dead, incorporated the sounds and styles of country music.³⁰ The counterculture's embrace of country also reflected the younger generation's search for roots and an alternative vision of American identity that differed from the one prescribed by normative patriotism and white middle-class values. In this musical movement, country and, by extension, Southern working-class identity could seem subversive. While some country-rock musicians leaned on the cowboy image, others incorporated Civil War memory into their search for Southern rootedness, using the historical symbols most readily at their disposal to make a statement about their connection to race and region. That return of Civil War memory made sense. In the late 1960s Americans were once again at war with themselves, clashing in the streets over the nation's commitment to Cold War liberalism, civil rights, and free speech. For some musicians, it was time to be rebels.

The International Submarine Band, a short-lived group led by the influential singer-songwriter Gram Parsons, expressed its countercultural rebellion by indulging in a Confederate image. Born into affluence in Florida and raised in Georgia with the help of Black domestic workers, Parsons had participated in the folk revival as a teenager and formed a group inspired by the Kingston Trio called the Shilos.³¹ He had also absorbed the sound of mainstream country music. The International Submarine Band showed those influences when it released its only album, *Safe at Home*, in 1968. The track list balanced covers of country songs with Parsons's originals while the group styled themselves in Old South/Confederate attire on the cover photograph. The image features three members, including Parsons, in suits and string ties that made them look like planters, while guitarist John Nuese wears a Confederate officer's uniform.³²

While inarguably insensitive by today's standards and the standards of many people at the time, Parsons's embrace of Confederate imagery falls more in line with misplaced expressions of regional pride than an explicit declaration of white supremacy. Parson briefly joined rock band the Byrds in 1968 and guided them into their country-rock phase. He left the group after refusing to tour South Africa and play to whites-only apartheid audiences, citing his Southern background and opposition to segregation for his reasoning.³³ He then formed the Flying Burrito Brothers, another pioneering group pursuing what Parsons called "Cosmic American Music" and known for their country-rock covers of Black soul songs like Aretha Franklin's "Do Right Woman."³⁴ None of these factors necessarily made Parsons an ally for racial justice, but neither did his planter image make him a closeted Klan member. Rather, it seems more likely that he relied on inelegant references to the past as a means of legitimizing and broadcasting his Southern roots. The Lost Cause interpretations of the past functioned as a default version of Southern and U.S. history for someone of Parsons's specific background in the 1960s. As he used Southern history to define his art, he took the most recognizable historical symbols of white Southern identity, almost inevitably connected to the Confederacy, and attempted to make them his own.

Of course, other rock, soul, and country-rock acts of the era used and abused Civil War memory in well-documented instances that are too numerous to name here in full. Throughout the 1960s, a label in Georgia called Confederate Records issued releases complete with the battle flag on the center sticker. The label's roster of artists included the Black soul singer Otis Redding, who signed with the company in 1962 and released his debut single "Shout Bamalama" before his storied run of records with the Stax/Volt label out of Memphis.[35] The roots-rock group the Band released its self-titled second album in 1969, featuring Arkansas drummer/vocalist Levon Helm singing "The Night They Drove Old Dixie Down." In this song, Helm voices a downtrodden Southern character named Virgil Caine who mourns the state of the South in the final days of the war, although critics still debate whether audiences should hear the lyrics as being sympathetic toward the Confederacy.[36]

The Nitty Gritty Dirt Band enlisted Civil War memory to offer a musical history lesson that also promised to bridge the generational divides between country and rock. The group had started as a jug band playing the coffee houses of the folk revival. They then embraced the burgeoning sounds of country-rock in the late 1960s but always maintained references to traditional folk by incorporating the mandolin, accordion, and banjo alongside electric guitars, drums, and modern production techniques. In 1972 the band traveled to Nashville and cut a landmark record with country music legends including Roy Acuff, Merle Travis, Earl Scruggs, and Mother Maybelle Carter for the album *Will the Circle Be Unbroken*. This melding of old and young sprawled across six sides of vinyl, sold as a triple-gatefold LP, with a track list of thirty-seven canonical country songs like "Wildwood Flower" and "I Saw the Light," traditional fiddle tunes "Black Mountain Rag" and "Soldier's Joy," and recent compositions by Jimmy Driftwood and Joni Mitchell.[37]

William E. McCuen served as the producer and the art director for the album. The front cover featured a portrait of Union Admiral David Dixon Porter flanked by Confederate and U.S. flags on each side in a conciliatory gesture. Purchasers could open the record to find color photographs of rural landscapes, antique trains and planes, and candid shots of the musicians in the studio. Other illustrations include what look like lithographs of ironclads, battles between white settlers and Native Americans, and Andrew Jackson's Hermitage. For the font, McCuen used an Old English–style type for the title, and he listed the personnel and song titles in cursive handwriting that evokes the entries from a nineteenth-century family Bible. All of this appears on a muted white background that appears stained on the back, suggesting the patina of aged parchment.[38]

The Nitty Gritty Dirt Band's turn to country music and Civil War memory aligned with the way much of the nation turned to the South in the 1970s. From the United States' military collapse in Vietnam to Watergate to the increasing influence of identity politics, the upheavals of the 1970s shattered the illusions of the Cold War liberal consensus. The South offered an optimistic story of redemption. The region's reputation had suffered during the civil rights movement of the 1950s and 1960s, but the South's reinvention as the Sunbelt seemed to shed the weight of its benighted past. White Americans from all over the nation embraced their inner Southerner. Country music enjoyed a boost in commercial popularity as radio stations converted to country formats, signaling what some scholars have referred to as the "reddening" or "southernization" of America. The album *Wanted! The Outlaws*, featuring Willie Nelson, Waylon Jennings, and Jessi Colter, became, in 1975, the first country LP to go platinum, while the *Urban Cowboy* soundtrack in 1980 ushered in the rise of the "redneck chic" fashion trend.[39] By the late 1970s, the mainstream caught up with the counterculture and where it had pointed in the late 1960s. Country was cool.

Pop culture sold markers of white Southern history in the new decade through the symbols of the Confederacy that fit easily alongside the music of the white South. When you wanted to listen to Willie and Waylon and the boys, perhaps you did so on the Magnavox Change of Face stereo console with a removable Confederate flag face plate.[40] Or you might pledge your allegiance to the New South as envisioned by country-rocker Charlie Daniels in his song "The South's Gonna Do It," with lyrics that praised many of the Southern acts of the day like Lynyrd Skynyrd, Grinderswitch, Barefoot Jerry, Wet Willie, and Dickey Betts of the Allman Brothers Band. "Be proud you're a rebel," Daniels sings, "because the South's gonna do it again."[41]

Daniels released the song as a statement of cultural pride, but his regional chauvinism could be mistaken for neo-Confederate sentiment. The Ku Klux

Klan in Louisiana briefly paired the song with their radio recruitment messages before Daniels disavowed the white supremacists. "I wrote that song about the land that I love and my brothers," Daniels told reporters. He added, "It was not written to promote hate groups."[42] Maybe not. But when Daniels coopted a slogan that resembled "the South will rise again" and failed to mention any Black artists in his list of brothers, the Klan could assume that regional and racial pride had melded under the heat of the band's hillbilly boogie.

The historical country albums *White Mansions* and *The Legend of Jesse James* provided another window into the way white musicians blurred regional and racial identities in the post–civil rights era. In the mid-1970s, an Englishman named Paul Kennerley discovered that he loved country music. He worked at an advertising firm in London, but he listened to American music and found inspiration in the works of Waylon Jennings, Willie Nelson, and Bob Dylan. Kennerley wanted to write country songs in the vein of these heroes, but he struggled with an approach that sounded authentic. "If you're from the South," he commented, "you can write about picking up Betsy in your Chevrolet. But for me that would be so fake and unreal. I couldn't become that character, but I did want to write this sort of music." Instead, Kennerley went with the historical turn: "That's when I decided to put myself in another time."[43]

To prepare for his time travel, Kennerley read several books on the Civil War and began composing songs about the characters he imagined populating the wartime South. They were the first songs he had ever written. A tape of the songs made its way to Glyn Johns, an English recording engineer and producer who worked on albums with the Who, the Rolling Stones, the Beatles, Eric Clapton, and the Eagles, to name but a few. Johns believed in Kennerley's work and enlisted his peers in rock's elite circles to play on the songs, including Eric Clapton and Bernie Leadon, an original Eagles guitarist. The producer also convinced country music power couple Waylon Jennings and Jessi Colter to join, as well as John Dillon and Steve Cash from the Ozark Mountain Daredevils. Jennings felt compelled to participate and wrote that the songs "touched me in a deeply personal way, as a man whose house is built on a Civil War battlefield and as a Southerner."[44]

This cast of performers began recording in 1978, and A&M Records released *White Mansions* later that year. The album art played into country's historical turn by featuring a photograph of a thirteen-year-old Confederate drummer boy named Charles Mosby centered on a stark gray background below the full title, *White Mansions: A Tale from the American Civil War, 1861–1865*. Record purchasers would have opened the record to find a twenty-eight-page booklet with Kennerley's lyrics and narrative interpretation of the war. The insert also includes photographer Ethan Russell's pictures of models dressed in Civil War–period clothes and posed as the characters depicted in the songs, alongside actual images from the 1860s.

The austere and scholarly tone of the cover and booklet belied the star power and cutting-edge production on the actual record. Jennings, Colter, Dillon, and Cash voice the main characters in these tales from the war. Jennings acts as an outside observer called "The Drifter," who comments on the state of the South at different points, from the early tempered optimism about secession heard in the song "Dixie, Hold On" to the depths of defeat heard in the final track, "Dixie, Now You're Done." Dillon provides the voice for Matthew J. Fuller, a slaveholding planter's son who joins the Confederate army as an officer, while Colter sings the part of his suitably aristocratic sweetheart, Polly Ann Stafford. Kennerley offers a critique of that aristocracy through the perspective of Cash's landless "white trash" character Caleb Stone. Black gospel singer Rodena Preston and her group Voices of Deliverance round out the cast to portray "The Slaves," who make an appearance on one song.[45]

White Mansions offered a fairly sophisticated interpretation of the war that undoubtedly benefited from Kennerley's cultural and physical distance from the South. The songs properly cite slavery as the motivation for secession. The four main characters reflect the way race, class, and gender shaped individual experiences, while Kennerley explained the minimal presence of Black voices on the record as a reflection of the fact that "despite the fact that they represented over a third of the population of the South, their voice was seldom heard." Yet his writing also falls into the Lost Cause trap of characterizing Reconstruction as a failure marked by Northern corruption and greed that ultimately forces Matthew, the former planter and Confederate officer, to resort to life as an outlaw in order to live by his own code of honor.[46] Although no one would mistake this album for a neo-Confederate screed, Kennerley's interest in and sympathy for white Southern stories, paired with the hip cachet of the country-rock soundtrack, opens the album to romantic interpretations of everything that white Southerners lost with the defeated cause of the Confederacy.

This sympathetic, underdog portrayal of the Confederates' rebellion reemerged on Kennerley's next project, *The Legend of Jesse James*, released in 1980, also on A&M Records. Another cast-led concept album, *Jesse James* features Levon Helm as the title character, Johnny Cash as Frank James, Charlie Daniels as Coleman Younger, and Emmylou Harris as Zerelda James, the mother of the outlaw brothers. Kennerley does not shy from the fact that the James–Younger Gang murdered and stole for their own benefit rather than the good of their community in the style of Robin Hood. His songs call out their brutality and describe their run of robberies as a wrongheaded, fatalistic death wish.

And still, the decision to voice these characters through Levon Helm, Johnny Cash, and Charlie Daniels and provide accompaniment by the top names in the business infused these tales of murder and treason with country-rock coolness. In the second song on the album, "Quantrill's Guerillas," Helm sings the opening lines "I could fill a hundred ditches / With them Yankee sonsabitches and not care."[47] Eleven years had passed since Helm's iconic voice had breathed life into Virgil Caine, a character who accepted defeat but not vengeance. As Jesse James in 1980, Helm sounded like he was out for retribution, even if that thirst for blood was ultimately short-lived and slaked only by the outlaw's own death. Kennerley may have found fault in the James–Younger Gang's murderous methods, but Helm's delivery imbued his character with a new sense of tragedy fit for the country-rock era. James became another romantic underdog mowed down in his prime by an overwhelming foe—a one-man lost cause who was gone but not forgotten.

Like Jimmy Driftwood, Kennerley had discovered an unlikely route toward a career in the country music business. He found that path by telling stories that emphasized the lives of everyday soldiers and Southern underdogs, making connections with some of the biggest names in country and rock music in the process. He succeeded in that regard. Although neither of Kennerley's historical albums generated much commercial success, he went on to a brilliant career as a country music songwriter, penning hits for the Judds, Juice Newton, Marty Stuart, Tanya Tucker, and Emmylou Harris, to whom he was also married for eight years.[48] Having searched for a way to write truthfully within a genre that values authenticity, Kennerley landed on the Civil War, placing an Englishman's stamp on one of the defining moments of Southern racial and political history at the very moment the nation looked to the South for its racial and political future.

Country artists continued using the Confederate flag and references to Dixie to brand themselves and sell their music throughout the 1980s. Waylon Jennings transitioned from his narrator role as "The Drifter" on *White*

Mansions to the "The Balladeer" on *The Dukes of Hazzard* television series, known for the Dodge Charger named the General Lee with a Confederate flag paint job and a horn programmed to play "Dixie."⁴⁹ The band Alabama used a Confederate flag as part of its logo and on album covers for *My Home's in Alabama, Feels So Right, Mountain Music,* and *Roll On.*⁵⁰ The Confederate flag likely functioned as another ill-conceived statement of regional pride in these cases, yet none should be divorced from the specter of the Lost Cause's most dangerous and racist ideologies.

Two country radio hits released in 1988 kept the Confederate connection active as well. Hank Williams Jr.'s "If the South Woulda Won" sounded a euphoric counterhistory in which "we woulda had it made" had the Confederacy survived, although the "we" in this scenario begs for more explanation.⁵¹ Dwight Yoakam, a transplant to Southern California's music scene from Kentucky, reached number one on *Billboard*'s country chart with "I Sang Dixie," about crooning the minstrel tune and unofficial Confederate anthem to a dying alcoholic Southerner on Skid Row. Yoakam's song delivers a balance of nostalgia and warning about life beyond the South. In his telling, the old days in the land of cotton were not "nearly as rotten / as they are on this damned old LA street," as if the woes of urban America and substance abuse might find a remedy back home below the Mason–Dixon line.⁵² While both of these songs fall within the Lost Cause tradition to varying degrees, neither attempt the historical turns of Driftwood's folk revival or Kennerley's historical fiction.

Country music and the Lost Cause collided again in force when the Sons of Confederate Veterans (SCV) booked part of their annual meeting at the Ryman Auditorium in 1997, one hundred years after the United Confederate Veterans had met there and added the balcony to accommodate the crowd. Local activists and journalists spoke out against the organization and its overt usage of the Rebel flag in its iconography and ceremonies. The SCV merely pointed to the Ryman's history and the construction of the Confederate Gallery to legitimize its use of the space. Dick Knight, a local attorney and cochair of the SCV convention, noted that many people associated the Rebel flag with hatred, but he defended the banner and what it meant to him. "It symbolizes country music and stock car racing," Knight argued. "It symbolizes freedom," he continued. "It symbolizes the South, Southern culture, Southern manners and civility." Marilyn Robinson, vice president of the Nashville NAACP, begged to differ. "Southern hospitality?" she asked. "You mean how many people you can lynch?"⁵³ The SCV meeting continued despite these objections. Country acts the Kentucky Headhunters, Highway

101, and Ronna Reeves performed for the SCV, and funds raised from the concert benefited local battlefield preservation efforts.[54] This time, the Lost Cause faithful had turned to country music's history and found a reason to call this genre their own. They had a point.

Despite such undeniable precedent, nothing about the relationship between country music and Civil War memory remains static, especially as the meanings of race and region change in the twenty-first century. On June 26, 2015, Charlie Daniels posted a column on his website clarifying his stance on the Confederate flag in the wake of the murder of nine Black churchgoers at Mother Emanuel African Methodist Episcopal Church by Dylann Roof in Charleston, South Carolina (see John M. Kinder's chapter in this volume). Daniels maintained that he only saw the flag as a symbol of defiant regional pride and that he had "no desire to reinstate the Confederacy." Yet he also recognized that "the Confederate battle flag has been adopted by hate groups—and individuals like Dylann Roof—to supposedly represent them and their hateful view of the races." He ended by calling for a colorblind Americanism and a prayer that God "will intervene in the deep racial divide that we have in this nation."[55] Where country music's Confederate connections once fit into an accepted historical narrative shaped by the Lost Cause, the genre's one-time defenders of the Rebel flag like Daniels needed to reassess in a new century.[56]

That reassessment continued in 2020 when the nation's present looked hauntingly like the past, and country musicians made a new historical turn. As the Black Lives Matter movement forced Americans to face the disproportionate murder of Black people at the hands of law enforcement officers, some artists within the country industry took the opportunity to reevaluate the genre's racial legacy, reconsider its connection to the most divisive moments in U.S. history, and at least make cosmetic changes. The Chicks dropped Dixie, and Lady Antebellum attempted to pay for its transgressions by appropriating the name Lady A, a name already in use by a Black artist named Anita White.[57] When white country artists pleaded ignorance at the hurtful nature of those names, they could do so with some justification. Generations of artists before them so embedded the Lost Cause within the genre that it remains as pervasive in Nashville as rhinestones and bachelorette parties, if not always as visible.

To fully examine the legacy of the Lost Cause requires digging deeper, past the obviously problematic names and the Rebel flags. There is value in examining country music's engagement with Civil War memory through the work of Driftwood, Kennerley, and other likeminded artists in country's historical turns. These songwriters attempted to take country audiences back to the Confederate past through the music most associated with white Southern culture. While these artists wrote and performed songs that could pass as nuanced and balanced at the time, each contained analytical cracks that allowed the Lost Cause to seep into their reimagining of Civil War history. This is not to vilify musicians for what were sometimes good-faith efforts to represent history. It is a reminder of how difficult it can be to hear the nuances of that history when it must compete with the deafening music of memory.

NOTES

1. Brad Paisley (featuring LL Cool J), "Accidental Racist," *Wheelhouse*, Arista Records 545539, 2013, CD.
2. For a sampling, see Ta-Nehisi Coates, "Why 'Accidental Racist' Is Actually Just Racist," *The Atlantic*, April 9, 2013, https://www.theatlantic.com/entertainment/archive/2013/04/why-accidental-racist-is-actually-just-racist/274826/; Brad Soderberg, "Dissecting Brad Paisley and LL Cool J's Politely Toxic Dud 'Accidental Racist,'" *Spin*, April 8, 2013, https://www.spin.com/2013/04/dissecting-brad-paisley-ll-cool-j-politely-toxic-accidental-racist/.
3. For an overview of country songs about the Civil War, see Smith and Akenson, "Civil War in Country Music Tradition," 1–25.
4. Kreiser and Allred, *Civil War in Popular Culture*; Cullen, *Civil War in Popular Culture*; Gallagher, *Causes Won, Lost, and Forgotten*; Chadwick, *Reel Civil War*.
5. Stephen Thomas Erlewine, "The South's Gonna Do It (Again): Charlie Daniels, the Confederacy and the Rise of the New South in the '70s," *Medium*, October 25, 2017, https://medium.com/@sterlewine/the-souths-gonna-do-it-again-charlie-daniels-the-confederacy-and-the-rise-of-the-new-south-in-ebbce1059d51. For more on the Outlaw/Southern rock usage of Confederate imagery, see Hughes, *Country Soul*, 152–56, 162–66.
6. Emily Yahr, "Luke Combs Apologizes for Confederate Flag Imagery as Tough Conversations Consume Nashville," *Washington Post*, February 19, 2021, https://www.washingtonpost.com/arts-entertainment/2021/02/19/country-singer-reaction-morgan-wallen/.
7. "CMA Fest Bans Confederate Flag Imagery at Country Music Fest," *Billboard*, June 3, 2022, https://www.billboard.com/music/country/2022-cma-fest-bans-confederate-flag-imagery-1235081037/.
8. Malone and Neal, *Country Music, U.S.A.*, 35. Others have claimed that both men dressed as cowboys. Either way, Gilliland and Robertson met at a Confederate reunion and bonded over their fiddling skills at that gathering in Richmond. For this alternate version, see Wayne Erbsen, "'Arkansaw Traveler' and 'Sallie Gooden'—Eck Robertson (1922)," Library of Congress, https://www.loc.gov/static/programs/national-recording-preservation-board/documents/ArkansawTraveler.pdf.
9. Huber, *Linthead Stomp*, 43, 58–59, 61, 69; Malone and Neal, *Country Music, U.S.A.*, 37; Campbell, *Music*, 134–35.

10. "Old Confederates," *Nashville American*, March 12, 1898, 3; Stephen Elliott, "Ryman's Confederate Sign Moved to Museum Exhibit," *Nashville Scene*, September 21, 2017, https://www.nashvillescene.com/news/pithinthewind/ryman-s-confederate-sign-moved-to-museum-exhibit/article_4c034c52-1860-5e87-8074-89efb3b0dd18.html; Wolfe, *A Good-Natured Riot*.
11. Malone and Neal, *Country Music, U.S.A.*, 283–86.
12. Bill Maples, "Unique," *The Tennessean*, December 22, 1957, 7-E.
13. Peter Stone, "Jimmy Driftwood," Association for Cultural Equity, https://www.culturalequity.org/alan-lomax/friends/driftwood; Jimmie Driftwood, *Jimmie Driftwood Sings Newly Discovered Early American Folk Songs*, RCA Victor LPM-1635, 1958, 33⅓ rpm.
14. Pecknold, *Selling Sound*, 135–43.
15. "Country Hoedown on Madison Avenue," *Country & Western Jamboree*, August 1956, 28–29, Box 56 Country and Western Jamboree, 1955–1959, Southern Folklife Collection, University of North Carolina–Chapel Hill. For more on Clement's promotion of the country music industry, see Pecknold, *Selling Sound*, 72, 80, 105–10; Thompson, *Cold War Country*.
16. Cantwell, *When We Were Good*.
17. Horton, *Johnny Horton Makes History*.
18. Stonewall Jackson, "Mary, Don't You Weep," Columbia 4-41533, 1959, 45 rpm; Claude King, "The Burning of Atlanta," Columbia 4-42581, 1962, 45 rpm. I am indebted to David Cantwell's insights regarding these songs and their potential political impact during the early 1960s. David Cantwell, "'The Battle of New Orleans,' 'Johnny Reb,' and the Civil Rights Movement" (presented at Sign o' the Times: Music and Politics, Museum of Pop Culture Pop Conference, April 22, 2017).
19. Tennessee Ernie Ford, *Tennessee Ernie Ford Sings Civil War Songs of the South*, Capitol Records T-1540, 1961, 33⅓ rpm; Tennessee Ernie Ford, *Tennessee Ernie Ford Sings Civil War Songs of the North*, Capitol Records T-1539, 1961, 33⅓ rpm.
20. Bill Vernon, liner notes, *Rebel Records, 1960–1995: 35 Years of the Best in Bluegrass*, RB CD 4000, 1997, CD. This label should not be confused with the Klan-affiliated company Reb Rebel Records, which released a series of white supremacist records in the 1960s. For more information on that label, see Tosches, *Country*, 226–27; Wade, "Johnny Rebel and the Cajun Roots of Right-Wing Rock," 493–512.
21. Reno and Smiley, *New and Original Folk Songs Written in Commemoration of the Centennial of the American Civil War, the War Between the States*, King Records K-12-756, 1961, 33⅓ rpm.
22. Jimmie Driftwood, *Songs of Billy Yank and Johnny Reb*, RCA Victor LSP-2316, 1961, 33⅓ rpm.
23. Driftwood, *Songs of Billy Yank and Johnny Reb*. Lester Flatt and Earl Scruggs also included "Poor Rebel Soldier" on their setlists in the mid-1960s. See Flatt and Scruggs, *Recorded Live at Vanderbilt University*, Columbia CS 8934, 1964, 33⅓ rpm.
24. Driftwood, *Songs of Billy Yank and Johnny Reb*.
25. "Jimmy Driftwood My Blackbird Is Gone (Demo Version!)," JimmyDriftwoodfan, YouTube, November 7, 2015, https://www.youtube.com/watch?v=6i-kks8srue.
26. Branch, *Parting the Waters*, 274–80.
27. Harris Martin, "Music City to Echo 'Civil War' Guns," *Music City News*, December 1964, 6; "Civil War Songs," *Music City News*, December 1964, 6, 13, Frist Library and Archive, Country Music Hall of Fame and Museum, Nashville TN.
28. "'Big Picture' in Country," *Music City News*, January 1965, 8, Frist Library and Archive.

29. La Chapelle, *I'd Fight the World*, 208–12; "Gov. Wallace Alabama's # One Citizen, Country & Gospel Fan," *Music City News*, July 1965, 8, Frist Library and Archive.
30. Mellard, *Progressive Country*; Stimeling, *Cosmic Cowboys and New Hicks*.
31. Meyer, *Twenty Thousand Roads*, 23, 108.
32. The International Submarine Band, *Safe at Home*, LHI Records LHIS-12001, 1968, 33⅓ rpm.
33. Meyer, *Twenty Thousand Roads*, 244; Greenbaum, "Hearing Waycross," 98–111.
34. The Flying Burrito Brothers, *Gilded Palace of Sin*, A&M Records SP 4175, 1969, 33⅓ rpm.
35. "Music as Written," *Billboard*, April 14, 1962, 16; "Reviews of New Singles," *Billboard*, May 12, 1962, 26.
36. Jack Hamilton, "The Troublesome Case of 'The Night They Drove Old Dixie Down,'" *Slate*, August 13, 2020, https://slate.com/culture/2020/08/night-they-drove-old-dixie-down-band-confederate.html; Ta-Nehisi Coats, "Virginia," *The Atlantic*, August 17, 2009, https://www.theatlantic.com/entertainment/archive/2009/08/virginia/23415/; Cullen, *Civil War in Popular Culture*, 118–23.
37. The Nitty Gritty Dirt Band, *Will the Circle Be Unbroken*, United Artists Records UAS-9801, 1972, 33⅓ rpm.
38. The Nitty Gritty Dirt Band, *Will the Circle Be Unbroken*.
39. Schulman, *Seventies*, 115–17; Martinez, "Redneck Chic," 128–43.
40. "Magnavox Compact Front Changeable," *Billboard*, October 6, 1973, 79.
41. The Charlie Daniels Band, "The South's Gonna Do It," *Fire on the Mountain*, KSBS 2603, 1974, 33⅓ rpm.
42. "KKK Lashed by Daniels on Song Use," *Billboard*, December 20, 1975, 4; Erlewine, "South's Gonna Do It (Again)."
43. Quoted in Robert K. Oermann, liner notes, various artists, *White Mansions* and *Legend of Jesse James*, Mercury Records 314-540 791-2, 1999, CD.
44. Oermann, liner notes, *White Mansions* and *Legend of Jesse James*.
45. *White Mansions*.
46. *White Mansions*.
47. "Quantrill's Guerillas," *Legend of Jesse James*.
48. "Juice Mixes Country Punch with Maher-Kennerley Tune," *The Tennessean*, February 28, 1988, 59; "Stuart 'Thumps' Charts," *The Tennessean*, September 9, 1990, 39; Juli Thanki, "Emmylou Harris Gives 'Sally Rose' Second Life," *The Tennessean*, September 19, 2018, 1F.
49. Lechner, *South of the Mind*, 163–64.
50. Alabama, *My Home's in Alabama*, RCA-AHL 1-3644, 1980, 33⅓ rpm; Alabama, *Feels So Right*, RCALP 5025, 1981, 33⅓ rpm; Alabama, *Mountain Music*, RCA-AHL 1-4229, 1982, 33⅓ rpm; Alabama, *Roll On*, RCA-AHL 1-4939, 1984, 33⅓ rpm.
51. Hank Williams Jr., "If the South Woulda Won," Warner Bros. 92 78672, 1988, 45 rpm.
52. Dwight Yoakam, "I Sang Dixie" b/w "Floyd County," Reprise Records 7-27715, 1988, 45 rpm.
53. Jay Hamburg, "Rebel Sons' Assembly Renews Flag Clash," *The Tennessean*, July 27, 1997, 1A.
54. Mark Blevins, "Rebel Sons Gather to Aid Battlefield," *The Tennessean*, July 31, 1997, 2B.
55. Charlie Daniels, "Flags," Charlie Daniels Band, June 26, 2015, https://www.charliedaniels.com/soap-box?b_id=518&pg=34.
56. Kristin M. Hall, "Country Acts Quietly Abandon Confederate Flag," *Seattle Times*, July 9, 2015, https://www.seattletimes.com/entertainment/music/country-music-acts-quietly-abandon-confederate-flag/.

57. Jon Freeman, "Lady A Drop 'Antebellum' from Their Name," *Rolling Stone*, June 11, 2020, https://www.rollingstone.com/music/music-country/lady-antebellum-change-name-1013602/; Chris Willman, "The Chicks Explain Dropping 'Dixie' From Their 'Stupid' Name: 'We Wanted to Change It Years Ago,'" *Variety*, July 8, 2020, https://variety.com/2020/music/news/dixie-chicks-explain-name-change-new-interview-1234701080/.

BIBLIOGRAPHY

Branch, Taylor. *Parting the Waters: America in the King Years, 1954–1963*. Simon and Schuster, 1988.

Campbell, Gavin James. *Music and the Making of a New South*. University of North Carolina Press, 2004.

Cantwell, Robert. *When We Were Good: The Folk Revival*. Harvard University Press, 1996.

Chadwick, Bruce. *The Reel Civil War: Mythmaking in American Film*. Alfred A. Knopf, 2001.

Cullen, Jim. *The Civil War in Popular Culture: A Reusable Past*. Smithsonian Institution Press, 1995.

Gallagher, Gary W. *Causes Won, Lost, and Forgotten: How Hollywood and Popular Art Shape What We Know About the Civil War*. University of North Carolina Press, 2008.

Greenbaum, Abigail. "Hearing Waycross." *Southern Cultures* 27, no. 4 (Winter 2021): 98–111.

Huber, Patrick. *Linthead Stomp: The Creation of Country Music in the Piedmont South*. University of North Carolina Press, 2008.

Hughes, Charles L. *Country Soul: Making Music and Making Race in the American South*. University of North Carolina Press, 2015.

Kreiser, Lawrence A., and Randal Allred, eds. *The Civil War in Popular Culture: Memory and Meaning*. University Press of Kentucky, 2014.

La Chapelle, Peter. *I'd Fight the World: A Political History of Old-Time, Hillbilly, and Country Music*. University of Chicago Press, 2021.

Lechner, Zachary J. *The South of the Mind: American Imaginings of Southern Whiteness, 1960–1980*. University of Georgia Press, 2018.

Malone, Bill C., and Jocelyn R. Neal. *Country Music, U.S.A.* 3rd rev. ed. University of Texas Press, 2015.

Martinez, Amanda Marie. "Redneck Chic: Race and the Country Music Industry in the 1970s." *Journal of Popular Music Studies* 32, no. 2 (June 2020): 128–43.

Mellard, Jason. *Progressive Country: How the 1970s Transformed the Texan in Popular Culture*. University of Texas Press, 2013.

Meyer, David N. *Twenty Thousand Roads: The Ballad of Gram Parsons and His Cosmic American Music*. Villard, 2007.

Pecknold, Diane. *The Selling Sound: The Rise of the Country Music Industry*. Duke University Press, 2007.

Schulman, Bruce J. *The Seventies: The Great Shift in American Culture, Society, and Politics*. Da Capo, 2001.

Smith, Andrew K., and James E. Akenson. "The Civil War in Country Music Tradition." In *Country Music Goes to War*, edited by Charles K. Wolfe and James E. Akenson. University Press of Kentucky, 2005.

Stimeling, Travis D. *Cosmic Cowboys and New Hicks: The Countercultural Sounds of Austin's Progressive Country Music Scene*. Oxford University Press, 2011.

Thompson, Joseph M. *Cold War Country: How Nashville's Music Row and the Pentagon Created the Sound of American Patriotism*. University of North Carolina Press, 2024.

Tosches, Nick. *Country: The Biggest Music in America*. Stein and Day, 1977.
Wade, Michael. "Johnny Rebel and the Cajun Roots of Right-Wing Rock." *Popular Music and Society* 30, no. 4 (October 2007): 493–512.
Wolfe, Charles K. *A Good-Natured Riot: The Birth of the Grand Ole Opry*. Vanderbilt University Press and the Country Music Foundation Press, 2008.

7

Love Is a Battlefield

Civil War Memory in Modern Romance Novels

SARAH HANDLEY-COUSINS

The Planter's Daughter, a romance novel published in 2017 by Michelle Shocklee, takes place on a Texas plantation called Rose Hill in the years before the Civil War. Adella Rose Ellis, the beautiful and tenderhearted daughter of the plantation owner, is friendly with the plantation's enslaved population while her greedy father plots to breed his "stock" like cattle, hoping to sell off resulting children for a juicy profit. When Seth Brantley, Rose Hill's new overseer arrives, Adella has mixed feelings—she's taken with the handsome young man but also knows that overseers have a reputation for cruelty. But this one is different. Seth has taken up work as an overseer only because his fledgling career in the Texas Rangers was put to an abrupt end when an escaping slave, desperate to flee to Mexico, shot Seth in the leg, leaving him with a painful limp. Seth is angry at the fugitive who ended his career, and his bitterness leaves "little room for sympathetic thoughts toward the dead runaway or his kind."[1]

Over the course of the novel, though, Adella's tenderness and faith soften Seth's steely resolve. Adella helps him let go of his anger toward Black men by introducing him to Jeptha, her enslaved childhood friend. She takes Seth to the local slave church, where he hears that Jesus died for the sins of all people, white and Black. As they fall in love, Seth finds himself disgusted by enslavers like Adella's father and brother, and when her father plots to keep them apart, she and Seth decide to run to Mexico to marry, taking Jeptha and a select group of Rose Hill's bondspeople with them to freedom. Seth is proud of being a kindly overseer, disdaining excessive cruelty but still believing that slavery is "natural" until he meets Adella. He doesn't truly understand the plight of the enslaved until he spends more time with Jeptha, who explains that all Black folks want is freedom. In a kind of conversion experience, Seth realizes that the fugitive who shot him was just like Jeptha, simply seeking freedom. He asks for forgiveness—from Jeptha, from the dead fugitive, and from God—and the pain in his wounded thigh miraculously disappears. By the final pages, Seth and Adella have successfully ushered the small group to freedom beyond the Rio Grande, where they eagerly await the arrival of the preacher who will unite them in marriage.

The Civil War era seems like a fitting backdrop for such dramatic romance novels. After all, the most famous book about the era is *Gone with the Wind* (1936), a romantic story about the life and loves of a Southern beauty living through the tumult of war and its aftermath. The war itself is often presented as a kind of romance, full of adventures and tragedies, heroes and heroines. And historical romance has consistently been one of the most popular subgenres of romance. In a 1983 study of romance reading conducted by American studies scholar Janice Radway, almost half of respondents identified historical as their favorite subgenre. More recently, a 2017 survey conducted by the Romance Writers of America (RWA) showed that historical romance is the third most popular romance genre. In the short years since that RWA survey, the subgenre's popularity has only grown due to the release of the massively successful Netflix series *Bridgerton*, based on Julia Quinn's book series set in Regency England.

But despite the voracious demand for historical romance, the long history of romantic plots in Civil War literature, and the appealingly dramatic backdrop it offers, there has been no recent bump in Civil War romance novels. Civil War romance had a mainstream moment in the 1970s through the early 1990s, but today, there are vanishingly few Civil War romances published by large, mass market romance presses. While certainly no scientific measure, Goodreads, a website that allows users to categorize books into virtual shelves, illustrates the discrepancy between Regency and Civil War romances. The site's users have shelved 13,728 titles as "Regency romance," but I was able to identify fewer than 150 titles for a shelf I built called "Civil War romance."[2] Readers might have an insatiable desire for Regency rakes and Victorian rogues, but they don't seem to want heroes wearing blue and gray. If the Civil War makes a good backdrop for a sweeping romance, why aren't there more modern mass market romance novels set during the conflict?

Historical romance novels like Quinn's *Bridgerton* series are popular because they offer a reader an escape into a fantasy not only of passion but also of glittering gowns and witty conversation. For many modern American readers, though, the white supremacy of the Civil War era and its continued impacts on modern society make it a painful, rather than delightful, setting.

The political upheaval and racist violence of the past decade have shifted the way that many think about the Civil War and its legacy. For example, a proposed television drama called *Confederate*, an alternate history in which the Confederacy won the Civil War, was roundly criticized before it even had a script and was officially scrapped by HBO in 2020. Roxane Gay summed up many Americans' feelings when she wrote in the *New York Times* that she "didn't want to watch slavery fan fiction." In a country where "vestiges of slavery" are still present in daily life, Gay warned, creators need to be aware that "we do not make art in a vacuum isolated from sociopolitical context."[3] Just weeks after Gay's op-ed was published, her warning proved prescient when white supremacists gathered in Charlottesville, Virginia, to protest the city's proposed removal of a statue of Robert E. Lee. As the doomed *Confederate* project demonstrated and Gay articulated, art about the Civil War is inextricably connected to white supremacy and violence, past and present. Within such fraught social context, a frothy romance set in the era is less sweet escapism and more an act of complicity.

However, there are two main exceptions to the general dearth of Civil War romance. First, the war era remains a very popular setting for inspirational romances—that is, novels with an explicitly evangelical Christian perspective, typically released by Christian publishing houses and consumed largely by conservative, evangelical readers. Authors such as Michelle Shocklee and Tamera Alexander have recently written book series that follow the travails of white, typically Southern women looking to God to bring them through the devastation of the war. In sharp contrast to Civil War inspirationals, the second exception is books by Black authors such as Beverly Jenkins and Alyssa Cole, who have reclaimed the Civil War setting to write bestsellers about Black heroes and heroines escaping slavery, spying for the U.S. Army, or building communities of freedpeople in the postwar South and West, all while finding love. While Civil War novels are no longer a major part of the mainstream historical romance market, those that do appear play a significant role in shaping the popular modern memory of the war, in ways both forward thinking and deeply damaging.[4]

During the war era, romances were common and popular, and they played an important cultural role as Americans processed regional and political divides. Writers both Northern and Southern imagined healing national wounds through fiction about intersectional romances. During the war, historian Megan Bever has shown, women writers penned stories in which Unionist women converted Confederate men through the power of their love.⁵ After the surrender, the most common romance trope was the Northern man who symbolically cemented the Confederate loss by marrying a Southern woman. "Marriage," writes Jane Turner Censer, "was the metaphor for northern male supremacy even while love was a euphemism for domination. Therefore, fictional northern soldiers conquered southern beauties with *billet-doux*, not bullets."⁶ John William De Forest's *Miss Ravenel's Conversion from Secession to Loyalty*, one of the most well-known novels written during the Civil War era, is many things: It's an early example of American literary realism, a novel about war, reunion, and modernization—but it's also a romance, featuring a love triangle between Southern belle Lillie Ravenel and military officers John Carter and Edward Colburne. Lillie marries the Virginian Carter, but she learns that he has been unfaithful to her just before he is killed in battle. Yankee Colburne overcomes a wartime illness and marries the now widowed former Miss Ravenel, successfully completing her "conversion from Secession to Loyalty."⁷

Across fiction genres, the Civil War has never lost its appeal to authors, and twentieth-century novels have been hugely influential in shaping Civil War memory. Irene Hunt's classic youth novel *Across Five Aprils* (1964); battle sagas *The Killer Angels* (1974), *Gods and Generals* (1996), and *The Last Full Measure* (2000) by Michael Shaara and Jeff Shaara; John Jakes's *North and South* trilogy (1982, 1984, 1987); and *Cold Mountain* (1997) by Charles Frazier were all bestsellers. Many of these novels feature romantic storylines—*North and South* includes many tangled relationships, and the central plot of *Cold Mountain* is deserter Inman's quest to return home to his beloved Ada. Two of the most impactful Civil War novels of the early twentieth century were also explicitly romantic. Thomas Dixon's Reconstruction novel and Ku Klux Klan romance *The Leopard's Spots: A Romance of the White Man's Burden* (1902), the sequel to which was later adapted to film as *The Birth of a Nation*, revolves around a love triangle, this one between scalawag Allan McLeod, Democratic politician Charles Gaston, and Sallie Worth, daughter of a Confederate war hero. And of course, *the* romance of the Civil War era is Margaret Mitchell's *Gone with the Wind* (1936), which with its 1939 film adaptation has done more to shape Civil War memory than nearly anything else.⁸

But while many Civil War novels have romantic plotlines and some, like *Miss Ravenel*, *The Leopard's Spots*, and *Gone with the Wind*, have sometimes been categorized as romances, they are *not* romance novels by today's genre conventions.⁹ Instead, they have more in common with an earlier genre known as romance, which might feature love stories but also included a great deal of manly swashbuckling. Such romances weren't defined by the love story of two characters—though they might include them, and they might even be central to the plot. Instead, romance typically referred to literature that placed love stories alongside tales of derring-do, heroism, and adventure. Sir Walter Scott's novels *Ivanhoe* and *The Pirate*, for instance, were both sold as romances.[10] In the wake of the Civil War, writers like Thomas Dixon and Thomas Nelson Page expanded Scott's romantic tradition in the service of the Lost Cause with the plantation romance, which mythologized and romanticized the Old South. Thomas Nelson Page's *Red Rock* (1898) exemplified the pattern that would be followed in later plantation romances such as *The Leopard's Spots* and *Gone with the Wind*. *Red Rock* included several romantic plotlines, but the story centered on Southern men who, despite being beset by carpetbaggers and scalawags, were fighting for justice in devastated the postwar South. The purpose of these novels, argues Bertram Wyatt-Brown, "was . . . shoring up the long-revered values that had been the justification for resolute action in secession, war, and redemption."[11] Indeed, Page wrote of Southern people in the prologue to *Red Rock*: "If they shone in prosperity, much more they shone in adversity; if they bore themselves haughtily in their day of triumph, they have borne defeat with splendid fortitude. . . . They were subjected to the greatest humiliation of modern times: their slaves were put over them—they reconquered their section and preserved the civilization of the Anglo-Saxon."[12]

Meanwhile, the romance novel was evolving along a different path. Samuel Richardson's *Pamela; or, Virtue Rewarded* (1740) is generally regarded as the first "romance novel," though it shares very little with the modern romances beside a plot centering on a courtship that leads to a wedding. The works of Jane Austen are more recognizable precursors to modern romance novels: *Pride and Prejudice* (1813), her most well-known novel, is entirely focused on the main couple, who must overcome obstacles to earn their happily ever after. The modern romance novel took shape in the early twentieth century, led by two British authors: E. M. Hull, author of *The Sheik* (1919), and Georgette Heyer, whose Regency romances established the era as the ideal setting for a historical romance and which were published at a staggering rate between 1921 and 1974.[13] In the midcentury, publishing houses like Harlequin and Silhouette, later joined by Avon Romance, began to pump out mass market paperbacks in lines that focused on different subgenres, such as contemporary, historical, and paranormal. By the 1980s, Harlequin and Silhouette were publishing at least eighty titles a month across their various lines, together producing nearly a thousand paperback romance novels a year.[14]

Most romance scholars, critics, and writers agree on the modern definition of the romance novel. Scholar Pamela Regis defines it as a "work of prose fiction that tells the story of the courtship and betrothal of one or more heroines."[15] The RWA, the professional organization for writers in the genre, gives a more specific, two-part definition. The main plot of a romance novel must revolve "around individuals falling in love and struggling to make the relationship work." Subplots are fine so long as the focus always remains on the central couple. The second part of the definition is equally crucial. While Regis identified the betrothal as key to the romance novel ending, the RWA does not limit the ending to an engagement or marriage but highlights the absolute necessity of the happy ending. "In romance," it declares, "the lovers who risk and struggle for each other and their relationship are rewarded with emotional justice and unconditional love."[16] So while *Gone with the Wind* might have a powerful romance in its dramatic plot, when Rhett tells Scarlett he does not give a damn and leaves her at the end of the book, he disqualifies the book as a romance novel.[17]

Though wildly popular and tremendously influential in its day, today *Gone with the Wind*'s troubled reputation casts a long shadow on the Civil War as a romance setting.[18] Several novels influenced by Margaret Mitchell's problematic classic appeared during the paperback boom of the late 1970s through the early 1990s. The first wave of mass market Civil War romances were "bodice-rippers," the romance community's term for the overtly erotic historicals with heavy elements of misogyny and dubious consent that were popular at that time. The war made an ideal setting for a bodice-ripper, which have high-adventure plots and often featured tumultuous romances with pirates, outlaws, or knights. These novels drew heavily on elements of plantation romances. Like their predecessors, they featured Lost Cause tropes: feisty and adventurous Southern belles, dashing Confederates, reserved but irresistible Federal officers, and, of course, faithful slaves.

Kathleen Woodiwiss, who revolutionized the romance genre with *The Flame and the Flower* (1972), published the exemplar Civil War bodice-ripper, *Ashes in the Wind*, in 1979. In the novel, heroine Alaina finds herself a wanted woman after she delivers a message from a dying Confederate soldier to General Richard Taylor. As a result, a white Yankee lieutenant and his Black soldiers arrive to investigate her home, Briar Hill. The lieutenant attempts to rape Alaina but is stopped when her loyal slave Saul rushes in: "Her screams had brought Saul crashing through the back door, and in the face of the huge black servant's rage, the chickenhearted coward had fled like a cur with its tail tucked between its legs, calling his men after him and vowing to see her hanged and that damned black right along with her."[19] Alaina and Saul flee the rapacious Yankees, but after a week's trek, they seize Saul in Baton Rouge. In occupied New Orleans, Alaina dresses as a boy to find work in a Union hospital, where she inevitably falls in love with a "bluebelly" Federal surgeon, Cole Latimer.

The pairing of spicy Southern belle with duty-bound Yankee is an ode to Civil War–era intersectional romances, but it's also a way to provide readers with a popular trope known as "enemies to lovers."[20] Conveniently, the transition from enemies to lovers also solves the crisis between North and South through marriage. Not only do Alaina and Cole marry and have a child, but even Alaina's un-Reconstructed Confederate brother, Jason, is won over by her kinship with Yankees. But while the intersectional romance has been slightly updated to fit a modern trope, other elements are just copy-and-paste bits of Lost Cause literature. There are loyal enslaved people, such as housekeeper Dulcie, who is "petulant and uncommunicative" when she learns Alaina's cousin will marry a Yankee, and Saul, who somehow returns from the Yankees' grasp to continue to protect Alaina. There are also menacing Black men, such as Gunn, a "big ox" who provides his villainous white mistress the muscle for her kidnapping plot. Slavery is referenced only in terms of these few alternately threatening and loyal individuals, and unfreedom serves as a metaphor for white characters rather than a reality for the Black ones. Toward the end of the novel, Cole tells Alaina she is no longer wanted by the U.S. Army, joking that aside from their marriage, she is a "virtually" free woman. Alaina responds: "As to that bondage, my love . . . I would that I be chained to you forever."[21]

In other novels of the 1970s and 1980s, race and slavery played a less metaphorical and more immediate role in setting the scene or driving the plot. Patricia Gallagher's *Mystic Rose* (1977), another Avon publication, is set at the "great plantation" Mystic Rose in South Carolina in the early nineteenth century. The novel follows the tumultuous romance of beautiful Star Lamont and Captain Troy Stewart. The atmosphere of Mystic Rose—both the plantation and the book overall—is set by the pervasive presence of the enslaved. Describing the plantation, Gallagher writes: "Some distance from the great mansion stood the rows of neat slave cabins. . . . The doors and shutters... are painted blue to keep away evil spirits. The gray morning mists hovering about the dark walls and the shadows of dusk creeping furtively into the moss-hung gardens cast an aura of mystery and enchantment over the place, which was keenly felt by the superstitious blacks, inspiring many awesome hallucinations of witches and 'haints.'"[22]

The enslaved are also treated as part of the landscape of the plantation. As heroine Star Lamont returns home after a long time away from Mystic Rose, she looks out admiringly at the beautiful lawn, lush gardens, and bountiful orchards, noting that nothing has changed in her time away, including the slaves, who, "as always," were tending to the beautiful landscaping. But the peculiar institution also drives the plot. Obah, an enslaved African man who was severely beaten at Mystic Rose as punishment for a rape, leads an uprising against the Lamonts. As a slave cabin burns, Obah is described as "drunk with power": "Obah was in his full glory as a leader. He was a magnificent black giant, naked except for a loincloth of deerskin, his face and body grotesquely painted with clay stained with the dyes of swamp plants. A chieftain's headgear of egret and flamingo feathers crowned his massive head. A necklace of alligator teeth adorned his throat and bracelets of rattlesnake tail buttons circled his wrists and ankles, rattling dismally as he changed and did a jungle dance of death around the roaring bonfire." But Obah's intention is not only to watch the plantation burn: He also wants to rape Star. He enjoys her struggle against him: "You wild woman! You make much fun for Obah."[23] Star fights him off, and by the end of the book, her virginity is despoiled only by the handsome Captain Stewart, safely within the bonds of marriage.

Other early Civil War romance novels were less focused on the plantation and instead used well-known events of the war to move the plot. Heather Graham is particularly well known for her Civil War romances during this period. Her first Civil War novels, the Cameron Saga trilogy, included *One Wore Blue* (1991), followed by *And One Wore Gray* and *And One Rode West*. In *One Wore Blue*, Jesse Cameron and Kiernan Miller, residents of Harpers Ferry, Virginia, live through John Brown's raid. They're childhood friends in love, but the politics of the sectional crisis have torn them apart—Jesse a loyal medical officer in the U.S. Army, Kiernan a slaver Southern belle. One pivotal scene takes place in the courtroom as John Brown's sentence is read. The lovers' eyes meet at the moment the martyr's fate is announced: "Kiernan looked across the court room. Jesse took his eyes from Brown and stared at her. He seemed sad—no, stricken, almost anguished. She felt his stare like a touch."[24] This powerful historical moment—when a white man demonstrated his willingness to die to protest enslavement, and the United States, in turn, reaffirmed its willingness to execute John Brown rather than admit the immorality of slavery—is thus transformed into a plot device in Kiernan and Jesse's love story.

That night, when Jesse comes to dine with the rest of the Miller family, Kiernan meets him by the livery stables. They kiss, but their passion turns to anger when the steadfastly Southern Kiernan refuses to agree to marry the Unionist Jesse. Eventually, Kiernan calls Jesse an arrogant Yank and the lovers part ways—one to the North, one to the South. Kiernan marries a good Virginian but is almost immediately widowed when her new husband dies at First Manassas. And she, of course, can't keep away from Jesse. By December 1861, she's pregnant with Jesse's baby, a child "conceived in love ... conceived in war."[25] Even then, Kiernan rails against Jesse's choice to serve the Federal army. But this is a romance novel, so not even a civil war can stand in the way of love. By the end, Kiernan and Jesse have been ordered to marry by his commanding officer (to avoid the accusation that the Federal army is "peopling the South with bastards"), fought off Reb deserters while Kiernan is in labor, delivered a son in Jesse's (now West) Virginia mansion, and accepted their happily-ever-after—all without Kiernan relinquishing her commitment to the Confederacy.

Likely due to the commercial success of the Cameron Saga and aided by the popularity of Ken Burns's *The Civil War*, Graham wrote more Civil War novels, including a six-book series set in her native Florida, and republished earlier books that hadn't gotten much notice. *Tomorrow the Glory*, first published pseudonymously in 1985 but republished in 1994, is particularly notorious today. The novel follows Confederate naval officer Brent McClain and heroine Kendall Moore, who Brent rescues from an abusive Yankee husband. While both Brent and Kendall express their distaste for slavery, they also think it's tangential to the real causes of the war—and when other characters express that opinion, they're depicted as unsophisticated or deluded. While its content is notorious enough, *Tomorrow the Glory* is better known now for the infamous cover art of the 1994 edition. On the cover is an innocuous painting of a pink magnolia, but the main characters' faces peek through a hole in the paperback. When that cover is opened, spread across the inside cover and first page (an illustration called a stepback) is a painting of the masculine hero clutching the lovely heroine in his arms—the classic "clinch" pose—set against a massive, waving Confederate flag. The hero and heroine in the image are Heather Graham and her husband, painted by artist Pino Daeni.[26] Uncontroversial when it was published, this stepback is now representative not only of the excesses of the bodice-ripper era but also of a generation of romances that recklessly embraced and endorsed the Lost Cause. In this case, though, not only did the characters embody that mythology, but by inserting herself into the cover art, Heather Graham also explicitly situated herself within that worldview. While there weren't a huge number of Civil War romances published in the 1980s and 1990s, those that did appear were more or less exactly like *One Wore Blue*, *Tomorrow the Glory*, *Ashes in the Wind*, and *Mystic Rose*: sensual plantation romances set in a mythical South, packed with sexy adventures and populated with loyal Black sidekicks and dangerous slaves.

By embracing tropes established by plantation and intersectional romances and spicing them up with sex scenes, Civil War bodice-rippers sold Lost Cause mythology to new audiences. Further, while the divide between North and South made for a natural enemies-to-lovers story, modern intersectional romances placed Northern and Southern causes on equal moral footing, where nothing—even the profoundly immoral institution of slavery—could stand in the way of love. Unsurprisingly, Civil War bodice-rippers now have a bad reputation for indulging in Lost Cause fantasies and trading in racist stereotypes.[27]

Today, historical romance readers still crave historical settings but want them to reflect progressive conceptions of race and gender. As the market shifts, big romance publishers have also shifted priorities, putting out books by increasingly diverse writers who have become more creative—and more feminist—in their storytelling. While many modern romance novelists do meticulous research for their historicals, they're also not afraid to imagine a more inclusive past. Writers such as Adriana Herrera, Cat Sebastian, and Alexis Hall have written queer historicals, for instance, and even Netflix's *Bridgerton* imagines a racially diverse *ton* in a fantasy Regency Britain.

Lost Cause romances no longer fit in the world of mainstream historicals. But they're far from gone—they've just adapted. While they may no longer be published by major romance presses, the inheritors of the plantation romance continue to live on in inspirational historicals, a thriving subgenre of evangelical Christian novels.

Inspirational historical romances are published by Christian publishing houses and marketed to conservative religious readers who prefer to read about American history. Key to the plot of an inspirational is the conversion experience, where a hero is brought to Christ by the moralizing influence of his ladylove. In stark contrast to the bodice-ripper, they don't include sex scenes. Lest they be accused of transparent white supremacy, though, Civil War inspirationals—which almost always take place in the South and are written by white Southern women—have to tread carefully when it comes to slavery. A common solution, as demonstrated by Seth's conversion in *The Planter's Daughter*, is to use slavery as the reason for the hero's conversion. Tamera Alexander, a prolific inspirational historical romance novelist, has also written several Civil War romances since 2011 that follow this narrative. *With This Pledge* (2019) is set at the Carnton Plantation near Nashville, Tennessee, and tells the story of Lizzie Clouston, a governess for the wealthy McGavock family. When the Battle of Franklin turns Carnton into a Confederate field hospital, Lizzie becomes a nurse and encounters Roland Ward Jones, a Confederate sharpshooter, who asks Lizzie to help ensure the surgeon does not amputate his wounded leg. Roland gets to keep his leg, and later Lizzie comes to his rescue again when she convinces U.S. Army officers to let the most severely wounded soldiers stay at Carnton to stabilize instead of going to Federal prison camps. Over the following weeks, Lizzie becomes the angel of the hospital, caring for the wounded men, ministering to her young charges, and, of course, falling in love with Roland. But Roland is a slaver and Lizzie is a closet abolitionist. When Lizzie undertakes a plan to educate two enslaved people, Roland's angry arguments against educating the enslaved seem taken directly from Southern slavery apologists. After another disagreement with Lizzie about slavery and the Confederate cause, Roland has a spiritual crisis resulting in his conversion. It's only when Roland accepts Jesus and reconciles himself to the immorality of slavery that he and Lizzie are finally united.

Just like turn-of-the-century plantation romances, the novel leans heavily on the Lost Cause trope of the loyal slave and never addresses the fact that the Confederate soldiers suffering in the halls of the Carnton mansion had put their lives on the line to protect slavery. Instead, Alexander repeatedly emphasizes the tragedy of the Confederate loss. In one scene, Roland weeps while he listens to the Battle of Franklin rage outside the mansion, needing to "remember what the Confederacy sounded like in its final moments."[28] Lizzie is the book's moral compass, yet she is only secretly antislavery while living with, working for, and falling in love with slave owners. The purpose of this plot isn't to convince the reader of the immorality of human bondage but rather to set up the Christian redemption narrative Alexander is building for

Roland. Even in marketing materials, Alexander hedges. In a supplemental essay intended to guide book club discussions, Alexander writes that "transatlantic slavery was an abhorrent evil."[29] That is undoubtedly true, but it's also a misdirection. By the time the novel takes place, the transatlantic slave trade had been banned in the United States for over fifty years. The domestic slave trade, the American institution of race-based chattel slavery, and white supremacy go unmentioned. Instead, Alexander follows this definitive statement on the transatlantic slave trade with another statement: "yet there is more slavery in the world today than in the 19th century," a reference to the human trafficking "epidemic" that has been repeatedly debunked as a conservative, evangelical moral panic with links to QAnon.[30]

Michelle Shocklee also uses enslaved characters in *The Planter's Daughter* to help drive the development of the white hero and heroine. At first glance, the novel might seem to turn the traditional plantation romance on its head: The hero and heroine turn against slavery, rather than shoring up the Southern patriarchal, white supremacist social order. But ultimately Adella and Seth do nothing to challenge the status quo. The enslaved are a foil for Seth's moral development and proof of Adella's inherent virtue. As is common in inspirational historicals by white authors, the Black characters, including Jeptha, are all written as speaking in dialect throughout the novel. As the group prepares to flee to Mexico, Jeptha eloquently thanks Adella and Seth for his (fraudulent) freedom papers, his speech written without dialect for the first time. When his enslaved friends ask how he learned to speak so beautifully, Jeptha responds, gesturing to Adella: "I had a good teacher."[31] As with Roland in *With This Pledge*, Seth's religious conversion stems from the fact that his proslavery beliefs cause a conflict with the woman he hopes to marry. Shocklee goes out of her way to assure the reader that neither Seth nor Adella are abolitionists—indeed, when Seth asks Adella directly in a conversation about the injustices of slavery, she replies, "I honestly don't know what I am." Moments later, she admits she enjoys having enslaved Black women available to do her hair, though it's increasingly making her squeamish. Ultimately, Adella and Seth flee for Mexico for their own purposes, taking Jeptha and others as an afterthought, and while they turn against slavery, it's only for the well-behaved, Christian enslaved people closest to them.

Modern Civil War romances that do not carry water for the Lost Cause are few and far between. To use the era as a setting without reproducing problematic narratives, the writer must also recognize the harm inherent in elements that may have been mainstays of earlier novels—such as dialect in dialogue or enslavement as a plot driver for white character development—and proceed with caution and intention while playing with romance tropes. While inspirational romances largely recycle storylines from older, outdated romances, in order to appeal to mainstream audiences, authors must be creative, even radical, in their reimagining of potential characters, plots, and relationships.

Take for instance *The Haunting* (2007) by Hope Tarr, published in Harlequin's extra spicy Extreme Blaze series, in which Civil War historian Maggie Holliday purchases a historical home in Fredericksburg, Virginia, where she enjoys sexy encounters with the ghost of Federal officer Captain Ethan O'Malley in her attic. Or Jamila Jasper's *Confederate Runaway*, a self-published ebook in which Ellen, a free Black woman, nurses Elijah, a Confederate draftee who deserted at the Battle of Gettysburg. Jasper deftly uses Ellen's tough character and Elijah's disdain for the Confederate cause to satisfy a popular romance couple profile (known as BWWM, or Black woman, white man) without replicating harmful plotlines. Authors sometimes also include content notes assuring readers of their careful navigating of potential harms. Jasper, for instance, includes an opening "Content Awareness" note that reminds the reader that the romance between a free Black woman and white Confederate deserter "isn't intended to glorify negative power dynamics and oppression."[32]

The most innovative and commercially successful Civil War romances since the 1990s have been written by Black women. In the mid-1990s, pioneering Black romance novelist Beverly Jenkins challenged the existing tropes of historical romance with books about nineteenth-century Black Americans, many with direct experience with bondage. Though most of Jenkins's historicals are Westerns, *Night Song* (1994), *Indigo* (1996), and *Rebel* (2019) are set in the Civil War era. In *Indigo* heroine Hester Wyatt, herself purchased from bondage as a child, works as a station master on the Underground Railroad in Michigan on the eve of the war. Hester is part of a community of free Blacks, some formerly enslaved and some born free, who help usher fugitives to freedom and are active in the abolitionist movement. Hester's life is upended when she must nurse Galen Vachon, a conductor on the Underground Railroad nicknamed Black Daniel, back to health after he's wounded by slavecatchers.

Jenkins weaves together sensual romance with the painful realities of life for Black Americans in the late 1850s. Hester was sold away from her enslaved parents as a baby, and her hands and feet are permanently stained by the indigo she helped to process as an enslaved child. Hester's aunt Katherine, a pillar of the community who recently died, was in love with neighbor Branton Hubble for decades, but their relationship went unconsummated because Hubble would not betray his vows to his enslaved wife, sold into the Deep South decades before, never to be heard from again. Jenkins also allows for complexity. While most of the Black people in the small Michigan town are part of the effort to get fugitives to freedom, others are more invested in their own survival—at one point, Hester's home is ransacked and her freedom papers stolen by a vigilante Black man working for a slavecatcher.

Published just five years apart, *Indigo*'s ending is an interesting contrast to Graham's *One Wore Blue*, in which Kiernan and Jesse's relationship evolves during John Brown's trial in Harper's Ferry. *One Wore Blue* presents John Brown with ambivalence and dread, depicting the raid and trial as tragic events that tore the couple—and the country—apart. But Jenkins emphasizes what Brown's abolitionist work and execution meant to Black Americans: "Black abolitionists called the day Martyr Day. In northern cities all over America, the multiraced opponents of slavery paused to mourn his death. Black businesses were closed. Church bells were rung. Members of the race fasted and wore black armbands to the many services and rallies held in his honor. Hester and Galen joined Detroit's Black citizens for the memorial held at Second Baptist Church. The Detroiters passed a resolution declaring John Brown 'our temporal leader whose name will never die.'"[33] And while Brown's death is devastating, Jenkins ends *Indigo* with Black joy: Hester is reunited with her mother after decades apart, and lives happily with Galen, awaiting the birth of their first child at home in Michigan and continuing the work to end slavery.

Alyssa Cole, another Black author, followed in Beverly Jenkins's footsteps with Civil War romance series The Loyal League, published between 2017 and 2019. In the introduction to the first novel, *An Extraordinary Union*, Cole notes that the idea for the series was sparked by the work of Ta-Nehisi Coates, who blogged about the Civil War for *The Atlantic* during the early part of the Trump administration and the height of the controversy of Confederate iconography, situating her books within modern debates over Civil War memory. Cole also did her homework—she includes a selected bibliography including primary sources, such as *Narrative of the Life of Frederick Douglass*, as well as classic historical texts like James McPherson's *Battle Cry of Freedom*. Like Alexander, Cole draws her hero and heroine in *An Extraordinary Union* from real figures—but unlike Alexander, Cole was inspired by individuals who worked to bring down the Confederacy: Mary Bowser, a formerly enslaved woman who acted as a spy in the Confederate White House, and Timothy Webster, a Pinkerton agent and spy. Cole turns the plantation romance on its head, even dropping tongue-in-cheek references to Sir Walter Scott throughout.

Cole's novels feature richly developed characters with diverse backgrounds, all touched in some way by the horrors of slavery and upheaval of war. There are no redemption narratives for bad whites and no attempts to justify the inhumanity of enslavement. The first book, *An Extraordinary Union*, follows the formerly enslaved Elle who uses her race (and eidetic memory) to pose as a slave in the households of prominent Confederates to gather information for the Loyal League, a network of Black and white people across the country spying for the federal government. While on assignment in Richmond in the household of a Confederate senator, Elle meets Malcolm McCall, another Loyal League spy disguised as a Confederate soldier. Malcolm's abolitionism isn't explained as simple evidence of Christian morality as in many inspirational romances. Instead, his opposition to slavery is drawn from his family's painful experience during the Scottish highland clearances. But despite his family's history, Malcolm understands he doesn't know what it means to be enslaved and takes Elle's testimony seriously. Angry on Elle's behalf for the outrages of slavery, he asks her why Black Americans haven't "set the country ablaze" yet. Elle is frustrated that he doesn't understand not only why this isn't an option, but why it misses the point. She responds with angry despair: "Don't you see? This is our homeland, too. We shouldn't have to wreak havoc on the land to be seen as citizens! We shouldn't have to!"[34] In the end, Elle and Malcolm help a group escape bondage on a commandeered Confederate warship (inspired by the real-life story of Robert Smalls), survive several near-death misadventures, and of course, marry. In a final, delightful, and modern twist, after his identity is discovered by the Confederates, Malcolm takes Elle's last name upon their marriage.

Despite the path laid by Beverly Jenkins and Alyssa Cole, such innovative Civil War romances remain rare. The Civil War was a painful, complex civic rupture stemming from our nation's original sin, and its memory—including nearly two centuries of cultural products such as romantic novels—has provided the historical and intellectual infrastructure for over a century of political division and racial terror. While there is a long history of turning that deep wound into the setting for a romance, it's largely been a damaging history, one that has traded on old, white supremacist storylines that have kept the Lost Cause alive to readers into the modern day. And with the romance market booming in recent years, the potential for modern harm shouldn't be understated: With romance readership growing and audiences getting younger, Civil War romances like those written by Tamera Alexander and Michelle Shocklee have the potential to introduce new generations of readers to a Civil War memory that historians and activists has worked hard, and sacrificed much, to combat. And a quick glance at Goodreads or Amazon reviews on inspirational Civil War romances show that there's no small audience who believe that they present a wholesome and accurate version of American history. As plantation romances in the late nineteenth century served the architects of Lost Cause, modern inspirationals provide a cultural foundation for a worldview that refuses to acknowledge the reality of the American system of enslavement or its lasting legacies of modern structural racism and white supremacy.

Writing a Civil War romance that doesn't perpetuate historical falsehoods or undergird racist ideologies requires the historical literacy to navigate the tricky connections between history, memory, and mythology. But nearly as important is imagination: the capacity to dream up characters, relationships, and plot lines that are often silent in our archives, invisible in histories and nonexistent in traditional romance. As the sparkling romances by Jenkins, Cole, and others demonstrate, writing a great Civil War romance isn't impossible, and further, it can be done in ways that help to challenge readers' assumptions and push back against harmful abuses of history. As historical romance continues to enjoy its *Bridgerton* bump, perhaps more brave and innovative writers will take up arms and use love to fight the ongoing war against the Lost Cause.

NOTES

1. Shocklee, *Planter's Daughter*, 18.
2. There are likely some Civil War romances that don't appear on Goodreads, since it doesn't always capture self-published books. Romances are extremely popular on Kindle Unlimited, for instance, where short self-published romances are very common. These books, however, tend to quickly "go out of print" and become unavailable. For the shelves compared here, see "Regency Romance Books," Goodreads, https://www.goodreads.com/shelf/show/regency-romance; and Sarah Handley-Cousins, "Civil War Romances," Goodreads, https://www.goodreads.com/review/list/18179277-sarah-handley-cousins?ref=nav_mybooks&shelf=civil-war-romances.
3. Roxane Gay, "I Don't Want to Watch Slavery Fan Fiction," *New York Times*, July 25, 2017.
4. There is a third exception: Civil War romances are also available through Amazon's Kindle self-publishing and reading platform Kindle Unlimited, where romance novels are hugely

popular. Without editorial or publisher oversight, novelists who self-publish don't have to worry about the whims of the market or avoiding potentially problematic storylines and characters. As such, these books can vary wildly in quality and historical representation. In this chapter, I have chosen to concentrate largely on traditionally published novels.

5. Bever, "Paths to Reconciliation."
6. Censer, "Reimagining the North-South Romance," 66.
7. See Fick, "Genre Wars and Manhood"; Silber, *Romance of Reunion*; Blight, *Race and Reunion*; Appleby, "Reconciliation and the Northern Novelist."
8. See Dickey, *Tough Little Patch of History*.
9. The question of whether *Gone with the Wind* is a romance novel is still debated by scholars and readers. Romance critic Bonnie Loshbaugh notes that while the novel includes several tropes that are now very common in historical romances, it's missing the critical happily-ever-after ending. Ultimately, she argues that it is not a romance novel. Bonnie Lashbaugh, "Romance Tropes in *Gone with the Wind*," Romance MFA, April 9, 2018, www.romancemfa.com/romance-tropes-in-gone-with-the-wind/.
10. Regis, *Natural History of the Romance*.
11. Wyatt-Brown, "Evolution of Heroes' Honor," 996.
12. Page, *Red Rock*, vii–viii. For an analysis of the plantation romance, see Wells, *Romances of the White Man's Burden*.
13. Regis, *Natural History of the Romance*, 125.
14. Regis, *Natural History of the Romance*, 156–57.
15. Regis, *Natural History of the Romance*, 22.
16. "About the Romance Genre," Romance Writers of America, accessed May 27, 2025, https://www.rwa.org/the-romance-genre. In recent years, the RWA itself has been embroiled in criticism for its failure to recognize and condemn racism in the industry.
17. *Cold Mountain* is thus also disqualified, since Inman dies at the close of the book and Ada is left a widow. Weirdly, Dixon's *Leopard's Spots*—despite being odious—arguably still qualifies because Charlie Gaston and Sallie Worth are able to overcome obstacles in order to marry.
18. For a detailed analysis of *Gone with the Wind*'s legacy, see Dickey, *Tough Little Patch of History*.
19. Woodiwiss, *Ashes in the Wind*, 30–31.
20. Tropes, plot conventions that readers specifically seek out, such as "enemies to lovers," "forced proximity," or "secret identity," are an essential part of romance novel writing. All romance writers, but especially those that self-publish, use tropes to connect with readers and sell books.
21. Woodiwiss, *Ashes in the Wind*, 523.
22. Gallagher, *Mystic Rose*, 242.
23. Gallagher, *Mystic Rose*, 248.
24. Graham, *One Wore Blue*, 180.
25. Graham, *One Wore Blue*, 469.
26. @romancehistorian, Instagram, September 20, 2022, https://www.instagram.com/reel/CivNDmdALyZ/.
27. More generally, bodice-rippers are also criticized today for their rape plotlines and romanticization of dubious consent.
28. Alexander, *With This Pledge*, 265.

29. Tamera Alexander, "Truth or Fiction?" https://tameraalexander.com/WTP_TruthorFiction.pdf.
30. See Kaitlyn Tiffany, "The Great (Fake) Child-Sex-Trafficking Epidemic: Dispatches from Moral Panic," *The Atlantic*, December 9, 2021.
31. Shocklee, *Planter's Daughter*, 266.
32. Jasper, *Confederate Runaway*, 1.
33. Jenkins, *Indigo*, 348.
34. Cole, *Extraordinary Union*, 82.

BIBLIOGRAPHY

Alexander, Tamera. *With This Pledge*. Thomas Nelson, 2019.

Appleby, Joyce. "Reconciliation and the Northern Novelist, 1865-1880." *Civil War History* 10 (June 1964): 117-29.

Bever, Megan. "Paths to Reconciliation: Northern Intersectional Romances of the Civil War Era." *Civil War History* 60 (2014): 32-57.

Blight, David. *Race and Reunion: The Civil War in American Memory*. Harvard University Press, 2003.

Censer, Jane Turner. "Reimagining the North-South Romance: Southern Women Novelists and the Intersectional Romance, 1876-1900." *Southern Cultures* 5 (1999): 64-91.

Cole, Alyssa. *An Extraordinary Union*. Kensington, 2017.

Dickey, Jennifer W. *A Tough Little Patch of History: "Gone with the Wind" and the Politics of Memory*. University of Arkansas Press, 2014.

Dixon, Thomas, Jr. *The Leopard's Spots*. Doubleday, 1902.

Fick, Thomas. "Genre Wars and Manhood in *Miss Ravenel's Conversion from Secession to Loyalty*." *Nineteenth Century Literature* 46 (1992): 473-94.

Gallagher, Patricia. *Mystic Rose*. Avon, 1977.

Graham, Heather. *One Wore Blue*. Loveswept, 1991.

Jasper, Jamila. *Confederate Runaway*. Self-published, 2019.

Jenkins, Beverly. *Indigo*. Avon, 1996.

Page, Thomas Nelson. *Red Rock: A Chronicle of Reconstruction*. Charles Scribner's Sons, 1898.

Regis, Pamela. *A Natural History of the Romance Novel*. University of Pennsylvania Press, 2007.

Shocklee, Michelle. *The Planter's Daughter*. Lighthouse Publishing of the Carolinas, 2017.

Silber, Nina. *The Romance of Reunion: Northerners and the South, 1865-1900*. University of North Carolina Press, 1993.

Wells, Jeremy. *Romances of the White Man's Burden: Race, Empire, and the Plantation in American Literature, 1880-1930*. Vanderbilt University Press, 2011.

Woodiwiss, Kathleen. *Ashes in the Wind*. Avon, 1979.

Wyatt-Brown, Bertram. "The Evolution of Heroes' Honor in the Southern Literary Tradition." *Georgia Review* 40 (Winter 1986): 990-1007.

8

Dixie Chic

Hoodies and Embodying Confederate Exceptionalism

NICOLE MAURANTONIO

The 2013 acquittal of seventeen-year-old Trayvon Martin's murderer is the oft-cited birth of the Black Lives Matter movement, igniting national and international efforts to highlight the racism, discrimination, and inequities experienced by Black and Brown people in the United States.[1] At the center of this story of a burgeoning twenty-first-century activist movement lies a complicated, albeit mundane, garment: the hoodie. Publicly vilified by media personality Geraldo Rivera, who claimed that "the hoodie is as much responsible for Trayvon Martin's death as George Zimmerman was," the hoodie became an object of intense national debate following Martin's death.[2]

For Rivera and others, the Black teen Martin had embraced a "part of a larger negative trend in young people's fashion: dressing like criminals and thugs."[3] Yet, as sociologists Erynn Masi de Casanova and Curtis Webb demonstrate, the garment's meanings have been shown to shift with the identity of its wearer. Invoking popularly circulating images of Facebook founder Mark Zuckerberg, "the social network's hoodie-wearing head honcho," de Casanova and Webb note that for Zuckerberg, a white man, the hoodie was the consummate marker of the "mystique of youth and coolness."[4] While de Casanova and Webb tell a "tale of two hoodies"—a "sign of social deviance" feared in one instance and admired in another—this chapter attempts to delve further into the racial, class, and gender dynamics underpinning this powerful garment by suggesting yet another story.

While the proliferation of consumer goods bearing symbols of the Confederacy—the Battle Flag most prominent among them—is by no means a new trend,[5] the choice of artifacts that appropriate Confederate symbols nonetheless deserves closer scrutiny. Contemporary T-shirts displaying the Stars and Bars and embracing rebellion as a source of aesthetic pride in Southern culture should not surprise, given the T-shirt's history as a canvas for political performance and public memory.⁶ Neo-Confederates', and particularly neo-Confederate women's, use of the hoodie, however, might seem a less natural extension of their propaganda efforts, given the garment's associations with Black criminality that echo in Rivera's words. This chapter considers this apparent dissonance by exploring how neo-Confederates transformed a garment allegedly worn by fearsome criminals into a cornerstone of a white supremacist aesthetic.

Taking as its point of departure a collection of hoodies sold under the moniker Simply Dixie through the Myrtle Beach, South Carolina–based online retailer the Dixie Shop, this chapter explores how a seemingly innocuous set of memory objects, hoodies, works to strategically forget history by embracing a color palette, set of fonts, and imagery designed to soften the stereotype of the Confederate "Rebel." Bestowing their mythical power on their wearer, Simply Dixie's hoodies work to dilute the realities of the Confederacy, submerging its connection to the history and legacies of enslavement. The hoodie, de Casanova and Webb note, "is not just good for covering up a bad hair day. It hides much more than flesh and face. The hoodie—and the debates over who should wear one and where—can reveal or conceal how power works, who has it and who doesn't."⁷ Building on this argument, this chapter considers how the fraught symbol is used in subtle yet powerful ways to normalize the Confederacy in the present through seemingly benign and playful appeals to fashion—to center whiteness and a specific feminized and elite version at that.

This chapter presents fashion as a form of communication and purveyor of memory, invested with symbolic and material meanings placing particular emphasis on the hoodie and its history. It continues by unpacking the meaning of "Dixie," with which the clothing line is associated. It next explores the Simply Dixie line specifically, analyzing its garments' colors, font, and icons as they attempt to make the (neo-)Confederacy simultaneously legible, trendy, and welcoming as a contemporary community among women. This chapter concludes by considering the larger implications of Simply Dixie's rhetorical move in a twenty-first-century context where the Confederacy and its attendant legacies are centered in public conversations surrounding race, racism, and the nation's reckoning with the past.

Fashion as Rhetoric

Clothing is associated with warmth and protection, modesty and concealment, immodesty and attraction, as it communicates cultural messages that are not only individualistic but also social, political, and economic.[8] Such associations are rooted in both form and function. In short, clothes, sociologist Joanne Finkelstein notes, "can . . . suggest, persuade, connote, insinuate, or indeed, lie," and as such are potent rhetorical artifacts.[9] Throughout history, what one wears, or doesn't, has been understood as an expression of occupation, regional identity, religion, and social class.[10]

These expressions have become all the more complicated in the twentieth and twenty-first centuries, given, as sociologist Diana Crane notes, "the increasing importance of fashion worlds in other countries, of fashion leaders in media culture, and of subcultures centered on leisure activities."[11] Far from a "mandate" that leaves some "victims," fashion is a choice used to construct an identity.[12] The recognition of fashion as a choice has meant that fashion and clothing are used, visual culture scholar Malcolm Barnard argues, "not only to constitute and communicate a position in [a] social order, but also to challenge and contest positions of relative power within it."[13] Skinheads are among the most visible groups where this shift in power can be witnessed. A movement initially tied to the Jamaican Rudeboys and ska music within working-class communities, skinheads were, at the time of their origins in the 1960s, a largely apolitical movement. The rise of white power skinheads throughout the 1970s, however, led to a shift in the association of the skinhead with racism and neo-Nazism, mapping onto their iconic dress: polo shirts of the Ben Sherman and Fred Perry variety, MA-1 flight jackets, and Doc Marten boots.

This association was made once again when white nationalists stormed the city of Charlottesville, Virginia, in August 2017 donning polo shirts, connecting the staple of the American prep uniform with historical exclusionary practices among predominantly elite white men. As fashion editor Robin Givhan noted, the Charlottesville marchers reminded that "just like polo shirts, racism, white nationalism, and KKK rallies are as American as apple pie."[14] The purportedly "wholesome" Americanness communicated by the prep aesthetic was exposed as a fraud. While the polo shirt's antisemitic history might seem to align quite obviously with the ideologies espoused by white supremacists, the polo shirt's history is not so politically linear. Adopted and adapted in the 1990s by rappers and hip-hop artists, the oversized polo was appropriated and reappropriated, eventually becoming connected to cultures its originators sought to oppress.[15]

The subversive power of garments has received perhaps greatest attention, however, where the T-shirt is concerned. In the wake of the Second World

Fig. 8.1. Members of the alt-right prepare to enter Emancipation Park at the Unite the Right Rally in Charlottesville, Virginia, on August 12, 2017. In addition to waving swastikas, Confederate battle flags, and Gadsden "Don't Tread on Me" standards, many of the participants sported a tacti-prep uniform of khakis, polo shirts, and tactical backpacks. Anthony Crider from USA, CC BY 2.0, https://creativecommons.org/licenses/by/2.0, via Wikimedia Commons.

War, the T-shirt, formerly a masculinist icon linked to patriotism and military prowess, came to stand in for "a quintessentially American mode of dress and expression"—"an emblem of individualism, a marker of identity, a space for free expression," serving as a canvas of sorts.[16] Known at once for its accessibility and ubiquity as a communication technology, the T-shirt embodies a series of tensions, between homogeneity and difference, and individualism and conformity.[17] Like the T-shirt, the hoodie holds liberatory as well as oppressive possibilities.

The sweatshirt found currency with college co-eds in the 1960s, who seized on the garment as a site to sport university pride, and the hoodie has a similarly long history. First marketed by Champion Athletic Wear for football players to use on the sidelines, the hoodie was an offshoot of the collarless, long-sleeved sweatshirt, whose origins are traced to 1925. Defined as oversized pullovers made of thick fleecy cotton, which "possessed the functional ability to induce and absorb sweat during exercise," sweatshirts had a wholly functional use: keeping their wearers warm.[18]

Embraced by surfers for its ability to keep one warm upon exiting the ocean, the hoodie was later appropriated by skateboarders and other extreme sport enthusiasts, who used the garment for another practical purpose: as a layer of cushion between the body and the pavement.[19] Like the T-shirt and polo before it, the hoodie was also adopted within the sphere of hip-hop, particularly within the 1970s and 1980s, Barnard notes, where the garment was "seen as a challenge to mainstream white middle-class styles. Young, ghetto-based black youth used fashion and music to challenge dominant white, middle-class ideologies."[20]

Beyond providing a medium to interrogate race, the hoodie is, too, a site to explore issues of gender and class. While historically a predominantly masculine artifact, the hoodie has been identified as a staple item for women, "a must-have in every wardrobe,"[21] due to its comfort, versatility, and adaptability to the latest in fashion trends. Hoodies can be classic or edgy, oversized or cropped. Like T-shirts, they can serve as a canvas for further expression through graphics printing. While the phrase "hoodie" might not have entered the popular lexicon until the 1990s, "locker room chic," inspired by designer Norma Kamali in the 1970s and early 1980s, was undoubtedly a style mainstay decades earlier.

The hoodie can range in cost from twenty dollars to thousands, whether purchased from a big box store or sold as haute couture. In sum, "The sweatshirt's ability to transcend its athletic origins by becoming both an influential component of sportswear and an element of various subcultural dress, testifies to its importance in fashion; furthermore, the fashion system's innate ability to recycle pre-existing motifs guarantees that the sweatshirt will evolve for years to come."[22] The hoodie's history of function and fashion, consensus and cultural disruption, makes it a profound artifact.

"Selling Dixie"

The Simply Dixie hoodies sold by the Dixie Shop cost between $25 and $30, depending on the size of the garment (i.e., whether it is a child's or adult's). Hardly commanding the prices of luxury brands like Balenciaga, the Dixie Shop as a retailer and Simply Dixie as a brand are accessible, capitalizing on their distinctly Southern identity and a tone of play. With advertising that shares a love for "exercising our first amendment right," the Dixie Shop includes a social media presence that is unabashed in its loyalty to the (neo-) Confederacy. Encouraging consumers to #GetYaDixieOn, the Dixie Shop sells a range of wares that feature the Confederate battle flag, from boxers and bikinis to onesies and wallets, with not even the slightest indication of the symbol's contentious nature.

Material objects aside, the retailer's decision to embrace the nomenclature of "Dixie" is not coincidental. If the South is a region, Dixie became, in the early twentieth century, a brand, incorporating "the mythology and traditions of the southern past," as historian Karen Cox notes.[23] Linked to Daniel Decatur Emmett's 1859 minstrel song of the same name, "Dixie" became a popular marching song for the Confederate army, and as such the unofficial anthem of the Confederacy.[24] According to historian Tammy Ingram, "By the time Dixie made it into minstrel shows, it was clearly understood to be more than just a place name. 'Dixie' was the antebellum South, and the lyrics evoke a very nostalgic and romanticized view of slavery."[25] While the origins of the song and term are difficult to ascertain, the label is nonetheless "indivisible from Black slaves and those grand plantations where they were forced to toil for free."[26] This romanticized South was one of Southern belles, cotton plantations, and happy slaves laboring in the fields, bearing little resemblance to the realities of life under the brutal institution. Part of the score of *The Birth of a Nation*, which bolstered the rise of the Ku Klux Klan, "Dixie" has been a significant part of popular culture, a notable car horn in the television show *The Dukes of Hazzard* (1979–85), and a rallying cry for aficionados of the University of Mississippi's sports teams, to name just a couple of examples.[27]

In recent years, a number of musicians and retailers have gone to great lengths to distance themselves from the term "Dixie" and the mythologized history it invokes—but not the Dixie Shop. If anything, the retailer has doubled down in the wake of the protests of 2020, continuing to use the Confederate battle flag on its home logo. Visitors to the site can purchase Confederate battle flags proclaiming "My Heritage Our History" and "I Ain't Coming Down," a less-than-subtle rejoinder to critics. Confederate battle flag belt buckles, board shorts, toothpicks, and charm necklaces are among the purchasable souvenirs. The Dixie Shop also sells a range of objects aimed at supporters of Donald Trump, reminding us that the "Dixie" iconography is a referent to both past and present.

Beyond displaying Confederate battle flags, garments sold under the Simply Dixie umbrella embrace an aesthetic designed to conflate the Confederacy with Americanness, manifesting what I have in other venues described as

"Confederate exceptionalism."[28] Fusing elements of Lost Cause ideology and American exceptionalism, the myth of Confederate exceptionalism nostalgically remembers "the South" through an amalgam of embodied and textual practices that alternately embrace and revise the Confederacy's racial history.[29] The outcome, I suggest, like antiracialism, "is whiteness by another name, by other means, with recruitment of people of color to act as public spokespersons for the cause."[30]

Confederate exceptionalism seeks to mask the perniciousness of slavery and racism with appeals to normalcy. Consumerism is, of course, one of the cornerstones of this approach. In this way, the Confederacy is equated with a certain, ostensibly benign, "Southern" aesthetic. According to the popular *Southern Living* magazine, "Southern style" is "classic elegance, bold and bubbly, modern, monogrammed simplicity. . . . Southern style is wearing a tailored dress or bow tie to the grocery store. Southern style is seersucker and gingham, eyelet and linen, and loving your signature scent. Southern style is dressing up your school colors. Southern style is channeling the best of the South—the culture, the people, the history—and wearing your look with pride."[31] This is, of course, a reductive distillation of regional style that captures a particular subset of Southerners who literally buy into this fiction. While the hoodies of the Simply Dixie line may not embrace all elements of this aesthetic, I argue that Confederate exceptionalism is articulated materially through the retailer's hoodies in three ways: the colors, the font, and icons, which work to center the Confederacy as not a defunct entity but rather one very much alive, manifest in an aesthetic that embraces play, patriotism, and a certain DIY culture to instill a sense of accessibility, presentness, and community.

The Colors

Visitors to the Simply Dixie merchandise section of the Dixie Shop will immediately confront a color palette distinctively softer than the Confederacy's bright and vibrant red, white, and blue. Instead, Simply Dixie is characterized by a palette of soft pastels—pinks, blues, and greens. If brands understand that "darker colors are symbolic of more 'respectable' products—that pastel colors mean softness, youthfulness, femininity, that yellows and browns are manly, [and] that red is exciting and provocative"—Simply Dixie has selected a palette that embraces this youthful femininity.[32] It is thus little surprise that the sweatshirts are not advertised explicitly in the sections tagged for men. When considering pastels, words like "serene, calm and ease pop up very frequently."³³ It is much easier to receive these colors generously, which, due to their lightness, are easier to miss than the primary colors one might otherwise expect to see in contexts where the palette of the Confederate battle flag is on display.

In some ways, such a move (eschewing the red, white, and blue) might appear antithetical to the staunch chauvinism espoused by (neo-)Confederates. Perhaps even more dissonant might be the embrace of a palette that once made Democrats the object of derision. One need only recall Republican keynote speaker Governor Tom Kean of New Jersey, who mocked Democrats' "pastel patriotism," claiming it would weaken the nation.³⁴ This color palette is, after all, known to communicate a "girly," sweet, and vulnerable sensibility, save for the "pastel goth" trend, which disrupts this somewhat by mixing goth and grunge. Yet the association of the nonthreatening feminine works strategically with the historical rhetorics deployed by Confederate heritage organizations like the United Daughters of the Confederacy, which at the turn of the twentieth century embraced the image of the "Southern lady," a conservative woman whose primary responsibility was to uphold gender hierarchies and elevate the myth of Southern manhood.³⁵

Simply Dixie is not the only clothing brand to use pastel colors to sell "Southernness." North Carolina–based apparel brand Simply Southern also relies on a decidedly feminine palette to paint an idealized (and highly simplified) vision of Southern culture.³⁶ According to founder Ginger Aydogdu, Simply Southern "is not just a brand but a lifestyle that customers, friends, and followers connect with for a happy, preppy, and classy existence." Aydogdu allegedly chose her company's name "to reflect the values of a southern lifestyle, where things run a little slower and you are always there to help your neighbor."³⁷ This communal sentiment is warm and welcoming, similar to Aydogdu's description of her company's vision for "loving the blessings we are so privileged to enjoy."³⁸ Simply Southern is a brand anchored in a deep gratitude, with the company's logo featuring a turtle, a gesture to Simply Southern's conservancy partner. Their "Simply Faithful" label donates money to ChildFund International. Taken together, Simply Southern embraces a color palette that is meant to evoke care and community as distinctive regional traits of which Southerners should be proud. It is also a brand that is itself an American "rags to riches" story, beginning as a small apparel kiosk in a mall, growing to now be sold by more than six thousand independent retailers. Simply Southern owns twenty-seven retail stores in twelve states, including Ohio and Delaware.³⁹

The expansion of the Simply Southern brand to states that extend beyond the geographic borders of the South points to the ways in which an imagined "Southern" aesthetic is both appealing and profitable. The brand captures a sentiment that is embraced and accessible, facilitating a strategic forgetting, if altogether erasure, of the less desirable elements of regional identity.[40]

By reusing Simply Southern's color palette, Simply Dixie capitalizes on an aesthetic that normalizes the Confederacy as part of a "look" that is not only mainstream but "trendy" and, at least nominally, altruistic. While the hoodies don't adhere to the price point of more high-end, haute couture brands, they are designed to mimic a Lilly Pulitzer look, defined by colorful printed cotton pinks, greens, yellows, and oranges that have become synonymous with American resort wear since the Palm Beach, Florida, hostess first launched her designs in the 1950s.[41] Pulitzer designs, her website boasts, "have been beloved for their casual glamour, vibrant optimism, and endlessly joyful spirit."[42] Simply Southern invokes a similar sentiment, upon which the Simply Dixie line shamelessly builds in an effort to soften the Confederacy, buoying it with an ahistorical optimism and casual joy.

The Font

The Simply Dixie sweatshirts, like the Simply Southern brand, use a variety of fonts across their hoodies, which signal the retailer's appeals to both past and present. While meant to communicate text—*content*—fonts, too, "can evoke a wide range of emotions, depending on their design characteristics." From "elegance and sophistication" to "strength and power" to "friendliness and warmth," the selected font can share a strong sentiment.[43] Simply Dixie does not adhere to a singular design aesthetic where fonts are concerned. Rather, the brand incorporates several different fonts, the range of which speaks to the line's efforts to toggle alternately between past and present.

Some Simply Dixie designs use a serif font—a type used to provide "a feeling of elegance, confidence, and trustworth[iness]. This usually makes them a good fit for companies who want to appear more reputable, established, and serious."[44] Others employ sans serif fonts, which are typically used to present a more decidedly modern and clean-looking aesthetic. One hoodie employs script, which is "considered personal and elegant as the general look itself promotes a dedicated approach and familiarity."[45] Taken together, Simply Dixie's use of fonts contribute to its aim of selling a "Dixie" shorn of its racist connotations. Coupling a "friendlier," more accessible font with a soft pastel color, Simply Dixie hoodies hearken to the Confederacy in a manner that divorces them from a less pleasant reality—the intimate connection to the history of slavery and its attendant legacies. While the use of both serif and sans serif fonts might signal a lack of brand identity—an imprecise set of goals and values—in this case, the typeface bricolage helps to establish Simply Dixie as an adaptable and not especially rigid brand, where one might as easily connect with the past as present, or delight in a classical aesthetic as well as a trendier one. Such a chameleonic identity serves Simply Dixie, making its core values difficult to pin down, offering a strategic and alluring ambiguity.

The resonances of Simply Dixie to the consumer familiar with Vineyard Vines, and controversially Simply Southern, are also impossible to miss. In 2018 Vineyard Vines filed a suit against the Greensboro, North Carolina–based Dazzle Up, claiming that Simply Southern's T-shirts bore an illegal resemblance—namely the use of a lower-cased serif font with lettering set against a pink backdrop with a white border.[46] As the *Chicago Tribune* has noted, Vineyard Vines' pink might be a shade or two darker, but the general aesthetic is pretty much the same. While the aesthetic similarities are unmistakable, what accompanies the clothing is a reminiscent ethos. Reflecting on the philosophy of the New England retailer, a purveyor of "preppy chic," brothers Shep and Ian Murray note, "We make ties so we don't have to wear them," leaning into their "image as freewheeling fun lovers less interested in money than barbecues and beer."[47] Known for whimsical ties sold out of their Jeep, the brothers envisioned Vineyard Vines as more than a clothier. It would be a lifestyle brand. Simply Southern and Simply Dixie leverage the successes of Vineyard Vines, creating a sort of Southern analog that trades in a "live in the now" sentiment, largely eschewing the past. This is a rhetorical strategy that works especially well when the past in question is a deeply problematic and difficult one.

The Icons

The Simply Dixie collection not only displays pastel colors against an array of font types but also embraces a series of seemingly disparate icons—deer, pigs, dogs, palmetto trees, mason jars, and, of course, the Confederate battle flag—that each hearken, in different ways, to a distinctively Southern aesthetic. These icons, too, gesture to Simply Southern's apparel, which regularly features "evocative southern iconography (bow ties, bird dogs, ducks, magnolias, etc.) the way Vineyard Vines traffics in Coastal New England iconography."[48]

While the mason jar might seem an icon out of place when thinking about the neo-Confederacy, the product's use makes it an especially powerful image for neo-Confederates to embrace in Simply Dixie's collection. Linked with farming culture, where goods were often pickled and jams made, mason jars are objects associated with thrift and preservation in American production. The most famous of the mason jar's manufacturers, the Ball Corporation, prints "Made in the U.S.A." near the bottom of each jar. They are thus, in essence, a quintessential "American" product both in terms of site of production as well as encapsulation of allegedly American values. For neo-Confederates, who argue that the Confederacy serves as the purest form of Americanism, the mason jar is more than an object used to store foods and keep them from spoiling. It is a marker of American antimaterialism and DIY culture that has, in recent years, seen a resurgence.

As freelance writer Ariana Kelly argues in *The Atlantic*, mason jars "suggest resistance to the mass production of food and culture; they emphasize the values of self-sufficiency and community."[49] These values are communicated in the various ways in which the mason jar's life has assumed a place outside food storage alone. Mason jars have become "oil lanterns, soap dispensers, terrariums, drinking glasses, speakers, vases, and snow globes," as just a few examples. At the same time, as a *Gawker* piece reflecting on news of 7-Eleven's decision to sell Slurpees out of mason jars reminds us, the mason jar is seen as the province of varied constituents: "hipsters, foodies, southern, weed growers, rednecks," and as such is seen as part of the frontier of gentrification.[50]

Beyond an embrace of the mason jar as an icon, Simply Dixie has paired the image, which, like all other products sold by the retailer, includes a Confederate battle flag, with an anchor. By taking an icon that has become virtually synonymous with the seafaring communities of New England and aligning it with the Confederate battle flag, Simply Dixie attempts to equate the regional identities in such a way as to amplify not only the so-called Americanness of "Dixie" but its ahistoricity.[51]

Unlike the mason jar, the pig's connections to "the South" and Southern heritage are more direct, with links to history, culture, and foodways that affirm and display a sense of pride in so-called Southern values. As historian Laura Dove notes, "Barbecue, like the recent 'chic' of the redneck, embraces the humble origins of Southern foodways. In the South, there is a tendency to glorify defeat and privation, and this is amply demonstrated in the popularity of barbecue. Pigs are smelly, slothful, and unattractive, but pigs are Southern."[52]

This pride in the Southern pig makes it a logo of note for a number of Southern-themed retailers, who embrace the animal to mark regional identity. Pink Pig apparel, based in Memphis, Tennessee, proclaims a love of barbecue and a desire to represent the "true self."[53] This "self," the online retailer admits, "do[es] not know anyone who plays polo, has seen a whale, caught and kept a bony fish or even wants to be close to a crocodile."[54] With this less-than-subtle jab at Ralph Lauren, Vineyard Vines, and Lacoste, mainstays of the American prep aesthetic with visible ties to the Northeast and Martha's Vineyard in particular, Pink Pig encourages its customers to "wear your pink pig with pride." While Southern Trend Clothing, a Fayetteville, Arkansas–based retailer, has similarly embraced the pig in its logo, the retailer emphasizes the diverse backgrounds of its customers: "From the trendsetters, to the outdoors men, and of course the sports lover; our products are designed to represent your favorite interests in a fresh, fashionable way."[55] Given Fayetteville's status as home to the University of Arkansas Razorbacks, a local affinity for the pig should be little surprise. Dallas-based Impeccable Pig's website proclaims that the retailer "prides itself on extending a family-like atmosphere to each customer. This means providing exceptional customer service and a personalized shopping experience."[56] "Family-like" is another descriptor intended to lean into community as a "Southern" value. The Maryland-based clothing retailer Live Oak Brand, a not-so-subtle nod to the iconic tree of the South, advertises a T-shirt that reads "Go pig or go home!" The warm embrace of the pig as a marker of regional pride and identity further distances the former Confederacy from its history by eliding the distinctions between the Confederacy and "the South."

If customers opt not to purchase a hoodie prominently displaying a pig, they can instead buy a hoodie featuring a dog. While there may not be something distinctly "Southern" about a dog, there is something distinctly American about one. The Black Dog company has become an icon of American prep. Tied to a historical dog owned by a seafaring captain, Black Dog is a Martha's Vineyard–based brand with locations scattered across New England but clustered along the eastern shoreline. Much like the popular Vineyard Vines brand, Black Dog hearkens to an equally preppy aesthetic.[57] Again, the dog's symbolism gestures much more to the region than to the Confederacy explicitly, even though the dog on display bears the Stars and Bars along its body. Yet with its cool pastels and accessible font, the dog, which might once have appeared potentially menacing, is playful. By extension, the Confederacy communicates a similar sense of play and ease. The sweatshirt hardly appears an embattled emblem.

Finally, customers can purchase a hoodie featuring the Sabal palmetto, South Carolina's state tree. While the image is recognizable as a likeness printed on the state flag, it is intended to connote peace and calm. Of the sweatshirts, this is perhaps the most potentially menacing, as the words "SIMPLY DIXIE" are boldest here and fairly difficult to miss. Yet, with the tree's trunk neatly wrapped in a bow, there is little to threaten the viewer.

Dixie Chic

In its line of hoodies, Simply Dixie has appropriated a garment vilified as a marker of Black men's criminality, as was observed in the wake of the murder of Black teen Trayvon Martin in 2012. Embracing a color palette, set of fonts, and imagery designed to soften the stereotype of the Confederate Rebel, Simply Dixie enables the Confederacy to creep into the twenty-first-century woman's closet in a way that underplays the perniciousness of Confederate ideologies and their attendant racism. Capitalizing on the popularity of New England retailers like Vineyard Vines and Black Dog, Simply Dixie's hoodies and T-shirts proffer a narrative of the Confederacy's accessibility, presentness, and community that fails to engage in any meaningful way with its legacies. Rather, like the white supremacists in Charlottesville in August 2017 who donned Fred Perry's eponymous polo shirt, Simply Dixie's wearers attempt to perform respectability through a fashion choice that is, at least in the case of the hoodie, casual and mundane. In this way, the Simply Dixie line reminds powerfully of the way in which the Confederacy lives not only in hearts and minds but in closets and on bodies.

NOTES

1. "About," Black Lives Matter, accessed October 9, 2023, https://blacklivesmatter.com/about/.
2. Rowley, "'It Could Have Been Me,'" 521.
3. de Casanova and Webb, "Tale of Two Hoodies."
4. de Casanova and Webb, "Tale of Two Hoodies," 119.
5. Artist Sonya Clark documented the appropriation of the Confederate flag in propaganda as part of her *Monumental Cloth* exhibit. For more on the exhibit, see Arielle Gray, "Sonya Clark Unravels American Propaganda in 'Monumental Cloth,'" WBUR, April 26, 2021. See also Coski, *Confederate Battle Flag*.
6. Neal, "Ideal Democratic Apparel."
7. de Casanova and Webb, "Tale of Two Hoodies," 121.
8. Barnard, *Fashion as Communication*, 51–63.
9. Finkelstein, *Fashioned Self*, 22.

10. Crane, *Fashion and Its Social Agendas*, 1.
11. Crane, *Fashion and Its Social Agendas*, 15.
12. Crane, *Fashion and Its Social Agendas*, 15.
13. Barnard, *Fashion as Communication*, 41.
14. Jared Michael Lowe, "How Polo Shirts Became a White Supremacist Uniform," *Teen Vogue*, August 29, 2017, https://www.teenvogue.com/story/polo-shirts-white-supremacist-white-nationalist-charlottesville-uniform.
15. Chavie Lieber, "Charlottesville White Supremacists Missed the Jewish Connection to Their Polos," *Racked*, August 16, 2017, https://www.racked.com/2017/8/16/16157838/charlottesville-white-supremacists-polo-shirts-jews.
16. Neal, "Ideal Democratic Apparel," 187.
17. Penney, "Eminently Visible"; and Neal, "Ideal Democratic Apparel," 201.
18. Park, "Sweatshirt."
19. Park, "Sweatshirt," 246.
20. Barnard, *Fashion as Communication*, 45.
21. Tarefaantf, "The History and Evolution of Hoodies for Women," *Medium*, November 3, 2023, https://medium.com/@tarefaantf/the-history-and-evolution-of-hoodies-for-women-14c0921b4c3c.
22. Park, "Sweatshirt," 247.
23. Cox, *Dreaming of Dixie*, 51.
24. Alaa Elassar, "How the Term 'Dixie' Came to Define the South," CNN, June 27, 2020, https://www.cnn.com/2020/06/27/us/dixie-term-south-racism-black-lives-matter-trnd/index.html.
25. Cited in Elassar, "How the Term 'Dixie.'" See also Cobb, *Away Down South*.
26. Cited in Ben Zimmer, "What *Dixie* Really Means," *The Atlantic*, June 26, 2020, https://www.theatlantic.com/culture/archive/2020/06/what-dixie-really-means/613585/.
27. Bilal Qureshi, "The Anthemic Allure of 'Dixie,' an Enduring Confederate Monument," NPR, September 20, 2018, https://www.npr.org/2018/09/20/649954248/the-anthemic-allure-of-dixie-an-enduring-confederate-monument.
28. Maurantonio, *Confederate Exceptionalism*.
29. Maurantonio, *Confederate Exceptionalism*, 2.
30. Maurantonio, *Confederate Exceptionalism*, 3.
31. "Fashion," *Southern Living*, accessed October 9, 2023, https://www.southernliving.com/fashion-beauty/southern-fashion.
32. Levy, "Symbols by Which We Buy," 434.
33. "How Pastels Become a Cultural Obsession," *Exposed Mag*, August 24, 2020, https://www.exposedmagazine.co.uk/features/how-pastels-become-a-cultural-obsession/.
34. David Greenberg, "How the Republicans Claimed the 'Patriotism' Mantle in Presidential Politics," *Slate*, July 2, 2008, https://slate.com/news-and-politics/2008/07/how-the-republicans-claimed-the-patriotism-mantle-in-presidential-politics.html.
35. Heyse, "Women's Rhetorical Authority."
36. "What Is Simply Southern?" Simply Southern, accessed October 9, 2023, https://simplysouthern.com/our-story/.
37. "Simply Southern Vision," Simply Southern Wholesale, accessed October 9, 2023, https://simplysouthernwholesale.com/giving-back/.

38. Kelly Magee, "Sustainable Fashion: Clothing Can Be Stylish and Eco-Friendly," *Flagler College Gargoyle*, December 9, 2018, https://gargoyle.flagler.edu/2018/12/sustainable-fashion-clothing-can-be-stylish-and-eco-friendly/.
39. "What Is Simply Southern?"
40. See Cobb, *Away Down South*.
41. "Lilly Pulitzer," 6pm, accessed October 9, 2023, https://www.6pm.com/b/lilly-pulitzer/brand/1048.
42. "About Us," Lilly Pulitzer, accessed October 9, 2023, https://www.lillypulitzer.com/about-lilly-pulitzer/about-us.html.
43. Gert Svaiko, "Font Psychology: Here's Everything You Need to Know About Fonts," *Designmodo*, January 12, 2023, https://designmodo.com/font-psychology/.
44. Joe Rinaldi, "Sans Serif vs. Serif Font: Which Should You Use and When?" *Impact*, May 30, 2019, https://www.impactplus.com/blog/sans-serif-vs-serif-font-which-should-you-use-when.
45. Svaiko, "Font Psychology."
46. Michael Gordon, "Preppy Retailer Vineyard Vines Says Competitor's Shirt Bears Striking—and Illegal—Resemblance to Logo," *Chicago Tribune*, March 6, 2018, https://www.chicagotribune.com/business/ct-biz-vineyard-vines-dazzle-up-lawsuit-20180306-story.html.
47. Eric Gershon, "Growing Tie Company Is Selling a Lifestyle," *Hartford Courant*, March 10, 2008, https://archive.boston.com/news/education/higher/articles/2008/03/10/growing_tie_company_is_selling_a_lifestyle/.
48. "The New Southern Preppy Brands," *Official Houston Preppy Handbook*, August 8, 2019, https://theofficialhoustonpreppyhandbook.wordpress.com/2019/08/08/the-new-southern-preppy-brands/.
49. Ariana Kelly, "The Mason Jar, Reborn," *The Atlantic*, September 24, 2015, https://www.theatlantic.com/technology/archive/2015/09/mason-jar-history/403762/.
50. Kelly, "Mason Jar."
51. See Cobb, *Away Down South*.
52. Laura Dove, "BBQ: A Southern Cultural Icon," Xroads, accessed October 10, 2023, https://xroads.virginia.edu/~MA95/dove/bbq.html.
53. "About + Contact," Pink Pig Apparel, accessed October 10, 2023, https://www.pinkpigapparel.com/about-contact/.
54. "About + Contact."
55. "About Us," Southern Trend Clothing, accessed October 10, 2023, https://southerntrend.com/pages/about-us.
56. "Our Story," The Impeccable Pig, accessed October 10, 2023, https://www.theimpeccablepig.com/pages/about-us.
57. "The Black Dog Legacy," Black Dog, accessed October 10, 2023, https://www.theblackdog.com/pages/the-black-dog-history-video.

BIBLIOGRAPHY

Barnard, Malcolm. *Fashion as Communication*. Routledge, 2002.
Cobb, James C. *Away Down South: A History of Southern Identity*. Oxford University Press, 2005.

Coski, John M. *The Confederate Battle Flag: America's Most Embattled Emblem*. Harvard University Press, 2005.

Cox, Karen. *Dreaming of Dixie: How the South Was Created in American Popular Culture*. University of North Carolina Press, 2008.

Crane, Diana. *Fashion and Its Social Agendas: Class, Gender, and Identity in Clothing*. University of Chicago Press, 2000.

de Casanova, Erynn Masi, and Curtis L. Webb III. "A Tale of Two Hoodies." *Men and Masculinities* 20, no. 1 (2017): 117–21.

Finkelstein, Joanne. *The Fashioned Self*. Temple University Press, 1998.

Gonzalez, Umberto. "Dolly Parton on Why She Dumped 'Dixie' Name from Her Theme Parks: 'Don't Be a Dumbass.'" *Yahoo! Entertainment*, August 18, 2020.

Heyse, Amy. "Women's Rhetorical Authority and Collective Memory: The United Daughters of the Confederacy Remember the South." *Women & Language* 33, no. 2 (Fall 2010): 31–53.

Levy, Sydney J. "Symbols by Which We Buy." In *Marketing: Critical Perspectives on Business and Management*, edited by Michael John Baker, 434–56. Taylor and Francis, 2001.

Maurantonio, Nicole. *Confederate Exceptionalism: Civil War Myth and Memory in the Twenty-First Century*. University Press of Kansas, 2019.

Neal, Lynn S. "The Ideal Democratic Apparel: T-Shirts, Religious Intolerance, and the Clothing of Democracy." *Material Religion* 10, no. 2 (2014): 182–207.

Park, Jennifer. "Sweatshirt." In *Encyclopedia of Clothing and Fashion*, vol. 3, edited by Valerie Steele, 246–47. Charles Scribner Sons. Accessed October 9, 2023. https://link.gale.com/apps/doc/cx3427500554/GVRL?u=vic_uor&sid=bookmark-GVRL&xid=57463b9f.

Penney, Joel. "Eminently Visible: The Role of T-Shirts in Gay and Lesbian Public Advocacy and Community Building." *Popular Communication* 11 (2013): 289–302.

Rowley, Michelle V. "'It Could Have Been Me': Really? Early Morning Mediations on Trayvon Martin's Death." *Feminist Studies* 38, no. 2 (2012): 519–29.

PART 4
Civil War Memory in the Age of Black Lives Matter

In 2020, just weeks after the murder of George Floyd, Donald Trump's reelection campaign announced that the embattled Republican would hold a rally in Tulsa, Oklahoma. It was a controversial choice, to say the least. A city in the beating heart of MAGA country, Tulsa became the site of the worst episode of racist violence in U.S. history when, in 1921, armed mobs of white Tulsans massacred their Black neighbors, killing hundreds of men, women, and children and reducing the once-prosperous Black neighborhood of Greenwood to ashes. Making matters worse was the rally's timing, which was initially set to be held on June 19, a date that would need little introduction to the nation's African American population. On June 19, 1865, shortly after arriving in Galveston Bay, Texas, Union Major General Gordon Granger issued General Order No. 3 announcing the end of slavery in the state. In subsequent decades, African Americans in Texas and, eventually, across the United States would come to celebrate Juneteenth as the nation's second Independence Day—a day as hallowed and ripe with memory, both hopeful and tragic, as any other.

Asked if the rally date was intentional, Trump initially answered in the affirmative, telling Fox News, "My rally is a celebration."[1] Within thirty hours of the announcement, however, the Trump campaign, already under fire for its candidate's knee-jerk hostility to antiracist protest, decided to move the date back by one day. Not to be outdone, Trump nevertheless managed to find an upside to the controversy. Reiterating his view that he had done more to help African American people since Abraham Lincoln, he took credit for making Juneteenth famous: "It's actually an important event, an important time. But nobody"—a formulation that negates the lives, fears, ambitions, and joy of millions of African American celebrants, past and present—"had ever heard of it."[2]

On June 17, 2021, President Joe Biden signed a bill making Juneteenth a federal holiday. Even so, it continues to inspire fierce backlash on the political right. On the first Juneteenth of his second term, President Donald Trump once again used the date to remember and reflect—this time ranting online that there are "too many non-working holidays in America. . . . Soon we'll end up having a holiday for every one working day of the year. It must change if we are going to, MAKE AMERICA GREAT AGAIN!"[3] Trump's dismissive attitude toward a Black-led holiday is telling, especially given his relentless crackdown on diversity, equity, and inclusion efforts throughout American society. However, Trump's pushback against Juneteenth is also part of a larger project: to deny the existence of racial inequality in America, both in the Civil War era and in the present.

NOTES

1. Annie Karnie, Maggie Haberman, and Reid J. Epstein, "How the Trump Campaign's Plans for a Triumphant Rally Went Awry," *New York Times*, June 18, 2020, https://www.nytimes.com/2020/06/18/us/politics/trump-rally-tulsa-juneteenth.html.
2. Morgan Chalfant, "Trump Says He Made Juneteenth 'Very Famous,'" *The Hill*, June 18, 2020, https://thehill.com/homenews/administration/503390-trump-says-he-made-juneteenth-very-famous/.
3. Alejandra Jaramillo, "Trump Criticizes 'Non-Working Holidays' on Juneteenth," CNN, June 19, 2025, https://www.cnn.com/2025/06/19/politics/trump-non-working-holidays-juneteenth.

9

"This Battle Was Fought Because Black Lives Matter"
How Black Lives Are (or Aren't) Remembered at Gettysburg

SCOTT HANCOCK

In 2020, during yet another sweltering summer of Black America's legitimate discontent, startling yard signs began appearing in the borough of Gettysburg, Pennsylvania. Stark black letters, popping out of a bright yellow background, mustered themselves into a shout: "THIS BATTLE WAS FOUGHT BECAUSE BLACK LIVES MATTER." Karl Mattson, a white borough resident and retired chaplain at Gettysburg College, said he created the signs "in response to what happened here on the Fourth of July" of 2020 and as a way to change the narrative of the battle at Gettysburg into "a celebration of emancipation and freedom."[1]

"What happened here" on that July 4, witnessed by Reverend Mattson, me, and the other seven thousand–plus people who live in the borough, was an invasion of this quaint town by hundreds of well-armed militia members. They were accompanied by hundreds more supporters, many of whom carried guns. They had been spurred to action by a hoax designed to prank white reactionaries. Three years earlier, a nearly identical hoax had generated a similar response, but in 2020 the reactionaries were more numerous, better organized, and even more thoroughly armed. Their fear: that Antifa was coming to burn Gettysburg's suburbs, torch American and Confederate flags, and deface or destroy Confederate monuments.[2]

Mattson's sign pushed back against that hysteria, but I'll admit that when I first saw it, the academic in me questioned its historical foundations. *Did* Black lives matter to the majority of white U.S. privates, sergeants, majors, and generals? To white civilians and politicians? I loved the way the sign tried to connect past and present—the way it spoke back to people like the white man who told me on that July Fourth that Black Lives Matter (BLM) is "burning cities" across America or the white man who stood next to me during one of the BLM protests on the town square later that summer,

Fig. 9.1. Gettysburg, June 2022. Courtesy of Scott Hancock.

shouting, "White lives matter!"³ Nonetheless, for me, the sign's message boiled down to two linked questions, one about our history and one about our present. Were the Civil War and this battle really fought because Black lives mattered in the way that Black Lives Matter, the most recent manifestation of the centuries-long Black Freedom Movement, says they do? And what threat did Black lives mattering pose to the nearly all-white militia and militia supporters who came to the Gettysburg battlefield on July 4, 2020?

How Did Black Lives Matter to White Militia in 2020?

On the one hand, it seems many of those militia members surely knew any social media posts claiming Antifa was going to burn Gettysburg's suburbs were a hoax. Gettysburg has about 7,500 residents. It doesn't have suburbs. The closest thing to a suburb is the borough's mid-twentieth-century, almost entirely white neighborhood of Colt Park, with its neatly trimmed lawns snuggled around ranch and split-level homes, less than a mile from the Virginia monument. Despite Antifa's allegedly murderous intent, and the ubiquitous white nationalist mantras ("white lives matter," "all lives matter") shouted by armed militia members on Gettysburg's town square later that summer, the July 4 militia folks apparently decided Colt Park's white lives were on their own. That neighborhood went strangely unpatrolled. One could conclude, then, that either Confederate flags and monuments mattered more than white lives, or militia members knew the threat was phony and were simply looking to flex their power in a tumultuous election year.

On the other hand, just a few weeks before, in the wake of George Floyd's murder, protesters had repurposed Robert E. Lee's statue in Richmond, Virginia, into a canvas of Black Lives Matter graffiti, ratcheting up efforts to remove the monument. They would eventually succeed. So, though there's little doubt some militia members were using the alleged threat as a pretext for riding into town locked and loaded, it's reasonable to acknowledge that others may have thought some level of genuine threat existed to the relics of the Confederacy at Gettysburg.

In either case, another question arose: Why did such inanimate objects as monuments and flags merit violence?

On that July 4, a handgun-carrying army-green-attired white woman at the North Carolina state monument told some friends and me that if she saw anyone burning a flag, she'd shoot them. She did not specify what kind of flag. Only Confederate flags, though, had been threatened with immolation by the hoaxer. When I asked, politely but seriously, if she thought a flag and a human life had the same value, she declined to answer.[4] Her nonanswer speaks volumes about the persistent pervasiveness of Lost Cause mythology: a romanticized, revisionist retelling of the American Civil War largely, though not exclusively, constructed by white Southerners, including former Confederate soldiers and efficient propaganda outfits like the United Daughters of the Confederacy. The Lost Cause sought "to present the war from the perspective of Confederates and in the best possible terms."[5] In its most generous retellings, Black lives are eased into a contented existence alongside white Southerners. Other retellings ignore Black lives: They simply disappear. This is white supremacy as well-oiled productivity, running almost noiselessly, smoothly, churning out rapidly replicated and easily used goods as uncomplicated stories that can, like the products of Adam Smith's ideal pin factory in *The Wealth of Nations*, be reproduced by the hundreds, the thousands, the hundreds of thousands, manufactured by teachers, docents, politicians, novelists, filmmakers, painters, sculptors, fathers, mothers, for generation after generation. This is white supremacy as an "industry of memory," a term Viet Than Nguyen explains as "the material and ideological forces that determine how and why memories are produced and circulated."[6] The industry of memory enables white Americans from red states, blue states, all states, to accept a relatively uncomplicated past, where steady movement toward greater and greater freedom was always the plan. And as long as none of us squints and looks closely, we can all supposedly see that plan coming to fruition.

When that story, which demands a fixed, pinpoint view of white supremacy as being only the worst excesses of the worst of the KKK, is confronted by the reality of Black lives mattering and *why* they mattered . . . well, the story shatters. Holding it together requires either trying to reassemble the pieces or making sure the story stays intact regardless of pesky facts. When you've got a lot of guns, the latter is probably easier. But in either case, the threat was never Antifa. The threat was always the reality of Black lives mattering.

For me and five friends of mine, this became shockingly, but unsurprisingly, obvious on that July 4, 2020, when we conducted a thirty-minute confab with some fellow American citizens, several of them very well armed in combat boots and military fatigues, at the Virginia monument that has stood on West Confederate Avenue since 1917. We arrived in battle gear, too: open-toed sandals, comfortable walking shoes, water bottles at the ready. We carried a few homemade signs like one reminding visitors of the 189 enslaved people that General Robert E. Lee and his wife inherited and profited from, and that Lee petitioned the Virginia legislature, twice, to keep those people enslaved longer than his deceased father-in-law's will legally allowed.

I also came armed with some miniature Black Lives Matter flags that I had printed out the previous night. If you've been to Gettysburg National Military Park, you may have seen miniature flags, American and Confederate, that visitors often place by monuments. We wanted to tell a different story with other flags, so my son fashioned some one-eighth-inch-diameter, six-inch-long dowel rods as flag posts that would break easily (we wanted to avoid the possibility that some militia member or supporter might find it gleefully ironic to stab one of us with our own BLM flag). With my friends on sentry duty, I gently hammered our homemade flags into the ground in front of the North Carolina State Memorial, and then at the Virginia State Memorial. In front of that imposing tower of concrete, we didn't think they posed a threat. We were wrong.

The BLM flags flapped warily in the light breeze for maybe one minute. Since the flags were standing bravely behind me, I less bravely preferred to keep my eyes forward on the AR-15-accessorized white men spreading out in a flanking maneuver around the cul-de-sac. I don't know, then, just how many visitors quick-marched up behind me to assault our modest flags. I did see one clearly infuriated white woman, muttering "oh, no, you don't,"

Figs. 9.2 & 9.3. Black Lives Matter flags at Virginia State Memorial, July 4, 2020. Courtesy of Scott Hancock.

rolling up my left flank, followed by the death knell sound of dowel rods being snapped. Thankfully, no attempted stabbing transpired. The handgun-carrying woman from the North Carolina monument was nowhere to be seen, but I'm fairly certain our flags weren't among those she was willing to kill to protect.

The refusal by this group of white visitors to permit four very small, very plain flags to stand for even one minute shows what they were really threatened by. As another friend of mine said afterward, what was exposed on that July 4 was the continued "inability to grapple with the centrality of Black lives" on the battlefield and in the story of this battle, this war, this country. Sixty years ago, James Baldwin advised his nephew that until white people understood history, "they cannot be released from it."[7] My friends and I had figured that July 4, 2020, was prime time for helping militia folks get free. And for twenty minutes or so at the Virginia monument, despite the capture and destruction of our flags, we found that some of the armed and not visibly armed visitors were willing to engage in conversation. Or at least engage in verbal exchanges oscillating between something close to a conversation and, on their part, yelling. But as we unfolded Lee and the Confederacy's story as committed enslavers, well grounded in evidence that threatened their heritage-based, white-supremacy-shaped memory, the oscillating did unfortunately, though not unexpectedly, escalate to insults and attempted intimidation.

Three of us who were there that day are Black. In many respects, I like to think that apart from all of us being male, we're a pleasingly historical snapshot of certain kinds of American Blackness. I'm a light mixed-race Brown, descended from early twentieth-century West Indian immigrants who can trace their stories back to enslavement on Barbados and Nevis. Shawn is darker skinned, descended from enslaved African Americans in Northampton County, Virginia, and may be descended from the first or second generation of enslaved Africans to arrive in British North America (and some of them came from Barbados, so who knows, we may be cousins). Clotaire, the darkest-skinned of our merry band, came to the United States in the late twentieth century from the first Black republic, Haiti, which has shaped so much of American history, a story that would no doubt surprise our militia confabulists had they been patient enough to hear it. After fifteen minutes or so, you didn't have to have a Black American's racial perspicacity gained from a lifetime of interacting with white folks, though, to figure out that our discussion, never exactly congenial, was rapidly deteriorating. It disintegrated completely with the shouts of "go back to Africa," "go pick up your welfare check," "socialists!" and whispers of "n——" (overheard by our white friends; interestingly, even holding AR-15s and other guns didn't embolden people enough to shout that, I'm guessing because they didn't want to out themselves as being *too* racist).

Minutes before all things fell apart, I asked what they were all so afraid of that required their presence and their guns. One man replied forcefully that they had all come to protect the Confederate monuments. When I asked him what he thought the six of us could do to the forty-one-foot concrete tower that Lee's horse Traveller stands upon, and upon whom Lee sits, he answered back that we might have ropes with us that we'd use to pull Lee off his pedestal. I politely challenged his ocular proficiency, noting that the only rope we had was the thin twine on the signs we held, and invited him to peek inside the small string bag on my back. He less politely declined.

He invented a nonexistent threat to the monuments. The threat to the twenty-first-century operative narrative of white supremacy, however, did exist. That's why they came out on this July 4 (as well as in July of 2017) equipped with AR-15s, AK-47s, a smorgasbord of handguns, and God knows what else. Many of them also brought an impressive display of Confederate flags to the festivities: flags with Trump's image, flags with AR-15s, large flags on six-foot poles, mini-flags on six-inch plastic sticks, flags on tattoos, flags on men's, women's, and kids' T-shirts, flags on bumper stickers, on hats, on dogs. Overlooking all this with staid approval, the Confederate state monuments stood placidly and majestically along Seminary Ridge, ground held by the Army of Northern Virginia for three days in 1863, a ground that has been telling the same Lost Cause, white supremacist story every day for over a hundred years, since Robert E. Lee and Traveller were installed atop the Virginia State Memorial in 1917.

Did Black Lives Matter to Gettysburg National Military Park in 2020?

There are, too, more subtle ways that narrative gets reified. A year after that July Fourth (and "Fourth" must be capitalized in order to demonstrate one's patriotism), on July Fourth of 2021, having just returned from a trip to the fabulous National Museum of African American Music in Nashville, wearing a bright yellow shirt with James Brown's lyrics "Black and Proud" on it, I rode my bike past the Virginia monument and saw a crowd of well over three hundred white people. One of the park's ranger-led "battlewalks"

Fig. 9.4. Stephen Lang at Virginia State Memorial, Gettysburg National Military Park, July 4, 2021. Author Scott Hancock is standing on edge of grass, behind and left of Lang. Screenshot from Addressing Gettysburg's YouTube video.

happened to be kicking off. I jumped off the bike, locked it up, and joined the crowd, virtually all white, mostly men. A PCN television crew (Pennsylvania's version of C-SPAN) was filming the festivities. Actor Stephen Lang was there, too, to everyone's pleasant surprise, except for mine, as I had not heard of him. I've never been able to get through more than the first thirty minutes of *Gettysburg*, the film that apparently, based on the enthusiastic applause when Lang stepped out in his boots and wide-brimmed hat, just about the entire crowd had seen, probably more than once. A fascinating discussion with Lang followed. He played General George Pickett in the film, and when he announced that he would be playing Robert E. Lee in an upcoming feature, he got another big round of applause. Toward the end of his Q&A with the crowd, I quickly raised my hand to ask a question but wasn't selected. Probably he never saw me. I did wonder, though, if I wasn't picked because of my blatant lack of whiteness.

    I wanted to ask Lang if he and his fellow actors ever discussed what it is like to play the roles of people who, enslavers themselves, were also fighting to protect the right to keep four million Black women, children, and men enslaved. I was genuinely curious. But I also wanted to point the crowd toward the centrality of slavery at Gettysburg, a place that existed because of Black lives that existed both in the shadows of the surrounding woods and out in the sun-drenched fields. But their lives had been sunk so deep under the weight of white supremacy that no hint of Blackness remained. On this summer day in 2021, no markers, no monuments, no signs, except for one that had been installed earlier that spring at the Abraham Brian farm, nothing else on the more than six thousand acres surrounding the Gettysburg Museum and Visitor Center even mentioned the word "slavery."[8]

During the first forty-five minutes of the battlefield walk, we stood in the warm sun, some people literally standing in the shadow of Lee, listening while a park ranger masterfully set the stage. We learned about Captain Michael Spessard and his eighteen-year-old son Hezekiah, both in the Twenty-Eighth Virginia Infantry. Hezekiah, a private who had enlisted just six months before Gettysburg, was shot soon after Pickett's Charge began. Some accounts say his father came across him as he lay wounded. After the failed assault, Michael searched briefly and unsuccessfully for his son in field hospitals before Lee's army began its retreat. He spent the rest of the month not knowing what happened to his son, until he received a letter from his wife at the end of July, informing him that Hezekiah had died in a field hospital at Gettysburg two weeks after the battle. The ranger told this story poignantly and brought us back to it two hours later, at the end of the walk inside the Federal line, commonly described as the "High-Water Mark." Captain Spessard, even though he had probably either seen or had been told that his son had been seriously wounded, had reached the High-Water Mark before falling back to Seminary Ridge with the rest of Lee's army.

The ranger humanized the Spessards, a vitally important mission of education on the battlefield for the nearly one million visitors who come here each year. Enslavers or not, the Spessards, along with all their fellow soldiers, were complex people whose humanity matters as much as those they fought against and those they fought to keep enslaved. Unfortunately, during the three-plus hours of standing in sun and shade, walking across grassy fields, and tramping up and down ridges, there was never even a vague reference to the fundamental reason why there was a war that had caused them to enlist and ultimately led them to Gettysburg.

I wondered if the Spessards had any connection to slavery. I walked a mile back to my bike, rode a mile back home, and started googling. In less than half the time of the battlefield walk, I learned that Captain Michael Spessard owned at least one Black man, and his father owned eight. They were enslavers in a county that did not have many—Spessard's father owned more human beings than most other enslavers in the county. A secretary of Virginia's Craig County Democratic Party, Captain Spessard was politically active before the war and a sheriff in 1860. When he wrote in an 1862 letter that the Union army would "invade our home, confiscate our property," he was surely thinking of all his family's legal property, including human beings.[9] That part of the Spessard story, though, was absent during our walk across the battlefield.

Even so, Captain Spessard's letter hints at an answer to the historical question posed by Reverend Mattson's sign: Did Black lives matter to Americans in the years and days leading up to the battle at Gettysburg? And if so, to whom, and why?

Did Black Lives Matter to Secessionist Southerners?

From a perverse perspective, you could answer that Black lives mattered tremendously to the Confederacy. During Mississippi's secession convention in January of 1861, legislators debated whether to levy an additional tax per enslaved person. The debate was not about whether owners would have to pay a tax, but if, in light of pending secession and likely war, there should be an additional tax. Delegate Joel Berry, representing mainly non-slaveholders, argued for an additional tax, noting that he was "utterly opposed" to anything that might be "prejudicial to the institution of slavery."[10] Berry certainly valued Black lives and, in fact, wanted them valued more. His proposal to do so via the additional tax was narrowly voted down, mainly by slaveholding legislators who thought the people they were busy exploiting were already valued plenty. Nonetheless, Berry's affection for the institution that he said blessed both Black and white Mississippians was deeply shared by his fellow legislators who voted against him. They had already come together in Mississippi's Declaration of Secession, declaring, "Our position is thoroughly identified with the institution of slavery—the greatest material interest of the world." Because of the legislature's stance on the value of Black lives, some of their relatives would subsequently be among the Mississippians who fought at Gettysburg, today memorialized by the Mississippi state monument's inscription, which blares out, "Our brave sires fought for their righteous cause."

And Black lives certainly mattered to Confederates after the war started, including during the Pennsylvania Campaign in 1863. For the Army of Northern Virginia, Black lives mattered in at least two important ways. The first was by impressing enslaved laborers from their owners to serve the looming military campaign (more on this below). The second was by kidnapping free Black American citizens as the army moved through Pennsylvania's Franklin and Adams counties. On occasion, I get to talk about the kidnapping of enslaved people with white visitors, some of whom are reenactors, a.k.a. "living historians." (This term strikes me as grossly inadequate when it comes to Confederate reenactors who rely upon misrepresentation, distortion, omission, and outright lies in conjuring the past. It seems a different term is needed to distinguish them from those Confederate reenactors who have done their homework. "Living caricatures"? "Living white supremacists"? I'm open to suggestions.) Mentioning Confederate soldiers' kidnapping of Black residents often elicits an eruption of vociferous denials: "That's not true!" "There's no evidence for that!" "That never happened!" What's fascinating yet troubling is the immediacy and vigor of the denials, which strongly suggest these visitors have heard these stories before. Apparently, they assume their ancestors, or those they wish were their ancestors, would have never thought that Black lives mattered so much in this particular manner. Their wistfulness notwithstanding, Black lives did matter to most white Southerners, whether they owned those lives or not.

Did Black Lives Matter to White Northerners?

Compared to white Southerners, white Northerners, in some respects, had a more complicated valuation of Black lives. Though many white Northerners supported the war that would end slavery, historians largely agree that in 1861 Abraham Lincoln and his white Northern supporters did not have emancipation and abolition of slavery as primary goals. Preserving the United States was the initial and guiding purpose. But by late June of 1863, as two armies were marching down the ten roads that led to Gettysburg, emancipation and abolition had arguably become equally important to the Union cause.

Many white Northerners bitterly resented that implication. This was certainly the case in Gettysburg and the surrounding counties. North of Gettysburg, on the last day of the battle at Gettysburg, the *Harrisburg Daily Patriot and Union* made sure to rebroadcast its daily pronouncement that "The Purposes of the War" had nothing, on their surface, to do with anybody or anything Black, but rather were "to defend and maintain the supremacy of the Constitution, and to preserve the Union." Once that was done, "the war ought to cease." A couple of weeks later, just west of Harrisburg, the *Carlisle American Volunteer* (also called the *Carlisle American Democrat*) reported on the "great indignation meeting at Chicago," where the speaker unknowingly foreshadowed a mockery of Lincoln's Gettysburg Address, declaring that "this war was started upon the ground that it was to be fought under the constitution, and for the constitution, and for the maintenance of the Union . . . but the object of this war has since been perverted into a war for the emancipation of the negro."[11]

In fact, white Northerners in the Union and Nothing but the Union Camp may have been the only group of Americans to whom Black lives did not matter. A couple weeks prior, the *Patriot and Union* sarcastically titled an article "The Negro Our Only Hope," complaining that for Lincoln and his fellow supporters of "this abolition war . . . it matters not to them how many *white* lives are sacrificed or how much treasure is wasted" (emphasis in the original) in order to "carry out their favorite idea of a negro insurrection in the South." As historians and people interested in history, we must be careful not to overlay what was said in the past onto the present. Yet it's hard to think that critically when the past seems to be echoing loudly from white men yelling almost identical words in 2020 during Black Lives Matter protests on the square in Gettysburg while sauntering around with AR-15s or sitting in the back of a World War II deuce-and-a-half truck. The same issue of the *Daily Patriot and Union* carried an advertisement for a minstrel show with "plantation scenes" and "Grand Ethiopian Soirees." Black lives did not matter to these white Northerners, but maybe Black life did, so long as it could be used for their entertainment. Hard not to hear those echoes today too.[12]

There were, however, plenty of white Northerners who either begrudgingly thought ending slavery had become an equal priority to preserving the Union or were passionate advocates of Black freedom, even if they did not want full Black social and legal equality. That complexity of white attitudes toward African Americans was true of white U.S. Army soldiers too. There's ample evidence of white soldiers' bitterly racist resentment about the presence of Black contrabands, teamsters, and soldiers, and there's ample evidence of soldiers who advocated for emancipation and sometimes even unflinching support for Black people's citizenship rights.[13]

You could argue, then, that because Black lives did matter to varying degrees to enough white Northern soldiers, politicians, and civilians, the United States maintained its commitment to fight this increasingly cruel war into the summer of 1863, which led to Gettysburg, and explains why there was a battle here. Maybe, then, Reverend Mattson's sign is legit. Maybe.

Did Black Lives Matter to the Armies at Gettysburg?

Among the Black people who caused such ambivalence among white U.S. Army soldiers, few were more involved, directly and indirectly, in the battle at Gettysburg than teamsters. Teamsters pop up in the stunning cyclorama painting at the Gettysburg Museum and Visitor Center; they stand out because . . . well, one, they are the only Black people in the painting, and two, they are the only men wearing bright red and blue shirts. On multiple occasions, I've asked the staff there who and why they are there, and every time the response has been polite versions of "I don't know." This isn't a critique of the staff but suggests there's more work to be done. Though the museum does an outstanding job dealing with issues of slavery and African Americans in the museum itself, outside the museum—whether the actual landscape or, in this case, the landscape as depicted in the painting—Black lives, even when they are visible, are still rendered effectively meaningless if nobody can explain their presence to the viewing public.

And their presence isn't all that hard to explain. While writing this essay, it took me only a few hours of research to document how Black teamsters, such as the ones depicted in figures 9.5, 9.6, and 9.7, provided crucial labor for the army in nearly every theater of the war, including taking care of horses and mules, setting up camp, cooking, or even posing for staged photographs. James Paradis's examination of quartermasters' pay records found that "the overwhelming majority of the teamsters were African American" during the Union's Gettysburg campaign.[14] Some of those teamsters worked in a critical transportation role as drivers in wagon trains, bringing supplies to Gettysburg upon which the army depended in an important battle in the war for union and emancipation.

The significance of their role also made them targets. One wagon train was described as "comprising one hundred and fifty vehicles, each drawn by six mules, driven by a very black and picturesque negro. This train must have been at least two miles long." Another report about the very same train noted that the "wagonmasters were instructed to move steadily but rapidly" out from Tenleytown, near the present-day site of the National Cathedral in Washington DC, two days before the battle would commence in Gettysburg. Almost immediately, in the twelve miles en route to Rockville, Maryland, they were attacked three times by Confederate raiders. Still a mile and a half from Rockville, "a citizen rode up in hot haste," warning that Confederates had occupied Rockville, followed by cavalry soldiers, who told them to turn back. While the drivers were trying to turn the wagon train around, "the rebels made their appearance on the road on both sides, firing on the fugitive teamsters." Other reports noted that 100 Black teamsters were captured—which meant 50 got away—adding to the 150 who would be captured the next

Fig. 9.5. "Bermuda Hundred, Va. African American teamsters near the signal tower." Library of Congress.

day while working on supply barges at Edwards Ferry on the Chesapeake and Ohio. Those 250 Black lives mattered enough to the Confederate army to be worth forcing into labor to support its war for slavery.[15]

The Confederate army used Black labor at Gettysburg too. Forcing enslaved laborers, nearly all men, to support the Confederacy's military campaign was standard operating procedure. Thousands were quite efficiently impressed from their owners by the Confederacy's centralized government throughout the war.[16] Supplementing impressment was the army's operational directive of stealing Black lives, which was especially needed to replace contrabands—the enslaved people who escaped to Union lines, and, in the Chambersburg area, allegedly gave into "excessive alarm." Enslaved workers did the necessary grunt work of the army—digging latrines, taking care of horses, carrying

Fig. 9.6. "Confederate and Union dead side by side in the trenches at Fort Mahone." The body in the foreground is a U.S. soldier. The body in the background is a Black teamster posing as a dead Confederate soldier. Library of Congress.

arms, and other work that was not entirely dissimilar from African American teamsters' labor.

Anywhere from six thousand to ten thousand enslaved workers marched to Gettysburg.¹⁷ We don't know the names of most of them. But we know the names of a few. Two months before the battle, General William Dorsey Pender, who would not survive his wounds from the battle, brought at least three enslaved men with him: Joe, Harris, and Columbus. Pender had a classically racist paternalistic view toward Joe, at one point wanting to "Christianize" him because he "seems to be a good boy." Interspersed with comments about how faithful Joe was, Pender wrote in October of 1862, "I gave Joe a tremendous whipping last night. I had been promising him some

Fig. 9.7. *Supply Train* by Edwin Forbes. Library of Congress.

time and finally he got it. He is a good and smart boy but like most young negroes needs correction badly."[18] In his last letter, Pender told his wife that "Joe enters into the invasion with much gusto and is quite active in looking up hidden property. In fact the negroes seem to have more feeling in the matter than the white men and have come to the conclusion that they will [im]press horses, etc., etc. to any amount. Columbus is laying in a stock for his sweetheart and sisters."[19]

Pender may have been right about Joe and Columbus's intent. Like Columbus, Joe had four sisters and perhaps other kin. Like most enslaved army workers, they would have been extremely reluctant to abandon their families. Or Pender may have been completely wrong. It's possible Joe or Columbus or both were in fact making connections with free Black communities and saving resources that they could later use to seek freedom. Pender had previously said that Joe was "a very smart boy" and that "the rascal seems to have plenty of money."

Colonel E. P. Alexander recounted how he had two enslaved men with him, Charley and Abram, throughout the war, including at Gettysburg. Abram, "small and pure black," was his driver, and he never saw him again after Abram was "captured a few days before the surrender" in April of 1865.

There's a good chance Abram led his wagon straight away from Alexander at the war's end, distancing himself from his former owner, as did millions of his new fellow African American citizens. Despite Alexander's claim that, when the war was drawing to a close, Charley wanted to go with him to South America, Charley did the same as Abram. Upon leaving from "the surrender," Alexander, probably feeling a bit emotional, gave Charley a ten-dollar gold piece as recompense for two and half years of unpaid wages that he said he had kept track of. Charley accepted the gold piece. And left. Alexander never saw him again.[20]

Some enslaved workers, probably those with few or no kin in the South, did not wait until the end of the war to leave their owners for good. Georgian Edgeworth Bird described to his wife Sallie that "a great many Negroes have gone to the Yankees" in the aftermath of the battle at Gettysburg. One was Willis, enslaved laborer of Captain Charles Waddell. Waddell had been laid up sick with typhoid fever; Willis, rather than exhibiting the tender care that Alexander seemed to see in slaves, took advantage of Waddell's illness and escaped—and took all of Waddell's camp gear with him.[21]

Did Black Lives Matter to White Gettysburgians?

As the Confederate army marched eastward through Franklin County toward Gettysburg, white Gettysburgians reflected on their Black neighbors with a mix of emotions. To some white observers, it seemed to be not Black lives, but Black life—parties, dance, music, family get-togethers, church—that mattered. Their narrow perceptions of Black people's behavior fascinated and entertained just as it did for the minstrel-loving white supremacists in Harrisburg. Tillie Pierce, a young civilian who endured the battle, wrote afterward that whenever news of a Confederate raid reached Gettysburg, "on these occasions it was also amusing to behold the conduct of the colored people. . . . They regarded the rebels as having an especial hatred toward them, and they believed that if they fell into their hands, annihilation was sure." Pierce concluded with a minstrel-show-like mimicry of African American Vernacular English.

More empathetic observers witnessed the terrors faced by Black people at the hands of Southern slave-catchers. Rachel Cormany described Confederates near her Chambersburg home "hunting up the contrabands & driving them off by droves," which she said "grated on our hearts to have to sit quietly & look at such brutal deeds."[22] Others reported that "quite a number negroes—free and slave, men, women and children—were captured, by

[General Albert G.] Jenkins and started south to be sold into bondage." Some escaped. One man "forced a gun from the rebel and fired, wounding him in the head." White Greencastle residents helped around fifty African Americans get away from their captors.[23] Though there are no similar existing accounts of such rescues in the Gettysburg area, there had been at least a few very active abolitionist allies in the Underground Railroad, such as the James McAllister family.[24] Though it is doubtful that every one of these witnesses advocated for full Black equality, at the very least, Black lives mattered to them.

Confederate raids were not new in June of 1863. Historian David G. Smith argues that the kidnapping of free Black people, as well as escaped enslaved people, could be considered as part of the Confederate army's operational directive. There had been a well-known pattern in Virginia and other states, of stealing Black people and selling them into the internal slave trade in Southern states. In one earlier campaign into Maryland in 1862, Confederate soldiers had kidnapped free African Americans. Many Black Gettysburgians maintained networks of family and friends that extended into Maryland and Virginia, and the strong oral culture no doubt communicated that news north of the Mason–Dixon line. Historian Kevin Levin records a soldier writing that a standard operating procedure was "capturing negroes and horses" and sending them south.[25] Similarly, historian Hilary Green cites a North Carolina infantry major who said his regiment had captured "many hundred slaves" but complained that he probably would not get more than one hundred dollars apiece. Confederate General Albert Jenkins—who until George Floyd's murder had a monument just north of Gettysburg in Mechanicsburg—used his calvary to persecute and round up African Americans in south central Pennsylvania.[26]

Even so, a Chambersburg newspaper went out of its way to characterize Jenkins as a honorable enemy.[27] While moving through Franklin County, the paper claimed, Jenkins "called upon the ladies of the house" and "acted in all respects like a gentleman." Of course, he and his soldiers did not act like the gentleman with Black women—but for the newspaper, and most Northern whites, such distinctions did not matter. The contrast—between the paper's depiction of Jenkins's honorable dealings and restraint and its reports of his troops kidnapping Black people, even children—hopefully stands out to us in 2024. For many white Gettysburgians in 1863, however, no such tension existed.

Today, some visitors I talk with, both by happenstance and as part of NPS programs, have similarly resolved what would be a problem in these twenty-first-century post–civil rights United States: They repeat with pride and respect the stories of how Confederates did not wantonly pillage the entire countryside and tried to pay for what they took. And there's good evidence that this was sometimes, though certainly not always, true during their time in Pennsylvania. These visitors' exercise in memory and heritage is often paired by recounting how Union soldiers utterly failed to reciprocate Confederates' allegedly honorable behavior in the South, such as Sherman's March to the Sea. The denial of Confederate kidnapping, then, is necessary: With the exception of today's most obvious and virulent white supremacists, who just might be quite proud of Confederate kidnapping, you can't shout that "all lives matter" and still see people like Jenkins as an honorable gentleman if he did indeed kidnap dozens, hundreds, maybe thousands of Black women, children, and men.

Black Lives Mattered to Black Gettysburgians

If we could step back in time and ask white Northerners whether and how much Black lives mattered, we'd get quite a spectrum of responses. Pose that same question to Black Northerners, like the two hundred or so who lived in Gettysburg, and there would have most definitely been a blunt response: What's wrong with you, asking such a question? Did somebody drop you on your head as a child? It was precisely because Black Gettysburgians knew their lives mattered a great deal that many of them got out of town fast in the days leading up to the battle. The march into Pennsylvania was at minimum the second campaign in which the army under the command of Robert E. Lee had a green light to kidnap free Black citizens and either use them as enslaved laborers for their army or sell them into slavery.[28] What, then, some white neighbors like Tillie Pierce thought was amusing hysteria and unorganized panic was instead an informed decision, carried out with deliberation. It is likely that the "bundles as large as old-fashioned feather ticks" as well as the bundles the children carried were what some people today call go-bags—the necessities of life, packed up in a backpack or carry bag, stored in a closet by the back door, that people who live in uncertain circumstances can grab on the way out when they have to leave at a moment's notice.[29]

James and Eliza Warfield had moved into the area just a year or two before the battle and owned a small house, filled with five children, aged six months to twenty years old, along with thirteen acres upon which Warfield Tower (a.k.a. Longstreet Tower) now sits. Jane Nutter, former president of Gettysburg Black History Museum, notes that her family's oral traditions maintain that there was at least one other Black family with a house on the Warfield property. The Warfields, and likely the other families living on their thirteen acres, left when they heard the Confederates were approaching. From their front porch, the Warfields could look across the gentle ridges that would prove daunting for the Confederate army and see Abraham and Elizabeth Brian's farm about a mile and half to the northeast. The Brians also left with their children. The Brians had probably bought their twelve acres in 1857 with funds from the selling of their house in town to Julia Ann and Jack Hopkins, leading members of Gettysburg's African American community. The Hopkinses got out of town too.[30]

What often gets missed in the stories of kidnapping and Black flight from Confederates are the stories of Black Gettysburgians who stayed. If you'd like to stir the ire of Jane Nutter, tell her about how "all" the Black folks left town. She knows there's more to that story. Because their lives mattered—if we understand "lives" as not only including the physiological actions of keeping your heart pumping blood and lungs filling with air, but also as *a life*, as what we build around those physiological actions, as giving meaning to a place through family, friends, going to church, skipping church, work, a house, a farm, a business. In other words, because *life* mattered, some people, like some of Jane's ancestors, decided to stay. Jane points out that the "narrative usually excludes any mention of those who stayed to protect their families and belongings." She also notes that many who stayed did so to take a stand against what they knew the Confederacy represented: continued support for owning Black lives, a reality that was a mere eight miles due south across the Mason–Dixon line.[31]

Black Gettysburgians pursued different strategies to preserve the totality of their lives. Some left. But not everybody. During the battle, as Jane tells the story that's been kept faithfully in her family for generations, some hid out in a basement, surviving a cannonball crashing through a ground-floor window. Presumably, they thought this was their best shot at maintaining their lives and the life they had built in Gettysburg, the life they had earned and had a right to hold onto. They no doubt experienced some measure of loss, probably some trauma, too, but as Black people living in these United States, they had been there and done that, so obviously they had managed to work through it—because Jane and her sister Mary Alice, as well as many other descendants of Black Gettysburgians who stayed as well as those who left but later returned, are still here.[32]

Their stories are rarely told, perhaps because they did not fit the narratives told in Civil War–era Gettysburg, by either racist white neighbors or well-meaning sympathetic neighbors. For the former, Black people who stayed were not entertaining. For the latter, Black people who did not fight back in obvious ways but simply endured and outlasted Confederate depredations were not exciting for white audiences (and, frankly, too often still are not). Nor did these more prosaic stories of endurance carry enough ethical outrage for righteous white neighbors. Viet Thanh Nguyen, writing about the similarities and differences between American and Vietnamese memories of what we call the Vietnam War, notes that memories of a war's predations too often convey an ethical outrage to "reassert the centrality of the person feeling that emotion, which justifies viewing the other as a perpetual victim."[33] That kind of self-centering whiteness forgets or ignores or just flat out doesn't care how the ordinary stuff of Black life matters to Black people and works to perpetuate white supremacy just as efficiently as the more patently racist narratives. And it's why the story of the Nutter family needs told too; it's a subtle yet critical tool in the kit for dismantling white supremacy.

We know, then, many of the Black lives that were here and that mattered. Their stories need to be made plain. And encouragingly, there are signs (some literal) that Gettysburg National Military Park is working to center Black lives in the story the park tells on the six thousand acres surrounding the museum.

Black Lives Matter

In July 2022 there was another battlefield walk across Pickett's Charge, this time starting from the North Carolina monument, with a crowd of about one hundred white people. The park ranger told us with no equivocation about how General Joe Davis, nephew of Confederate President Jefferson Davis, enslaved dozens of Black people and increased that number as war approached. That was a big step forward. However, three hours later, there was a big step backward while we stood three feet from the side of Abraham and Elizabeth Brian's house, the free African Americans who owned the twelve acres we stood upon. We heard dramatic and tragic stories about soldiers from North Carolina and Mississippi hiding behind the Brians' house and barn, desperately trying to stay alive as the charge disintegrated. Not a word was spoken about the Brians, nor that they and other Black Gettysburgians knew enslavers like Joe Davis had abetted the Army of Northern Virginia's kidnapping of free Black Pennsylvanians. Despite being close enough to

Fig. 9.8. Seventy-fifth anniversary, Battle of Gettysburg. A Union and Confederate veteran join hands. National Archives and Records Administration.

reach out an arm and touch the back of their house, the Brians and Blackness were not part of the narrative.

It was because of Black lives that 160,000 white soldiers came to these fields. It was because of Black lives that the undulating ridges were transformed, in a mere three days, into a massively jumbled graveyard. There are few markers for those Black lives—now two restored small houses, the Brian and Warfield homes, and six wayside markers that mention issues of race, slavery, or African Americans.

There is, though, one sense in which the disappearance of Black lives was historically appropriate. During the 1938 reunion of soldiers who fought on this landscape, the Brians and Blackness vanished, a vanishing epitomized in a staged handshake of veterans. In a staged photo (fig. 9.8), the U.S. and Confederate veterans are standing right on the edge of the Brians' twelve acres, with their house and barn easily visible in the background.

Whenever Black lives are absented from the Gettysburg narrative, white supremacy is reinforced by permitting, even encouraging, visitors to see white sacrifice and valor as disconnected from ugly complications like the exploitation and brutalization of other people. The narrative of whiteness, lauded by flags and reunions and monument and gun-carrying monument

Fig. 9.9. Marker at North Carolina Memorial, Gettysburg National Military Park, March 2022. Courtesy of Scott Hancock.

protectors, must be challenged every July, and every day for that matter, by including the ugly, repressive, unpalatable stories of white supremacy.

I was on my bike on West Confederate Avenue on a cool and cloudy March day in 2022 when I saw a new three-foot-high wayside marker in front of the five-foot-high plaque erected by the United Daughters of the Confederacy, which in turn stood in front of the dominating twelve-foot-high North Carolina state monument, designed and made by KKK advocate and Mount Rushmore sculptor Guzton Borglum, both installed almost a hundred years earlier. The marker, titled "War for Memory," included the sentence that "the causes that precipitated the war—especially slavery—were largely ignored." To the best of my knowledge, as well as the park rangers that I asked, it is only the second sign on the battlefield landscape to contain the word "slavery."[34] It still, though, doesn't note how Black lives matter.

That said, Gettysburg National Military Park is moving carefully toward a deeper and broader history—not erasing history, as we so-called revisionist historians are often accused of doing, but rather adding more history. At several fairly high-traffic areas, new signs are challenging the century-long white supremacist industry of memory on the battlefield. A sign at the bottom of the Warfield Tower now concisely tells the story of the Warfield family, with their restored house in the background. Another new marker at the Peace Light Memorial mentions that issues of race were ignored at 1938 reunion speeches there, which were attended by a quarter of a million people. Yet another new marker at the High-Water Mark that displays the photo of the 1938 handshake makes a similar point—though, ironically, it says nothing about the Brian farm, so it still needs improving. And most recently, in March 2024, a new sign atop the Warfield Tower points visitors to the mountains that lie to the south and west of the battlefield, prompting them to consider how the role of escaping slaves and their allies pushed the nation to the war that led to the battle at Gettysburg.

Additionally, there are a growing number of thoughtful battlewalks focused on African Americans. Ranger John Hoptak has done impressive research for years on Black life in Gettysburg during and after the war, and now offers a regular battlewalk on that subject. Ranger Rachael Nicholas's battlewalk on monuments in the summer of 2023 brilliantly concluded the walk at the Warfield house—making an impassioned and well-grounded case that the house, too, is a monument. It's a monument to Black lives on the battlefield. Chief of Interpretation Christopher Gwinn and I conducted a "reverse Pickett's charge" in September of 2022, walking with about eighty visitors from General Mead's statue down to the Virginia Memorial to disinter the buried stories of Black lives from Abraham and Elizabeth Brian to Black laborers at the 1913 reunion to enslaved workers during the battle. In 2023 the late historian Peter Carmichael led a provocative battlewalk on the anniversary of the battle, the three days when the park gets the most visitors, centered on enslaved laborers and the complicated relationship they had with Confederate officers.

Much, much more needs to be done. The six four-foot wayside markers that note issues of race, slavery, or African Americans are important—but they can't really compete with the 1,300-plus other monuments and markers, many of which tower to twenty, forty, sixty, or one hundred feet high. Battlewalks that draw, at most, a few hundred people total are just a start to better educating the nearly million annual visitors.

Nonetheless, all these signs and stories do begin to unpack the message of Reverend Mattson's sign. And this forces Americans to grapple with the consequences of the Battle of Gettysburg and the American Civil War, questions that are particularly important in such an age of polarization. Gettysburg was, after all, fought because Black Lives Matter.

NOTES

1. "In Gettysburg, This Summer's Black Lives Matter Protests Have Bled into Fall and Become a War of Words," Pennlive.com, October 13, 2020, https://www.pennlive.com/news/2020/10/in-gettysburg-this-summers-black-lives-matter-protests-have-bled-into-fall-and-become-a-war-of-words.html.
2. In 2017 the hoax was that Antifa was conspiring to desecrate Confederate graves on the battlefield. According to a *Washington Post* investigation, both hoaxes were perpetrated by the same person, Adam Rahuba. Antifa individuals said on both occasions they had no such plans, and there has been no evidence that I'm aware of that Antifa showed up on either of these two dates (though small numbers have been present on at least two other occasions). "The Troll: A Fake Flag Burning at Gettysburg Was Only His Latest Hoax," *Washington Post*, July 17, 2020, https://www.washingtonpost.com/investigations/2020/07/17/gettysburg-antifa-flag-burning-troll/.
3. The evidence is clear that at most, only a small, single-digit percentage of the tens of millions of protesters engaged in anything that could be remotely considered violent behavior. See Roudabeh Kishi and Sam Jones, "Demonstrations and Political Violence in America: New Data for Summer 2020," ACLED, September 3, 2020, https://acleddata.com/2020/09/03/demonstrations-political-violence-in-america-new-data-for-summer-2020/; and Tara Adhikari, "BLM and Floyd Protests Were Largely Peaceful, Data Confirms," *Christian Science Monitor*, July 8, 2021, https://www.csmonitor.com/USA/Politics/2021/0708/BLM-and-Floyd-protests-were-largely-peaceful-data-confirms. Many incidents of violence were due to either counterprotesters, or simply mishandling by police, something I witnessed myself on May 30, 2020, during a large Harrisburg, Pennsylvania, BLM protest that was loud but peaceful until police placed a vehicle and three officers directly in the path of thousands of protesters who were marching down a street that had already been cleared and blocked off for the express purpose of the march. The result was a confrontation that was limited to angry shouting, until a phalanx of additional officers came down the street equipped with riot shields and tear gas, which they employed against protesters who had not used, and did not use, any physical violence against persons or property.
4. Pennsylvania has no explicit law permitting or prohibiting open carry. Therefore, so long as a person has a gun license, open carry is permitted. The exception is in the city limits of Philadelphia, where an open carry permit is required. See Commonwealth of Pennsylvania State Police, "Carrying Firearms in Pennsylvania," https://www.pa.gov/en/agencies/psp/programs/firearms/carrying-firearms-in-pennsylvania.html.
5. Caroline E. Janney, "The Lost Cause," Encyclopedia Virginia, https://encyclopediavirginia.org/entries/lost-cause-the/.
6. Nguyen, *Nothing Ever Dies*, 106.
7. Baldwin, *Fire Next Time*, 11.
8. Gettysburg Foundation owns and operates the museum and visitor center. The foundation is "a 501(c)(3) non-profit philanthropic, educational organization that operates in partner-

ship with the National Park Service to preserve Gettysburg National Military Park and the Eisenhower National Historic Site, and to educate the public about their significance." "About Us," Gettysburg Foundation, https://www.gettysburgfoundation.org/about-us. The museum and visitor center do work closely with the National Park Service, and NPS rangers have been and still are the beating heart of the museum, which does a fine job situating slavery as the central cause of the American Civil War and includes African Americans, enslaved and free, among the exhibits.

9. *Richmond Semi-weekly Examiner*, October 31, 1854; U.S. Census 1860, New Castle, Virginia; "Craig County Gave Its All at the Battle of Gettysburg," *Roanoke Times*, July 3, 2013.
10. Power, *Proceedings of the Mississippi State Convention*, 87. See Declaration of Secession, 47.
11. *Gettysburg Compiler*, June 1, 1863, 1; *Gettysburg Compiler*, June 22, 1863, 2; *Harrisburg Daily Patriot and Union*, July 3, 1863, 2; *Carlisle American Volunteer*, July 16, 1863, 1. On the *Patriot and Union*'s political bent, see Dahlen, "Harrisburg's Civil War *Patriot and Union*."
12. *Harrisburg Daily Patriot and Union*, June 20, 1863, 2.
13. For an example of the spectrum of the relationship between Black teamsters and white officers, see Teters, *Practical Army of Liberation*, ch. 4, "Officers, Servants and Race," 83–105. Though, as Teters notes, many of the officers in the Western theater were from the Midwest and had little previous experience interacting with African Americans, the spectrum of their responses were not atypical from white Northerners who had had a great deal more interaction.
14. Paradis, *African Americans and the Gettysburg Campaign*, 15–16.
15. Moore, *Rebellion Record*, 325–26; *New York Herald*, June 29, 1863; *Boston Daily Advertiser*, June 30, 1863, 1.
16. For a thorough analysis of Confederate impressment, see Martinez, *Confederate Slave Impressment*. The North also at times impressed African Americans into service; for example, when it appeared that during the Gettysburg campaign Lee's Army of Northern Virginia may also be threatening Maryland, newspapers reported that "the defences of Baltimore are now very strong. All the negroes that can be found, without distinction, are impressed into the service and made to work in building fortifications." *New Haven Palladium*, June 30, 1863, 2.
17. Brown, *Retreat from Gettysburg*, 49–50.
18. Hassler, *General to His Lady*, 108–9, 186.
19. Hassler, *General to His Lady*, 254–55.
20. Gallagher, *Fighting for the Confederacy*, 507–8.
21. Rozier, *Granite Farm Letters*, 119; Brown, *Retreat from Gettysburg*, 300. Edgeworth Bird records the name of Waddell's enslaved young man as being Antony, not Willis. It's entirely possible that Waddell had two enslaved men with him and both worked together to escape, as other officers brought more than one slave on military campaigns, and escaping slaves, especially during the war, often departed in groups.
22. Valley of the Shadow, "Franklin County," June 16, 1863.
23. *Franklin Repository*, July 8, 1863, 1.
24. Paradis, *African Americans and the Gettysburg Campaign*, 4–7.
25. Kevin Levin, "The Terror of Being Black at Gettysburg," History News Network, July 2, 2013, https://www.historynewsnetwork.org/article/the-terror-of-being-black-at-gettysburg.

26. Green, "Persistence of Memory," 133.
27. On the connection between gentlemanliness and the military, see Foote, *Gentlemen and the Roughs*, in particular chapter 2, "'The Model of the Gentleman': Gentility and Self-Control," 41–65. Foote notes that "gentility had been the special province of a distinct social class in both the north and the south when the nineteenth century began. . . . Military law in the Civil War, with its 83rd Article of War, was one legacy of the eighteenth-century assumption that all officers would be products of this distinct social class. According to Caroline Cox, the Americans who created and led the Continental Army during the American Revolution took it for granted that poor men would be soldiers and that the officers leading them would be gentlemen" (42–43). For other examples of perceiving officers as gentlemen, see Griffin, *"A Gentleman and an Officer"*; Frederick Law Olmsted's characterization of Meade as a "gentleman and old soldier" in Olmsted and Page, "After Gettysburg," 437; and General Alpheus William's letter on June 29, 1863, expressing relief that "*now with a gentleman and a soldier in command*" the Army of the Potomac was in better hands than it had been with General Joseph Hooker.
28. Smith, "Race and Retaliation"; Allen C. Guelzo, "Robert E. Lee and Slavery," Encyclopedia Virginia, https://encyclopediavirginia.org/entries/lee-robert-e-and-slavery/; Levin, "Terror of Being Black at Gettysburg."
29. Historian Tiya Miles notes that in the antebellum era, enslaved African Americans forced to travel, often by foot, in coffles over long distances when they were sold or rented habitually carried "tow sacks." See Miles, *All That She Carried*, 91.
30. Christopher Gwinn, "Trials and Triumphs: A New Opportunity to Explore the Abram Brian Farm," *Blog of the Gettysburg National Military Park*, May 15, 2015, https://npsgnmp.wordpress.com/2015/05/15/trials-and-triumphs-a-new-opportunity-to-explore-the-abram-brian-farm/; Vermilyea, "Jack Hopkins' Civil War," 4–21. For a thorough recounting of James Warfield's time in Gettysburg, see Jared Frederick's 2022 Winter Lecture at GNMP, "Gettysburg Roots: A Family, a Farm, and the Fight for Freedom," https://www.youtube.com/watch?v=evl7jVkBXHI.
31. Jane Nutter, conversation with author, March 16, 2023.
32. Nutter, conversation with author, March 16, 2023.
33. Nguyen, *Nothing Ever Dies*, 75.
34. The first sign on the battlefield landscape, outside the museum, to have the word "slavery" was installed in 2021, next to the Abraham and Elizabeth Brian house.

BIBLIOGRAPHY

Baldwin, James. *The Fire Next Time*. Modern Library, 1995.

Brown, Kent Masterson. *Retreat from Gettysburg: Lee, Logistics and the Pennsylvania Campaign*. University of North Carolina Press, 2005.

Dahlen, Richard L. "Harrisburg's Civil War *Patriot and Union*: Its Conciliatory Viewpoint Collapses." *Cumberland County History* 15, no. 2 (Winter 1998): 115–27.

Foote, Lorien. *The Gentlemen and the Roughs: Violence, Honor, and Manhood in the Union Army*. New York University Press, 2010.

Gallagher, Gary W., ed. *Fighting for the Confederacy: The Personal Recollections of General Edward Porter Alexander*. University of North Carolina Press, 1989.

Green, Hilary N. "Persistence of Memory: African Americans and Transitional Justice Efforts in Franklin County, Pennsylvania." In *Reconciliation after Civil Wars: Global Perspectives*, edited by Paul Quigley and Jim Hawdown, 131–49. Routledge, 2019.

Griffin, James B. *"A Gentleman and an Officer": A Military and Social History of James B. Griffin's Civil War*. Edited by Judith N. McArthur and Orville Vernon Burton. Oxford University Press, 1998.

Hassler, William W., ed. *The General to His Lady: The Civil War Letters of William Dorsey Pender to Fanny Pender*. University of North Carolina Press, 1962.

Martinez, Jaime Amanda. *Confederate Slave Impressment in the Upper South*. University of North Carolina Press, 2013.

Miles, Tiya. *All That She Carried: The Journey of Ashley's Sack, a Black Family Keepsake*. Random House, 2021.

Moore, Frank, ed. *The Rebellion Record: A Diary of American Events*. Vol. 7. 1864. Reprint, Arno Press, 1977.

Nguyen, Viet Thanh. *Nothing Ever Dies: Vietnam and the Memory of War*. Harvard University Press, 2016.

Olmstead, Frederick Law, and Elizabeth Page. "After Gettysburg: Frederick Law Olmsted on the Escape of Lee." *Pennsylvania Magazine of History and Biography* 75, no. 4 (October 1951): 436–46.

Paradis, James M. *African Americans and the Gettysburg Campaign*. Scarecrow Press, 2013.

Power, J. L. *Proceedings of the Mississippi State Convention*. Power & Cadwallader, 1861. https://docsouth.unc.edu/imls/missconv/missconv.html.

Rozier, John, ed. *The Granite Farm Letters: The Civil War Correspondence of Edgeworth and Sallie Bird*. University of Georgia Press, 1988.

Smith, David G. "Race and Retaliation: The Capture of African Americans during the Gettysburg Campaign." In *Virginia's Civil War*, edited by Peter Wallenstein and Bertram Wyatt-Brown, 137–51. University of Virginia Press, 2005.

Teters, Kristopher A. *A Practical Army of Liberation: How the Union Army Carried Out Emancipation in the West*. University of North Carolina Press, 2018.

The Valley of the Shadow, Valley Personal Papers. "Franklin County: Diary of Rachel Cormany (1863)." https://valley.lib.virginia.edu/papers/FD1006.

Vermilyea, Peter C. "Jack Hopkins' Civil War." *Adams County History* 11 (2005): 4–21.

10

The Black Confederate Myth and Civil War Memory in the Trump Era

KEVIN M. LEVIN

In June 2023 Mississippi Republican State Senator Kathy Chism called for the readoption of the state's Confederate-themed flag, which the state had abandoned three years earlier as a result of a ballot initiative. Voters chose to adopt a new state flag by a wide margin after a similar ballot initiative had failed two decades earlier. The new flag featured a magnolia blossom above the words "In God We Trust." It replaced one that featured a Confederate battle flag, approved in 1894, following the Civil War and Reconstruction, and which marked the beginning of legalized segregation that would come to define the Jim Crow era for decades to come (see Brett A. Barnett's chapter).

During the debate over the state flag, Senator Chism explained her defense of the old state flag by claiming that it had been designed by an "African American Confederate Soldier." "I can only imagine," she wrote on a Facebook post, "how proud he was that his art, his flag design was chosen to represent our State and now we want to strip him of his pride, his hard work." Chism's claim about the origins of the state flag is part of a long history of mythologizing about the Confederacy and the role that its Black population played during the war. Individuals and organizations like the Sons of Confederate Veterans (scv) and United Daughters of the Confederacy have long embraced the Black Confederate myth as a means to countering any attempt to saddle their ancestors with the baggage of slavery and white supremacy. If Black men served as equals in the Confederate army, so the argument goes, then their ancestors and the Confederacy could not have been fighting to maintain the institution of slavery. As one scv commander put it, the presence of Black men in Confederate ranks "wipes out the whole segregation and hate and racism issue."[1]

This Lost Cause myth remains a persistent belief and potent political weapon within the Confederate heritage community and increasingly among their conservative Republican allies. For a number of reasons they have embraced this narrative to minimize the history of slavery and race in America, to assert that the nation has fundamentally solved its racial problems, and to push back against the Black Lives Matter movement and the increased calls to remove Confederate monuments and other symbols of the Confederacy in public spaces—all of which was heightened during the Trump era. Though the Black Confederate myth can still be heard in certain circles, it has largely been eclipsed by an "emancipationist" memory of the war that emphasizes the end of slavery as the Civil War's most important result and the military service of roughly 180,000 Black men in the U.S. Army.[2]

Most people are surprised to learn that references to Black Confederate soldiers only first appeared as recently as the 1970s, following the civil rights era of the 1950s and 1960s. Real Confederates would be confused and utterly befuddled by the outlandish claims made by their descendants on their behalf about the supposed service of large numbers of Black soldiers in the army. Confederate military and political leaders, the rank and file, and those on the home front were never in doubt about the legal status of Black men who were forced to provide labor for the benefit of the war effort. Tens of thousands of enslaved men labored for the Confederacy by constructing earthworks, building and maintaining rail lines, and working in foundries producing war matériel in places like Richmond, Atlanta, and Selma. Confederate armies were supported by thousands of forced laborers who functioned as teamsters and hospital attendants, as well as accompanying their enslavers into the army as body servants or camp slaves.[3] It was not until the final weeks of the war in March 1865 that the Confederate Congress approved the enlistment of slaves as soldiers, but by then it was too late.[4]

For generations after the war white Southerners remembered the thousands of enslaved men who labored for the Confederacy in the army and on the home front not as soldiers but as "loyal slaves." The emphasis on slave loyalty and fidelity fit neatly into a burgeoning Lost Cause narrative that attempted to vindicate the Confederacy and that allowed postwar writers to assert that the war was a constitutional dispute rather than a war to protect and expand the institution of slavery. Former Confederates and other writers relished retelling stories of enslaved men coming to the rescue of their masters on the battlefield, escorting wounded soldiers home, and even ensuring that their bodies arrive home safely in the event of their death.[5] Former body servants, such as Jefferson Shields and Steve "Eberhart" Perry, attended numerous Confederate veteran reunions, entertaining large white crowds with their own wartime accounts that reinforced their continued loyalty to former masters and the Lost Cause.

At the height of the Jim Crow era, white Southerners leveraged the past to justify legalized segregation with references to loyal slaves inscribed on monuments, such as the one in Fort Mill, South Carolina, dedicated in 1896, or more boldly through the inclusion of the images of the loyal "Mammy" figure and uniformed body servant on the Confederate monument in Arlington National Cemetery, dedicated in 1914.[6]

During the 1950s and 1960s, civil rights activists focused on the goal of political empowerment, in part by challenging the Lost Cause narrative and reminding the nation of Black military service in the U.S. Army and their sacrifice in saving the Union.[7] At the same time, new scholarship on slavery and in the field of Civil War military history underscored the myriad ways in which the actions of enslaved people on the plantation, in contraband camps, and eventually in the army itself contributed to Union victory and the end of slavery. This ultimately led to significant changes in how the war was interpreted at museums and historical sites in the decades to follow. The civil rights movement itself underscored the "unfinished work" of interpretation that was needed at historical institutions and historical sites.[8]

By 1979 the first Black reenactors, who performed roles as slaves and free Blacks, could be found at Colonial Williamsburg and later at reconstructed slave quarters at nearby Carter's Grove. Changes in interpretation at individual parks in the national park system also took place during the 1980s. Park staff at Petersburg National Battlefield began to focus more intentionally on the massacre of United States Colored Troops at the Crater in their tours as well as through the placement of new wayside exhibits.[9] A groundbreaking exhibit in 1991 called Before Freedom Came at the Museum of the Confederacy in Richmond—originally established as a shrine to the Confederacy in 1896—addressed the violence of slavery through the display of slave shackles.[10] Hollywood movies and popular television shows also reflected this shift in Civil War memory.

The first references to significant numbers of Black Confederate soldiers came in direct response to these shifts in interpretation at museums and historical sites as well as a shift in popular memory of the Civil War era in Hollywood movies, documentaries, and television series such as Roots, which aired in 1977. At the time, the leadership within the scv expressed concern over how the institution of slavery and race relations were portrayed in the film as well as the Confederacy itself. Commander in Chief Dean Boggs called on members to research the contributions of African Americans to the Confederate war effort to counter the movie's "propaganda": "Suddenly, after more than 100 years, it seems to have become 'good politics' to assert that the flags, uniforms, and songs of the Confederacy are repugnant to negroes. This is childish nonsense. Politics often ignores the truth, and the truth is that the majority of Southern Negroes, slave and free, sided [with] the Confederate war effort tremendously. Some were under arms and in combat." Boggs and others issued a call to their members to uncover stories of their own loyal Black soldiers.[11]

The push on the part of Confederate heritage organizations like the SCV to find their own Black soldiers only intensified in the following decades, especially after the release of *Glory* in 1989 and the PBS series *The Civil War*, directed by Ken Burns, which aired the next year. Both the movie and documentary emphasized the importance of emancipation through the story of the service and sacrifice of two hundred thousand Black U.S. soldiers and sailors, including the Fifty-Fourth Massachusetts Volunteer Infantry. At the time the SCV relied on a few books written by its members and released by small publishing houses. Articles also appeared throughout this period in the organization's magazine, *Confederate Veteran*, but none of these efforts had much of an impact beyond a small group of readers within the Confederate heritage community.[12]

It was only with the widespread use of the internet by the turn of the twenty-first century that the Black Confederate narrative had any chance of spreading. And it did. References that placed the number of Black soldiers in Confederate ranks in the hundreds and as high as one hundred thousand could be found on thousands of websites. A few high-profile stories, including a fourth-grade Virginia textbook that referenced thousands of Black men serving with Stonewall Jackson in the Shenandoah Valley in 1862, made the mainstream news in 2011, but the mythical Black Confederate soldier never posed a serious challenge to the growing awareness that slavery had caused the Civil War, that the Confederacy was fighting to preserve slavery and white supremacy, and that Black U.S. soldiers played a crucial role in winning the war and preserving the Union. This "emancipationist" narrative of the war was on full display throughout the years of the Civil War Sesquicentennial between 2011 and 2015, especially within the National Park Service, which acknowledged that for far too long, "we as a Nation (consciously or unconsciously) have assigned the rights of memory to a few select groups.... They, in turn, fostered a swift but incomplete reconciliation—one that passed over but did not extinguish lingering bitterness, one that was based on selective memory, and forged, in part, at the expense of liberty for free blacks and newly freed slaves."[13] Any attempt to claim victory in the continuing clash over Civil War memory during the sesquicentennial was overshadowed by one of the worst racial massacres in recent American history.

On June 17, 2015, Dylann Roof, a twenty-one-year-old white supremacist, walked into Emanuel African Methodist Episcopal Church in Charleston, South Carolina, and murdered nine church members, including senior pastor and state senator Clementa Pinckney, who were taking part in a Bible study. The release of photographs of Roof posing with Confederate battle flags as well as a manifesto that highlighted his racial hatred and desire to start a race war led to calls to remove the Confederate battle flag on the State House grounds in Columbia and other symbols of the Confederacy (see John M. Kinder's chapter). In his eulogy for Reverend Pinckney, President Barack Obama urged his audience and the nation to acknowledge that the Confederate battle flag was "a reminder of systemic oppression and racial subjugation." Removing it, he said, "would not be an act of political correctness; it would not be an insult to the valor of Confederate soldiers. It would simply be an acknowledgment that the cause for which they fought—the cause of slavery—was wrong—the imposition of Jim Crow after the Civil War, the resistance to civil rights for all people was wrong."[14]

In the wake of the murders, the South Carolina Division of the scv issued a statement in an attempt to reclaim Confederate symbols from their association with Dylann Roof. It was the same argument that the scv had embraced since the 1970s: "Historical fact shows there were Black Confederate soldiers. These brave men fought in the trenches beside their White brothers, all under the Confederate Battle Flag." The scv offered this argument not only to stem the tide of calls to lower the Confederate flag in Columbia and remove monuments but to suggest that the flag had nothing at all to do with racial divisions in South Carolina in the present or the past. The history of the Confederate military—properly understood—it argued, ought to unite Black and white South Carolinians. According to the scv's spokesman, Roof's violent act and close identification with the Confederate flag was the product of the "deranged mind of a horrendous individual."[15] According to the scv, it was Roof who hijacked the meaning of the Confederate battle flag—a flag under which both Black and white men had fought side by side.

The president's words proved to be a rallying cry for activists across the county, who demanded that cities and towns across the country divest themselves of all Confederate symbols, especially Confederate monuments. By 2017 cities including New Orleans, Saint Louis, Kansas City, Louisville, and even Boston had removed public monuments honoring the Confederacy while many other communities were in the process of deciding whether to follow suit.[16] The debate over Confederate monuments quickly divided the nation along political and racial lines, with Democrats and a significant percentage of African Americans largely supporting their removal, while Republicans followed the president's lead in defending them, going so far as to pass legislation in some former Confederate states preventing communities from making these decisions on their own. Republicans have largely aligned themselves with a belief among many conservative voters that the call to remove Confederate symbols is little more than "political correctness" and "wokeness" run amok. Race relations would be more peaceful, they contend, if minorities and others stopped talking about the history and legacy of slavery and segregation along with mass incarceration, economic inequality, and voter suppression.

South Carolina Republican State Representatives Bill Chumley and Mike Burns embraced this argument in the wake of the Charleston murders in an attempt to speak for constituents who believed that their "heritage" and political outlook were under attack from the "Radical Left." Neither representative supported the removal of the Confederate battle flag from the State House grounds in 2015. Writing in *USA Today*, Burns appealed to the public to consider the "descendants of Confederate soldiers" who were concerned about how their ancestors were being portrayed, "many of whom were poor or middle-class farmers who thought they were going to war to defend their homeland."[17] Confederate soldiers, according to Burns, were fighting for the very same things that many of his constituents were working to attain 150 years later. In 2017 Chumley and Burns attempted to distance the Confederacy and slavery even further by introducing a bill calling for a monument honoring African Americans who fought for the Confederacy to be erected at the State House in Columbia. The two representatives believed the monument would "help educate current and future generations of a little known" chapter of South Carolina history.[18] Like the SCV, they justified the need for a new monument by suggesting that white and Black South Carolinians had fought together for the Confederacy: "These African-Americans, like many of their Caucasian contemporaries," argued Burns, "stepped up to defend their home state during a tumultuous time in our country's history." Burns added, "Their service has largely been overlooked or forgotten."[19]

The timing of this proposed new monument came just as Donald Trump entered the White House in early 2017. Trump had previously called for the removal of Confederate flags from public spaces, suggesting that "they should put it in the museum and let it go," but he quickly reversed course as his campaign increasingly attracted supporters who viewed the removal of Confederate symbols as an attack on their shared "heritage" and as a growing indication of minority political power and fear of the effects of liberalism and modernity.[20] Trump supporters routinely waved Confederate flags at campaign rallies, while Trump himself spoke out in defense of Confederate leaders like Robert E. Lee. On August 12, 2017, white nationalists rallied in Charlottesville, Virginia, to defend a monument honoring Robert E. Lee after the city council voted to have it removed. Members of the Unite the Right Rally clashed with antiracist demonstrators throughout the day in Emancipation Park, the violence ultimately leading to the death of Heather Heyer. Anyone expecting or hoping for a blanket condemnation of openly racist agitators by the president was sorely disappointed. Instead, President Donald Trump concluded that "there were good people on both sides."

The violence in Charlottesville brought about a new wave of Confederate monument removals and a deepening public rift over their meaning. The Confederate heritage community and their conservative allies rallied around President Trump. "Sad to see the history and culture of our great country being ripped apart with the removal of our beautiful statues and monuments," the president tweeted. "You can't change history, but you can learn from it. Robert E. Lee, Stonewall Jackson—who's next, Washington, Jefferson? So foolish! Also the beauty that is being taken out of our cities, towns and parks will be greatly missed and never able to be comparably replaced!"[21]

The SCV routinely relied on Black Confederates in their defense of Confederate monuments. Todd Kern, commander of the Turner Ashby Camp, SCV, referred to a "new narrative of the cultural Marxist" to dismiss any suggestion that the monuments were erected to reinforce white supremacy and Jim Crow segregation at the beginning of the twentieth century. "All one has to do is read the inscriptions on the memorial markers," he asserted. "There are even monuments [of] Black Confederates! None of this will help to unify the country."[22] References to Black Confederates allowed Kern and others to deflect attention away from the monuments as exacerbating racial tension throughout the country and instead depicted the Confederacy and the South as a multiracial paradise.

This distorted picture of a strong interracial bond has been aided in recent years by a small but vocal community of African Americans who have embraced the Black Confederate myth for various reasons. Some families have embraced the Black Confederate narrative as a means to identify and to celebrate stories of ancestors who they believe have been long forgotten or intentionally ignored in the scholarly literature and popular memory well into the twentieth century. Nelson Winbush, for example, has found a supportive audience among SCV members in Tennessee. According to Winbush, his grandfather fought bravely alongside Confederates to defend his home against "Yankee" invaders, despite the overwhelming evidence that Louis Napoleon Nelson accompanied his master to war while enslaved.[23]

Since the early 2000s, the SCV has leveraged this interest among Black families by dedicating new military-style gravestones in honor of supposed Black Confederate soldiers. These ceremonies attract local and sometimes national media and offer an opportunity for the SCV to highlight this historical myth as a way to rebrand their organization as welcoming to all races. For the descendants of these men, it is an opportunity to honor their bravery and heroism on the battlefield even if the basis for such praise is historically misplaced.

In 2008 the North Carolina Division of the SCV honored Weary Clyburn, a former body servant from South Carolina who was now remembered as a soldier. The SCV welcomed the descendants of Clyburn as "one of their own." The headstone itself makes no mention that Clyburn was enslaved, ensuing that future visitors would conclude that he was indeed a soldier. The family was satisfied that their ancestors received proper recognition, while the SCV succeeded in distorting not only Clyburn's personal history but also the larger story of the Confederacy's commitment to keeping men like Clyburn enslaved. Following the death of Clyburn's daughter in 2014, the SCV and a number of other Confederate heritage organizations held an elaborate ceremony next to the grave of her father. Former SCV Commander in Chief Michael Givens referred to Mattie as a "true daughter of the Confederacy" and used the occasion to suggest that Black and white Southerners have always been closely linked around the bonds of brotherly affection. "The same blood that coursed through Weary's veins when he stood on the front lines and he fired at the enemy that was invading his home land, the same blood that was coursing through his veins when he took his friend Frank [his enslaver] and put him on his shoulders and carried him home," Givens stated confidently, "is the same blood that coursed through her veins when she stood up for her own heritage. . . . It's the same as yours and the same as mine."[24]

These ceremonies continue to this day, most often during February and Black History Month.[25] SCV camps have also held ceremonies in cemeteries on Veterans Day, thus further obscuring the distinction between slave and soldier. In 2021 members of the Forty-Eighth Alabama Infantry Reenactors, along with members of a local SCV camp, held a ceremony honoring three enslaved men as Confederate veterans. A descendant of one of the enslaved men being honored used the occasion to remind the audience, "We want to remember the sacrifice that these men gave for our country and the sacrifice of Black Americans that their story has never been told."[26]

Regardless of motivation, the SCV has welcomed African Americans into their ranks, over the past three decades, to lend legitimacy to the Black Confederate narrative, while other conservative groups have used the opportunity to forge what they see as an interracial alliance against organizations like Black Lives Matter and in support of traditional values and an understanding of American history that downplays the history of slavery and white supremacy. In 2016 Derek Boyd Hankerson, an African American university lecturer and author, served as Trump's Northeast Florida field director and touted that he helped him win "sixty-six of sixty-seven counties in Florida." The previous year he coauthored a book with Judith Hearer titled *Belonging: The Civil War's South We Never Knew*, which made the claim that a large number of Black men fought for the Confederacy. "It's a misnomer or incorrect history," claimed Hankerson in an interview, "believing blacks didn't fight for the south when the majority or 80 percent of black people are originally from the south. . . . To classify them as coward is false." Not surprisingly, Hankerson also maintained that slavery "was not the key issue" of the Civil War. Anyone looking to minimize the nation's complicity in chattel slavery would have nodded along in approval as he exclaimed that "slavery was started in Egypt by Africans enslaving Jews" and that the Civil War was fought over "trade, tariffs, states' rights, and religion."[27]

No African American has been more vocal in support of the Black Confederate myth than H. K. Edgerton. Over the past twenty years, Edgerton—a onetime president of the Asheville branch of the NAACP—has become one of the most popular attractions in the Confederate heritage movement. His transition from the NAACP to Confederate apologist is difficult to explain, but Edgerton has come to embrace a vision of the nation that ignored the long history of racial violence and white supremacy for one that centered peaceful race relations at the center of the history of the South. Edgerton's championing of the Black Confederate narrative resonated with SCV and United Daughters of the Confederacy audiences, vindicating their Lost Cause belief that the Confederacy did not fight to preserve the institution of slavery. In 2002 Edgerton, dressed in a Confederate uniform and carrying a Confederate battle flag, set out on a 1,300-mile "March Across Dixie for Southern Heritage" from Asheville, North Carolina, to Austin, Texas. Edgerton has maintained a close working relationship with the Southern Legal Resource Center—an organization founded by Kirk Lyons and declared a hate group by the Southern Poverty Law Center—and the Sons of Confederate Veterans Heritage Defense Fund.[28]

Edgerton has demonstrated in front of Confederate monuments and has spoken up at numerous city council meetings against their removal. In Knoxville, Tennessee, in 2017, Edgerton asserted that the push to remove monuments "is a continuation of the attacks upon our southern heritage, our ancestors, the Confederate army, [and] the flag." Following the attempt of others to depict race relations in the South and the Confederacy as peaceful, Edgerton argued, "Those monuments weren't just for the white soldier, its for the red, yellow, black, [and] white."[29] A year later and just days after students at the University of North Carolina at Chapel Hill removed a Confederate statue popularly known as "Silent Sam," H. K. Edgerton proudly boasted that the monument "should be embraced by black folks." "It's always slavery," he went on to say. "The evil white man and the south land of America. That's the biggest lie they've ever told."[30]

Unfortunately for Edgerton, his suggestion that African Americans should embrace the symbolism of Confederate monuments was roundly ignored. In fact, no number of mythical Black Confederate soldiers or Black men dressed in Confederate uniforms has been able to stem the tide of calls for the removal of monuments and other symbols of the Confederacy from public spaces. The subject remains politically divisive, with Republicans largely calling for the monuments to remain in place, including those located in the U.S. Capitol building's Statuary Hall, where each state is allowed two representative statues. In addition, state laws have been passed barring the removal of Confederate monuments in a number of Republican-controlled legislators across the South.

A record number of monument removals occurred in the wake of the police murder of George Floyd in May 2020.[31] Activists in Virginia vandalized or "tagged" all of the Confederate monuments on Richmond's famed

Monument Avenue and set fire to the United Daughters of the Confederacy's national headquarters. SCV members once again trotted out the Black Confederate narrative but with little impact. In Texas an SCV member insisted, "There were people of all races and backgrounds on both sides of the war that fought for their beliefs. It was about state rights; it wasn't just about slavery. If it was about slavery, you wouldn't have had a single Black person fighting for the Confederacy."[32] While the Black Confederate soldier continued to struggle to gain credibility, the history of Black Union soldiers increasingly appeared in popular culture—the result of decades of new scholarship and access to traditional and digital resources in the classroom.

Hollywood movies now routinely feature the stories of these men. Steven Spielberg's Oscar-winning movie *Lincoln* (2012) begins with a scene depicting the fighting at Jenkin's Ferry on April 30, 1864, along the Saline River in Arkansas. The brief scene depicts soldiers in the Second Colored Kansas Infantry and Confederates engaged in close-quarters fighting in the mud and hard rain. Men on both sides are brutally killed and wounded with bayonets, fists, and strangulation. Nate Parker's *The Birth of a Nation* (2016) ends with a young boy looking on as Nat Turner hangs from the gallows only to be transformed into a Black Union soldier marching forward with his comrades in line of battle. Black soldiers appear at the end of the movie *Harriet* (2019) in a scene in which the famous conductor of the Underground Railroad leads the Second Regiment South Carolina in what became known as the Combahee River Raid on June 2, 1863.[33]

In 2022 Will Smith starred in the movie *Emancipation*, playing an enslaved man named Peter who is impressed by the Confederacy to work on earthworks in Louisiana and who later joins the Union army in 1863. The movie accurately depicts the vital role that enslaved men played in the Confederate war effort, as well as the violence they experienced—a depiction that stands in sharp contrast to the mythical Black Confederate soldier. In the movie's penultimate scene, Peter lines up with the rest of his regiment to take part in an assault against an enemy position at Port Hudson on May 27, 1863.[34] The increased attention to United States Colored Troops points to a broader recognition in popular memory of the war that the Confederacy was fighting to maintain the institution of slavery and that Black men played a vital role in saving the Union and ending slavery.

The clearest evidence that the Black Confederate narrative, along with the larger Lost Cause narrative with which it is associated, have failed to capture the attention of the public can be found in in the recent flurry of new monuments honoring Black Union or United States Colored Troops that have appeared across the country, especially in former Confederate states. The dedication of the African American Civil War Memorial in Washington DC in 1998 was the first memorial to honor Black Union soldiers since the dedication of the Robert Gould Shaw and Fifty-Fourth Massachusetts Memorial in Boston in 1897. These new monuments reflect both an increased awareness that African American men served in the army as well as the political influence at the local and state level that for a long time was solely in the hands of white residents committed to maintaining a Lost Cause memory in public spaces.

Among the places in which monuments have been erected are Pulaski, Tennessee, the birthplace of the Ku Klux Klan; Natchez, Mississippi; and Culpeper, Virginia. In Wilmington, North Carolina, sculptor Stephen Hayes utilized local descendants of United States Colored Troops as models for his monument. *Boundless* depicts eleven men marching, three rows of three soldiers, a drummer boy, and a color bearer. "Everybody has a certain history they want to put forward," Hayes shared in an interview. "We've washed over certain types of history and at the end of the day, I want to see what conversations the sculpture will bring."[35]

The prevalence of Lost Cause symbolism in public spaces has long overshadowed the kinds of stories and conversations that Hayes and others now champion through their public art. The shift in how Americans now think about and commemorate the American Civil War is visible with every Confederate monument removed and every new one raised, along with the ending of other forms of public commemoration of the Confederacy. But even in these changing times, the Black Confederate myth is never far from view. In February 2023, just days after a bust honoring Nathan Bedford Forrest—slave trader, Confederate general, and Ku Klux Klan leader—was removed from inside the state capitol building in Nashville, Tennessee, two Republican state legislators signed a proclamation declaring April Confederate History Month.[36] The proclamation recognized the Confederacy as engaging in a "heroic struggle for states' rights, individual freedom, local government control, and a determined struggle for deeply held beliefs." No attempt was made to define the specific "rights" and "beliefs" that were under threat, though it is well documented that the central issue in the state's debate over secession was slavery.[37] Though it was likely overlooked by many, the proclamation also includes a nod to the Black Confederate and "loyal slave" myth in its recognition of the "noble spirit and inspiring leadership of the officers, soldiers, and citizens, free and not free, of the Confederate States." The implication that enslaved people supported, if not fought for, the Confederacy as soldiers could not be clearer.

Tennessee's proclamation is an important reminder that despite the waning influence of the Black Confederate myth and its Lost Cause parent, they remain potent weapons in the ongoing debate about the meaning and legacy of the Civil War era. In the words of historian David Blight, "As long as we have a politics of race in America, we will have a politics of Civil War memory."[38] What is at stake is not simply the question of whether African Americans fought as soldiers in the Confederate army, but whether Americans are willing to confront difficult questions about the legacy of the Confederacy's fight to preserve slavery and the even longer history of white supremacy—subjects that the promotion of the Black Confederate narrative and the Lost Cause has long attempted to obscure.

The ways in which the Black Confederate narrative has been deployed in recent years by Confederate heritage groups and their conservative allies suggests that the history and legacy of racism and white supremacy will likely continue to divide Americans over how to interpret and commemorate the Civil War era for the foreseeable future.

NOTES

1. Stephanie Garry, "In Defense of His Confederate Pride," *Tampa Bay Times*, October 7, 2007, https://www.tampabay.com/archive/2007/10/07/in-defense-of-his-confederate-pride/. On the history of the Confederate flag in Mississippi, see Coski, *Confederate Battle Flag*, 80–81, 236–37.
2. Not everyone in the Confederate heritage community has embraced the Black Confederate narrative, especially those who openly embrace white supremacy. Neo-Confederate organizations, like the League of the South, for example, refer to people who believe in the Black Confederate myth as "Rainbow Confederates." See "Racial Division Along the Neo-Confederate Spectrum," Southern Poverty Law Center, March 2, 2017, https://www.splcenter.org/hatewatch/2017/03/02/racial-division-along-neo-confederate-spectrum.
3. On the use of enslaved labor in the Confederacy, see Levin, *Searching for Black Confederates*, 12–36.
4. On the slave enlistment debate, see Levine, *Confederate Emancipation*.
5. On the Lost Cause, see Janney, *Remembering the Civil War*, 133–59.
6. Levin, *Searching for Black Confederates*, 68–99.
7. On African Americans and the Civil War Centennial, see Cook, *Troubled Commemoration*, 155–92.
8. On changing interpretations in the academic field and at historical sites, see Brundage, *Southern Past*, 293–303; Greenspan, *Creating Colonial Williamsburg*.
9. Levin, *Remembering the Battle of the Crater*, 131.

10. Coleman, "Among the Ruins," 5.
11. Levin, *Searching for Black Confederates*, 129–30.
12. Levin, *Searching for Black Confederates*, 130–32.
13. Quoted in Cook, *Civil War Memories*, 201. On the NPS and the sesquicentennial, see Rudy, "From Tokenism to True Partnership," 61–76.
14. Barack Obama, "Remarks by the President in Eulogy for the Honorable Reverend Clementa Pinckney," White House, June 26, 2015, https://obamawhitehouse.archives.gov/the-press-office/2015/06/26/remarks-president-eulogy-honorable-reverend-clementa-pinckney.
15. Levin, *Searching for Black Confederates*, 177–78.
16. "From 2017: Confederate Monuments are Coming Down Across the United States. Here's a List," *New York Times*, August 28, 2017, https://www.nytimes.com/interactive/2017/08/16/us/confederate-monuments-removed.html.
17. Mike Burns, "South Carolina Rushed to Erase Heritage: Opposing View," *USA Today*, July 9, 2015, https://www.usatoday.com/story/opinion/2015/07/09/south-carolina-confederate-flag-mike-burns-editorials-debates/29938783/.
18. Levin, *Searching for Black Confederates*, 183–84.
19. Doug Criss, "Republicans in South Carolina Want to Honor Black Confederate Soldiers. There's Just One Problem . . . ," CNN, January 4, 2018, https://www.cnn.com/2018/01/03/us/black-confederate-monument-trnd/index.html.
20. Michael Tesler, "In 2015, Donald Trump Said the Confederate Flag Should Go in a Museum. Here's What Changed," *Washington Post*, August 18, 2017, https://www.washingtonpost.com/news/monkey-cage/wp/2017/08/18/in-2015-donald-trump-said-the-confederate-flag-should-go-in-a-museum-heres-what-changed/.
21. Quoted in Karen L. Cox, "The Whole Point of Confederate Monuments Is to Celebrate White Supremacy," *Washington Post*, August 16, 2017, https://www.washingtonpost.com/news/posteverything/wp/2017/08/16/the-whole-point-of-confederate-monuments-is-to-celebrate-white-supremacy/.
22. Josh Janney and Cathy Kuehner, "Local Officials Majority Opinion Stands on Side of Confederate Statues," *Winchester Star*, August 18, 2017, https://www.winchesterstar.com/news/clarke/local-officials-majority-opinion-stands-on-side-of-confederate-statues/article_cbefa9d5-4d18-54a2-aefc-c303e29857f5.html.
23. Kimberly Kindy, "His Grandfather Was a Slave. Now He's a Vocal Champion of Confederate Monuments," *Washington Post*, October 9, 2017, https://www.washingtonpost.com/news/post-nation/wp/2017/10/09/his-grandfather-was-a-slave-now-hes-a-champion-for-confederate-monuments/.
24. Levin, *Searching for Black Confederates*, 168–69.
25. "Rabun Gap Riflemen Honor, Salute Black Confederates during Black History Month," *Clayton Tribune*, February 23, 2023, https://www.theclaytontribune.com/local-news-newsletter/rabun-gap-riflemen-honor-salute-black-confederates-during-black-history-month.
26. Hadley Hitson, "Group Honors Black Men as 'Confederate Veterans,'" *Montgomery Advertiser*, November 28, 2021, https://eu.montgomeryadvertiser.com/story/news/2021/11/24/heritage-group-honors-black-men-says-were-confederate-veterans/6347517001/. For a thoughtful discussion of the SCV's commemoration of Richard Poplar in Petersburg, Virginia, see Smith, *How the Word Is Passed*, 147–51.

27. Danielle Dougall, "Meet the Self-Described Historian Responsible for Helping Donald Trump Win the Florida Primary," History News Network, August 2, 2016, http://historynewsnetwork.org/article/163533.
28. "A 'March Through Dixie' Has Onlookers a Bit Bewildered," Southern Poverty Law Center, December 18, 2002, https://www.splcenter.org/fighting-hate/intelligence-report/2002/march-through-dixie-has-onlookers-bit-bewildered.
29. Kelly Reinke, "Debate Continues over Confederate Monument in Knoxville," Wate.com, August 18, 2017, https://www.wate.com/news/local-news/debate-continues-over-confederate-monument-in-knoxville/.
30. "Black Confederate Supporter Says Flag, Silent Sam Aren't Race Related," WBTV, August 23, 2018, https://www.wbtv.com/story/38948569/black-confederate-supporter-says-flag-silent-sam-arent-race-related/.
31. Bonnie Berkowitz and Adrian Blanco, "A Record Number of Confederate Monuments Fell in 2020, but Hundreds Still Stand. Here's Where," *Washington Post*, March 12, 2021, https://www.washingtonpost.com/graphics/2020/national/confederate-monuments/.
32. Liz Landers, "We Talked to the Sons of Confederate Veterans About Why They're Defending Racist Monuments," *Vice*, July 28, 2020, https://www.vice.com/en/article/ep4mpk/we-talked-about-black-lives-matter-with-the-sons-of-confederate-veterans.
33. Levin, "Violence and Forgetting in the Crater," 118–19.
34. Levin, "Violence and Forgetting in the Crater," 120.
35. Liz Vinson, "'Boundless': New Sculpture in North Carolina Honors Black Soldiers Who Helped Win the Civil War," Southern Poverty Law Center, December 10, 2021, https://www.splcenter.org/news/2021/12/10/boundless-new-sculpture-north-carolina-honors-black-soldiers-who-helped-win-civil-war.
36. Daniel Feller, "White Tennessee Lawmakers Speak Out for Insurrection in Honoring Confederate History," *Tennessee Lookout*, April 21, 2023, https://tennesseelookout.com/2023/04/21/white-tennessee-lawmakers-speak-out-for-insurrection-in-honoring-confederate-history/.
37. Pitcaithley, *Tennessee Secedes*.
38. Blight, *Race and Reunion*, 4.

BIBLIOGRAPHY

Blight, David W. *Race and Reunion: The Civil War in American Memory*. Harvard University Press, 2001.

Brundage, W. Fitzhugh. *The Southern Past: A Clash of Race and Memory*. Harvard University Press, 2005.

Coleman, Christy S. "Among the Ruins: Creating and Interpreting the American Civil War in Richmond." In *Interpreting the Civil War at Museums and Historic Sites*, edited by Kevin Levin, 1–12. Rowman and Littlefield, 2017.

Cook, Robert J. *Civil War Memories: Contesting the Past in the United States since 1865*. Johns Hopkins University Press, 2017.

———. *Troubled Commemoration: The American Civil War Centennial, 1961–1965*. Louisiana State University Press, 2007.

Coski, John M. *The Confederate Battle Flag*. Harvard University Press, 2005.

Greenspan, Anders. *Creating Colonial Williamsburg*. Smithsonian Institution Press, 2002.

Janney, Caroline E. *Remembering the Civil War: Reunion and the Limits of Reconciliation*. University of North Carolina Press, 2013.

Levin, Kevin M., ed. *Interpreting the Civil War at Museums and Historic Sites*. Rowman and Littlefield, 2017.

———. *Remembering the Battle of the Crater: War as Murder*. University Press of Kentucky, 2012.

———. *Searching for Black Confederates: The Civil War's Most Persistent Myth*. University of North Carolina Press, 2019.

———. "Violence and Forgetting in the Crater." In *The Civil War and Pop Culture: Favorite Stories and Fresh Perspectives from the Historians at Emerging Civil War*, edited by Chris Mackowski and John Tracey. Savas Beattie, 2023.

Levine, Bruce. *Confederate Emancipation: Southern Plans to Free and Arm Slaves during the Civil War*. Oxford University Press, 2006.

Mackowski, Chris, and John Tracey, eds. *The Civil War and Pop Culture: Favorite Stories and Fresh Perspectives from the Historians at Emerging Civil War*. Savas Beattie, 2023.

Pitcaithley, Dwight T. *Tennessee Secedes: A Documentary History*. University of Tennessee Press, 2021.

Rudy, John M. "From Tokenism to True Partnership: The National Park Service's Shifting Interpretation at the Civil War's Sesquicentennial." In *Interpreting the Civil War at Museums and Historic Sites*, edited by Kevin Levin, 61–76. Rowman and Littlefield, 2017.

Smith, Clint. *How the Word Is Passed: A Reckoning with the History of Slavery Across America*. Little, Brown, 2021.

PART 5
The Next Civil War

On May 2, 2023, the YouTube channel SensiblePrepper live-streamed a sixty-three-minute video about how to survive a second U.S. civil war. Just one of innumerable blog posts, online seminars, and TikToks on the topic, the video offers practical, hands-on advice about what to do (and, just as importantly, what not to do) in the increasingly likely event that Americans take up arms against each other. Viewers are advised, among other things, to secure their supplies against enemy confiscation (a lesson gleaned from Sherman's march through the South), keep a short-wave radio to scan for dangers, and have multiple "bug-out" plans in the event of sudden emergencies.[1]

However, the video's two hosts, both middle-aged white men living in the South, aren't content to limit their discussion to such matters as potassium iodide (used to inhibit radiation sickness) and the effects of EMP attacks. In between doling out advice on survival techniques, they mock the "LGBQT LMNOP . . . mindset," dismiss climate change as a hoax, criticize wokeism in the military, and downplay the January 6 insurrection ("Tucker" [Carlson] showed it was "blown up" by the media). Unlike many flag-waving Lost Causers and neo-Confederate types, however, the hosts of SensiblePrepper aren't itching for an armed conflict—not now, at least. The first Civil War "didn't turn out so well" for the South (by which they mean the white South in 1865, of course), and a second one would be "devastating" for everyone involved, even those who hope to avoid taking sides.

Then again, sometimes violence is all but inevitable. If people's liberties are "pecked away at and pecked away at," they tell us, there will eventually be tipping point—after which all hell will break loose.

NOTES

1. "2nd Civil War? Things to Do to Survive," SensiblePrepper, YouTube, May 2, 2023, https://www.youtube.com/watch?v=0s4uWVjvQbg.

11

The Confederate Battle Flag's Symbolic Shorthand

Appropriation, Dissemination, and Proliferation by U.S.-Based White Supremacists in Post–Civil War America

BRETT A. BARNETT

Since time immemorial, symbols have been subject to appropriation, the act of acquiring something used by others for one's own purposes, often without permission or acknowledgment, by persons of varying beliefs and motivations. Over the span of centuries, white supremacists in the United States and abroad have seized upon a multitude of symbols, ranging from the culturally significant (e.g., Christian cross) to the seemingly benign (e.g., Pepe the Frog cartoon character). Arguably the most notorious example of symbol appropriation by persons embracing extremist ideologies is the swastika, or *svastika* in Sanskrit, an ancient symbol often associated with peace, well-being, and good fortune still used by many cultures (e.g., Hindus, Buddhists, Jains) on several continents.[1] In the early twentieth century, followers of the right-wing Völkisch movement in Germany, a movement largely dedicated to discovering an idealized and largely mythological German Aryan past, appropriated the swastika, something that in turn motivated Adolf Hitler to adopt it as the Nazi Party's primary symbol in 1920.[2] The Nazi Party's appropriation of the symbol, in effect, converted the swastika into one of the most powerful symbols of hate, especially antisemitic hate, inextricably linked to the atrocities committed during the Holocaust.

Like the Nazi swastika, the Confederate battle flag is a potent visual symbol. Championed as an icon of the Confederacy, the Civil War emblem has deep historical ties to the defense of slavery and to violence against communities of color. At the same time, the battle flag's status as an all-purpose symbol of "rebellion" is ubiquitous in American culture thanks to its wide dissemination in films, television shows, and online forums. Thus, it is hardly surprising that U.S.-based white supremacists have long appropriated the Confederate battle flag for their own purposes. Use of the flag serves as an effective marketing device of white supremacy in mainstream (that is, nonracist) media outlets. U.S.-based white supremacists' publicity-seeking efforts have been aided, and their association with the Confederate flag has been further strengthened, by their activities involving public displays of the flag. Indeed, U.S.-based white supremacist groups, entities reliant on publicity to recruit and maintain members, have developed a symbiotic relationship with U.S.-based media organizations, entities tending to gravitate toward sensational and controversial subject matter like that offered by white supremacists to generate audience interest. In effect, dissemination of content through mass-mediated means serves as a force multiplier, proliferating white supremacists' display of the flag to the masses. Consequently, white supremacists have ushered the Confederate flag into the twenty-first century as a modern-day symbol of hatred, igniting unprecedented calls to eradicate Confederate symbols from public view throughout the United States.

In this chapter, I offer a brief survey of white supremacists' efforts to deploy the Confederate flag from the nineteenth century to the present day. While display of the Confederate flag still endures, so too does the appropriation of the emblem by an ever-growing array of white supremacists and racists interested in repurposing the emblem for their ends. Ironically, some of the most vocal champions of the Confederate battle flag are not especially interested in redeeming Confederate memory. Rather, they are invested in a different project, using the flag as an immediately recognizable visual symbol of white resistance to any form of racial progress.

The Battle Flag's Association with the Confederacy

Conceived in 1861 during the American Civil War, the Confederate battle flag remains among the most recognizable and controversial symbols in America. Although there were three national flags of the Confederate States of America, the Stars and Bars (1861–63), the Stainless Banner (1863–65), and the Blood-Stained Banner (1865), the emblem most associated with the Confederacy is the battle flag designed by William Porcher Miles, a South Carolina politician and leading secessionist. Ironically rejected by the Confederate Congress as the Confederacy's first national flag, Miles's motif, a white-outlined dark blue saltire adorned with thirteen white stars representing the Confederate states on a red field, soon pervaded other Confederate flags.[3] After the first major engagement at Manassas, Virginia, Brigadier General P. G. T. Beauregard favored Miles's saltire motif for battle over the Stars and Bars as it was more easily distinguished from the U.S. Stars and Stripes carried by Federal soldiers.[4] Miles's motif was also adopted as the flag of General Robert E. Lee's Army of Northern Virginia, the Confederacy's primary military force. Later, the saltire was incorporated into the second and third national flags of the Confederacy as a canton occupying two-thirds of the flag's hoist.[5] In 1863 Miles's battle flag was embraced by the Confederate Navy as the jack flown from the bows of its fleet, although its design was rectangular in shape and thus similar in proportion to Confederate-style flags seen today.[6] The incorporation of Miles's saltire motif into several Confederate flags, along with its association with Lee and the Army of Northern Virginia, go a long way toward explaining why the battle flag is most commonly affiliated with the Confederacy, an affiliation further strengthened even after the end of the Civil War.

The Battle Flag's Association with U.S.-Based White Supremacists

On December 24, 1865, only months after the last battle of the Civil War, six Confederate veterans formed the Ku Klux Klan in Pulaski, Tennessee. Duplicitously introduced as members of a social club with the purpose of defending America by maintaining the old order, Klansmen were not opposed to using violence to subordinate Blacks and enforce racial segregation. Although the KKK is frequently associated with the Confederate flag, the inaugural Klan did not appropriate the flag for organizational purposes but rather personal and enduring ones. For instance, in May 1913, *Confederate Veteran* magazine ran an obituary of John B. Kennedy, a Confederate veteran and one of the Klan's founding members, accompanied with a later-in-life photo of Kennedy in Confederate uniform along with a battle-torn, bloodstained flag from his infantry, the Third Tennessee (that same flag would be later draped over his funeral casket).[7]

Unlike the first Klan, however, other U.S.-based white supremacists vigorously displayed the emblem in public for organizational purposes. Formed in July 1869 under the inconspicuous facade of a social sporting club, the Carolina Rifle Club of Charleston, South Carolina, was among the first U.S.-based white supremacist groups to appropriate the Confederate flag. Although the Carolina Rifle Club's official flag featured a blue monogram (the club's initials, motto *Patriae Infelici Fidelis*, and inception date superimposed over two crisscrossed rifles and a palmetto tree) on a white field, in 1875 the organization's new president, C. Irvine Walker, resurrected a Confederate flag carried by his regiment, the Tenth South Carolina.[8] The first of many

U.S.-based white supremacists to publicly display the Confederate flag, armed members of the Carolina Rifle Club carried the battle flag through the streets of Charleston as part of a statewide white supremacist movement aimed at intimidating Black voters.[9]

Throughout the remainder of the nineteenth century, public display of the Confederate battle flag was largely attributed to ceremonial events (e.g., monument dedications, veterans' parades, reunions and funerals) organized by Confederate organizations such as the United Confederate Veterans, Sons of Confederate Veterans, and United Daughters of the Confederacy. It also popped up in commemorative photographs, murals, paintings, and lithographs as a revered symbol of Confederate honor. Soon thereafter, public display of the Confederate flag would proliferate on a grander scale with myriad visual-based communications afforded by the motion picture industry.

A landmark of early cinema, both lauded for its technical flair and reviled for its pro-Klan themes and imagery, D. W. Griffith's 1915 silent film *The Birth of a Nation* forged a connection between the Confederacy and a romanticized Klan with battlefield scenes of troops, including General Lee's regiment, carrying Confederate flags, followed by a portrayal of the Klan engaged in its own battle to save the South. Griffith's film, based on Thomas Dixon Jr.'s 1905 novel *The Clansman: An Historical Romance of the Ku Klux Klan*, presented Klansmen as heroically fighting to maintain a white supremacist status quo and, accordingly, rendered the Klan as accomplishing something the Confederacy had failed to achieve. Far from Griffith's heroic portrayal of the Klan, however, the first Klan was a short-lived terrorist organization engaging in activities worthy of federal investigation, something that likely contributed to a significant decline in the group's activities and virtual disbandment of the Klan by the mid-1870s. Nevertheless, while cultivating a connection between the Confederacy and a romanticized Klan, *The Birth of a Nation* effectively resurrected the battle flag and helped to popularize both it and the Klan, providing mediated publicity the Klan would benefit from, and exploit, for decades. Although *The Birth of a Nation* is rarely screened publicly today due to its overtly racist themes and profound lack of historical authenticity, modern-day Klan leaders still use Griffith's film, along with their own narration, as a recruitment device.[10]

Not only did one of the film industry's first blockbusters generate Klan-related publicity, so too did a cross-burning in the same year at Stone Mountain in Georgia, the site of an emerging Confederate monument featuring Robert E. Lee, Jefferson Davis, and Thomas "Stonewall" Jackson, carved from a colossal granite structure, and later a KKK ceremonial site. Upon learning *The Birth of a Nation* would be released in Atlanta on December 6, 1915, William J. Simmons, a former-Methodist-clergyman-turned-salesman, put a plan in motion to revive the Klan.[11] Just days before the movie's premiere in Atlanta, Simmons drove fifteen friends in a hired bus from the city to nearby Stone Mountain, where he assembled a wooden cross and set it ablaze, signaling the birth of the second Klan.[12] Simmons publicized the event in a newspaper ad that ran alongside an advertisement for *The Birth of a Nation*'s premiere, something that certainly helped to spread the word of the cross-burning.[13] Acutely aware of the film's promotional value, Simmons used the publicity surrounding *The Birth of a Nation* to garner new recruits.[14]

Fueled by Klan-related publicity generated by *The Birth of a Nation* and Stone Mountain, KKK membership peaked in the mid-1920s to an estimated three to five million. Reminiscent of similarly garbed Klansmen portrayed in Griffith's film, the 1920s Klan wore white robes and conical, face-concealing hoods with eyeholes during parades and marches. Embracing a pro-American and nativist ideology, however, the 1920s Klan explicitly vowed allegiance to the American flag rather than the Confederate flag, a sentiment explicitly conveyed in August 1925 when an estimated forty thousand participants, including women, marched while prominently displaying American flags in Washington DC.[15]

Confederate Flag Appropriation
During the Civil Rights Movement

Although *The Birth of a Nation* cultivated a Confederate-Klan connection and subsequent movies (e.g., *The General*, *Gone with the Wind*) disseminated Confederate-related imagery to mass audiences, an organizational connection between the Klan and the Confederate battle flag was not known, at least widely, until 1946, when author and civil rights activist Stetson Kennedy infiltrated an Atlanta Klan group. Kennedy's description of his initiation ceremony appeared, along with photos of a Confederate-flag-draped altar alongside an American flag and a Christian cross, in an article titled "The Ku Klux Klan Tries a Comeback," featured in a May 27, 1946, edition of *Life* magazine.[16] Kennedy's article was aptly titled as the burgeoning second Klan had quickly waned after its peak in the 1920s due to legal woes and friction among its members to such an extent that by the mid-twentieth century, the Klan would almost certainly seize any opportunity to make a comeback.

Cultivated in part by publication of the *Life* article, the Klan's appropriation of the Confederate flag also occurred around the time when support for civil rights was gaining momentum in the United States, strengthened by Democratic President Harry S. Truman's assuming office in April 1945. As support for civil rights intensified in the late 1940s, display of the Confederate flag increasingly shifted to the political realm as some white Southerners opposed the Democratic Party's pro–civil rights agenda. On May 17, 1954, a day regarded as "Black Monday" among Southern segregationists, political opposition to civil rights became palpable when the U.S. Supreme Court handed down a unanimous *Brown v. Board of Education of Topeka* decision asserting the unconstitutionality of "separate but equal" schools for white and Black students. In response to *Brown*, many Southern political leaders and state legislators committed to do everything in their power to undermine the court's decision, a concerted effort branded the "massive resistance." Amid special sessions throughout the South to pass legislation in an effort to thwart *Brown*, Georgia's state legislature also voted to incorporate the Confederate flag into their state flag in 1956.[17] Similarly, in April 1961 a Confederate flag was hoisted over the South Carolina statehouse dome, along with other flags (i.e., state, American), purportedly to commemorate the Civil War Centennial but widely interpreted as symbolic opposition to civil rights, especially since legislators officially voted to keep the flag flying over the statehouse dome the following year.[18]

Together with the growing prominence of the Confederate flag in the political realm, the Klan's appropriation of the emblem became not only more pronounced but also more calculated in the sense that Klansmen were opposed to civil rights activists, many of whom carried the American flag during public events. During rallies throughout Alabama, Klansmen displayed the Confederate flag, while Klan leaders hung flags in their offices and, even more prominently, on their business fronts. As reporters looked on, small groups of men with Confederate flags and wearing Confederate clothing confronted civil rights activists participating in the 1965 march from Selma to Montgomery, Alabama, in support of a federal voting rights act. The Confederate flag was also featured in articles published to mark the end of the Civil War Centennial.[19] For example, an edition of *Time* on April 9, 1965, contained an article on Klan violence, "The Various Shady Lives of the Ku Klux Klan," along with a photograph of Tuscaloosa Imperial Wizard Robert Shelton with a Confederate flag. In December 1967, just two hours after Dr. Martin Luther King Jr. delivered an antiracism speech at a Baptist church in Montgomery, Alabama, forty-three robed Klansmen paraded through the city's streets displaying, among other symbols, the Confederate flag, images of which appeared in the city's newspaper, the *Southern Courier*.[20] Consequently, the publication of sensational and controversial images reinforced the Klan's appropriation of the Confederate flag throughout the 1960s, an era in which the Klan, perhaps not coincidentally, experienced an uptick in membership.

U.S.-Based Klan and Neo-Nazi Collaborations

As support for civil rights grew during the twentieth century, so too did collaborations among U.S.-based white supremacists of varying ideologies. Although the KKK generally held an anti-Nazi sentiment around the time of World War II, that sentiment morphed over time, and some Klanspersons and American neo-Nazis (i.e., persons embracing ideologies akin to the German Nazi Party) began to work together. The 1970s brought what scholar John Drabble termed "the Nazification of the Ku Klux Klan" when figures such as neo-Nazi David Duke, former Klan leader and Louisiana politician who today is among the most recognizable persons in the American racist right, began to "fuse Klan iconography with Nazi racialism."[21] On November 3, 1979, the Klan–American Nazi Party collaboration turned violent when members of both organizations shot and killed five participants and wounded at least a dozen others in a Communist Workers' Party Death to the Klan march in Greensboro, North Carolina.[22] Precipitated in part by the burning of two Confederate flags by communist protesters less than four months before, the incident, dubbed the "Greensboro Massacre," drew national attention and signaled to Americans that some Klanspersons and neo-Nazis had begun to operate on a unified front.[23]

While Klan groups still organized some in-person public demonstrations independently in the wake of Greensboro, Klan and neo-Nazi collaborations became more frequent in public spaces (e.g., streets, courthouses), particularly in the South (e.g., Texas, Tennessee). A political science professor familiar with American racial politics, Steven White, writes, "By the end of the 1970s, these new Nazi-KKK hybrid groups became more popular than traditional Klan organizations, marking an important shift in both the symbolism and tactics of white supremacist groups."[24] Confederate flags were often, if not always, on display during public demonstrations held by Klan groups, entities that had become more dependent on publicity-generating events to counteract their decline in influence and recruitment within the

U.S.-based hate movement amid an ever-growing universe of non-Klan white supremacist groups. For example, a group of nearly sixty hooded Klan members holding Confederate flags, among other symbols, held an anti-immigration march in downtown Dallas, Texas, in July 1983.[25]

On other occasions, Klan members and neo-Nazis operated in concert when conducting activities in public spaces such as a march through the streets of Pulaski, Tennessee, in October 1989. The Pulaski march was significant because it was not only a demonstration of Klanspersons and neo-Nazis operating on a unified front but also evidence that U.S.-based neo-Nazis were displaying Confederate flags as well as imagery fashioned after the flag, including a shield bearing the "Crossed Hammers." Comprised of two crisscrossed claw hammers superimposed over the Confederate saltire, the Crossed Hammers was conceived by the Confederate Hammerskins, an ultra-violent neo-Nazi skinhead group formed in the late 1980s in Dallas.[26] Thus, the Pulaski march coupled with the existence of the Crossed Hammers revealed that U.S.-based neo-Nazis had also appropriated the Confederate symbol, something other non-Klan U.S.-based white supremacists would do in subsequent decades.

Public Display of the Confederate Flag and Modern Media

Like other public displays of the Confederate flag by U.S.-based white supremacists, the sensational and controversial nature of the marches in Dallas and Pulaski predictably garnered coverage from the mainstream media, including the *Fort Worth Star-Telegram* and *The Tennessean*, both of which published photos of the Confederate flag and flag-related imagery (e.g., Crossed Hammers). White supremacists often rely on media coverage to disseminate their visual-based content (e.g., photos, video) to an audience altogether removed from their in-person events. What is more, the advent of the internet means that any U.S.-based white supremacist media coverage can reach a universe of potential sympathizers online, an appealing prospect for entities reliant on publicity to recruit and maintain members. Indeed, media coverage of U.S.-based white supremacists' activities often results in content, including past stories about U.S.-based white supremacist activities, being posted on the respective media organization's website where it can be accessed by anyone. For example, images of Klanspersons and neo-Nazis marching through the streets of Pulaski, Tennessee, in October 1989 can be accessed from a picture gallery on *The Tennessean* website.[27] Moreover, non-media organizations have posted media content regarding U.S.-based white supremacists' activities in some instances. For example, images of Klanspersons holding Confederate flags during the anti-immigration march in Dallas, Texas, in July 1983 can be accessed at a digital gallery maintained by the University of Texas at Arlington Libraries.[28] Thus, the internet allows for a seemingly boundless array of images, new and old, of the Confederate flag and flag-related imagery being displayed by U.S.-based white supremacists.

Shortly after the emergence of the internet, Alabama-Klan-leader-turned-neo-Nazi Don Black, an American racist right icon whose white supremacist activities date back to the 1970s, demonstrated that the U.S.-based white supremacist community was no longer reliant on traditional media to receive exposure online. In March 1995 Black established the stormfront.org online message board that is widely regarded as the first major internet "hate site," a website containing content that denigrates a particular class of persons.[29] In establishing the Stormfront message board, Black showed persons in the U.S.-based white supremacist community they could independently disseminate content (e.g., textual, visual, aural) online, and before too long several other U.S.-based white supremacist hate sites existed. By the century's end, there were more than four hundred U.S.-based hate sites, with the majority maintained by white supremacist groups (e.g., KKK, neo-Nazi, racist skinhead).[30]

Not surprisingly, an array of Confederate flags and flag-related imagery, in the form of photos or computer-generated images (CGIs), has been posted by U.S.-based white supremacists on their hate sites. While much of the Confederate flag-related imagery appeared on sites maintained by U.S.-based Klan groups (e.g., American White Knights of the Ku Klux Klan, Mississippi White Knights of the Ku Klux Klan), some other white supremacist groups have also posted flag-related imagery on their hate sites. For example, Detroit-based National Socialist Movement (NSM), one of the largest U.S.-based neo-Nazi groups, has been known to post CGIs of the Confederate flag. In the early 2000s, the racist skinhead group Tualatin Valley Skins posted computer-generated artwork of Confederate flags along with photos portraying persons with flags. Also in the early 2000s, a hate site operated by the now-defunct California-based Orange County Assembly of Christ (OCAC), a group affiliated with Christian Identity (i.e., racial interpretation of Christianity wherein whites are viewed as the "chosen people"), contained CGIs of the Confederate flag. Indeed, the most prominent CGI on OCAC's site, appearing on its home page as well as interior pages, was a Confederate flag superimposed with Christian iconography including a man, a lion, an ox, and an eagle (i.e., "Four Living Creatures"), each occupying their own quadrant of the saltire, along with the word "GLORY" emblazoned across the saltire's center. Reminiscent of the prophet Ezekiel's message to the Israelites amid their exile in the sixth century BCE, the living creatures parallel his description of the winged throne bearers. Thus, in fusing Christian iconography regarding the divine with the Confederate flag, a symbol of white supremacy, OCAC seemingly reinforced a racist tenet of Christian Identity, upholding the white race as God's chosen people.

Since various U.S.-based white supremacist groups have appropriated the Confederate flag, it is hardly surprising the emblem is a mainstay of groups characterized as "neo-Confederate," a term used to describe persons supportive of reviving the ideologies, including racist dogmas, of the Confederacy.[31] By the early 2000s, the Alabama-based League of the South, the largest U.S.-based neo-Confederate group at the time, was maintaining a Confederate-themed website with myriad images, photographic and computer generated, of the Confederate flag as well as images of Confederate leaders, the Confederate South, and Confederate-style military uniforms.[32] Indeed, the most common CGI on League of the South's site, situated at the bottom of virtually every web page, was an icon that incorporated in its design a man, a Confederate flag, and graphic-style lettering that formed the group's website address (www.dixienet.org).

Even as a variety of U.S.-based white supremacist groups were posting Confederate flag imagery online in the first decade of the 2000s, in-person public display of the flag did not cease. For example, in 2004 the once-prominent white supremacist group Aryan Nations held its annual parade in downtown Coeur d'Alene, Idaho, during which a large Confederate flag was prominently displayed behind the group's now-deceased founder, Richard Butler, who was seated in the bed of a pickup truck.[33] What is more, U.S.-based white supremacists' in-person public displays of the Confederate flag continued into the 2010s. For example, the neo-Nazi group NSM held an anti-immigration rally in the streets of Knoxville, Tennessee, in August 2010, during which multiple Confederate flags, among other symbols (e.g., NSM flag), were displayed.[34] Like other in-person public displays of the Confederate flag by white supremacists, Coeur d'Alene and Knoxville garnered media coverage. The *Spokesman-Review* newspaper and *Inside of Knoxville* blog covered the respective white supremacist events, and both posted photos online where they could be, and can still be, viewed by a mass audience.

Backlash Against Confederate Symbols and a Pro-Confederate Movement

U.S.-based white supremacists continued to appropriate the Confederate flag in the 2010s, often posting Confederate flag imagery online, including on social media sites that have increasingly populated the internet landscape. However, it was the online images of one white supremacist waving a Confederate flag that caused a profound chain reaction in the mid-2010s, igniting unprecedented calls to eradicate Confederate symbols from public view throughout the United States while also sparking a reactionary movement among pro-Confederate supporters, including some white supremacists. On June 17, 2015, twenty-one-year-old high school dropout Dylann Roof gunned down nine Black worshippers participating in Bible study inside the historic Emanuel African Methodist Episcopal Church in Charleston, South Carolina (see John M. Kinder's chapter in this volume). When photos of Roof waving a Confederate flag later surfaced online, a backlash against the Confederate flag and other Confederate symbols ignited across the United States.[35] U.S.-based media were quick to incorporate images of Roof waving a Confederate flag into their stories, making them visible to an audience of potentially millions. For example, an image of Roof with a Confederate flag appeared at the top of an article posted online by the *New York Times* on June 20, 2015, just three days after the church shootings.[36] Predictably, other U.S.-based media incorporated images of the now-convicted mass murderer waving a Confederate flag into their online articles (e.g., CNN, *New York Post*) and televised video content (e.g., NBC News). As it became evident the murders committed by Roof were motivated by racial hatred, the nationwide backlash against the Confederate flag and other Confederate symbols reached a fever pitch.

After a decades-long push to remove the Confederate flag from South Carolina's statehouse where the flag had flown since 1961, on July 10, 2015, less than one month after Roof's images surfaced, South Carolina officially removed the Confederate flag from its statehouse grounds.[37] In October 2015 the University of Mississippi acquiesced to calls to rid the campus of the state's flag, which at the time was the only remaining state flag incorporating the Confederate battle emblem, although several other state flags (e.g., Alabama, Arkansas, Florida, Tennessee) arguably still evoked aspects of the emblem.[38] Both flag removals prompted pro-Confederate counterprotests, including events organized by U.S.-based white supremacists that predictably garnered media coverage. At the South Carolina statehouse, the North Carolina–based Loyal White Knights of the Ku Klux Klan (LWKKKK) angrily displayed a multitude of Confederate flags, including flags incorporating the battle emblem.[39] LWKKKK's counterprotest drew a variety of Confederate flag supporters, among them other white supremacists (e.g., NSM, other Klan factions) who further contributed to the sea of Confederate flag imagery at the event.[40] What is more, LWKKKK's counterprotest attracted coverage from U.S.-based media such as NBC News, which not only televised footage of the event but also posted images and video online. Likewise, the University of Mississippi's decision to remove the state flag from campus prompted a counterprotest from multiple U.S.-based white supremacist groups (including League of the South as well as an Arkansas-based Klan group), photos and videos of which were disseminated by U.S.-based media (e.g., *Huffington Post*, Action 5 News in Memphis, Tennessee). Certainly, pro–Confederate flag rallies, which had become havens for U.S.-based white supremacists, were not rare in 2015. The Southern Poverty Law Center, a group that monitors hate and extremist activity in the United States, documented more than 350 pro–Confederate flag rallies occurring in the South during the six months following the Charleston church shootings.[41] While pro–Confederate flag rallies were overwhelmingly concentrated in the South, rallies were also held as far north as Michigan and as far west as Oregon, in more than twenty states.[42]

Calls for removing Confederate flags and other Confederate symbols from public properties continued to reverberate throughout the 2010s, sustaining a reactionary movement among pro-Confederate supporters, including U.S.-based white supremacists. Predictably, media were often quick to report on pro-Confederate rallies that almost inevitably included Confederate flag and flag-related displays. What is more, individuals who organized or simply attended pro-Confederate events were increasingly posting photos and video of the events online, further contributing to the proliferation of Confederate flag imagery already thriving on the internet. There is no greater example of this occurring than when, in response to a decision made by officials to remove a statue of Confederate General Robert E. Lee in Charlottesville, Virginia, hundreds of U.S.-based white supremacists (e.g., Klan, neo-Nazis, neo-Confederates, white nationalists) descended upon the city in August 2017.[43]

Billed as Unite the Right, the rally was organized by the "alt-right," a white nationalist subculture that emerged in the United States during the late aughts, and was heavily promoted by U.S.-based white supremacists by means such as posting digital posters, some of which contained images of the Confederate flag, to their websites and social media accounts. For example, David Duke posted a promotional Unite the Right digital poster, which incorporated a CGI of a Confederate flag amid text (i.e., speaker names, event name and date) and other imagery (e.g., CGI of the Robert E. Lee statue), to his Twitter account the day before the event. The Unite the Right's heavy promotion attracted many U.S.-based white supremacists and resulted in a clash with antiracists, antifascists, and other community members who opposed their presence in Charlottesville. The rally tragically turned deadly when a neo-Nazi from Ohio plowed his car into a group of counterprotesters, killing thirty-two-year-old Heather Heyer and wounding several others,[44] thus garnering extensive coverage from various media outlets, local (e.g., the *Daily Progress*), national (e.g., *Time*, CNN, *New York Times*), and even international (e.g., BBC News, Reuters). The extensive media coverage of the rally resulted in a proliferation of Confederate flag imagery, not only in the immediate wake of the event but also for years to come, as the media organizations posted stories to their respective websites and social media accounts.

In addition to the abundance of Confederate flag imagery pertaining to the rally posted online by media affiliates, Unite the Right participants posted their own photos and video content, some merely moments after being taken, to social media sites such as Facebook and Twitter, while others equipped with video cameras on their vests and helmets live-streamed events on social media.[45] Thus, Confederate flag imagery displayed at the rally was also delivered synchronously, or near synchronously, to an audience of potential viewers altogether removed from the event by non-media-affiliated persons. Consequently, the internet abounds with Confederate flag imagery from the Unite the Right Rally in various online forums (e.g., Wikipedia, video-sharing sites) where it remains readily accessible, and perhaps not coincidentally, the demand for Confederate flags reportedly surged nationwide in the wake of the rally.[46]

The backlash against Confederate symbols throughout the United States was reenergized in 2020 following the highly publicized officer-involved killings of Black Americans, most notably Breonna Taylor in Louisville, Kentucky, and George Floyd in Minneapolis, Minnesota. Taylor's and Floyd's deaths, which received extensive media coverage for several months, reignited nationwide protests on an unprecedented scale and renewed calls for ridding public properties across the United States of Confederate imagery, particularly Confederate flags. Following the Taylor-Floyd protests spearheaded by the Black Lives Matter movement, the Pentagon banned Confederate flags from all military bases, some online companies (e.g., Twitch) banned Confederate imagery from their services, and various organizations similarly denounced the flag. For example, on October 8, 2020, the Board of Education for the Howard County Public School System in the Baltimore area unanimously voted to ban Confederate flags and other symbols "promoting hatred" (e.g., swastikas) from school property, and the State of New York enacted a similar ban on public properties in December 2020.[47] Even more significantly, the nationwide Taylor-Floyd protests prompted Mississippi, the only remaining state incorporating the Confederate emblem as a canton within its flag, to pass a November 3, 2020, referendum adopting a new flag devoid of the battle emblem, and "The New Magnolia" was officially approved on January 11, 2021.

Conclusion

Much as the Nazi swastika remains a potent symbol of hate decades after World War II, the Confederate battle flag continues to inspire violent anger more than a century and a half after the end of the Civil War. While white supremacists' continuing appropriation of the Confederate flag has certainly helped to keep the emblem in the realm of public consciousness, the symbol has also endured as a multi-meaning shorthand to convey a host of ideologies, some connected to Civil War memory (e.g., white supremacist) and some disconnected (e.g., antisemitic, antigovernment, antiestablishment). With images of the Confederate flag disseminated to mass audiences in the early part of the twentieth century via films such as *The Birth of a Nation* and *Gone with the Wind*, it is hardly surprising that the Ku Klux Klan would be motivated to appropriate the flag. Mass-mediated Confederate flag imagery generated a renewed popularity of the flag, not only in the South but elsewhere in the United States, and by associating themselves with the flag white supremacists could tap into this popularity.

Just as Klanspersons' appropriation of the Confederate flag aided their publicity-seeking efforts, so too did their proclivity over the years to attach themselves to certain public controversies (e.g., opposition to civil rights) that garnered extensive media coverage. More recently, Klanspersons, and other U.S.-based white supremacists (e.g., neo-Nazis, neo-Confederates, white nationalists) following their lead, have associated themselves with controversy surrounding the public display of Confederate flags and other Confederate symbols. Certainly, U.S.-based media have often been quick to cover pro-Confederate events counterprotesting the removal of Confederate symbols from public spaces, though ironically media coverage has almost always resulted in further proliferation of Confederate flag and flag-related imagery. Moreover, even in the absence of media coverage, the emergence of the internet, especially social media, allows non-media-affiliated persons, and even white supremacists themselves, to disseminate content, sometimes even synchronously, to a mass audience of potential viewers altogether removed from the event, as was witnessed during the Unite the Right Rally.

And just as Klanspersons and other U.S.-based white supremacists are dependent on publicity to attract and maintain their memberships, so too are media reliant on audiences for their survival. While the media's proper role in covering U.S.-based white supremacists' public display of the Confederate flag is certainly worthy of examination by researchers, media ethicists, and media professionals, there can scarcely be a debate as to whether media coverage of such displays has further cultivated white supremacists' appropriation of the Civil War–era emblem. While the media has a duty to report newsworthy events and information that is in the public's interest, news reportage should not come at the cost of providing extremists like U.S.-based white supremacists a public forum to proliferate hate. If U.S.-based white supremacists' activities are indeed newsworthy, media organizations should provide coverage. However, just as media organizations covering terrorism take precautions to avoid garnering support or sympathy for terrorists, entities covering hate and extremism should make ethical decisions so as not to provide extremists like U.S.-based white supremacists with self-serving publicity regarding their activities and ideologies.[48]

Despite unprecedented denouncements and prohibitions against the public display of Confederate symbols, recent events, especially those events garnering extensive media coverage, seem to motivate people to appropriate the Confederate flag for their own purposes. On January 6, 2021, the world witnessed Confederate flags on public display, among a sea of other flags, when a mob of then-President Donald Trump's supporters, including U.S.-based white supremacists, stormed the U.S. Capitol to protest what they believed was Trump's being cheated out of a second term in office. The protest-turned-siege understandably garnered, and continues to garner, extensive media coverage, resulting in a proliferation of images, particularly the image of one Confederate flag-draped protester inside the U.S. Capitol, marking the first time the battle flag had entered the building as part of an insurrectionist act. Intriguingly, less than two days after the U.S. Capitol siege, it was a flag bearing the Confederate emblem rather than a Nazi swastika that was surreptitiously tied to the front door of the Museum of Jewish Heritage—A Living Memorial to the Holocaust in New York City, an apparent act of antisemitism demonstrating just how diverse the universe of persons to whom the flag has been intended as a symbol of hatred.[49] Thus, in helping to usher the Civil War–era emblem into the twenty-first century, U.S.-based white supremacists have effectively weaponized the Confederate battle emblem as a modern-day symbol of hatred, still capable of inflicting trauma, both emotional and psychological, in a large universe of persons.

NOTES

1. Mukti Jain Campion, "How the World Loved the Swastika—Until Hitler Stole It," BBC News, October 23, 2014, https://www.bbc.com/news/magazine-29644591; "Swastika," Anti-Defamation League, https://www.adl.org/resources/hate-symbol/swastika.
2. "Swastika."
3. Daniel Costa-Roberts, "8 Things You Didn't Know About the Confederate Flag," PBS, June 21, 2015, https://www.pbs.org/newshour/politics/8-things-didnt-know-confederate-flag.
4. Coski, *Confederate Battle Flag*, 8.
5. Costa-Roberts, "8 Things You Didn't Know."
6. Coski, *Confederate Battle Flag*, 14.
7. Coski, *Confederate Battle Flag*, 86.
8. Walker, *Carolina Rifle Club*, 21, 42, 47.
9. Askia Muhammad, "Sorry Governor, the Confederate 'Heritage' Is Hatred," *Washington Informer*, December 11, 2019, https://www.washingtoninformer.com/muhammad-sorry-governor-the-confederate-heritage-is-hatred/.
10. Staff of the Klanwatch Project, *Ku Klux Klan*, 21. The scholarly literature on *The Birth of a Nation* is vast; however, useful starting points include Stokes, *D. W. Griffith's "The Birth of a Nation"*; Lehr, *"Birth of a Nation"*; and Martin, *"Birth of a Nation."*
11. Barnes, "Another Look Behind the Masks," 192.
12. Alexis Clark, "How 'The Birth of a Nation' Revived the Ku Klux Klan," *History*, May 4, 2022, https://www.history.com/news/kkk-birth-of-a-nation-film; Staff of the Klanwatch Project, *Ku Klux Klan*, 17.
13. Clark, "How 'The Birth of a Nation' Revived."
14. Staff of the Klanwatch Project, *Ku Klux Klan*, 21.
15. Staff of the Klanwatch Project, *Ku Klux Klan*, 22, 46, 22, 23.
16. Kennedy, "Ku Klux Klan Tries a Comeback," 42–43.
17. Coski, *Confederate Battle Flag*, 138.
18. Justin Worland, "This Is Why South Carolina Raised the Confederate Flag in the First Place," *Time*, June 22, 2015, http://time.com/3930464/south-carolina-confederate-flag-1962/.
19. Coski, *Confederate Battle Flag*, 134.
20. Lottman and Heggie, "Dr. King Hits Racism," 1.
21. Shaun Assael and Peter Keating, "The Massacre That Spawned the Alt-Right," *Politico*, November 3, 2019, https://www.politico.com/magazine/story/2019/11/03/greensboro-massacre

-white-nationalism-klan-229873/; "David Duke," Southern Poverty Law Center, https://www.splcenter.org/fighting-hate/extremist-files/individual/david-duke; Steven White, "Confederate Flags and Nazi Swastikas Together? That's New. Here's What It Means," *Washington Post*, August 14, 2017, https://www.washingtonpost.com/news/monkey-cage/wp/2017/08/14/confederate-flags-and-nazi-swastikas-together-thats-new-heres-what-it-means/.
22. White, "Confederate Flags and Nazi Swastikas Together?"
23. Assael and Keating, "Massacre That Spawned the Alt-Right."
24. White, "Confederate Flags and Nazi Swastikas Together?"
25. "Confederate Flags," University of Texas at Arlington Libraries, https://library.uta.edu/digitalgallery/subject/confederate-flags.
26. "Hammerskin Nation (a.k.a. Hammerskins)," Counter Extremism Project, https://www.counterextremism.com/supremacy/hammerskin-nation-aka-hammerskins.
27. "Cradle of the Klan," *The Tennessean*, September 27, 2014, https://www.tennessean.com/picture-gallery/news/2014/09/26/cradle-of-the-klan/16311917/.
28. "Confederate Flags."
29. Barnett, *Untangling the Web of Hate*, 3; "Don Black," Southern Poverty Law Center, https://www.splcenter.org/fighting-hate/extremist-files/individual/don-black.
30. Barnett, *Untangling the Web of Hate*, 8.
31. Potok, *Intelligence Report*, 57.
32. "Neo-Confederate," Southern Poverty Law Center, https://www.splcenter.org/fighting-hate/extremist-files/ideology/neo-confederate.
33. Bill Morlin and Jim Camden, "Richard Butler, Founder of Aryan Nations, Dies at 86," *Spokesman-Review*, September 9, 2004, https://www.spokesman.com/stories/2004/sep/09/richard-butler-founder-of-aryan-nations-dies-at-86/.
34. "Rebel Flags in the City," *Inside of Knoxville*, August 13, 2015, https://insideofknoxville.com/2015/08/rebel-flags-in-the-city/.
35. Barnett, "League of the South's Internet Rhetoric," 151.
36. Frances Robles, "Dylann Roof Photos and a Manifesto Are Posted on Website," *New York Times*, June 20, 2015, http://www.nytimes.com/2015/06/21/us/dylann-storm-roof-photos-website-charleston-church-shooting.html.
37. Ben Brumfield, "The Confederate Battle Flag in South Carolina: From the Battlefield to the Capitol to a Museum," CNN, July 10, 2015, http://www.cnn.com/2015/07/10/us/south-carolina-confederate-battle-flag-journey/; Worland, "This Is Why South Carolina."
38. Mason Adams, "How the Rebel Flag Rose Again—and Is Helping Trump," *Politico*, June 16, 2016, https://www.politico.com/magazine/story/2016/06/2016-donald-trump-south-confederate-flag-racism-charleston-shooting-213954/.
39. Craig Stanley and Elisha Fieldstadt, "KKK, Black Panther Group Clash over Confederate Flag Outside South Carolina Capitol," NBC News, July 19, 2015, https://www.nbcnews.com/storyline/confederate-flag-furor/south-carolinians-urged-ignore-ugly-opposing-confederate-flag-rallies-capitol-n394401.
40. Max Blau, "'Still a Racist Nation': American Bigotry on Full Display at KKK Rally in South Carolina," *The Guardian*, July 19, 2015, https://www.theguardian.com/us-news/2015/jul/19/kkk-clashes-south-carolina-racism; Stanley and Fieldstadt, "KKK, Black Panther Group Clash."
41. Adams, "How the Rebel Flag Rose Again."

42. Christopher Ingraham, "All 173 Confederate Flag Rallies since the Charleston Massacre, Mapped," *Washington Post*, August 17, 2015, https://www.washingtonpost.com/news/wonk/wp/2015/08/17/all-173-confederate-flag-rallies-since-the-charleston-massacre-mapped/; "Mapping Hate: Pro–Confederate Battle Flag Rallies Across America," Southern Poverty Law Center, August 10, 2015, https://www.splcenter.org/hatewatch/2015/07/16/mapping-hate-pro-confederate-battle-flag-rallies-across-america.
43. Patrick Strickland, "'The Foot Soldiers': A Neo-Nazi Skinhead Gang Terrorized Dallas in the Late 1980s," *Dallas Observer*, June 9, 2021, https://www.dallasobserver.com/news/the-confederate-hammerskins-a-neo-nazi-skinhead-gang-terrorized-dallas-in-the-1980s-12024541.
44. Strickland, "'Foot Soldiers.'"
45. Blout and Burkart, "White Supremacist Terrorism in Charlottesville," 19.
46. Erin Blakemore, "How the Confederate Battle Flag Became an Enduring Symbol of Racism," *National Geographic*, January 12, 2021, https://www.nationalgeographic.com/history/article/how-confederate-battle-flag-became-symbol-racism.
47. Leah Asmelash, "New York Bans Display of Confederate Flag and Other Hate Symbols on State Grounds," CNN, December 17, 2020, https://www.cnn.com/2020/12/17/us/confederate-flag-ban-new-york-trnd/index.html; Jacob Calvin Meyer, "Confederate Flag, Swastikas, Other Hate Symbols Banned from Howard County School System Property," *Baltimore Sun*, October 19, 2020, https://www.baltimoresun.com/maryland/howard/cng-ho-hcpss-bans-hate-symbols-20201019-pme4moakvzfkpc7r5z4djvqcoi-story.html.
48. Barnett, "'Lone Wolf' Extremists," 54–55.
49. "Museum Statement on Confederate Flag Tied to the Museum's Front Door Overnight," Museum of Jewish Heritage—A Living Memorial to the Holocaust, January 8, 2021, https://mjhnyc.org/press/museum-statement-on-confederate-flag-tied-to-the-museums-front-door-overnight/.

BIBLIOGRAPHY

Barnes, Kenneth C. "Another Look Behind the Masks: The Ku Klux Klan in Bentonville, Arkansas, 1922–1926." *Arkansas Historical Quarterly* 76, no. 3 (2017): 191–217. https://www.jstor.org/stable/10.2307/26291365.

Barnett, Brett A. "League of the South's Internet Rhetoric: Neo-Confederate Community-Building Online." *Journal of Hate Studies* 13, no. 1 (2016): 151–73. https://doi.org/10.33972/jhs.137.

———. "'Lone Wolf' Extremists and the US News Media." *Ethical Space: The International Journal of Communication Ethics* 13, no. 4 (2016): 50–58.

———. *Untangling the Web of Hate: Are Online "Hate Sites" Deserving of First Amendment Protection?* Cambria, 2007.

Blout, Emily, and Patrick Burkart. "White Supremacist Terrorism in Charlottesville: Reconstructing 'Unite the Right.'" *Studies in Conflict & Terrorism* (2021): 1–29. https://doi.org/10.1080/1057610x.2020.1862850.

Coski, John M. *The Confederate Battle Flag: America's Most Embattled Emblem*. Harvard University Press, 2005.

Lehr, Dick. *"The Birth of a Nation": How a Legendary Filmmaker and a Crusading Editor Reignited America's Civil War*. PublicAffairs, 2014.

Lottman, Michael S., and Sarah Heggie. "Dr. King Hits Racism; Klan Stages a Parade." *Southern Courier* 3, no. 51 (December 16–17, 1967). http://www.southerncourier.org/low-res/Vol3_No51_1967_12_16.pdf.

Martin, Michael T., ed. *"The Birth of a Nation": The Cinematic Past in the Present*. Indiana University Press, 2019.

Potok, Mark, ed. *Intelligence Report* 121 (Spring 2006). Available from the Southern Poverty Law Center.

Staff of the Klanwatch Project, comp. *Ku Klux Klan: A History of Racism and Violence*. 6th ed. Southern Poverty Law Center, 2011. https://www.splcenter.org/sites/default/files/Ku-Klux-Klan-A-History-of-Racism.pdf.

Stokes, Melvyn. *D. W. Griffith's "The Birth of a Nation": A History of the Most Controversial Motion Picture of All Time*. Oxford University Press, 2008.

Walker, C. Irvine. *Carolina Rifle Club, Charleston S. C., July 30th, 1869*. 1905. https://babel.hathitrust.org/cgi/pt?id=wu.89072984933.

12

Dylann Roof's Civil Wars

JOHN M. KINDER

On the evening of June 17, 2015, a black Hyundai pulled into the parking lot of Charleston's Emanuel African Methodist Episcopal (AME) Church, the oldest African American congregation in the city.[1] The driver, a gangly twenty-one-year-old white man wearing a gray sweatshirt and carrying what looked to be a fanny pack, entered the side door and sat down for Wednesday Bible study. Dylann Storm Roof was a stranger there, but that didn't matter. Although "Mother Emanuel" was established in 1816, a time when African Americans were forbidden to attend white churches in Charleston, it had long welcomed Black and white alike to seek religious solace. Over the next forty-five minutes, the high school dropout chuckled at the gentle humor of his fellow worshippers. Finally, as the assembled group shut their eyes for the closing prayer, Roof pulled out a Glock .45 caliber semi-automatic pistol and opened fire. As men and women dove for cover, he screamed racial epithets and unloaded magazine after magazine on the people who had welcomed him so warmly just a few minutes earlier. When it was over, nine of the congregants were dead. Roof was captured the following day with a Confederate flag decal on his car and a list of six African American churches, potential tinder in a "race war" he hoped would burn the nation down to its foundations.

What could possibly inspire such madness? Was Roof a proverbial "lone wolf"? Or was he part of a larger conspiracy of backward-looking extremists eager to undo the racial progress of the last century? In the immediate aftermath, both survivors and the millions looking on from afar grappled for answers. Among the many clues Roof left behind was a hastily scrawled online "manifesto" titled "The Last Rhodesian," a reference that would have been familiar to anyone in white supremacist circles.[2] Internet sleuths also discovered a cache of digital photographs that could be used to track the fledgling terrorist's movement in the days prior to the assault. In a kind of farewell tour of the Palmetto State, Roof visited a series of historical sites across South Carolina, including a Confederate history museum in Greenville, a Confederate cemetery in the state capital of Columbia, and several plantations and Civil War memorials in and around Charleston—evidence, critics assumed, of the killer's deep ideological commitment to the Lost Cause.[3] Indeed, well before he was convicted and sentenced to death, Roof had become a poster child for the racism, rage, and grievance that seemed to roil just below the surface of much pro-Confederate sentiment.

As other chapters in this book attest, the 2015 massacre at Charleston's Emanuel AME Church is regularly cited as an important pivot point in Civil War memory. After Dylann Roof's murderous rampage, it became increasingly difficult for politicians to dredge up old justifications in support of Confederate monuments (though some certainly tried). Starting in South Carolina, cities across the South increasingly took down the Confederate standard and worked to backtrack from decades of neo-Confederate sympathies. Ironically, Roof has done more to discredit the mantra of "heritage not hate," a common talking point of Confederate sympathizers, than anyone in recent memory.

Despite such developments, predictions of a second civil war—to be fought along divisions of ideology and race—seem to get louder every day.[4] "We keep saying, 'It can't happen here,' but then, holy smokes, it can," remarked national security expert Keith Mines just days after Charlottesville's Unite the Right Rally in August 2017.[5] Five years later, *Politico* writer John F. Harris was more definitive: "Serious people now invoke 'Civil War' not as metaphor but as literal precedent."[6] Asked about the failed effort to assassinate Donald Trump at a campaign rally on July 13, 2024, political scientist Arie Perliger told an interviewer, "The first thing I thought about is that we were basically one inch from a potential civil war," a sentiment that would be repeated on the left and right throughout the weeks that followed.[7] If anything, the murder of George Floyd in 2020, the conspiratorial culture exacerbated by the COVID-19 pandemic, and rising levels of political violence have brought us even closer to the kind of national conflict Dylann Roof hoped his racist bloodbath would ignite.

This chapter explores the toxic mix of fear, lies, and anger that gave birth to Dylann Roof and that continues to feed others like him. Drawing heavily upon his online writing and prison diaries, I attempt to reconstruct Dylann Roof's "civil wars," from the killer's ahistorical claims about pre–Civil War Southern culture to his proclamations about twenty-first-century political violence. In December 2022, wanting to get a sense of what Roof might have seen (and thought about) in the days preceding the Charleston Massacre, I packed up my car and drove east to South Carolina, where celebrations of Confederate memory remain part and parcel of the state's political culture.[8] I returned home both deeply worried and tentatively hopeful about the future. More than anything, though, I came away convinced of the danger Roof continues to represent nearly a decade after his vicious crime. In white supremacist circles, Roof is more than a hero; he's the living embodiment of a centuries-old tradition that, in sociologist Ashley C. Rondini's words, views "White violence against people of color . . . as a legitimate form of 'pre-emptive self-defense.'"[9]

Museum and Library of Confederate History, Greenville, South Carolina

I pull up to a small bungalow in a quiet neighborhood. It's early still, the sky gray and overcast. On one side, an apartment complex; across the street, what looks like some kind of retirement home. As I wait, SUVs and Jeeps with kids in the backseat roll past, probably on their way to school. No one stops to gape at the heavy cannon and the Confederate battle flag hanging limply out front. Perhaps they've seen them so many times they've become invisible. Or perhaps the passersby choose not to acknowledge the scene, as if the mere act of looking would somehow legitimate the museum and the stories it tells.

Inside, I encounter no other people except for the staff: all white men, like me. I scan the walls. Coins, uniforms, paintings, guns (lots of guns), trinkets—the stuff you'd expect to find at any small-town military history museum, with one exception: All of it was meant defend the Confederacy and condemn the Union. I stare blankly at a grotesque image of Lincoln on his deathbed, with various figures showing the trajectory of the bullet as it pierced his skull.

"You know John Wilkes Booth didn't kill Lincoln, don't ya?" I turn around. A caricature of an aged Johnny Reb—gray jacket, white pants, with what looked like a Celtic cross dangling from his neck. He's at least seventy. "It was the surgeons poking around that did it," he says, smiling. "Some folks don't like that display. It's not politically correct."

For the next two hours, he is my personal guide, leading me from one display case to the other, pointing out minute details. He is a higher-up in the state chapter of the Sons of Confederate Veterans, and when I mention I'm from Oklahoma, he practically beams. "Hey fellas," he announces to the other volunteers, "we have a visitor all the way from Oklahoma" (where, he tells me, all the Indians sided with the South). The museum, I learn, began as a place to show off all their memorabilia. Now it attracts sixteen thousand visitors a year (many Black, I'm assured). At one point, I'm holding a rifle, impossibly heavy, my eye to the sight, scanning the room like a sniper. It's meant to be fun.

But my guide, a former high school history teacher and wrestling coach, is worried. Nowadays, he tells me, all kids learn is "cookie cutter history." They don't know that the English (who settled the North) and the Celts (who settled the South) had been fighting each other for hundreds of years.[10] They don't hear about how the first Thanksgiving took place in the South (a fact Lincoln "banned" from official history books) or about the great men who made South Carolina unique. "Do you know some people don't believe the Holocaust took place? Can you believe that?" If we can forget the Jews, we can forget the South Carolinians who suffered at Northern hands.

The lesson: History is a battle—know it or else you will be defeated. Memory is something to cultivated and sustained; without places like this museum, people will inevitably forget.

A few hours later, I'm standing in the museum gift shop, surveying the Confederate knickknacks on display. Bumper stickers, pamphlets, pins, copies of Shirley Temple's *The Littlest Rebel*. I can't help but hear my guide, not trying to shield his voice, as he chats to a fellow visitor. "When I was growing up, after my granddaddy was caught stepping out on my grandmother, the KKK pulled him out of the house and tied him to a tree. They said they'd bullwhip him if he ever stepped out on her again. I'll bet you never heard a story like that before," he says, turning to me.

But I have, and I tell him so. I am a history professor. His smile fades, and within five minutes I'm on my way.

As it turns out, Dylann Roof did not step foot inside the museum. His visit lasted just long enough for him to snap a selfie in front of the Confederate flag that hung near the front door before he moved on to his next destination. There is something revealing about this decision. For all his later posturing about the intellectual roots of his violence, Roof was (and, I assume, remains) a vapid student of history—even of the sort of nostalgic, grievance-based history on display in Greenville. Rather, Dylann Roof was a child of the internet age, his "inarticulate, pre-emergent racist logic" curdled into violent hatred by white supremacist websites, Nazi fan art, and the online scribblings of far-right provocateurs.[11]

Fig. 12.1. Museum and Library of Confederate History in Greenville, South Carolina. Dylann Roof did not venture inside to peruse the Lost Cause displays and stock up on Confederate merch. Instead, he was content to snap a photograph of the outside of the museum, visual proof of his halfhearted attempt to use Confederate memory to legitimize his future violence. Courtesy of John M. Kinder.

According to his online manifesto, the future mass murderer did not grow up in a "racist home" (whatever that means). His road to racial "awakening" began after reading about the killing of Trayvon Martin in 2012, when George Zimmerman, a Neighborhood Watch captain in Sanford, Florida, stalked and shot the African American teenager after he strayed into Zimmerman's suburban community. Incensed that, in his mind, the media was blowing Martin's killing out of proportion, Roof googled "black on white crime" and landed on the website of the Council of Conservative Citizens, one of the largest and most influential white supremacist groups in the nation.[12] "There were pages upon pages of these brutal black on White murders," he recalled. "I was in disbelief. At this moment I realized something was very wrong."[13] Roof's knee-jerk response to white supremacist "danger narratives" is hardly unique.[14] As the Southern Poverty Law Center points out, "White Americans' unsubstantiated views about the potential violence from black people was the number one excuse they used to justify slavery, lynching, and various forms of mass incarceration."[15] Indeed, in the aftermath of the Trayvon Martin shooting, far-right racist groups like Stormfront, the National Socialist Movement, and the Traditionalist American Knights of the Ku Klux

Klan have attempted to mobilize fears about an epidemic of "black crime" to recruit new members.[16]

Once introduced to the world of online hate, Roof made little effort to formulate a coherent worldview. In the years leading up to the massacre, he embraced what historian Gordon Fraser describes as a "mixed up, even contradictory, set of political projects," from neo-Nazism to a form of "Lost Cause nationalism" rooted in a generalized sense of historical defeat.[17] Like many of the white supremacists he encountered online, he celebrated the (ultimately failed) efforts of white mercenaries to prop up the openly racist government of South Rhodesia in the 1960s and 1970s. (In photos posted online, Roof is pictured wearing a green and white Rhodesian flag on his jacket.) "Claiming ties to white Rhodesia is a way to build street cred in white racist circles," notes writer Robert Beckhusen.[18] In Roof's case, it also prefigured his eventual embrace of the Confederacy in the weeks preceding the 2015 massacre. Although Roof says nothing about the Civil War of 1861–65 in his manifesto and jailhouse journal, he increasingly wrapped himself in the mantle of Confederate memory, waving the battle flag in photos, visiting Fort Sumter and other Civil War sites, and paying homage to his home state's secessionist past. Perhaps he was hoping to lay claim to a neo-Confederate tradition of righteous anger, a sense of historical injury that only violence can avenge.[19] Or perhaps he was hoping to win the sympathies of extremist hate groups like the Council of Conservative Citizens, which condemned Roof's actions yet nonetheless acknowledged that the mass murderer had "legitimate grievances."[20] Or perhaps—and this would be my guess—he was simply trolling, using Confederate iconography to provoke angry response from his perceived enemies.

If there was a central theme to Roof's pre-massacre thinking, it was a deep and abiding hatred of African American people. While he devoted several sections of his manifesto to different racial groups (he claimed not to "understand" Jews but considered "Northeast Asian races" to be potential "allies" to the white nationalist cause), he reserved 1,481 words of his 2,440-word manifesto to outlining his belief in Black inferiority.[21] His arguments ranged from biology ("Negroes have lower IQs, lower impulse control, and higher testosterone levels in generals [sic]") to social policy (school segregation existed to "protect us from them"). Echoing nineteenth-century race scientists, he asserted that "blacks are subconsciously viewed by White people [as] lower beings." Above all, he claimed to believe that twenty-first-century whites are victims of a vast historical conspiracy. "I wish with a passion that n——s were treated terribly throughout history by Whites, that every White person had an ancestor who owned slaves, that slavery was an evil [and] oppressive institution, and so on," he proclaimed. That would make it "easier for me to accept our current position," referring to his belief that whites now constitute an oppressed people. Like my guide at the Confederate history museum, Roof held that today's understanding of the past is rooted in "historical lies, exaggerations and myths." Someone (he doesn't say who) had pulled the wool over people's eyes. Only he—and the other keyboard warriors in his circles—knew the truth.[22]

Elmwood Cemetery, Columbia, South Carolina

I park my car near the entrance of Elmwood Cemetery in Columbia. Roof was here, not long before the shooting, a pilgrim to the famous Confederate cemetery nestled inside. It's drizzling, the sky still gloomy. At first glance, I could be at any graveyard: expansive, grassy, a jumble of stone monuments and wrought iron, all of it slippery from wet and mud.

Walking, I reach where Roof must have stood. Above me, an arched metal gateway reads "Confederate soldiers 1861–1865," like the entrance of some now disappeared cathedral. Stepping through, I'm greeted with neat rows of graves, each one capped with a small plastic Confederate flag. All look new, unweathered by the sun, recently added by some unknown hand. I bend down in search of provenance (I know that Alibaba sells made-in-China Confederate flags . . . and iPhone covers . . . and dog collars), but I can't find a tag. I wonder who planted them there, tending them like orange flowers. Is it someone at the cemetery? No, I think. It's someone else, someone compelled to honor these Confederate dead. This is how memory is made—one flag at a time, over and over again.

Of course, there's a danger in taking such efforts too seriously. Glancing around, I see that Confederate flags are outnumbered—what, three to one?—by the Stars and Stripes, that the Confederate dead pale in comparison to those who died of other causes. There is something absurd, pathetic in a literal sense, about building a memorial landscape out of something that (here at least) seems to matter so little.

Thirty minutes later I head toward my car. There is nothing to keep me here. Cheap flags, rocks in the dirt, and below it all bones. Roof would have spent far less time, in part because he cared less about the Confederate dead than I do. Just another opportunity to snap a pic, to forge enough ideological armor to make it seem like he's more than a homicidal loser with a gun.

Fig. 12.2. Elmwood Cemetery in Columbia, South Carolina. The Confederate section of Elmwood Cemetery has attracted Lost Causers, Southern apologists, and neo-Confederate types since the nineteenth century, future mass murderer Dylann Roof included. Courtesy of John M. Kinder.

The bones of the Confederate dead had barely started to settle before would-be prognosticators began to raise alarms about the next "civil war" looming on the horizon. Few agreed about what would cause this seemingly inevitable conflict, only that it was just around the corner. In 1876 inventor and Greenback Party presidential nominee Peter Cooper warned that fraud in that year's election would lead to "trouble—perhaps a second civil war."[23] During the Great Depression, the liberal theologian Charles Francis Potter predicted that America was on the precipice of violent internal division. Speaking before the Humanist Society of New York in 1937, Potter warned: "If [competitive capitalism] will not permit Rooseveltian compromise with labor, the United States will be plunged into its second civil war, with a semi-Fascist capitalism on the one side and a semi-Communistic labor party on the other."[24] Nightmarish tales of "Civil War 2.0" (and its aftermath) such as Philip K. Dick's *Flow My Tears, the Policeman Said* (1974), Orson Scott Card's *Empire* (2003), and Omar El Akkad's *American War* (2017), which imagines a conflict in an America rent by the effects of climate change, have long comprised a subgenre of speculative fiction. In recent years, advocates of President Donald Trump have routinely invoked the threat of civil war to "take America back" from the myriad forces (leftists, Marxists, drag-show-friendly librarians, the FBI, the so-called deep state) that they deem hostile to the MAGA vision.²⁵ After @realDonaldTrump retweeted that his removal from office would "cause a Civil War like fracture in this Nation from which our Country will never heal" in 2019, the hashtags #CivilWar2 and #CivilWarSignup started trending, and the radical antigovernment group the Oath Keepers affirmed the seriousness of the situation. "This is where we are," tweeted the group's leader Stewart Rhodes in response to Trump's musings. "We ARE on the verge of a HOT civil war. Like in 1859."²⁶

Since the 1960s, warnings of a second civil war have frequently revolved around issues of race. No political ideology has a monopoly on such talk; as such, references to the "next civil war" differ widely depending upon the context. Among civil rights leaders and the liberal left, Civil War rhetoric often reflects a critique of the United States' failure to make good on constitutional promises to Black people. Touring the segregated Watts neighborhood of Los Angeles in 1968, longtime politician and civil rights leader Adam Clayton Powell Jr. declared that a "second civil war" began with the Watts Rebellion of three years earlier, when allegations of police abuse against an African American motorist sparked a six-day uprising against discrimination and police injustice.²⁷ "The nation was not 'reconstructed' as a single thing," observed journalist Garry Wills in his 1968 book *The Second Civil War: Arming for Armageddon*. "The two things were reshuffled along different lines—instead of North and South, white and black."²⁸ For observers like Wills, the "second civil war" describes less a traditional armed conflict than an effort to maintain the structural, violent, and intentional inequality of Black people by the powers that be.

White supremacists and their fellow travelers, on the other hand, tend to imagine the second civil war as a "race war," a genocidal conflict in which whites and people of color take up arms against each other. An affirmed "n—— hater" who wanted to be a "hero to segregationists," James Earl Ray told biographers that he saw the assassination of the Reverend Martin Luther King as the "first shot in a social or racial conflict, a second Civil War, which will result in his being freed."²⁹ (He wasn't.) In a study of cyberfascism and social media, political scientist Cathrine Thorleifsson notes that white supremacist terrorists such as Brenton Tarrant, who murdered fifty-one Muslims in a mass shooting in Christchurch, New Zealand, in March 2019, "dismiss the 'softer' alt-right as cowards unwilling to take matters into their own hands." Instead, they hope to "accelerate violent societal collapse, that will lead to apocalyptic end times, and a race war, and then eventually to restoration and rebirth" in a "white-dominated future."³⁰ Accelerationists, as adherents of such thinking are often called, don't fear a future civil or race war—they welcome it, if only because of the racially "pure" paradise they imagine waiting on the other side.[31]

Dylann Roof shared this exact vision. Despite his neo-Confederate trappings, the twenty-one-year-old South Carolinian had little interest in provoking a fight between North and South (or even, as some far-right provocateurs would have it, between gun-toting conservatives and "woke" liberals). According to his confession to police, he had a larger goal: to "kill black people" to "agitate race relations" and inflame a "race war."[32] Much like other accelerationists, Roof was not content to wait around for society to fall apart on its own. As he wrote in his forty-two-page jailhouse journal, which was confiscated from his cell in early August 2015, "Unless we take real, possibly violent, action, we have no future, literally. I am 21 years old and I don't play pretend."[33] Did Roof think that murdering African American church folk would trigger an actual "race war" on a national or international scale? It's impossible to say for sure. During his appeal, Roof's lawyers claimed their delusional client "believed his sentence didn't matter because white nationalists would free him from prison after an impending race war."[34] In the end, though, his personal beliefs aren't important. His use of homicidal violence on June 17, 2015, was meant, in feminist rhetorician Karma R. Chávez's words, to "rupture or intervene in history, in the present, with the aim of a better future."[35] Roof murdered to change the world—to kickstart a final bloody confrontation between whites and anyone who stood in their way.

Boone Hall Plantation and Magnolia Plantation, Charleston, South Carolina

First stop, Boone Hall Plantation. As I approach, I'm forced to turn around because the roadway is flooded; one day, perhaps in the next few decades, all of Charleston will flood. Climate change will do to the city what Sherman never could.

When I finally arrive, I discover a desolate place, lonely in the way that only places that were once teeming with bodies can be. A talk at the slave cabins begins. Did Roof listen to this same recitation? Did he ingest the lesson about the laws that forbade teaching enslaved people to read? Does it matter? I imagine he went straight to the main house. It's a relic of the 1930s, after Boone Hall stopped being a brick-making plantation and became what it is today: part of Charleston's memory industry, selling the antebellum South back to the millions who flock there. The guide pauses the tour to mention the discovery of an 1848 ledger in the house: It was for a young "negro" girl purchased for breeding purposes. A moment of awkward silence. Then it's back to the matter at hand: all the movies that have been filmed on the plantation grounds. *North and South* with a young Patrick Swayze. *The Notebook* with Ryan Gosling and Rachel McAdams. "See that staircase? That's where Halle Berry came down in *Queen*." Nods and the click of digital cameras. "And in here is where they shot the dinner scene." A young African American woman, excited, pulls up a screenshot on her phone. The plantation hosts a hundred weddings a year nowadays.

Leaving, I ask a couple of tour guides about *why* folks like Dylann Roof feed on plantation nostalgia. One, nearly shaking with anger, won't comment. Another, outraged, rejects the proposition entirely. Boone Hall, I'm told, doesn't sugarcoat the truth: "We tell it as it is." I hear echoes of my guide the day earlier. Sugarcoat . . . cookie-cutter history . . . as if it's all a matter of swapping one recipe for another. Roof believes in such sentiments. If he spent much time at Boone Hall, I don't think he'd have been disappointed.

Later that afternoon, I make a second stop. Magnolia Plantation, on the other side of the city, makes Boone Hall seem like a modest farm. From the road, you pass through an entranceway lined with live oak and Spanish moss. The place advertises itself as the South's most romantic garden, a legacy of the former owner's decision to open the erstwhile slave plantation to the public not long after the war.

While most of the crowd tours the lush gardens and petting zoo, I trudge with a small group to the former slave cabins and await the historical interpreter. It's night and day from the brief talk at Boone Hall. Our interpreter, a young history graduate, places enslaved labor at the center of Magnolia's working history as a rice plantation. Because of the disease, poor food, and environmental threats, an enslaved person typically died in their thirties, and 50 percent of kids died before age ten. When I ask about unhappy visitors, our guide repeats a familiar set of stories: the Virginia woman, daughter of ex-plantation owners, who told him he needed a "lesson in history"; the folks flashing the Stars and Bars during his presentation, as if they could somehow bully the past into silence.

I wonder what Roof might have said, had he stood where I now stand. For some reason, I imagine him smiling awkwardly, politely, too scared to say much of anything. He was no good at using words. He would use a gun.

In his online manifesto, Roof wrote that he chose to target Charleston "because it is the most historic city in my state, and at one time had the highest ration [sic] of blacks to Whites in this country."³⁶ For once, the high school dropout seemed to have paid attention in his social studies classes. In their book *Denmark Vesey's Garden: Slavery and Memory in the Cradle of the Confederacy*, historians Ethan J. Kytle and Blain Roberts describe Charleston as the "capital of American slavery." "By the 1850s," the two authors write, "the city boasted more than thirty slave-trading firms and many more slave-dealing brokers, auctioneers, and commission agents—euphemisms locals preferred to the more accurate 'negro trader.'" More than a hub of slave labor, Charleston played host to some of the loudest proslavery voices of the antebellum period, the bulk of which celebrated organized human trafficking as a munificent institution that benefited all involved. In the Civil War's aftermath, white Charlestonians usually downplayed the centrality of slavery to the Confederate project. Instead, like many Southern whites, they tended to embrace the Lost Cause defense of Confederate secession: the belief that Southern armies had fought in a noble yet ultimately doomed campaign in defense of their principles.³⁷ This is the story that Greenville's Museum of Confederate History still tells, and one need only spend a day or two in Charleston to hear echoes of it today.

Starting in the 1870s, the city began to remake itself into a mecca of plantation tourism. With the local economy devastated by the war and the end of chattel slavery, boosters hoped to lure interested visitors to see the numerous agricultural estates, once teeming with trafficked people, within a day's ride of the city. At places like Magnolia Plantation, which opened to the public in 1870, local freedmen who lived on the grounds guided curious sightseers through lush gardens, reassuring the overwhelmingly white visitors about the benevolence of their former masters. "These portraits of blacks function[ed] like magnolias and Spanish moss, as a 'signifier of the Old South' to northern tourists not only seeking novelty but also taken with fantasies of white supremacy and black docility," observe Kytle and Roberts. In 1924 Mayor Thomas Stoney declared Charleston "America's Most Historic City," a slogan that would be repeated on tourist brochures, pamphlets, and postcards for years to come.³⁸ City maps pointed out spots of historical interest and traced scenic walking routes, erasing any vestige of the cruelty upon which the city's wealth was made.³⁹ In recent decades Charleston has tried to make amends for its racist culture of forgetting, opening the Old Slave Mart as a historical site and museum in 2007 and the $125 million International African American Museum in 2023.[40] To this day, however, many Charlestonians are reluctant to abandon their whitewashed memories of the city's past. Critics single out the powerful Charleston Area Convention and Visitors Bureau for trying, in journalists Tariro Mzezewa and Kim Severson's words, to "soften the city's history of enslavement with a big serving of genteel Southern charm."[41]

Somewhere along the line, Roof seems to have acquired a similar sense of nostalgia, an unshakable longing for—and belief in—a past that never existed, a past wiped clean of its worst horrors. The South did not need to apologize for its past misdeeds. "Only a fourth to a third of people in the South owned even one slave," he insisted in his online manifesto, reflecting a sentiment familiar to those seeking to unmoor the Confederacy from human trafficking and exploitation. Slavery was not a cauldron of cruelty. Roof claimed to have read "hundreds" of slave narratives—nearly all of them "positive." (We can only infer what that means.) White people were not oppressors; they were victims in need of saving. On June 17, 2015, only seconds away from his own death, twenty-six-year-old Tywanza Sanders, the youngest victim of the Emanuel AME Massacre, asked Roof why he was killing men and women he'd never met, men and women he'd never know. "You are raping our women and taking over the country," he responded, invoking a stereotype of Black rapacity used to (preemptively) jail, lynch, and torture untold numbers of Black men throughout the Jim Crow era.[42]

Writing about the historical roots of Roof's racism not long after the massacre, historian Eric Foner noted that the killer's "complaints that blacks were 'taking over' the state echo justifications for racist violence during and after Reconstruction and the disenfranchisement of black voters in the 1890s."[43] Roof's justification also anticipates many Trump-era claims about Mexicans, Muslims, the unhoused, and others running rampant across the American landscape, leaving a nation of victimized white innocence in their wake. Indeed, many of the basic tenets of Roof's message—his insistence on white victimhood, his belief that talk of past injustices is overblown, and his paranoia that racial minorities are unfairly usurping white power—are at the center of Trump's promise to Make (White) America Great Again.

McLeod Plantation, Charleston, South Carolina

I'm eager to leave Charleston. I'm not going to visit Mother Emanuel to stalk Roof's final movements. Folks do such things—make a pilgrimage of hate.

Instead, I make a final stop at McLeod Plantation, just outside the city. It's not like Boone and Magnolia, where the story of slavery comes across as an afterthought. McLeod is a member of the International Coalition of Sites of Conscience. Here, you visit for one reason: to learn about the past to foster justice in the present.

As the tour begins, we're asked to look around us. All of it is a lie. In the 1920s, we learn, hot on the release of the Klan epic *The Birth of a Nation*, McLeod was remade to fit visitors' expectations of what a plantation should be. The columns bolted to the back of the main house—architectural fakery. The great live oak that straddles the yard—planted decades after the last slaves were freed. This was not some *Gone with the Wind*-style Southern manse. It was a factory farm, where human beings were consumed from dawn to dusk to fuel the greed and ambitions of its owners.

Black and white, old and young, we follow the tour in near silence. We're told of the backbreaking labor endured by the plantation's captive residents and the sexual violence perpetrated by its white owner. Like penitents, we run our fingers over the seedy coastal cotton, sequestered to a small patch of ground. Once there were acres of the stuff. Now there are just a few meager plants, removed at the end of each growing season to prevent their spread. We glance at the "big house," but few seem interested. The story is out here: in the fields, in the work buildings, in the cabins inhabited by generations.

When it is over, I speak to Isa, the interpreter, about his experiences as an African American man telling a history of Charleston—of America—that many visitors don't want to hear. He recalls the open hostility, the people yelling in his face, the postures (back up, chest out, arms crossed) of barely contained fury. That's why, he points out, they now carry radios—so that no one is ever alone. The problem of the Dylann Roofs of the world, he tells me, is that they look just like everyone else.

Not like everyone, I think. Then again, the next mass killer might do even less to hide his intentions.

As of this writing, Dylann Roof is serving time on death row at a federal prison in Terre Haute, Indiana. At some point in the future, he will likely become the first person executed for a federal hate crime. If reporting is correct, he is not especially popular with his fellow prisoners. (In 2016 Dwayne Stafford, a fellow inmate at Charleston County Detention Center, was showered with gifts and cash after assaulting Roof during the trial phase.)[44] In the darkest corners of the online hate sphere, however, Roof's influence

Fig. 12.3. Slave quarters at McLeod Plantation in Charleston, South Carolina. Guides at McLeod Plantation tend to downplay the significance of the "big house," the focus of so much plantation tourism. Instead, they highlight the importance of the slave quarters, which were occupied by descendants of enslaved people well into the twentieth century. We have no evidence that Dylann Roof ventured inside the slave quarters in his visit to McLeod in the days leading up to the Charleston massacre. Courtesy of John M. Kinder.

continues to grow. References to Roof's signature bowl-style haircut, which the New York–based Anti-Defamation League added to its database of hate symbols in 2019, proliferate on forums like 4chan and Gab, where supporters with screennames like "The Bowlfather" and "The Final Bowlution" have elevated the Charleston killer to the status of a secular saint. Roof's online acolytes, known collectively as the "Bowl Gang," profess that "Dylann Roof did nothing wrong" and enjoin fellow white supremacists to "take them to the church," a slang phrase meant to encourage further violence against their racial enemies.[45]

Much of this is just shitposting, the sort of thing that people would be too embarrassed or scared to say in real life. But as the Anti-Defamation League and others have pointed out, Roof's celebrity is not confined to internet hate-mongers. Over the past several years, white supremacists from Ohio to Washington state have attempted to "pull a Dylann Roof" against people of color in their home communities. On May 14, 2022, eighteen-year-old Payton Gendron opened fire at a Tops Friendly Market in an African American neighborhood of Buffalo, New York, killing ten and injuring three others. In the aftermath of the live-streamed attack, researchers at the Anti-Defamation League's Center on Extremism produced a descriptive key for interpreting the numerous white supremacist symbols and messages scrawled on the shooter's weapons and gear. Along with references to Anders Breivik, the Norwegian terrorist who murdered seventy-seven people (mainly kids) in July 2011, and Robert Bowers, author of the deadly shooting at Pittsburgh's Tree of Life Synagogue in October 2018, Gendron's rifle name-checked Dylann Roof, whom the Buffalo killer's own 180-page manifesto cited as a fellow "partisan/freedom fighter/ethno soldier" in the fight against "ethnic and cultural genocide."[46] Most telling of all, Gendron had decorated his weapons with the names of several alleged victims of Black-on-white crime, taking us back to where Roof's own radicalization began a decade earlier.

Nearly three years after following Dylann Roof to South Carolina, I'm left with many questions and not enough answers. For starters, how do we distinguish folks like Roof and Gendron from the untold numbers eager to spout off about the "next civil war" on social media? For most people, it would seem, talk of civil war is just that—empty talk. The "next civil war" is less an anticipated event than all-purpose signifier of, well, just about anything. Fail to reelect Donald Trump? The next civil war. Reinstate mask mandates? The next civil war. Virtually none of this has to do with the conflict of 1861–65, why it was fought, and how it shaped the nation. If anything, casual predictions that America is on the brink of another civil war trivialize the viciousness of the nation's first such conflict. Given that few, outside of fiction writers, pause to describe what form the next civil war might assume (Black versus white? urban versus rural? rich versus poor?), it's difficult to take such warnings seriously. And yet, we must—and not simply because armed man-children feel compelled, in Roof's words, to take the fight from the internet to the "real world." The invasion of the Capitol building on January 6, 2021, suggests that, for some at least, the line between online conspiracy and violent action has become increasingly blurred. That day did not mark the start of a civil war, but it was something, the ramifications of which might take decades to unfold.

Second, I am struck by the question of how to tell the story of Roof's violence without further elevating his reputation among those sympathetic to his views. It's a dilemma that's befuddled historians of crime for generations, and I can't claim to have stumbled upon a solution. For all his intellectual pretensions, Roof was not a studied adherent of neo-Confederate dogma; his manifesto reads like the raving of a semiliterate teenager; and, in the run-up to the 2015 massacre at Charleston's Emanuel AME Church, he appeared more concerned with crafting an online persona than anything else. Yet it would be a mistake to dismiss him as a wholly marginal figure. As historians Chad Williams, Kidada Williams, and Keisha Blain argue in *The Charleston Syllabus*, a crowdsourced project produced following the 2015 attack, "Dylann Roof was not an anomaly but, in fact, a product of American history, a legacy of white supremacist thought dating back to the founding of the country." In their reading, Roof matters because he represents centuries of white terrorism against Black people—the fear, violence, and racial denigration Southern apologists once defended as "heritage" and that places like Greenville's Museum and Library of Confederate History are now content to ignore altogether.[47] On top of that, it's worth noting another sad truth. What allowed Roof to make history was, above all else, his access to inexpensive firearms and his willingness to use them. In this sense, Roof himself tells us less about Civil War memory in today's polarized America than he does about the United States' deranged misremembering of an earlier period, when—according to Second Amendment evangelists—the Founding Fathers granted each one of us the right to amass an arsenal in the name of personal defense.

Finally, I'm left pondering an even more disturbing set of questions: What if Roof had not taken selfies waving a Confederate flag? What if he'd skipped the museum, bypassed the cemetery, and driven directly to Emanuel AME and opened fire? Would it have provoked the same sort of reckoning with symbols of the Confederacy? Or would it have been just *another* shooting, to be fretted over, prayed on, and chalked up to "mental illness"? True, memory activists, especially in the African American community, had already spent years working to dismantle the worst of Confederate nostalgia. I think back to Isa, my guide at McLeod Plantation, who spoke openly about the fight to revise the City of Charleston Tour Guide Training Manual, which for decades had ignored ugly truths about the history of slavery and white supremacy in the Palmetto State. Even so, I remain skeptical of Lost Causers' newly found moral courage. If nothing else, it's clear that the battle over Civil War memory is far from over—and there will be casualties.

NOTES

1. This opening description of the mass murder draws upon details from *United States v. Dylann Storm Roof*.
2. This title, as I explain later in the chapter, refers to the government of Rhodesia (now Zimbabwe) in the 1960s and 1970s, which white supremacists continue to venerate for its forthright support of white minority rule.

3. Neely Tucker and Peter Holley, "Dylann Roof's Eerie Tour of American Slavery at Its Beginning, Middle, and End," *Washington Post*, July 1, 2015, https://www.washingtonpost.com/news/post-nation/wp/2015/07/01/dylann-roofs-eerie-tour-of-american-slavery-at-its-beginning-middle-and-end/. Although it's difficult to nail down the exact dates and route of Roof's final excursions, journalists Neely Tucker and Peter Holley contend they went something like this: After leaving his home in Columbia, he drove to Sullivan's Island north of Charleston Harbor, the disembarkation point for some 40 percent of enslaved Africans to the British colonies, where he paused just long enough to snap a photo with a road sign and draw some pro-Hitler numerology in the sand. He visited three nearby plantations (Boone Hall, Magnolia Plantation and Gardens, and McLeod) before, at some point, driving three hours north to make the briefest of visits to the Museum and Library of Confederate History. He also dropped by the Confederate section of Elmwood Cemetery in Columbia around this time. Roof's final trek took him to 110 Calhoun Street in Charleston, home of Emanuel AME Church. Tucker and Holley, "Dylann Roof's Eerie Tour."
4. For a creative look at how some future Civil War might unfold, see Marche, *Next Civil War*.
5. Quoted in Robin Wright, "Is America Headed for a New Kind of Civil War," *New Yorker*, August 14, 2017.
6. John F. Harris, "We Are in a New Civil War . . . About What Exactly?" *Politico*, January 6, 2022, https://www.politico.com/news/magazine/2022/01/06/new-civil-war-about-what-exactly-526603.
7. Naomi Schalit, "'One Inch from a Potential Civil War': Attempted Assassination of Trump Sets American Democracy on Edge," *U.S. News and World Report*, July 14, 2024, https://www.usnews.com/opinion/articles/2024-07-14/one-inch-from-a-potential-civil-war-attempted-assassination-of-trump-sets-american-democracy-on-edge.
8. See Brown, *Civil War Canon*.
9. Rondini, "White Supremacist Danger Narratives," 60.
10. My guide's reference to the so-called Celtic character of the Confederacy is by no means unique. McWhitney and Jamieson's *Attack and Die* famously argues that Confederate military leaders cited the South's "Celtic" heritage when insisting on frontal assaults.
11. Fraser, "End of Reconstruction, Again," 177.
12. Edward Ball, "The Mind of Dylann Roof," *New York Review of Books*, March 23, 2017, 12, https://www.nybooks.com/articles/2017/03/23/mind-of-dylann-roof/.
13. Quoted in Josh Sanburn, "Inside the White Supremacist Group That Influenced Charleston Shooting Suspect," *Time*, June 22, 2015, https://time.com/3930993/dylann-roof-council-of-conservative-citizens-charleston/.
14. Rondini, "White Supremacist Danger Narratives," 60.
15. Cassie Miller, "The Biggest Lie in the White Supremacist Propaganda Playbook: Unraveling the Truth About 'Black-on-White Crime,'" Southern Poverty Law Center, June 14, 2018, https://www.splcenter.org/20180614/biggest-lie-white-supremacist-propaganda-playbook-unraveling-truth-about-%E2%80%98black-white-crime.
16. "White Supremacists Use Black-on-White Crime as a Propaganda Tool," American Defense League, September 7, 2012, https://www.adl.org/resources/news/white-supremacists-use-black-white-crime-propaganda-tool.
17. Fraser, "End of Reconstruction, Again," 177.

18. Robert Beckhusen, "Why White Supremacists Identify with Rhodesia," *War Is Boring*, January 19, 2015, https://warisboring.com/why-white-supremacists-identify-with-rhodesia/. On the embrace of Rhodesia in white supremacist circles, see Dan Murphy, "Why Would an American White Supremacist Be Fond of Rhodesia?" *Christian Science Monitor*, June 18, 2015, https://www.csmonitor.com/World/Security-Watch/Backchannels/2015/0618/Why-would-an-American-white-supremacist-be-fond-of-Rhodesia; John Ismay, "Rhodesia's Dead—but White Supremacists Have Given It New Life Online," *New York Times Magazine*, April 10, 2018, https://www.nytimes.com/2018/04/10/magazine/rhodesia-zimbabwe-white-supremacists.html; and Burke, *Revolutionaries for the Right*.
19. On neo-Confederate ideology, see Barnett, "League of the South's Internet Rhetoric," 155.
20. Catherine Thompson, "Group That May Have Influenced Charleston Killer: He Had Some 'Legitimate Grievances,'" *Talking Points Memo*, June 22, 2015, https://talkingpointsmemo.com/livewire/ccc-dylann-roof-legitimate-grievances.
21. On the word count of the manifesto, see Chebrolu, "Racial Lens of Dylann Roof," 48.
22. The quotes in this paragraph are taken from his online "manifesto," a copy of which can still be found on the Internet Archive at https://web.archive.org/web/20150620182210/http://lastrhodesian.com/data/documents/rtf88.txt.
23. "Letter from Peter Cooper. He Corrects a Misstatement of His Political Views—No Preference for Tilden over Hayes, but Much Confidence in the People," *New York Times*, November 18, 1876, 1.
24. "Civil War Threat Seen: Rev. C. F. Potter Says Capital and Labor Struggle Menaces U.S.," *New York Times*, February 15, 1937, 20.
25. See, for example, Charlie Warzel, "Why Trump Tweeted About Civil War," *New York Times*, September 30, 2019, https://www.nytimes.com/2019/09/30/opinion/trump-civil-war.html; Andrew Mitrovica, "Sorry Trumpers, There Won't Be a US Civil War for 2024," *Al Jazeera*, September 7, 2023, https://www.aljazeera.com/opinions/2023/9/7/sorry-trumpers-there-wont-be-a-us-civil-war-for-2024; Max Burns, "Republicans Just Can't Stop Calling for Civil War," *The Hill*, September 6, 2023, https://thehill.com/opinion/campaign/4187490-republicans-just-cant-stop-calling-for-civil-war/.
26. Caitlin O'Kane, "'Civil War 2' Trends on Twitter after Trump Quotes Speculation That Impeachment Would Spark a 'Civil War,'" CBS News, September 30, 2019, https://www.cbsnews.com/news/trump-civil-war-tweet-civil-war-2-is-trending-on-twitter-after-trump-suggested-what-might-occur-if-removed-from-office/.
27. "Powell Says '2d Civil War' Began in Los Angeles," *New York Times*, January 10, 1968, 28.
28. Wills, *Second Civil War*, 23.
29. Martin Waldron, "Huie Thinks Ray Killed Dr. King to Gain 'Status,'" *New York Times*, April 1, 1969, 14.
30. Thorleifsson, "From Cyberfascism to Terrorism," 292.
31. Zack Beauchamp, "A Neo-Nazi Idea to Spark a Race War Inspired the Buffalo Killings," *Vox*, May 16, 2022, https://www.vox.com/policy-and-politics/2022/5/16/23074812/buffalo-shooting-accelerationism-great-replacement-neo-nazi.
32. *United States v. Dylann Storm Roof*, 13.
33. Dylann Roof, jailhouse journal, confiscated from cell search on August 3, 2015, Government Exhibit 500, US-060652, https://www.scd.uscourts.gov/cases/2-15-472/exhibits/index.asp.
34. Quoted in Salazar, "I, Dylann Roof," 371.

35. Quoted in Chebrolu, "Racial Lens of Dylann Roof," 49.
36. Dylann Roof Manifesto.
37. Kytle and Roberts, *Denmark Vesey's Garden*, 6, 17, 27, 81.
38. Kytle and Roberts, *Denmark Vesey's Garden*, 170, 180.
39. See, for example, "The City of Charleston, South Carolina," a tourist map released by the Office of Port Development in 1939. A copy can be found at the Low Country Digital Library at https://lcdl.library.cofc.edu/lcdl/catalog/lcdl:25897.
40. Jennifer Berry Hawes, "Activists Have Long Called for Charleston to Confront Its Racial History. Tourists Are Now Expecting It," *ProPublica*, July 29, 2023, https://www.propublica.org/article/tourism-helping-charleston-confont-racial-history.
41. Tariro Mzezewa and Kim Severson, "Charleston Tourism Is Built on Southern Charm. Locals Say It's Time to Change," *New York Times*, August 12, 2020, https://www.nytimes.com/2020/08/12/travel/charleston-tourism-black-lives-matter.html.
42. On the myth of the "Black rapist" in American society and culture, see Rondini, "White Supremacist Danger Narratives," 61; Pieterse, *White on Black*, 174–78; Davis, *Women, Race, and Class*, especially chapter 11, "Rape, Racism and the Myth of the Black Rapist"; Kendi, *Stamped from the Beginning*, 249, 274.
43. Eric Foner, "The Historical Roots of Dylann Roof's Racism," *The Nation*, June 25, 2015, https://www.thenation.com/article/archive/the-historical-roots-of-dylann-roofs-racism/.
44. "Things Are Going Great for the Guy Who Attacked Dylann Roof in Jail," *Vice*, August 15, 2016, https://www.vice.com/en/article/5gqbax/dwayne-stafford-assaulted-dylan-roof-jail-vgtrn.
45. "Hardcore White Supremacists Elevate Dylann Roof to Cult Hero Status," ADL, February 6, 2019, https://www.adl.org/resources/blog/hardcore-white-supremacists-elevate-dylann-roof-cult-hero-status. On the addition of the bowl cut to the Anti-Defamation League's database of hate symbols, see Michael Kunzelman, "'OK' Hand Gesture, 'Bowlcut' Added to Hate Symbols Database," Associated Press, September 26, 2019, https://apnews.com/article/48ae1303568b4b21813adb3bd6d592e5.
46. Payton Gendron Manifesto.
47. Williams et al., *Charleston Syllabus*, 2.

BIBLIOGRAPHY

Barnett, Brett A. "League of the South's Internet Rhetoric: Neo-Confederate Community Building Online." *Journal of Hate Studies* 13, no. 1 (January 2016): 151–73.

Brown, Thomas J. *Civil War Canon: Sites of Confederate Memory in South Carolina*. University of North Carolina Press, 2015.

Burke, Kyle. *Revolutionaries for the Right: Anticommunist Internationalism and Paramilitary Warfare in the Cold War*. University of North Carolina Press, 2018.

Chebrolu, E. "The Racial Lens of Dylann Roof: Racial Anxiety and White Nationalist Rhetoric on New Media." *Review of Communication* 20, no. 1 (2020): 47–68.

Davis, Angela Y. *Women, Race, and Class*. Random House, 1981.

Fraser, Gordon. "The End of Reconstruction, Again: Dylann Roof, Thomas Dixon, Jr., and the Transhistorical Structures of Racist Feeling." *Forum: Afterlives of 19th Century Racism* 19, no. 6 (2018): 174–81.

Gendron, Payton. Manifesto ("You Wait for a Signal While Your People Wait for You"). https://www.hoplofobia.info/wp-content/uploads/2022/05/pg-Manifesto.pdf.

Kendi, Ibram X. *Stamped from the Beginning: The Definitive History of Racist Ideas in America.* Nation, 2016.

Kytle, Ethan J., and Blain Roberts. *Denmark Vesey's Garden: Slavery and Memory in the Cradle of the Confederacy.* The New Press, 2018.

Marche, Stephen. *The Next Civil War: Dispatches from the American Future.* Avid Reader, 2022.

McWhitney, Grady, and Perry D. Jamieson. *Attack and Die: Civil War Military Tactics and the Southern Heritage.* University of Alabama Press, 1982.

Pieterse, Jan Nederveen. *White on Black: Images of Africa and Blacks in Western Popular Culture.* Yale University Press, 1992.

Rondini, Ashley C. "White Supremacist Danger Narratives." *Contexts* 17, no. 3 (Summer 2018): 60–62.

Roof, Dylan. Manifesto ("The Last Rhodesian"). https://web.archive.org/web/20150620182210/http://lastrhodesian.com/data/documents/rtf88.txt.

Salazar, Philippe-Joseph. "'I, Dylann Roof'—White Voice v. the Force of Law." *Javnost—The Public* 27, no. 4 (2020): 369–79.

Thorleifsson, Cathrine. "From Cyberfascism to Terrorism: On 4chan/pol/culture and the Transnational Production of Memetic Violence." *Nations and Nationalism* 28, no. 1 (January 2022): 286–301.

United States v. Dylann Storm Roof. Defendant-Appellant, No. 17-3 (4th Cir. November 16, 2020). https://www.justice.gov/crt/case-document/file/1339781/dl.

Williams, Chad, Kidada E. Williams, and Keisha N. Blain, eds. *The Charleston Syllabus: Readings on Race, Racism, and Racial Violence.* University of Georgia Press, 2016.

Wills, Garry. *The Second Civil War: Arming for Armageddon.* New American Library, 1968.

Epilogue

"Wow, That Was a Big Mistake"

JENNIFER M. MURRAY AND JOHN M. KINDER

In mid-April 2024 Republican presidential candidate Donald Trump held a rally in Schnecksville, Pennsylvania, a battleground state for the upcoming November election. Seeking to curry favor with the Commonwealth residents gathered that afternoon, Trump turned the conversation to the Battle of Gettysburg, the Civil War's bloodiest battle fought some 120 miles to the southeast. Donning his red "Make America Great Again" hat, Trump declared, "Gettysburg. Wow. I go to Gettysburg, Pennsylvania, to look and to watch." While it was not clear what Trump "watched" or "looked" at while visiting the landscape where fifty-one thousand U.S. and Confederate soldiers became casualties, he continued to ruminate on the battle's implications in contemporary America. In perhaps a reference to the removal of Confederate monuments and tributes in recent years, Trump pivoted to the commander who *lost* at Gettysburg, Robert E. Lee. He offered, "And the statement of Robert E. Lee—who's no longer in favor, did you ever notice that? No longer in favor—'Never fight uphill, me boys, never fight uphill.' They were fighting uphill. He said, 'Wow, that was a big mistake.' He lost his great general, and they were fighting. 'Never fight uphill, me boys!' But it was too late."[1]

Trump's incoherent and historically incorrect ramblings quickly drew fire from an array of politicians, pundits, and historians. In the opening segment of *The Daily Show*, host Jon Stewart evaluated "Trump's Gettysburg Address," sardonically noting, "If you thought Lincoln consecrated Gettysburg with his soaring rhetoric, well, buckle up."[2] Others noted the irony of Trump's reference to Lee, a man who abdicated his oath to the Constitution and took up arms against the very government he had sworn to protect. Michael Steele, former lieutenant governor of Maryland and chair of the Republican National Committee, observed: "Oh and 'Robert E. Lee is no longer in favor'! Do you know why he is no longer in favor? Because he was a damn insurrectionist! On June 7, 1865, Robert E. Lee was indicted for treason, and charged with 'wickedly, maliciously, and traitorously' carrying on war against the Constitution and the 'peace and dignity' of the United States of America. Sound familiar?"[3]

We can't be surprised by Trump's effort to repurpose Lee (who, in the former president's understanding, spoke with a distinctive Irish brogue) into a vessel of MAGA grievance. As we've demonstrated throughout this volume, many Americans are content to treat the Civil War, in David Blight's words, as a "political plaything," using and abusing its memory to serve their own interests.[4]

Nor should we expect the Civil War to fade from American consciousness any time soon. And perhaps that is "altogether fitting and proper." More than a century and a half after the subjugation of Confederate forces and the triumph of Federal armies in the spring of 1865, the deadliest conflict in U.S. history continues to inspire fiery, even violent, debate on all sides of the ideological spectrum. Civil War iconography permeates American culture in eclectic and surprising ways, and the conflict remains, for better or worse, a go-to reference against which contemporary traumas (from the levels of political polarization to deaths from COVID-19) are measured.[5] For millions of African Americans, the Civil War represents the first—but by no means the last—step in making good on the nation's promise of liberty and justice for all. Meanwhile, predictions of the next "civil war" seem to grow louder every day. Not long after the attempted assassination of Trump in July 2024, Stephen Marche, author of *The Next Civil War: Dispatches from the American Future*, warned that the threat of armed conflict was higher than he had imagined even a few years earlier: "The United States has entered a period of anocracy, a shadowy realm between autocracy and democracy. Any expert of civil war will tell you that anocracy is the most dangerous political state to inhabit, with the greatest tendency to violence."[6] For all that, an increasingly vocal subset of Americans seems to welcome the prospect of national collapse, if only because it will allow them to carry out violent retribution against their perceived persecutors. In 2020 a group of extremists plotted to kidnap Michigan Governor Gretchen Whitmer in the hopes of starting a civil war. Since that time, the United States has experienced a surge in political violence, from the hammer attack on the husband of then–House Speaker Nancy Pelosi to the assassination attempts on Trump to the June 2025 killing of Minnesota State Representative Melissa Hortman and her husband, Mark (along with the slaying of the family dog, Gilbert).[7]

What's more, those who cling to notion that "It can't happen here!" (at least, not again) are likely to be disappointed. War, not peace, is the natural state of humankind (according to one account, humans have been at war for approximately 92 percent of recorded history), and Americans are decidedly *unexceptional* when it comes to taking up arms against each other.[8]

As political scientist and Vietnam veteran Andrew Bacevich has pointed out, Americans have a singularly unique obsession with war. Too many of us are seduced into viewing war as the solution to all the nation's problems— and the military as the be-all and end-all of citizenship in action. The militarization of American sports offers just one example of the acceptance, either active or passive, of warfare and the men and women who wage it. One need only to watch the martial pageantry at a Major League Baseball game, note the NFL's Salute to Service Award, or sit in an SEC stadium and gawk at the splendor of a military flyover before kickoff.[9]

No doubt, to some observers the conflict of 1861–65, made by soldiers carrying single-shot rifles making frontal assaults that closely resembled the battlefields of Napoleonic Europe, seems primitive by its absence of tanks, drones, F-35s, and assorted weapons of mass destruction. But that four-year conflict ended in the deaths of at least seven hundred thousand people, representing 2 percent of the 1860 population. Imagine what havoc we could create today. Were the United States to become involved in a war where 2 percent of our population died, over six million Americans would find their eternal resting places. As a point of comparison, Oklahoma, the state where the coeditors live and teach, has a mere four million residents.[10]

For all these reasons, Civil War memory is not something to be taken lightly, and historians have a special responsibility to push back against anyone who would have us do so. That means sharpening our rhetorical sabers to take on the latest generation of Confederate apologists, who continue to repackage the Lost Cause for twenty-first-century audiences. Most Americans engage with history outside the confines of an academic classroom. This is particularly true for the public, whose insatiable appetite for the Civil War is fed in any number of museums, national park sites, state parks, films, and community events.[11] More than most scholars, Civil War historians are presented with a unique opportunity to engage in meaningful conversations with the public and facilitate a dialogue of how we can better come to terms with that conflict and its legacies. We must hold museums accountable to the latest developments in scholarship and encourage communities to develop novel practices of memorializing the war and its participants. Faced with

Fig. Epi.1. Counterprotesters at a KKK rally in Columbia, South Carolina, on July 18, 2015. A monument to Confederate General Wade Hampton looms in the background. Dedicated in 1906, the monument was originally placed near Hampton's grave but was relocated in 1969 to the Wade Hampton State Office Building. At the time of this writing, this monument still stands. Photographer Edwin Shelton via Flickr.

calls for another civil war, we should arm ourselves with facts about the first one, reminding would-be warriors of the terrible price paid in death, destruction, and mental suffering. And rather than waxing, "Never fight uphill, me boys!" we must be clear-eyed about who Robert E. Lee really was: a wealthy enslaver who, in casting aside his oath of loyalty to the United States, was "responsible for the deaths of more U.S. Army soldiers" than any other "enemy officer in American history."[12]

None of this will be easy, particularly in our current climate of hyperpartisanship. When President Abraham Lincoln traveled to Gettysburg in mid-November 1863, he came to a war-torn community not only to dedicate the Soldiers' National Cemetery, the "final resting place" for more than 3,500 Federal soldiers, but to articulate a vision of a unified nation. Lincoln understood that the survival of the American experiment, a "nation conceived in liberty," was not guaranteed nor perpetual. Standing among scores of freshly dug graves and surrounded by some fifteen thousand spectators who gathered that day, Lincoln spoke of the fragility of a democratic government.[13]

Today, the threat to American democracy lies not in soldiers wielding rifles in gray uniforms and charging Little Round Top but in armed insurrectionists storming the U.S. Capitol, vigilantes dressed as cops gunning down politicians, and federal agents roughing up elected officials who dare question Trump administration immigration policies. It lies not in a secessionist government in Richmond, Virginia, but in the deceitful allegations that the 2020 election was stolen and fraudulent. On July 12, 1864, Federal soldiers repulsed a Confederate offensive at Fort Stevens, seven miles north of Washington DC, securing the capital and turning the tide of the last Rebel invasion. Fast-forward to January 6, 2021. In a singularly vile act of desecration, the January 6 insurrectionists achieved what Confederate soldiers in 1864 could not—the unfurling of a Confederate flag in the Capitol building. On that hot summer day in 1864, Lincoln observed the repulse of the Confederate attack from a parapet; in the early winter days of 2021, the president encouraged followers to a "Big protest in DC!" adding, "Be there! Will be wild!"[14]

The submission of Confederate armies, the triumph of Federal armies, and the preservation of the United States of America was in no way inevitable in the 1860s. Our nation's most divisive and deadly epoch resolved the question of secession, but many social and political inequities remained unsettled for generations. The complexity of that conflict, as this volume underscores, resonates in many familiar and unfamiliar places in this country and demands our attention. We, the stewards of this American experiment and the denizens of the men who wore the uniform of the U.S. government between 1861 and 1865, are responsible for ensuring that "government of the people, by the people, for the people shall not perish from the earth."

Postscript

On November 5, 2024, more than seventy-seven million Americans voted to return former President Donald J. Trump, now a convicted felon, to the White House on a platform of fearmongering, anti-"wokeism," and revenge. As a candidate, he had promised to roll back many of the social justice initiatives that followed the 2020 murder of George Floyd, including congressionally authorized efforts to remove the names of Confederate generals from U.S. military bases (a pledge that he made good on—sort of—just months after his inaugural). Trump's victory did not signal a political mandate, no matter how much the reality-TV-star-turned-politician claimed otherwise. As his detractors rightly point out, the Trump ticket earned less than half the popular vote. (Of course, Trump's opponent, Vice President Kamala Harris, earned less than that.) Yet the ability to manipulate historical memory does not require overwhelming support. It's a function of power. And since taking office a little less than five months ago at the time of this writing, the Trump administration and the Republicans have proven willing and eager to use every lever of power at their disposal to rewrite the nation's past to serve their own interests—from pausing special remembrances of so-called identity months (Women's History Month, Pride Month) to firing National Park Service employees at Civil War battlefields and sites to scrubbing references to race and gender on federal websites. After years of promoting a whitewashed version of the Capitol Insurrection of January 6, 2021 (he once called it a "day of love"), Trump pardoned some 1,500 participants, including those convicted of attacking police officers. Who knows? In a few years, he might declare January 6 a federal holiday and dare those of us who lived through that day to protest.[15]

Without question, we live in a polarized America, and the struggle for our country's future, as well as its past, is at stake. When President Lincoln offered his annual message to Congress in early December 1862, the nation had endured two years of bloody campaigns and unprecedented carnage. The president reminded listeners of the burden of the past in stating, "Fellow-citizens, *we* cannot escape history." The same is as true in 2025 as it was in the wake of Shiloh, Antietam, and Fredericksburg. Whatever happens, one thing is clear. If we want to avoid a second civil war, we cannot forget the first one.

NOTES

1. "Trump Re-Writes Battle of Gettysburg: 'Never Fight Uphill, Me Boys!'" Pennlive.com, April 16, 2024, https://www.pennlive.com/politics/2024/04/trump-re-writes-battle-of-gettysburg-never-fight-uphill-me-boys.html.
2. *Daily Show*, episode 3885, April 15, 2024.
3. Michael Steele (@MichaelSteele), "So @realDonaldTrump Gettysburg was 'Beautiful' and 'it represented such a big portion of the success of this country,'" X, April 14, 2024, https://x.com/MichaelSteele/status/1779582795611885594. Steele was referring to a federal judge in Norfolk, Virginia, John C. Underwood, who called for Lee and a handful of other Confederates to be indicted for treason in the wake of Lee's surrender at Appomattox. Lee believed that the military terms signed at Appomattox, stating that he (and all other former Confederates) would be protected as long as they did not violate the terms of their parole, guaranteed his protection. Lee appealed to Grant, who urged that Lee be pardoned and not tried for treason. Judge Underwood dropped the proceedings. For a discussion of Grant's handling of this situation, see Simpson, *Ulysses S. Grant*, 451–53.
4. Marianne LeVine, "Trump Says 'Civil War Could Have Been Negotiated.' Historians Disagree," *Washington Post*, January 6, 2024, https://www.washingtonpost.com/politics/2024/01/06/trump-says-civil-war-could-have-been-negotiated-historians-disagree/.

5. For such a comparison of the Civil War and COVID-19 deaths, see Jonathan Jones, "Lessons Learned—and Forgotten—from the Horrific Epidemics of the U.S. Civil War," *State News*, April 18, 2021, https://www.statnews.com/2021/04/18/lessons-learned-forgotten-horrific-epidemics-us-civil-war/.
6. Stephen Marche, "I Predicted the Next US Civil War Would Be in 2040—But I Was Wrong. It Feels Closer Than That . . . ," *The Independent*, July 17, 2024, https://www.independent.co.uk/news/world/americas/us-politics/trump-jd-vance-biden-american-civil-war-b2580822.html.
7. Tim Sullivan, Steve Karnowski, and Alanna Durkin Richer, "Authorities Still Searching for Suspect in Shooting of 2 Minnesota State Lawmakers," Associated Press, June 14, 2025, https://apnews.com/article/minnesota-lawmakers-shot-d7983e1e4f1a7573a487cab1a98cd172.
8. Hedges, *What Every Person Should Know*, 1.
9. For the best treatment on America's thirst for war, see Bacevich, *New American Militarism*.
10. McPherson, "Out of War, a New Nation."
11. Burkholder and Schaffer, *History, the Past, and Public Culture*, 18–24.
12. Seidule, *Robert E. Lee and Me*, 216–19.
13. The text of Lincoln's Gettysburg Address can be found at https://www.abrahamlincolnonline.org/lincoln/speeches/gettysburg.htm.
14. Tom Dreisbach, "How Trump's 'Will Be Wild!' Tweet Drew Rioters to the Capitol on Jan. 6," NPR, July 13, 2022, https://www.npr.org/2022/07/13/1111341161/how-trumps-will-be-wild-tweet-drew-rioters-to-the-capitol-on-jan-6. U.S. Senator Alex Padilla was forcibly removed from Homeland Security Secretary Kristi Noem's press conference on June 12, 2025, after his efforts to ask Noem questions about Trump's immigration policies.
15. Tom Dreisbach, "Donald Trump Calls Jan. 6 a 'Day of Love.' Here Are the Facts," NPR, October 29, 2024, https://www.npr.org/2024/10/29/nx-s1-5159868/2024-election-trump-harris-capitol-riot; Max Matza, "Proud Boys and Oath Keepers Among Over 1,500 Capitol Riot Defendants Pardoned by Trump," BBC, January 20, 2025, https://www.bbc.com/news/articles/c5y7l47xrpko.

BIBLIOGRAPHY

Bacevich, Andrew. *The New American Militarism: How Americans Are Seduced by War*. Oxford University Press, 2005.

Burkholder, Peter, and Dana Schaffer. *History, the Past, and Public Culture: Results from a National Survey*. American Historical Association, 2021. https://www.historians.org/wp-content/uploads/2024/06/History-Past-Public-Culture-Survey-Report-2021-08.pdf.

Hedges, Chris. *What Every Person Should Know About War*. The Free Press, 2003.

McPherson, James M. "Out of War, a New Nation." *Prologue* 42, no. 1 (2010). https://www.archives.gov/publications/prologue/2010/spring/newnation.html.

Phillips, Jason. *Looming Civil War: How Nineteenth-Century Americans Imagined the Future*. Oxford University Press, 2018.

Seidule, Ty. *Robert E. Lee and Me: A Southerner's Reckoning with the Myth of the Lost Cause*. St. Martin's, 2021.

Simpson, Brooks D. *Ulysses S. Grant: Triumph over Adversity, 1822–1865*. Houghton Mifflin, 2000.

Timeline of Key Events from the Civil War Centennial to 2025

1957

September 7 — Congress approves the establishment of the Civil War Centennial Commission

1961

April — Civil War Centennial commemorations kick off at Fort Sumter

July 21–23 — Centennial commemorations at Manassas National Battlefield Park

1963

July 1–3 — Centennial events at Gettysburg, Pennsylvania

August 8 — Martin Luther King's March on Washington

1990

September 23 — The first episode of Ken Burns's nine-part documentary *The Civil War* airs on PBS, reigniting widespread interest in the conflict and its memory

2001

February 2 — Confederate flag removed from the state capitol in Tallahassee, Florida

2015

June 17 — Emanuel AME shooting, Charleston, South Carolina

July 10 — Confederate flag removed from South Carolina's state capitol, Columbia

2017

August 11–12 — Unite the Right Rally, Charlottesville, Virginia

2020

May 5 — Murder of George Floyd, Minneapolis, Minnesota

July 1 Removal of Stonewall Jackson monument, Richmond, Virginia
July 4 Antifa rally at Gettysburg National Military Park, Pennsylvania
December 11 Congress approves a bill that includes the renaming of nine U.S. Army bases no later than January 1, 2024

2021

January 6 Insurrectionists attack the U.S. Capitol
January 11 Mississippi adopts a redesigned state flag that removes the Confederate battle flag
September 8 Removal of Robert E. Lee monument, Richmond, Virginia

2023

October 27 Fort Gordon renamed Fort Eisenhower, marking the last of the nine U.S. Army bases to be renamed

2024

July 13 Twenty-year-old Thomas Matthew Cook attempts to assassinate former President Donald J. Trump at a rally near Butler, Pennsylvania, renewing online predictions of a looming civil war
November 5 Donald Trump elected for a second (nonconsecutive) term

2025

March 7 Secretary of Defense Pete Hegseth orders Fort Liberty to be renamed Fort Bragg, in honor of Roland Bragg, a World War II soldier
March 27 Trump signs executive order "Restoring Truth and Sanity to American History"
June 10 President Trump visits Fort Bragg and promises to change the names of U.S. Army bases
June 14 Minnesota State Representative Melissa Hortman and her husband, Mark, are assassinated by a political extremist

Contributors

BRETT A. BARNETT is a professor of strategic communication and media at Slippery Rock University of Pennsylvania and author of *Untangling the Web of Hate: Are Online "Hate Sites" Deserving of First Amendment Protection?* His research has also been published in the international journals *Perspectives on Terrorism*, *Journal of Hate Studies*, and *Ethical Space: The International Journal of Communication Ethics*.

TIM GALSWORTHY is a lecturer in history and military history at Lincoln Bishop University in Lincoln, UK. He is a specialist in modern U.S. politics and history. His book *The Republican House Divided: Civil War Memory, Civil Rights, and the Transformation of the GOP* was published in November 2025.

SCOTT HANCOCK is an associate professor of history and Africana studies at Gettysburg College.

SARAH HANDLEY-COUSINS is an associate teaching professor of history at the University at Buffalo. She is the author of *Bodies in Blue: Disability in the Civil War North*.

JOHN M. KINDER is director of American studies and professor of history at Oklahoma State University. He is the author of *Paying with Their Bodies: American War and the Problem of the Disabled Veteran* and coeditor of *Service Denied: Marginalized Veterans in Modern American History*. His most recent book is *World War Zoos: Humans and Other Animals in the Deadliest Conflict of the Modern Age*. He is currently working on a book about murder in World War II Mississippi.

KEVIN M. LEVIN is a historian and educator based in Boston. He is the author of numerous books and articles about the Civil War, including *Searching for Black Confederates: The Civil War's Most Persistent Myth* (2019) and a forthcoming book about Robert Gould Shaw.

NICOLE MAURANTONIO is a professor of rhetoric and communication studies and American studies at the University of Richmond. She is the author of *Confederate Exceptionalism: Civil War Myth and Memory in the Twenty-First Century* (2019) and coeditor, with David W. Park, of *Communicating Memory and History* (2019).

JENNIFER M. MURRAY is an assistant professor of history and the director of the George Tyler Moore Center for the Study of the Civil War at Shepherd University. She is the author of *On a Great Battlefield: The Making, Management, and Memory of Gettysburg National Military Park, 1933–2013* (2nd ed., 2023) and is working on a biography of Union General George G. Meade.

STEVE T. PHAN is the chief of interpretation at Camp Nelson National Monument in Nicholasville, Kentucky.

BROOKS D. SIMPSON is the ASU Foundation Professor of History at Arizona State University.

JOSEPH M. THOMPSON is an associate professor of history at Mississippi State University. He is the author of *Cold War Country: How Nashville's Music Row and the Pentagon Created the Sound of American Patriotism*.

JOSHUA WOLF earned his doctorate from Temple University and is an assistant professor at Point Park University.

Index

"Abraham Obama," 5–6
accelerationists, 262–63
"Accidental Racist" (LL Cool J and Paisley), 131–32
Adams, Charity, 65, 74
African Americans. *See* Black lives
Agnew, Spiro, 54, 56
Antifa, 284. *See also* Antifa hoax (Gettysburg, July 2020)
Antifa hoax (Gettysburg, July 2020), 189, 190, 192, 213n2
Appomattox Court House, 2, 3, 17, 72, 73, 99, 136, 280n3
Arlington National Cemetery, 25, 28, 219
Army of Northern Virginia, 17, 72, 73, 79, 99, 195, 198, 209, 214n16, 237
Army of the Potomac, 63, 215n27
Aryan Nations, 244
Ashes in the Wind (Woodiwise), 157–58, 161
Atkinson KS, 111–12; demographics and growth of, 113–14; Juneteenth Celebration (2021) in, 122–23; KKK presence in, 121–22; and lynching, 115–17; Molly's Hollow in, 111, 120; sued for George Johnson's murder (1872), 117–18
Austin, Lloyd, 65, 71

Barfoot, Van T., 73
"Battle Cry of Freedom" (Root), 63
Battle of Liberty Place obelisk, 22
"The Battle of New Orleans" (Horton), 135
Belknap, William W., 33
Benning, Henry, 75
Biden, Joseph R., Jr., 7, 27, 29, 31, 55, 188
"Billy Yank and Johnny Reb" (Driftwood), 137

The Birth of a Nation (Griffith), 17, 19, 155, 175, 238–39, 248, 267
The Birth of a Nation (Parker), 227
Black, Don, 243
Black Confederates: endorsement of, by African Americans, 224, 225–26; initial references to, 219–20; and the Lost Cause, 226, 227–28, 229; myth of, 217, 218, 220, 226, 227–28, 229; and the Sons of Confederate Veterans, 219, 221, 223, 225
Black Dog, 181–82
Black History Month, 1, 225
Black lives: and the armies at Gettysburg, 200–205; and Black Gettysburg residents in 1863, 207–9; and the Gettysburg narrative, 210, 211, 213; Gettysburg National Military Park views of, in 2020, 195–98, 209, 211–12; Southern secessionist views of, 198–99; and "This Battle Was Fought Because Black Lives Matter" yard signs, 189; and white Gettysburg residents in 1863, 205–7; white militia views of, in 2020, 190–95; white Northerners' views of, 199–200. *See also* Black Lives Matter (BLM) movement
Black Lives Matter (BLM) movement: birth of, 170; and the Black Confederate narrative, 225; and Black Freedom movement, 190; and Civil War, 7, 9; and Confederate monuments, 55, 191; era of, 187; fears about, 189–90; flags for, 192–94; and the Lost Cause, 218; and 2020 protests, 55, 129, 146, 200, 248; violent policing of, 213n3. *See also* Black lives
Blight, David, 2–3, 66, 229

bluegrass, 136
Boone Hall Plantation, 263–64
Bragg, Braxton, 28, 75–76, 81
Bragg, Roland L., 82
Bridgerton (Quinn), 153, 166, 167
Brown v. Board of Education of Topeka, 240
Burns, Mike, 222

Camp Nelson: as bastion of freedom, 99; and Camp Nelson Heritage Park, 101; Civil War usage of, 93, 96–97; exclusion of, from Kentucky's Civil War legacy, 95; and impressed African American labor, 97; interpretation at, 94, 104–5; and Long Range Interpretive Plan, 104–5; national significance of, 101, 102; preservation of, 94, 100–103; and refugees, 93, 94, 97–99, 103, 104, 106; and USCT units, 96, 98, 99, 105
Camp Nelson National Monument, 94, 102–6
Carlson, Tucker, 233
Cavazos, Richard E., 76–77
Charleston Massacre (2015), 254; and antiracist protest, 8; and *The Charleston Syllabus*, 270; Charlie Daniels on, 146; and debate about Confederate symbols, 1, 21–22, 26, 67, 146, 221, 222, 245, 255; as important moment in Civil War memory, 25, 255, 283; media coverage of, 245; pro–Confederate battle flag rallies after, 246. *See also* Roof, Dylann
Charleston SC: as "America's Most Historic City," 265; as capital of American slavery, 265; and Carolina Rifle Club, 237–38; and Charleston County Detention Center, 267; and memory industry, 263; and plantations, 263–64, 266–67; and start of Civil War, 21; and tourism, 265–66, 270. *See also* Charleston Massacre (2015)
Charlottesville VA, 8, 23, 26, 27, 172, 182, 247. *See also* Unite the Right Rally (Charlottesville VA)
Chism, Kathy, 217
Christian identity, 243–44
Chumley, Bill, 222

civil rights movement, 4, 46, 52, 57, 101, 138, 141, 219, 239–41
Civil War: as analogy for contemporary polarization, 7; and Black Lives Matter movement, 7; contemporary relevance of, 11–12, 276; as "felt history," 10; as "political plaything," 276; and pop culture, 132. *See also* Civil War memory; next civil war; Reconstruction; second civil war
The Civil War (Burns), 19, 220, 283
Civil War Centennial, 4, 10, 20, 46, 133, 136, 137, 138, 240, 283
Civil War Centennial Commission, 138, 283
Civil War memory: battles over, 2–3, 8, 25, 52, 80, 82, 165, 221, 270; and collective identity, 12; commodification and consumption of, 9, 128–29; divisions over, 21; and Dylann Roof, 270; and *Gone with the Wind*, 155; historiography of, 10–11, 24; malleable nature of, 112; and memory spaces, 8; periphery of, 94; in politics, 8; and politics of race, 229; and power, 280; and race, 9; and rebellion, 138; recent interest in, 6–7; reclamation of, 63; as reconciliation, 3; shift in, 219; significance of, 11, 66, 83, 277; as usable past, 2; and violence, 9. *See also* Black Confederates; Charleston Massacre (2015); Civil War; Civil War romance novels; Confederate battle flag; country music; industry of memory; January 6, 2021 (Capitol insurrection); Lost Cause; Reconstruction; renaming of military bases; Republican Party
Civil War romance novels: *Ashes in the Wind*, 157–58, 161; Black female authors of, 154, 164–66; and Civil War memory, 154–55, 165, 166, 167; *Confederate Runaway*, 164; and debate about *Gone with the Wind*, 157, 168n9; depictions of slavery in, 152, 158–59, 162–63, 166; and evangelical Christian perspectives, 154, 161; *An Extraordinary Union*, 165–66; *The Haunting*, 164; *Indigo*, 164–65; and intersectional romances, 154, 158–61; and the Lost Cause, 156–58, 161–62, 163–64, 167; *Miss*

Ravenel's Conversion from Secession to Loyalty, 155; *Mystic Rose*, 158–59, 161; *One Wore Blue*, 159–60, 161, 165; *The Planter's Daughter*, 152–53, 162, 163; *Tomorrow the Glory*, 160; *With This Pledge*, 162–63

Civil War Sesquicentennial (2011–15), 20, 21, 101, 220–21

Clement, Frank C., 135

clothing, 171–72

Clyburn, Weary, 224

Cold Mountain (Frazier), 155, 168n17

Cold War, 133, 135, 136, 139, 141

Cole, Alyssa, 154, 165–66, 167

Commission on the Naming of Items of the Department of Defense that Commemorate the Confederate States of America or Any Person Who Served Voluntarily with the Confederate States of America. *See* Naming Commission

Community Remembrance Project, 122, 124

Confederacy: alternate history of, 154; built on white supremacy, 3, 208, 220; defense of, 220; and defense of slavery, 24; image of, 178, 227; mythologizing of, 217; normalization of, 53, 171, 178–79, 181–82, 222, 223; political affiliations of, 45; as purest form of Americanism, 175, 180; representations of, 219–20; and Southern aesthetic, 176; and states' rights, 228; symbols of, 141, 170, 218, 221, 226. *See also* Black Confederates; Black lives; Confederate battle flag; Confederate monuments; Dixie (concept/place); Lost Cause; neo-Confederates; the South

Confederate (proposed television project), 154

Confederate battle flag: and army heritage, 81; backlash against, 221, 245–48, 283; and the Black Confederate narrative, 226; at the Capitol insurrection (January 6, 2021), 2, 7, 30–31, 44, 57, 249, 279; at cemeteries, 260–61; after the Charleston Massacre (2015), 1, 22, 146, 222, 245; and Christian iconography, 243–44; and the civil rights movement, 239–41; and Confederate heritage groups, 26; and country music, 131, 132, 136, 140, 141, 144, 145; and culture wars (1990s), 51–52; and Donald Trump, 54, 223; and Dylann Roof, 22, 221, 245, 254, 257, 270; in fashion, 173, 175, 177, 180; at Gettysburg National Military Park (2020), 195; as "heritage not hate," 21; history of, 236–37; on internet hate sites, 243–44; and the KKK, 239–42, 243, 246, 248; in mainstream media, 242–44, 246–47; and neo-Confederates, 244; in popular culture, 129, 145; and propaganda, 182n5; and regional heritage, 1, 145; and romance novels, 160; and the Sons of Confederate Veterans, 145, 221; and Southern politics, 47, 48, 50, 52; and state flags, 217, 240, 248, 284; and the summer of 2020, 189, 191, 248–49; as symbol, 56, 235–36, 238, 248, 250; and white supremacy, 26, 235–38, 242, 244

Confederate cemetery. *See* Elmwood Cemetery (Columbia SC)

Confederate exceptionalism, 176

Confederate Hammerskins, 242

Confederate heritage, 22–23, 26, 54, 82, 177, 217, 220, 223–25, 229, 229n2. *See also* Sons of Confederate Veterans (SCV); United Daughters of the Confederacy

Confederate History Month, 1, 228

Confederate iconography: debates about, 24–26, 165; Donald Trump's embrace of, 57; and Dylann Roof, 259; Early Cuyler's love of, 129; in fashion, 170–71; in Kentucky, 93; normalization of, 171. *See also* Confederate battle flag; Confederate monuments

Confederate monuments: defacing of, 226–27; defense of, 52–53, 56; Donald Trump's opposition to removing, 54–55; efforts to protect, 195, 226; and Jim Crow, 8; and the Lost Cause, 17, 195; and monument debate, 7–8, 222; removal of, 22–24, 28, 221–22, 226–27, 228, 255; scholarly focus on, 10; and Sons of Confederate Veterans, 223, 226–27; targeted by Black Lives Matter movement, 55; and white supremacy, 68

Confederate Records, 140

Confederate Runaway (Jasper), 164
Cook, Thomas Matthew, 284
Council of Conservative Citizens, 258, 259
country music: and American exceptionalism, 134–35; and Confederate memory, 9, 138; and the counterculture, 139; and historical songs about the Civil War, 134–38, 142–44; industry, 132, 133, 134, 135–36, 138, 146; and the KKK, 141–42; and the Lost Cause, 132–34, 135, 145–47; and Robert E. Lee, 131, 136; and the "southernization" of America, 141; and white supremacy, 132, 148n20
Country Music Association (CMA), 135
Cox, Karen L., 8, 14n22, 68, 175
Cox, Patrick, 112–14, 115, 118–19
Crossed Hammers, 242
culture wars, 51

Daniels, Charlie, 141–42, 144, 146
Davis, Jefferson, 48, 51, 54, 94, 209, 238
Dixie (concept/place), 132, 137, 143, 144, 146, 171, 175, 178, 180, 226
"Dixie" (song), 47, 49, 50, 52, 55, 135, 145, 175
Dixie chic, 182
Dixie Shop, 171, 174–76
dogs, 181
Douglass, Frederick, 4
Driftwood, Jimmy, 133–38, 140, 147
Duke, David, 241, 247
The Dukes of Hazard, 145, 175
Dunning School, 24, 123

Edgerton, H. K., 225–26
Eisenhower, Dwight D., 79
Elmwood Cemetery (Columbia SC), 260–61
Emancipation (Fuqua), 227
Emmanuel African Methodist Episcopal Church, 254. *See also* Charleston Massacre (2015)
English, Ron, 6
Equal Justice Initiative, 122, 123, 126n42
An Extraordinary Union (Cole), 165–66

fashion, 171–72

Floyd, George, murder of, 7, 8, 27, 55, 68, 187, 191, 206, 226, 247, 255, 279, 283
Forrest, Nathan Bedford, 23–24, 49, 78, 228
Frost, Malcolm, 67–68

gender, 74, 86n22, 94, 143, 161, 170, 174, 177, 280
Gendron, Payton, 268–69
George Johnson Community Remembrance Project, 122–23, 126n43
Gettysburg: and Abraham Lincoln, 199, 275, 278, 279; and capture of enslaved people, 202–5; in Civil War romance novel, 164; fiftieth anniversary of battle of, 3; in film, 196; and John Bell Hood, 76; and narrative of emancipation, 189; newspaper narratives of, 199–200; 150th anniversary of battle of, 21; and Pickett's Charge, 73. *See also* Black lives
Gettysburg (Maxwell), 196
Gettysburg National Military Park: and Abraham Brian farm, 197, 209–10, 212; absence of references to slavery at, 197; Antifa rally at, 284; and Civil War Centennial, 283; efforts to center Black lives at, 209, 211; First Michigan Infantry Monument dedication at, 84; and interpretive marker at the North Carolina Memorial, 211; and interpretive marker at the Peace Light Memorial, 212; and interpretive marker at the Warfield Tower, 212; interpretive programs at, 196, 197–98, 209, 211–12; July 4, 2020, incident at, 194–95; 105th Pennsylvania Infantry Monument at, 12; and "Trump's Gettysburg Address," 275; Virginia State Memorial at, 192, 195, 196. *See also* Antifa hoax (Gettysburg, July 2020); Black lives
Goldwater, Barry, 48–50, 56
Gone with the Wind (Fleming), 19, 239, 248, 267
Gone with the Wind (Mitchell), 153, 155, 156, 157, 168n9
GOP. *See* Republican Party
Gordon, Gary I., 91n69
Gordon, John B., 28, 79, 84n2

Grant, Ulysses S., 17, 25–29, 30, 31–33, 38, 71, 87n25, 280n3
Greene, Marjorie Taylor, 52–53
Greensboro Massacre, 241
Gregg, Arthur, 65, 73–74

Haley, Nikki, 1–2, 3, 53
Harriet (Lemmons), 227
hate websites, 243–44
The Haunting (Tarr), 164
Hegseth, Pete, 82, 83, 284
Helm, Levon, 140, 144
"heritage not hate," 21, 23, 57, 255
Hill, Ambrose Powell, 74
Hill, Lister, 47
hillbilly music, 133, 142
Holding the High Ground (Sutton), 101
Hood, John Bell, 76
Hood, Robert B., 91n69
hoodies, 170–71, 173–74, 182
Hortman, Melissa, 276, 284
Horton, Johnny, 135–36

Indigo (Jenkins), 164–65
industry of memory, 191, 212
"I Sang Dixie" (Yoakam), 145

Jackson, Thomas "Stonewall," 22, 52, 54, 72, 136, 220, 223, 238
James, Jesse, 144
January 6, 2021 (Capitol insurrection): aftermath of, 33, 34; and Civil War analogy, 7, 63; Confederate battle flag at, 2, 7, 30–31, 44, 57, 249, 279; and Donald Trump, 30, 31, 34–37, 279–80; downplaying of, 233; as first battle of a second civil war, 6–7, 269; as important moment in Civil War memory, 284; as insurrection, 32, 35; and Josh Hawley, 69; and parallels with Reconstruction, 31–32; and section 3 of the Fourteenth Amendment, 34–35
Jefferson Davis statue (Richmond VA), 28
Jenkins, Beverly, 154, 164–66, 167
Jennings, Waylon, 141, 142, 143, 144
Johnson, Andrew, 25, 27, 74, 87n25, 96

Johnson, George: absence of accountability for lynching of, 116; and Eliza Ann Johnson, 116; lynching of, 111, 115; in memory, 112, 120–21, 122, 124; reporting on murder of, 114–15, 117–20; response in Atchison to murder of, 115–16, 126n34; and shooting of Patrick Cox, 112–14; and surrender to Marshal Jesse Crall, 112. *See also* George Johnson Community Remembrance Project
Johnson, William Henry, 77–78
Juneteenth, 122, 187–88

Kennerley, Paul, 133, 142–44, 147
Kentucky Heritage Council, 100
Kentucky in the Civil War, 94–99
King, Martin Luther, Jr., 4, 240, 262, 283
Ku Klux Klan (KKK): as "American as apple pie," 172; and anti-Klan rally, 122, 278; birthplace of, 228, 237; and collaboration with neo-Nazis, 241–42; and the Confederate battle flag, 239–42, 243, 246, 248; and country music, 133, 141–42; as enforcers of values, 257; and fears of "Black crime," 259; in fiction, 155, 238; and first Klan, 237–38; and Guzton Borglum, 211; and John B. Gordon, 28, 79; in Kansas, 121; and Ku Klux Klan Act, 31; march of, in Dallas, 242–43; media coverage of, 239, 240; and Nathan Bedford Forrest, 23, 228; and neo-Nazi march (Pulaski TN), 242; opposition of, to the civil rights movement, 239–41; and second Klan, 175, 239; Ulysses S. Grant's actions against, 31, 32, 37. *See also The Birth of a Nation* (Griffith)

Lang, Stephen, 196
League of the South, 239n2, 244, 246
Lee, Fitz, 83
Lee, Robert E.: and Army of Virginia, 237; and country music, 131, 136; and deaths of U.S. Army soldiers, 73; Donald Trump on, 28–29, 54, 55, 223, 275–76; as enslaver, 192, 207, 278; in film, 196; as insurrectionist,

Lee, Robert E. (*cont.*)
276; and Lost Cause myth, 54; relief of, at Stone Mountain GA, 54, 238; statue of, in Charlottesville VA, 8, 22, 52, 154, 223, 246–47; statue of, in Richmond VA, 28, 191, 195; surrender of, at Appomattox Court House, 2, 17, 280n3; tributes to, 65, 67, 68, 73, 81; and Virginia, 72

The Legend of Jesse James (Kennerley), 133, 142–44

The Leopard's Spots (Dixon), 155, 156, 168n17

Lincoln (Spielberg), 227

Lincoln, Abraham: and Barack Obama, 4–6; and "Battle Cry of Freedom," 63; and country music, 131, 136; and Donald Trump, 56, 187; election of (1860), 7, 13n19, 114; and emancipation, 199, 200; and Gettysburg, 199, 275, 278, 279; image of, 256; and Kentucky, 94, 105; and message to Congress (1862), 280; and Republican Party, 33, 45, 51, 56, 57; and Thanksgiving, 257

Lincoln administration, 96

Lincoln Memorial, 4

LL Cool J, 131

Lost Cause: and Barry Goldwater, 48–49; and the Black Confederate myth, 226, 227–28, 229; challenge to, in the civil rights era, 219; and Civil War romance novels, 156–58, 161–62, 163–64, 167, 265; and Confederate exceptionalism, 176; and country music, 9, 132–34, 135, 145–47; as default interpretation of Civil War, 4, 17, 65, 68, 84, 94, 104, 105, 132, 140, 228; defenders of, 25, 52, 56, 277; disassociation of, with slavery, 3, 17, 44, 46, 53, 218; and Donald Trump, 54, 55; and Dylann Roof, 255, 259; and memory, 46, 47, 51, 105; and monuments, 17, 195; and Museum and Library of Confederate History, 258; as myth, 21, 53, 54, 191, 217–18; and Nikki Haley, 2; and nostalgia, 130; and Reconstruction as "failure," 143; and Republican politics, 18, 44–45, 47–50, 52–53, 55–56, 57; and Richard Nixon, 51, 54; and Robert E. Lee, 73; and the "Southern Strategy," 54; and Spiro Agnew, 54; and states' rights, 8, 17; and white supremacy, 80, 191; and World War I, 66. *See also* new Lost Cause

The Lost Cause (Pollard), 17

Lott, Trent, 51

Loyal White Knights of the Ku Klux Klan, 246

lynching: erasing the history of, 9, 119–20, 123; of George Johnson, 111, 114–18, 120–22, 124, 126n24; and monument construction, 8; sites of, 122, 123; as tool of white supremacy, 121, 258

MAGA (political ideology), 18, 81, 82, 83, 187, 262, 276

Magnolia Plantation, 263–65

Make America Great Again (slogan), 188, 275. *See also* MAGA (political ideology)

Marche, Stephen, 6, 276

Marie Tharp, USNS, 81

Martin, James, 47–48

Martin, Trayvon, killing of, 170, 182, 258

mason jars, 180

McLeod Plantation, 266–68, 270

Miss Ravenel's Conversion from Secession to Loyalty (De Forest), 155

Moore, Hal, 75

Moore, Julia, 75

Museum and Library of Confederate History, 255, 256–58, 265, 270

Museum of the Confederacy, 219

"My Black Bird Has Gone" (Driftwood), 137

Mystic Rose (Gallagher), 158–59, 161

Naming Commission, 28, 69, 70–72, 76, 82, 87n25

National Association for the Advancement of Colored People (NAACP), 126n40, 145, 225

National Defense Authorization Act (NDAA) of 2020, 68–69, 82

National Defense Authorization Act (NDAA) of 2021, 69

National Park Service (NPS), 11, 21, 101–4, 105, 106, 206, 214n8, 220, 280

neo-Confederates, 1, 136, 141, 143, 171, 180, 229n2, 233, 244, 246, 248, 255, 259, 261, 263, 269
neo-Nazis, 9, 241–43, 244, 246, 247, 248, 259
new Lost Cause, 18, 44, 57. *See also* Lost Cause
next civil war, 6, 233, 262, 269. *See also* second civil war
The Next Civil War (Marche), 6, 276
"The Night They Drove Old Dixie Down" (Helm), 140
Nitty Gritty Dirt Band, 140–41
Nixon, Richard, 27, 50, 54, 56
nostalgia, 4, 81, 130, 132, 145, 264, 266, 270
Novosel, Michael J., 78–79

Obama, Barack, 4–6, 89n52, 103, 131, 221
One Wore Blue (Graham), 159–60, 161, 165

Paisley, Brad, 131
palmetto, 182
Parsons, Gram, 139–40
pastels, 177
Pence, Mike, 28–30, 55
Pender, William Dorsey, 203–4
Phillips, Rubel, 46–48
Pickett, George E., 68, 72–73, 87n25, 196
Pickett, Vernon W., 91n69
Pickett's Charge, 197, 209, 212
pigs, 180–81
plantation tourism, 265
The Planter's Daughter (Shocklee), 152–53, 162, 163
police abuse and killings of African Americans, 7, 146, 226, 247, 262
political polarization, 2, 6, 9, 51, 53, 80, 95, 107, 213, 270, 276, 280
political violence, 6, 32, 38, 213n3, 255, 276
Polk, James H., 91n69
Polk, Leonidas, 77
Pollard, Edward, 17
polo shirts, 172–73, 182
"Poor Rebel Soldier" (Driftwood), 137, 148n23
presidential election (2020), 18, 29, 30, 34, 35, 44, 279

presidential election (2024), 6, 37, 53, 55, 63, 76, 81, 82, 86n16, 279–80, 284
Pulaski TN, 228, 237

"Quantrill's Guerillas" (Kennerley), 144

race: Black Republicans on, 53; and Civil War memory, 9, 229; and Civil War romance novels, 158, 161, 166; and the Confederate battle flag, 146; and Confederate myth, 226–27; Dylann Roof on, 259; erasing references to, at federal battlefields, 280; and the Lost Cause, 218; and the monument debate, 222; and new understanding of Reconstruction, 20, 23, 24, 38; and reconciliation, 3; references to, at Gettysburg, 210, 212; and regional identity, 139; and a second civil war, 255, 262; and violence, 121, 122, 124. *See also* Black lives; race war; racism; white supremacy
race war, 221, 254, 262–63
racism: and Civil War memory, 102; and the Confederate battle flag, 52; and Confederate exceptionalism, 176, 182; and Confederate heritage, 23; of Dylann Roof, 266; and legacy of Civil War, 66; and pro-Confederate sentiment, 255; public reckoning with, 171; and romance novel industry, 168n16; and skinheads, 172; structural and systemic, 7, 9, 27, 68, 79, 167; in United States, 122, 170; in U.S. Army, 79–81; and white supremacy, 167, 229
Reconstruction: and calls for "third Reconstruction," 27; and Civil War memory, 20; contemporary relevance of, 38; and Dunning School, 24; as failure, 143; historical parallels to, 49, 266; and January 6, 2021, 31–32; marginalization of, 19–21, 112, 119, 123–24; new scholarship on, 20–21, 24, 37–38; and racist violence, 123, 266; reassessment of, by the National Parks Service, 102, 103; and reassessment of Ulysses S. Grant presidency, 25–26; and the Republican Party, 46, 47, 50, 56, 57; resistance to, 79; and section 3 of the

Index 293

Reconstruction (*cont.*)
  Fourteenth Amendment, 33–36; as source of inspiration, 7; and terrorism, 20; as "tragic era," 46; and white supremacy, 21, 22, 23
reenactors, 199, 219, 225
renaming of military bases: congressional approval of, 284; conservative opposition to, 28, 69–70; Donald Trump's decision to undo, 66, 82–83; Fort A. P. Hill, 74, 83; Fort Barfoot, 73; Fort Benning, 75; Fort Bragg, 75–76, 284; Fort Cavazos, 76–77; Fort Eisenhower, 79; Fort Gordon, 78–79, 284; Fort Gregg Adams, 65, 73–74; Fort Hal and Julia Moore, 75; Fort Hood, 76, 80; Fort Johnson, 77–78; Fort Lee, 65, 73–74; Fort Liberty, 76, 81–82, 84, 284; Fort Novosel, 78–79; Fort Pickett, 72; Fort Polk, 77; Fort Rucker, 78; Fort Walker, 74; historical precedents for, 66–68; loophole in, 82; as MAGA talking point, 81–82; methodology and criteria of, 71, 72; momentum toward, 68; polls about, 80; and Removing Confederate Names and Symbols from Our Military Act, 68; and "Restoring Names That Honor American Greatness" agenda, 83. *See also* Naming Commission
Republican Party: and Abraham Lincoln, 33, 45, 51, 56, 57; and backlash to civil rights movement, 45, 48–49, 56, 57; and Confederate battle flag at South Carolina Capitol, 51–52; and election (1964), 49–50; and election (1968), 50–51; and embrace of Confederate iconography, 50; and the Lost Cause, 18, 44–45, 47–50, 52–53, 55–56, 57; and Reconstruction, 46, 47, 50, 56, 57; and the Sons of Confederate Veterans, 51; and the "Southern Strategy," 54–55
"Restoring Truth and Sanity to American History," 11, 284
Rhodesia, 243, 259, 270n2
Roberts, Needham, 78
Robert Smalls, USS, 81

romance (genre), 155–56
romance novels, evolution of, 156–57
Roof, Dylann: and Charleston Massacre (2015), 1, 21, 146, 221, 245, 254; and the Confederate battle flag, 22, 221, 245, 254, 257, 270; historical tour by, before the massacre, 254–55, 271n3; influence of, 267–69; and the internet, 257–59; and the Lost Cause, 255, 259; online manifesto of, 254, 258–59, 265–66; in prison, 267; and "race war," 263; second civil war predictions of, 255, 261–63, 269; as symbol, 255–56, 270; worldview of, 259. *See also* Charleston Massacre (2015)
Roots (Haley), 220
Rucker, Edward W., 91n69

second civil war, 6, 255, 261, 262, 280. *See also* next civil war
section 3 of the Fourteenth Amendment, 33–37, 43n45
SensiblePrepper, 233
Simply Dixie, 171, 174–76, 178–80, 182
Simply Southern, 177–79
skinheads, 172, 242, 243
Solid South, 45, 50
Songs of Billy Yank and Johnny Reb (Driftwood), 136
Sons of Confederate Veterans (SCV): African American involvement in, 225; and Black Confederate myth, 217, 219–27; and Black History Month, 225; and Charleston Massacre (2015), 221; and the Confederate battle flag, 238; and Confederate monuments, 223, 226–27; and country music, 145–46; and Museum and Library of Confederate History, 256; and Pete Hegseth, 82; and reenactments, 138; and Republican politics, 51; and Weary Clyburn, 224
the South: aesthetic of, 178–79; and Civil War inspirationals, 162; color palette of, 176–78; and the Confederacy, 181; and Confederate exceptionalism, 176; and fonts, 178–79; and gentility, 215n27; and

294 Index

glorification of defeat, 180; icons of, 179–82; and narrative of peaceful race relations, 223, 226; as region, 175; reinvention of, 141; resistance of, to Black freedom struggle, 56, 240; romanticization of, 175; shift of, toward Republican Party, 45, 56, 57; and "Southern lady" image, 177; style of, 176; as white, 233. *See also* Dixie (concept/place)
Southern Republicans. *See* Republican Party
"The South's Gonna Do It" (Daniels), 141
Spessard, Michael, 197–98
Squidbillies, 129–30
Stewart, Corey, 52
Stone Mountain (GA), 54, 238, 239
Stonewall Jackson monument (Richmond VA), 284
summer of 2020, 27–28, 68, 187, 189, 190
Supreme Court, U.S., 35–37, 54, 240
swastika, 173, 235, 248, 250
sweatshirts, 173–74

terrorism, 9, 20, 24, 32, 38, 124, 249, 270
Thurmond, Strom, 49, 50, 51
Tomorrow The Glory (Graham), 160–61
Tops Friendly Market shooting, 268–69
Tree of Life Synagogue shooting, 269
Truesdale, J. C., 12
Trump, Donald J.: assassination attempt on, 255, 276, 284; and Camp Nelson National Monument, 103; comments of, after Unite the Right Rally, 26, 70, 223; comparison of, to Andrew Johnson, 27; on Confederate flags and monuments, 54–55, 223; election of (2024), 82, 279, 284; election of (2024), 6, 279; impeachments of, 27, 33; and January 6, 2021, 30, 31, 34–37, 279–80; on Juneteenth, 187–88; and the Lost Cause, 54, 55, 57; and the new Lost Cause, 2, 44; opposition of, to renaming of military bases, 66, 70, 72, 81, 82, 83; and pro-Confederate memories, 55, 56–57, 70, 72; and "Restoring Truth and Sanity to American History," 11, 284; on Robert E. Lee, 28–29, 54, 55, 223, 275–76; on the threat of civil war, 261–62; and "Trump's Gettysburg Address," 275; on voter fraud in the 2020 election, 29–30
T-shirts, 170–74
Tulsa OK, 187

United Daughters of the Confederacy, 17, 24, 67, 75, 138, 177, 191, 211, 217, 226–27, 238
United States Colored Troops (USCT), 63; depicted in movies, 220, 227; interpreted at Petersburg National Battlefield, 219; in Kentucky, 96, 98, 99, 105; represented in monuments, 227–28
United States Military Academy, 28, 54, 65, 67, 68, 72, 74, 77, 81, 84n2, 87n25
United States Naval Academy, 81
Unite the Right Rally (Charlottesville VA), 23, 52, 54–55, 68, 70, 154, 173, 223, 246–47, 249, 255, 283

Vernon, Justin, 63
Vineyard Vines, 179, 182
Voting Rights Act of 1965, 21, 50, 240

Walker, Mary Edwards, 74
war, obsession with, 277
Warfield, Eliza, 207, 212
Warfield, James, 207, 212
Warren, Elizabeth, 68, 69, 90
Warren, Robert Penn, 10
West Point. *See* United States Military Academy
White Mansions (Kennerley), 133, 142–43, 144–45
white supremacy: aesthetics of, 171–72; and Black Confederate myth, 223, 225; and Charleston SC, 265; and the Civil War era, 153–54; collaboration between groups of, 241–42; Confederacy's fight to preserve, 220, 229; and country music, 132, 148n20; Equal Justice Initiative's challenge to, 126n42; as industry of memory, 191–92; and Lost Cause, 80, 191; and lynching, 121, 258; military base names as legacy of, 68, 80; narratives of, 195, 211;

Index 295

white supremacy (*cont.*)
    and Reconstruction, 21, 22, 23; rise of, 80; and the self-centering of whiteness, 209, 210; symbols of, 235–36, 242, 250; in traditional and online media, 242–43, 247, 249; unquestioned in Civil War romance novels, 163; and U.S. history, 11. *See also* Confederate monuments; Ku Klux Klan (KKK); neo-Confederates; neo-Nazis; racism; Roof, Dylann

Williams, Hank, Jr., 138, 145
Will the Circle Be Unbroken (Nitty Gritty Dirt Band), 140–41
With This Pledge (Alexander), 162, 163
Wolford, Frank, 105–6
Workman, William, 46–48

Yoakam, Dwight, 145

Studies in War, Society, and the Military

*Military Migration and State Formation:
The British Military Community in
Seventeenth-Century Sweden*
Mary Elizabeth Ailes

*Managing Sex in the U.S. Military:
Gender, Identity, and Behavior*
Edited by Beth Bailey, Alesha E. Doan,
Shannon Portillo, and Kara Dixon Vuic

The State at War in South Asia
Pradeep P. Barua

*Marianne Is Watching: Intelligence,
Counterintelligence, and the Origins
of the French Surveillance State*
Deborah Bauer

*Death at the Edges of Empire: Fallen Soldiers,
Cultural Memory, and the Making of an
American Nation, 1863–1921*
Shannon Bontrager

An American Soldier in World War I
George Browne
Edited by David L. Snead

*Beneficial Bombing: The Progressive
Foundations of American Air
Power, 1917–1945*
Mark Clodfelter

*Fu-go: The Curious History of Japan's
Balloon Bomb Attack on America*
Ross Coen

*Imagining the Unimaginable: World War,
Modern Art, and the Politics of Public
Culture in Russia, 1914–1917*
Aaron J. Cohen

*The Rise of the National Guard: The
Evolution of the American Militia, 1865–1920*
Jerry Cooper

*The Thirty Years' War and German
Memory in the Nineteenth Century*
Kevin Cramer

*Political Indoctrination in the U.S. Army
from World War II to the Vietnam War*
Christopher S. DeRosa

*The Korean War Remembered: Contested
Memories of an Unended Conflict*
Michael J. Devine

*In the Service of the Emperor:
Essays on the Imperial Japanese Army*
Edward J. Drea

*American Journalists in the Great War:
Rewriting the Rules of Reporting*
Chris Dubbs

*America's U-Boats: Terror Trophies
of World War I*
Chris Dubbs

*The Age of the Ship of the Line: The British
and French Navies, 1650–1815*
Jonathan R. Dull

*American Naval History, 1607–1865:
Overcoming the Colonial Legacy*
Jonathan R. Dull

*Soldiers of the Nation: Military Service
and Modern Puerto Rico, 1868–1952*
Harry Franqui-Rivera

*You Can't Fight Tanks with Bayonets:
Psychological Warfare against the
Japanese Army in the Southwest Pacific*
Allison B. Gilmore

*A Strange and Formidable Weapon: British
Responses to World War I Poison Gas*
Marion Girard

Civilians in the Path of War
Edited by Mark Grimsley and
Clifford J. Rogers

*A Scientific Way of War: Antebellum
Military Science, West Point, and the
Origins of American Military Thought*
Ian C. Hope

*Picture This: World War I Posters
and Visual Culture*
Edited and with an introduction
by Pearl James

*Indian Soldiers in World War I: Race and
Representation in an Imperial War*
Andrew T. Jarboe

*Death Zones and Darling Spies: Seven
Years of Vietnam War Reporting*
Beverly Deepe Keever

*They Are Dead and Yet They Live: Civil War
Memories in a Polarized America*
Edited by John M. Kinder and
Jennifer M. Murray

*For Home and Country: World War I
Propaganda on the Home Front*
Celia Malone Kingsbury

*I Die with My Country: Perspectives
on the Paraguayan War, 1864–1870*
Edited by Hendrik Kraay and
Thomas L. Whigham

North American Indians in the Great War
Susan Applegate Krouse
Photographs and original documentation
by Joseph K. Dixon

Remembering World War I in America
Kimberly J. Lamay Licursi

*Citizens More than Soldiers: The Kentucky
Militia and Society in the Early Republic*
Harry S. Laver

*Soldiers as Citizens: Former Wehrmacht
Officers in the Federal Republic of
Germany, 1945–1955*
Jay Lockenour

*Deterrence through Strength: British
Naval Power and Foreign Policy
under Pax Britannica*
Rebecca Berens Matzke

*Army and Empire: British Soldiers on the
American Frontier, 1758–1775*
Michael N. McConnell

*Of Duty Well and Faithfully Done: A History
of the Regular Army in the Civil War*
Clayton R. Newell and Charles R. Shrader
Foreword by Edward M. Coffman

*The Militarization of Culture in the
Dominican Republic, from the Captains
General to General Trujillo*
Valentina Peguero

*A Religious History of the American
GI in World War II*
G. Kurt Piehler

*Arabs at War: Military Effectiveness,
1948–1991*
Kenneth M. Pollack

*The Politics of Air Power: From
Confrontation to Cooperation in Army
Aviation Civil-Military Relations*
Rondall R. Rice

*Andean Tragedy: Fighting the War
of the Pacific, 1879–1884*
William F. Sater

The Grand Illusion: The Prussianization of the Chilean Army
William F. Sater and Holger H. Herwig

Sex Crimes under the Wehrmacht
David Raub Snyder

In the School of War
Roger J. Spiller
Foreword by John W. Shy

Empire between the Lines: Imperial Culture in British and French Trench Newspapers of the Great War
Elizabeth Stice

On the Trail of the Yellow Tiger: War, Trauma, and Social Dislocation in Southwest China during the Ming-Qing Transition
Kenneth M. Swope

Friendly Enemies: Soldier Fraternization throughout the American Civil War
Lauren K. Thompson

The Paraguayan War, Volume 1: Causes and Early Conduct
Thomas L. Whigham

Policing Sex and Marriage in the American Military: The Court-Martial and the Construction of Gender and Sexual Deviance, 1950–2000
Kellie Wilson-Buford

The Challenge of Change: Military Institutions and New Realities, 1918–1941
Edited by Harold R. Winton and David R. Mets

To order or obtain more information on these or other University of Nebraska Press titles, visit nebraskapress.unl.edu.

www.ingramcontent.com/pod-product-compliance
Lightning Source LLC
Chambersburg PA
CBHW030609230426
43661CB00053B/1900